Children Talking Television

Critical Perspectives on Literary and Education

Series Editor: Allan Luke
James Cook University of North Queensland
Australia

Literacy remains a contentious and polarized educational, media and political issue. What has emerged from the continuing debate is a recognition by many critical researchers and theorists that literacy in education is allied closely with matters of language and culture, ideology and discourse, knowledge and power.

This new series of monographs and anthologies draws together critical, cross-disciplinary work on language and literacy in a format accessible to researchers and students of education. Its aim is to provide competing discourses and alternative practices to the extant technical literature which offers 'state of the art' insights and 'how to' formulas for the achievement of literacy narrowly conceived as individual, psychological skills. Drawing perspectives variously from critical social theory and cultural studies, poststructuralism and feminisms, sociolinguistics and the ethnography of communication, social history and comparative education, the contributors to this series begin a critical interrogation of taken-for-granted assumptions which have guided educational policy, research and practice.

Children Talking Television:
The Making of
Television Literacy

by

David Buckingham

 The Falmer Press

(A member of the Taylor & Francis Group)
London • Washington, D.C.

UK   The Falmer Press, 4 John St., London WC1N 2ET
USA The Falmer Press, Taylor & Francis Inc., 1900 Frost Road, Suite 101, Bristol, PA 19007

First published 1993

A catalogue record for this book is available from the British Library

Library of Congress Cataloguing-in-Publication Data are available on request

ISBN 0 75070 109 9
ISBN 0 75070 110 2 (pbk)

Jacket design by Benedict Evans
Typeset in 9.5/11 pt Bembo
by Graphicraft Typesetters Ltd., Hong Kong

Printed in Great Britain by Burgess Science Press, Basingstoke on paper which has a specified pH value on final paper manufacture of not less than 7.5 and is therefore 'acid free'.

Contents

Contents

Part Four

Preface and Acknowledgments

The relationship between children and television is a topic that provokes considerable anxiety for many people. Television is held to be the root of most, if not all, evil among the young. It destroys the imagination, provokes delinquency and violence, undermines family life, and is the primary source of sexism, racism, consumerism and any other obnoxious ideology one might care to name.

As a parent, teacher and researcher, I have encountered these concerns in many areas of my work and leisure — and it would be wrong to pretend that I am somehow magically immune from them. Nevertheless, I have constantly been struck by how much of this anxiety about children and television is misplaced. It often appears to reflect much wider social, moral and political concerns, in which the role of television is far from being the most significant, and may in fact be highly ambiguous. Furthermore, this anxiety often prevents us from acknowledging the complexity of children's relationship with the medium, and taking seriously what they have to say about it.

This is not to suggest that I believe television's role is merely neutral, nor that its influence is wholly benign. This would, in my view, be equally simplistic. In a sense, my aim in this book is to question the notions of 'influence' and 'effect' on which these anxieties about television are often based. Children's relationship with television is typically regarded as a one-way process of cause-and-effect, in which children themselves are seen merely as powerless victims. By contrast, my aim in this book is to investigate the complex ways in which children actively make meaning and pleasure from television, particularly in the context of small-group talk.

The book emerges primarily from an extensive two-year research project, although my interest in this field extends back many years beyond this. It also reflects my own professional involvement in teacher education, training new and experienced teachers who are developing innovative, contemporary approaches to English and Media Studies in schools. The research is necessarily interdisciplinary, and draws on theories and perspectives developed within Media and Cultural Studies, English, education, psychology, sociology, linguistics and other related areas. Nevertheless, I have attempted to write a book which will be accessible both to students and teachers in the field, as well as to the general reader with an interest in children and the media.

The book is in four parts. The two chapters in Part One outline the context of popular debates about children and television, and the contribution of previous academic theory and research. Chapter 1 offers a general overview of the field, while Chapter 2 considers the problematic notion of 'television literacy' and the theoretical assumptions on which it might be based. These chapters (particularly the second) are inevitably fairly theoretical: readers primarily interested in 'getting to the data' might choose to begin with Chapter 3 and return to them later.

Part Two contains three chapters which in different ways consider the general characteristics of children's talk about television. Chapter 3 raises some broad questions about the *status* of talk as data, in relation to previous work on television audiences. Chapter 4 offers an overview of different styles of talk, focusing on the social context of talk and the different positions children take up in discussing television. Finally, Chapter 5 considers how children and to a lesser extent parents talk about 'family viewing' in the home.

The five chapters in Part Three each look at different 'key concepts' which appear to inform children's talk about television, and which have also emerged as the major organizing principles of media education. These are, in turn, genre, narrative, character, modality and agency. In each case, these concepts are explored through a detailed examination of different styles of talk, some of it comparatively open-ended, some gathered in the context of highly focused research activities.

The concluding part seeks to offer some conclusions from the study, and to outline issues for further research. These chapters return to the theoretical and educational contexts from which the research emerges — in Chapter 11, that of academic audience research, and in Chapter 12, that of media education.

Many people have been involved in different ways in assisting and discussing the research reported here. Most of the work was undertaken as part of a project on 'The Development of Television Literacy in Middle Childhood and Adolescence', funded by the Economic and Social Research Council UK (grant number: R000221959). I would particularly like to thank Valerie Hey, Susan Howard and Gemma Moss for their help in conducting and transcribing some of the interviews, and in discussing the results: responsibility for the analysis and the arguments contained here remains my own.

I would also like to thank the following people who offered advice and support in various forms: Basil Bernstein, Margaret Spencer, Michael Stubbs, Richard Paterson, Phil Cohen and Bill Melody for their support in getting the project off the ground; Pete Sanders, Jackie Simmonds, Kathy Kelly, Peter Maxwell, Paul Ratledge, Miriam Rinsler, Vijay Bhanault, Richard Quarshie, Andrew Lavis, Jackie Fenn, Pete Fraser and their colleagues for allowing access to their students; Cary Bazalgette for her encouragement and commitment; and Julian Sefton-Green, Bob Ferguson and Allan Luke for their detailed critical comments on the manuscript. Thanks are particularly due to the children and parents who took part in the research, who necessarily remain anonymous. And, most of all, to Celia Greenwood, for continuing to put up with me.

Various parts of this book have been published previously, although in a different form. Parts of Chapter 1 are taken from a paper entitled *Children and Television: An Overview of the Research*, published by the British Film Institute in 1987. Chapter 2 is a reduced version of 'Television Literacy: A Critique', published in *Radical Philosophy*, no. 51, 1989. Chapter 3 is an amended version of 'What are

Words Worth? Interpreting Children's Talk about Television', published in *Cultural Studies*, vol. 5, no. 2, 1991. Chapter 12 draws on 'Media Education: The Limits of a Discourse', published in *Journal of Curriculum Studies* in 1992. Versions of Chapters 2 and 5 were presented at the International Television Studies Conferences in London in 1988 and 1991.

This book is dedicated to my own children, Nathan and Louis Greenwood.

Transcription Conventions

(. . . .)	Words undeciphered
.	Talk omitted which is irrelevant to the issue being discussed
.	
.	
=	Contributions follow on without a break
/	Pause of less than two seconds
//	Pause of more than two seconds
CAPITALS	Emphatic speech
[. . . .]	Interjections by unidentified speaker
(?. . .)	Approximate wording
[. . . .]	Stage directions (e.g. [*laughter*])
[	
[	Simultaneous or interrupted speech
(&)	Continuing speech, separated in the transcript by an interrupting speaker

Lists of Tables

Series Editor's Introduction

Following World War II, the proliferation of television set out new material possibilities for the construction of discourses, texts, and indeed, social and economic 'reality'. Within a decade of its introduction as an affordable household appliance and the establishment of national broadcast networks, television had become the mainstay of leisure activity and mass pedagogy in Western countries. In these same countries, the multi-set household is now typical, where children, the elderly, and parents constitute multiple, and often competing, interpretive communities within the same home. The unprecedented economic and population expansion of the 1950s and 1960s also marked the building of Western technocratic societies — characterized and driven by military/industrial/corporate complexes, mass consumer culture, emergent youth markets and, ultimately, new forms of social identities and relations. Given this historical backdrop, it is hardly surprising that TV had become the target for what David Buckingham aptly describes as postmodern 'moral panic'.

Blaming the technology is itself mass spectator sport, with TV cited as a cause of virtually every social ill from drug culture, sexual violence, government dishonesty, budget deficits, the breakup of the family, and, of course, the decline of print literacy. This rhetoric offers simple explanations and equally simple answers. By focusing blame on an inanimate technology, it provides a convenient way of avoiding coming to grips with complex and competing interests at work in cultures where signs and symbols have become principal modes of value and exchange, and where economies are dominated by diversified media corporations. But communications technologies — alphabetic writing, print, radio, cinema, computers — have no intrinsic or inevitable social and cognitive consequences. While they enable and encourage particular kinds and relations of knowledge and power, they cannot be taken as simple causes or solutions for social phenomena. To assess the consequences of any communications technology and its attendant literacies requires that we look closely at its uses and practices in specific locales and communities, a task here undertaken by David Buckingham.

Even though mass media have been a focus of educational policy and curriculum since the 1960s, most school administrators, teachers and teacher educators still consider the transmission of print culture as their prime directive. As Pierre Bourdieu has pointed out (1977), in schools one never simply learns 'language' and 'literacy', but, more importantly, one learns a 'disposition' towards language and literacy, a social relation to texts and textuality. It is this relation which comes to count as a marker for the achievement of literate competence, perhaps more so than any single identifiable skill or knowledge. At the heart of modern school curriculum — whether progressivist or classicist, skills-based or child-centred — is the teaching of the authority of print culture. Beginning in early childhood education children are taught variously to 'understand' and 'comprehend', 'appreciate' and 'experience' literature. Where it is dealt with at all, a sceptical, questioning relation to written texts and text knowledge is considered a subsequent developmental achievement, often in elite secondary school literature study.

It is instructive to contrast this mainstream 'disposition' towards the book with the varied approaches to critical viewing analysed by Buckingham. All tend to begin from a fundamental mistrust of television and its messages — ranging from those American psychological models which aim to generate 'receivership skills' and 'attitude change', to those British and Canadian models which encourage students to identify ideological representation. My point here is that all literacy instruction builds and teaches differing relations of authority between readers/viewers and texts, enabling some 'readings' and disenabling others. The very stress on criticism in media literacy programs — however fallible — highlights a telling principle at work in schools: print literacy programs place the book beyond criticism, and assess students on the degree to which they have internalized *this* acquiescent relationship to the text.

Children Talking Television begins with a comprehensive overview of debates about the consequences and educational possibilities of television culture. These debates are closely connected with the issues dominating educational policy in the 1990s: controversies about the status and purpose of education in postmodern culture and work; about the possibilities of 'common culture' in the midst of ethnic and linguistic difference; about changing home, school and community practices and relations; and, of course, about the continued centrality of print literacy in schooling. Britain is considerably further down the track than most other countries in implementing approaches to critical viewing and media literacy, in part due to the continuing influence of British Cultural Studies. While educators in other countries are still debating whether television has a legitimate place in the curriculum, many British teachers and curriculum developers already have over a decade of experience using varied, at times competing, approaches to media literacy.

Buckingham's approach is multidimensional and multifocal. He has here gathered extensive data on: household family viewing practices; children's talk about the narrative structures, genres and ideologies of media texts; and their responses to curricular activities around television texts. His readings of these data are richly detailed, at each turn engaging with relevant theory from discourse analysis and critical linguistics, structuralist cinema theory and semiotics, poststructuralist and neomarxian social theory, and social psychology. The children studied here use talk about television to build and sustain their relations with others and to stake out and construct their own gendered identities. In this regard, the key question of whether the effects of television can be explained best by reference to the properties of the texts or the responses of the audience may be a theoretical dead end. Buckingham's analysis suggests that the relationship between media text and audience response, sociocultural structure and human agency, is one which, by definition, is always played out in relation to childrens social locations, purposes and competences. For example, the extent to which the 'narrative logic' of the latest MTV video or mini-series fixes a dominant cultural ideology, or makes available multiple identities and reading positions, is itself a product of the complex interactions of home, community, school and peer cultures documented here.

Thus, *Children Talking Television* is far more than an evaluation of teaching and learning about television. It begins to build a case that any curriculum which casts its principal goals as 'skills' or 'competences' of media literacy *per se*, may be missing the point altogether. Its detailing of the 'uptake' of curricula raises questions for all critical literacy programs: What are the consequences of 'critical' approaches to texts? What shape does 'critique' take in children's everyday talk and lives? And, of what value is 'becoming critical' in the first place? Buckingham points to the limits of media literacy curricula, much of which appears to service the panoptic aim of getting children to 'police their own viewing behaviour'. This can take various forms. Approaches which emphasize 'demystification' of the media, can 'end up reinforcing existing power-relationships between teachers and students', such that 'children may learn to "do" critical analysis in the same way they "do" medieval poetry or history'. At the same time, progressivist approaches which stress 'one's own' reading and writing of media texts, 'run the risk of simply leaving students where they are . . . [of] validating existing knowledge and resulting in a form of "institutionalised under-achievement"'. As an alterative, Buckingham lays out the parameters for a model of literacy which stresses systematic reflection on reading, writing and criticism as social practices, and on how these practices can be used to mediate conceptual, social and ideological relations with the world. In this emphasis, his proposals fit well with recent work by Fairclough, Kress and others on the importance of 'critical language awareness' in language and literacy learning.

Children Talking Television is a key work for those teachers, researchers and teacher educators involved in media education and for those exploring critical approaches to print literacy. It is the most extensive, empirically documented discussion of television literacy in classrooms and children's lives yet undertaken. As such, it offers powerful pedagogical and political lessons for the development of a critical social literacy and cultural studies *across* media and curricula. That some of the most productive work in literacy curriculum is being undertaken in media and cultural studies may itself be a potent message for those educators who continue to see educational work and practices solely in terms of the book.

Allan Luke
Townsville, Australia
October 1992

Part One

Chapter 1

Children and Television:
The Context of Research and Debate

An Ordinary Parent Speaks Out

On September 15th 1988, just as the research reported in this book was being devised, Prince Charles, heir apparent to the throne of Great Britain, delivered a speech at the opening of the Museum of the Moving Image, London's hyperactive museum of film and television. His comments were enthusiastically reported by many popular newspapers the following morning. The *Daily Mail* ran the story on its front page:

> Charles, speaking not just as Prince of Wales but as the father of two young sons, chose the opening of the new Museum of the Moving Image on London's South Bank and an audience of top TV and film executives to deliver his message.
> He said: 'A museum of this kind draws our attention to the past — the kind of standards which used to exist throughout the film-making profession.'
> And, he argued, it was not difficult to draw comparisons and to ask a few basic questions.
> 'For instance, do we have to tolerate an incessant menu of utterly gratuitous violence on both cinema and television — especially television — and most particularly videos?
> 'Those of us with children are very concerned by the appalling lack of restraint shown by those who make such films and videos, and who define their so-called art by insisting on the absolute necessity of portraying real life.
> 'They say that all you have to do if you don't like it is to switch the television off. And if, as parents, you complain that a diet of freely-available and insensate violence is likely to influence the way some people behave and relate to others, then you are told there is absolutely no proof that violence on TV has any effect on people's behaviour.
> 'But that, as we all know, is palpable nonsense.'
> The Prince, who wrote the speech himself, labelled this an attempt by 'so-called experts' to confuse people — to make them feel they didn't know what they were talking about and that what they were seeing with their own eyes was an illusion.

'But it is not an illusion and it is high time someone told these self-appointed experts that it is like the emperor's set of new clothes — that they are not wearing anything at all.'

Charles, who has video recorders at his homes in Kensington Palace and Highgrove, Gloucestershire, continued: 'I suspect that a great many people up and down the country are deeply concerned, for example, at the type of videos on sale — and, as we all know, available to children who cannot be prevented officially from obtaining them.

'So many people feel utterly powerless to alter this situation and so I hope that this museum will entertain and educate, while at the same time help to show people just how far good taste has been diminished during the last 20 years.'

The *Daily Mail*'s report was supplemented by an inside story entitled 'Why Charles speaks for every parent', in which Jeannette Kupfermann congratulated Charles for the 'finger-on-the-pulse wisdom of that attack on screen violence'. On the following day, its lead story was headed '25 KILLINGS ON YOUR TV NEXT WEEK', and reported that 'the flood of television violence is continuing unabated despite Prince Charles's heart-felt attack on it'.

The *Daily Mirror* also supported Charles's statements. Its editorial claimed that increases in crimes of violence were directly caused by increases in TV violence, and that 'those who say it has no effect on people's behaviour must know they are talking rubbish'. Here too, the lead story was supplemented by a feature article, in which newsreader and 'mum-of-two' Carol Barnes argued for the need to 'turn off the violence'.

This kind of controversy about 'screen violence' is familiar enough; but it is worth taking a little time to investigate what is taking place here. Firstly, consider how the key participants in the debate are defined. Previous media representations of Prince Charles have tended to portray him as an eccentric with little sense of everyday realities. Stories about how he talks to his plants or attempts to 'get in touch with nature' by escaping to the Scottish islands have provided extensive opportunities for satire. Indeed, as the *Mail* itself is bound to admit, Charles has often been criticized for leaving 'the mundane tasks of child-rearing' to his wife. Yet in this case Charles suddenly acquires the right to 'speak for every parent'. Rather than declaiming his usual quasi-mystical beliefs, he is seen to be the embodiment of common sense, to have his 'finger on the pulse', to 'voice what so many people feel' yet are somehow powerless to say. In effect, the press reports redefine Charles as a responsible parent, and as the voice of consensus.

Ranged against Prince Charles, two main parties can be identified. Firstly, there is the film and television industry, which is implicitly defined as cynical and irresponsible — although it is hardly aided here by the fact that its primary advocate is none other than Michael Winner, director of the *Death Wish* films. The *Daily Mail* reports Winner's 'astonishing outburst' in response to Charles's speech, although it is given little credence. The point, made by Winner and by representatives of the video industry, that video rentals are now extremely tightly censored, is effectively buried. The second major party here is the 'so-called experts', the researchers who talk such 'palpable nonsense' and attempt to deny the evidence of ordinary people's experience — although these experts are neither named nor consulted.

Significantly, the reports in both the *Mail* and the *Mirror* conclude with the words of Mary Whitehouse, Britain's leading 'moral majority' campaigner. Whitehouse expresses her 'immeasurable gratitude' for Charles's remarks, which she claims will 'echo in hearts just about everywhere, certainly among parents'.

Secondly, let us consider how the object of concern — 'screen violence' — is defined. Apart from the tendency to overstatement — 'incessant', 'utterly gratuitous', 'insensate violence' — one curious but significant aspect here is the recurrent food metaphor. Children are shown a 'menu' of violence, 'served up' a 'diet' of violence, 'fed' with gratuitous violence every day. It is obviously a metaphor of consumption, in which children have to 'eat' what they are given, yet it is also strangely physical, suggesting an almost visceral disgust.

Perhaps more significantly, there is the assumption that the object can be defined quantitatively — most notably in the *Mail*'s '25 killings' headline. 'Violence' is defined here exclusively as acts of physical aggression, which are to be counted irrespective of the contexts in which they occur or the characters who commit them. The argument would seem to be that the more 'violence' there is, the worse the effects will be: we can judge the influence of television simply on the basis of counting what is shown.

Insofar as the context of 'screen violence' is addressed, however, there is a significant emphasis on fiction rather than non-fiction. The *Daily Mail*'s '25 killings' refer exclusively to drama and feature films. Carol Barnes in the *Mirror* spells this out more explicitly: she is not concerned about the effects of television news on her children (although she obviously has a vested interest here!) but about movies and programmes like *The A-Team*. Perhaps paradoxically, fiction is seen to be capable of exerting effects in a way that factual material is not. According to Barnes, fictional programmes like this give children 'a completely wrong idea about life . . . children think that after people have been zapped or beaten on the head they just get up and walk away'.

However, when it comes to defining the *process* through which effects are presumed to occur, there is some confusion. In most cases, the process is implicitly seen as one of direct imitation: the *Daily Mirror*, as we have seen, attributes the rising crime rate to increasing levels of television violence, and its influence on 'impressionable minds'. The industry's claim that the incidence of television violence — at least in terms of counting aggressive acts — has steadily declined since the 1970s is dismissed as mere 'cynicism'. The *Mail*'s TV critic, Jeannette Kupfermann, offers a bewildering range of explanations of this process:

> Young children can still buy videos that degrade, humiliate and desensitize, and while we don't know exactly why screened violence will trigger real-life violence in one person and not another, the indisputable fact remains that it creates a climate that not only acts as a catalyst for the disturbed but will raise our level of tolerance and even expectation of violence. The Prince is right: common sense dictates that eventually television violence seeps through and has an effect on people's behaviour.

Violence, according to Kupfermann, appears to work in a number of different ways simultaneously: it 'triggers' and 'acts as a catalyst', yet it also 'desensitizes', 'creates a climate' and 'seeps through'. Yet among these diverse and seemingly contradictory hypotheses, it is the notion of 'direct effects' that wins through. Any request for a more complex explanation is merely academic quibbling.

Finally, how is the solution to this problem defined? The answer would seem to be two-fold. Firstly, there are calls for stricter censorship by the state — although, as I have noted, the censorship apparently being called for here already exists in the form of the Video Recordings Act, which itself arose from a previous 'moral panic' around the so-called 'video nasties' (see Barker, 1984). Yet just as the term 'video nasty' remained undefined, so in this case the precise nature of the 'violence' being condemned remains unclear. Apart from the *Mail*'s litany of '25 killings', there are very few actual films or programmes mentioned throughout the debate, and none by Charles himself. Here again, a consensus is being presumed — or rather constructed — around a shared abomination of something which remains conveniently vague.

However, there is another kind of regulation being promoted here, which is more 'private' than 'public'. Carol Barnes, for example, is implicitly held up by the *Mirror* as a model parent, who limits the amount of television her children watch and encourages them to select more 'educational' programmes. Similarly, Jeannette Kupfermann in the *Mail* contrasts the approach of the 'responsible' family, exemplified by 'family man' Prince Charles, with that of the 'worst' families, where 'latch-key children' watch TV alone, and are 'barraged with messages, none of which get filtered through mediating values'. The problem, according to Carol Barnes, is that new technologies like video and satellite TV are much harder to control. 'Deviant' families, such as single-parent families or those in which both parents work, are implicitly seen to be failing in their responsibilities, and it is up to the state to intervene.

What is at stake here, therefore, are much broader questions about knowledge and authority — about what children of different ages should be allowed to see and to know. Prince Charles, for example, argues that film-makers attempt to justify their 'lack of restraint' by 'insisting on the absolute necessity of portraying real life'; while Michael Winner counters this by suggesting that Charles's views would lead to 'endless programmes about flower-arranging and cookery'. While both parties somewhat overstate the case, the underlying issues here are much more fundamental than the mere local anxiety about what children might or might not watch on TV. In effect, they are about who defines 'real life' and who decides how far children should be 'exposed' to it. As this example illustrates, the topic of 'children and television' condenses much broader social, moral and political concerns — to the extent that a more open, less judgmental investigation of the issue is often extremely difficult.

Terms of Debate

Prince Charles's contribution to the debate about children and television was one moment in a continuing controversy. Stories about the evil effects of television on children make good copy, and they are rarely absent from the headlines. At the time of writing, for example, there have been stories about a killing apparently inspired by *Teenage Mutant Ninja Turtles*; and television has also been drawn into the debate about declining standards of literacy, which is currently enjoying one of its perennial revivals.

As a number of writers have argued (e.g. Pearson, 1984, Lusted, 1985), this public anxiety about children and television is the latest manifestation of a long-standing concern about the effects of popular media forms on young people. Over 2000 years ago, the Greek philosopher Plato proposed to ban the dramatic poets from his ideal Republic, for fear that their stories about the immoral antics of the gods would influence impressionable young minds. Just as in the case of concerns about *The A-Team*, Plato argued that young people were unable to tell the difference between what was 'allegorical' and what was 'literal', and would therefore be likely to copy what they saw. In more recent times, popular literature, music hall, the cinema and children's comics have all provoked 'moral panics' which have typically led to stricter censorship designed to protect children from their allegedly harmful effects. More recent public controversies — such as the 'video nasties' scare of the early 1980s (Barker, 1984) or Mary Whitehouse's attacks on the soap opera *EastEnders* (Buckingham, 1987a) — are merely heirs to this long tradition.

While Prince Charles's concern about 'screen violence' derives primarily from a right-wing 'moral majority' position, anxiety about the negative effects of television on children is manifested right across the political spectrum. The work of Marie Winn (1985) and Neil Postman (1983), among others, derives from a more 'liberal' position, which has considerable currency, especially among middle-class parents. The concern here is not so much with the effects of television on children's behaviour as on their thought processes. Here, it is the activity of viewing itself — irrespective of content — which is seen to be 'bad for children's brains'.

Winn's symptomatically-titled book *The Plug-In Drug* provides a barrage of evidence — much of it anecdotal — in support of the view that television destroys children's capacity for intelligent thought. Television, she asserts, retards the physical development of the brain, blunts the senses and encourages mental laziness. It impairs children's sense of their own identity, their attention span and their linguistic abilities. As a result of their addiction to television, Winn argues, children are deprived of play and of the opportunity to participate in the everyday rituals of normal family life. The metaphor of television-as-drug recurs throughout: television is 'an insidious narcotic', children are 'TV zombies' who watch in a 'trance-like state', which 'blots out' the real world. By contrast, Winn provides a series of glowing testimonials from parents who have helped their children 'kick the TV habit'.

For these writers, television is also regarded as a primary cause of social unrest. It is no coincidence, Postman (1983) argues, that the generation which rebelled so spectacularly against adult authority in the 1960s was the first to be brought up on television. By making adult 'secrets' freely available to children, television effectively undermines their respect for their elders and betters. As with the so-called 'moral majority', this argument is informed by a powerful nostalgia for a 'golden age' which apparently existed before television; and here too, the most effective response to the problem of television is seen to lie in a reassertion of traditional family values.

While there are definite affinities between these ideas and those of the 'moral majority', they also connect with anxieties about the negative effects of television voiced by many on the political left. Here, television is often regarded as an extremely powerful agent of the 'dominant ideology' — a kind of 'propaganda machine' which is responsible for brainwashing children into 'consumerism' and other forms of false consciousness.

Rose Goldsen's book *The Show and Tell Machine* (Goldsen, 1977) provides a typical example of this more 'popular' left-wing perspective. Goldsen describes television as a system of 'mass behaviour modification', which anaesthetizes the emotions, distorts authentic art and culture and maintains ideological hegemony. Significantly, she draws on the imagery of dystopian novels such as Aldous Huxley's *Brave New World* and George Orwell's *1984*, and on the equally apocalyptic theories of Marshall McLuhan. What emerges here is a view of television as enormously powerful — as 'irresistible' and 'insidious' — and of audiences as passive consumers, who are simply 'manipulated' by television and thereby 'sold' to advertisers. Yet again, it is children who are seen to be most at risk: their 'authentic' culture has been replaced by the 'imagineers', who have turned them into mere victims of merchandising.

On one level, this account of media effects would appear to be directly opposed to that of the 'moral majority'. If Whitehouse and her ilk condemn television for its attack on traditional moral values, many on the left condemn it for supporting them, and thereby upholding the dominant political order. Yet they are united in a view of television as extremely powerful, and as capable of seducing children away from their 'better nature'. Indeed, despite their overt political differences, there are significant similarities in the rhetoric used by these popular critics of television: in each case, the medium is seen as an attack on 'authentic' or 'essentially human' values, and on 'true' art and culture.

The different positions I have briefly sketched here often unite around particular controversies. Indeed, in reporting Prince Charles's speech, the *Daily Mail* notes the common ground which has been established on the issue of 'screen violence' between moral watchdogs like Whitehouse, feminists like Germaine Greer (described here as 'one of the darlings of the Sixties revolution') and Charles himself ('the prince of the counter culture', no less!).

Another recent example of this may be found in the controversy surrounding 'new wave' US cartoons such as *Thundercats*, *Ghostbusters* and *Teenage Mutant Ninja Turtles*. In this instance, it is often hard to distinguish traditional right-wing anxieties about violence from left-wing criticisms of 'war toys' and militarism. The cartoons serve as a focus for left-wing concerns about gender stereotyping and about merchandising, as well as liberal arguments about the way in which television is 'colonizing' children's play (see Engelhardt, 1986; Carlsson-Paige and Levin, 1990). The anxieties about these cartoons are also part of a broader concern about the potential impact of the deregulation of broadcasting. In the British context, these arguments are heavily informed by a fear of 'Americanization' (see Hebdige, 1982) and by a kind of nostalgia for a 'golden age' of 'quality' children's television, represented by programmes like the long-running factual magazine *Blue Peter* and 'classic' serials like *The Chronicles of Narnia*.

As these examples suggest, debates about children and television frequently serve as a vehicle for much broader concerns. Genuine, often deep-seated anxieties about what are perceived as undesirable social or moral changes lead to a search for a single, causal explanation. Blaming television may serve to deflect attention away from other possible causes of change or decline — causes which may well be closer to home and much more painful to examine.

For example, Mary Whitehouse has constantly looked to television as a primary explanation of the post-war decline in organized religion and in traditional 'family values' (Tracey and Morrison, 1979). Her attacks on the BBC, and in particular on its more 'populist' representatives such as Sir Hugh Greene and (more recently) Michael Grade, have been motivated by a much broader anxiety about the secularization of British society. To look for more complex explanations of these phenomena would mean acknowledging some of the contradictions and limitations of those institutions — such as the church and the family — themselves. Similarly, as Ian Connell (1985) has argued, blaming the media has become part of the popular mythology of the political Left. Yet regarding the failure of socialism to win the support of the masses as a direct result of media manipulation relieves us of the painful necessity of looking at some of the contradictions and weaknesses of the left's own political strategies.

In the case of the 'video nasties' scare of the early 1980s, this process of displacement can be traced quite clearly. Martin Barker (1984) argues that the debates and legislation in this area arose in response to the Conservative government's need to revive its image as the party of 'law and order' following the widespread social unrest of the time, which culminated in the inner city disturbances of 1981. Here again, blaming television deflected attention away from the more deep-seated structural causes of those disturbances, and provided a useful means of laundering the government's public image. As in the controversy surrounding Charles's speech on 'screen violence', much of the concern here focused on 'deviant' parents who were seen to be neglecting their responsibility for controlling their children's behaviour. In this instance, shifting the ground to a debate about the media — with the collusion of a largely Tory press — served the government's political purposes very well.

Setting the Agenda

These public debates about children's relationship with television and other popular media would make a fascinating topic of study in their own right, and I have only been able to scratch the surface of them here. Yet even from this brief sketch, it is possible to identify a number of their major limitations.

Firstly, there are significant problems here in terms of what counts as evidence. Books like *The Plug-In Drug* (Winn, 1985) combine highly selective accounts of research with great quantities of unsubstantiated anecdote. In many cases, an analysis of television itself — generally in statistical terms — is seen as sufficient evidence of its effects. More frequently, however, as in the case of Charles's speech, research is simply dismissed as foolish or irrelevant: 'common sense' and 'the evidence before our eyes' will tell us all we need to know.

In addition, the kinds of questions which are asked here remain extremely limited. As I have indicated, the concern is almost exclusively with the *negative* effects of television. Whether the emphasis is on children's behaviour, their mental development or their attitudes and beliefs, the role of television is predominantly assumed to be harmful. Many of these questions implicitly assume that complex social phenomena — violence, the decline of the family, social unrest, sexism or 'consumerism' — can be explained primarily in terms of a single, powerful cause. What is often ignored here is the question of why children might choose to watch television in the first place, and the pleasure they might experience in doing so. This can only be explained in terms of the apparently 'mesmerizing' or 'addictive' properties of the medium, or as a consequence of parental irresponsibility.

The theoretical model of media effects which is employed here is essentially behaviourist: it conceives of the relation between television and children as a process of stimulus and response. The stimulus has a fixed meaning, which is the same for all, and the response is a direct reaction to it: both can be quantified and compared. Television is seen as an extremely powerful influence, which moulds children's consciousness and behaviour, and which they are largely powerless to resist. Children themselves are implicitly regarded as passive victims — as impressionable and highly vulnerable.

In this respect, debates about children and television reflect much broader ideologies of childhood. Indeed, many critics of television would appear to hark back to a vision of childhood which has much in common with the Victorian ideal. From this perspective, the inadequacies and immaturities of children often provide a source of quaint amusement, sometimes tempered with a rather patronizing Wordsworthian belief in their essential purity and wisdom. Yet as Barker (1989) has argued, this view often masks a fear of children — and particularly of working-class children — as potential 'monsters'. The power of media such as television is seen to lie in their ability to penetrate the veneer of civilization and release the darker forces which lie beneath. Adult intervention is therefore needed in order to protect children from temptation and the ever-present possibility of corruption.

As histories of childhood have indicated, this view of children is a comparatively recent development, which has largely been confined to Western industrialized societies (e.g. Aries, 1973; de Mause, 1976; Pollock, 1983). These studies suggest that childhood must be seen, not as an essential and unchanging state, but as a social, historical construction. As Allison James and Alan Prout (1990, p. 7) have argued, 'the immaturity of children is a biological fact of life but the ways in which this immaturity is understood and made meaningful is a fact of culture'. Furthermore, the social construction of childhood is far from being a neutral process: the notion of children as innocent — or at least the attempt to keep them that way — can be seen as a function of the broader power-relationships between adults and children which obtain in contemporary society.

One inevitable consequence of this construction of childhood is that children themselves have largely been silenced. Certainly, children's voices have been almost entirely excluded from the debates I have described: it is adults who know best, and who take it upon themselves to argue on children's behalf.

What Research has (not) Shown . . .

So what of the 'self-appointed experts', the researchers who talk such 'palpable nonsense'? Ironically perhaps, given Charles's criticisms, the deep-seated assumptions and anxieties which underlie much of the public debate about children and television have largely set the agenda for academic research. What 'the public' wants — or rather what those who claim to speak on its behalf say that it wants — is *proof* of the negative effects of television, and this is largely what researchers have sought to provide. While this is partly down to the motivations of the researchers themselves — the majority of whom appear to share the view of television as somehow inherently 'bad' for children — it is also a result of the ways in which research is funded. Certainly in the United States, research in the area has often been funded from the mental health budget, suggesting that the issue is primarily conceived in pathological terms.

More fundamentally, the relationship between children and television has largely been defined as a *psychological* phenomenon. It is a question of what television 'does' to individual children's minds — or, more recently, what their minds 'do' with television. To all intents and purposes, children appear to be regarded as not fully social — or indeed even as 'pre-social' — beings.

The consequences of this situation are apparent in many of the areas to be addressed in this book, and will be discussed in more detail in due course. Yet the issue of television violence raised by Charles's speech provides a useful illustration of many of the broader shortcomings of mainstream research in this field.

Despite the considerable economic and intellectual resources which have been expended upon it, research into the effects of television violence has been generally inconclusive — and at least in this respect, Charles's criticisms are near the mark. The reasons for this are partly to do with the limitations of the methods which have been employed, but they are also a function of the ways in which the basic research questions have been formulated. (For a more extensive review of this research, see Buckingham, 1987b.)

While some of the early research on film and television violence took great care to emphasize the influence of 'intervening variables' such as the family and social class, and to caution against the more alarmist views which were already circulating in public debate (e.g. Blumer and Hauser, 1933; Himmelweit *et al.*, 1958; Schramm *et al.*, 1961), much of the research conducted since that time has been based on the notion of 'direct effects'. Using behaviourist models, researchers have attempted to identify the various ways in which a violent stimulus would produce an aggressive response. In this area, as in many others, the history of media research has not been one of steady and consistent development, but rather one of 'perpetual recurrence' (see Reeves and Wartella, 1985). The questions about television violence which were being investigated in the 1960s were very similar to those which had largely been surpassed by researchers studying the effects of the cinema in the 1930s.

Thus, laboratory experiments have been seen as the primary source of evidence of the effects of television violence — although their ability to predict real-life behaviour is clearly limited. As a number of critics have argued, the 'classic' experiments in this field tend to measure artificial responses to artificial stimuli in artificial situations. They largely ignore the distinction between 'fantasy' and real-life violence, both in the stimulus itself and in the behaviour it is presumed to cause.

While surveys are possibly less artificial, they do raise similar problems of reliability and validity. Apart from the difficulty of gaining accurate measures of children's television viewing and (to a greater extent) of their violent behaviour, the ability of surveys to establish *causal* connections — as opposed to correlations — is limited. One may well discover that children who are violent watch a lot of violent television, but this does not in itself prove that violent television causes real-life violence. As in the case of laboratory experiments, it is often assumed that other variables which might play a part in this process can be 'controlled' — which of course presumes that we know what they all are, and can measure their significance. Despite some sophisticated attempts to get around these problems, the findings of such surveys have often been contradictory or inconsistent.

Ultimately, however, the major limitations of mainstream research on television violence derive from its failure to address the *meaning* of violence, both on television and in everyday life. In these studies, 'violence' is predominantly defined in terms of acts of physical aggression — thereby ignoring what might be termed 'psychological' or 'institutional' violence. Much of the research takes 'violence' as a homogeneous category, and tends to ignore crucial distinctions between different types of violence, and the different contexts in which they may take place. Yet the meaning of a 'violent' act — whether it occurs on television or in real life — depends upon a whole series of factors: a given act may be regarded as more or less violent according to the identity and motivations of the person who commits it, the reasons which may have provoked it, and the circumstances which surround it. Violence directed against inanimate objects or toys is very different from violence directed against other human beings. Violence which is presented in a less 'realistic' dramatic context — such as in a cartoon — may be perceived as less 'serious', and thus have quite a different meaning from that which is portrayed more 'realistically' — although individuals will obviously vary in their judgments here.

While there have been attempts to classify types of television violence — for example, by genre (crime series as opposed to cartoons) or by context ('justified' as opposed to 'unjustified' violence) — these have typically been based, not on the judgments of viewers who are actually exposed to the programmes, but on the supposedly objective judgments of researchers. Yet viewers' own definitions of 'violence' may be based on extremely diverse and even contradictory criteria (Gunter, 1985). As Dorr and Kovaric (1980) argue, children's definitions of 'violence' may well not coincide with those of adults, and girls may perceive certain actions as aggressive which boys would not perceive in this way.

As Murdock and McCron (1979) have indicated, we can only begin to identify the *meaning* of these behaviours — of aggression and of watching violent television — if we situate them within broader social and cultural processes. By isolating 'violence' from other aspects of television, and 'aggression' from other aspects of social life, researchers have effectively failed to explain either phenomenon.

Active Viewers?

Following the so-called 'cognitive revolution' of the 1960s, psychological research has generally moved away from the behaviourist assumptions exemplified by 'effects' research — although that 'revolution' was slower to manifest itself in this area than in many others, for reasons I have intimated above.

At least outwardly, the cognitive paradigm stands in direct opposition to behaviourism. Viewers are seen here as having an active role in constructing meaning from television: rather than merely responding to stimuli, they are consciously processing, interpreting and evaluating what they watch. According to cognitive researchers, viewers make sense of television by using 'schemas' or 'scripts' — sets of plans and expectations which they have built up from previous experience, both of television and of the world in general (for overviews of this approach, see Wartella, 1979; Bryant and Anderson, 1983; Dorr, 1986).

In studying children's understanding of television, cognitive psychologists have tended to concentrate on the 'micro' rather than the 'macro' aspects — on detailed processes of attention and comprehension, and on the effects of specific formal features, rather than on broader responses to different television genres, or the role of television in forming attitudes and beliefs. There has also been an increasing use of developmental psychology — primarily the work of Piaget — in attempting to define the ways in which children's understanding changes as they mature.

An illustration of this approach may be found in research on children's attention to television. Early research in this field tended to adopt a stimulus-response model, attempting to identify specific formal features which increased or decreased attention. For example, Levin and Anderson (1976) found that factors such as adult females, puppets, rapid scene changes and animation tended to increase attention, while adult males, animals and stationary activity had the opposite effect. However, the work of Anderson and his colleagues (e.g. Anderson and Lorch, 1983) has moved away from the view that attention is a kind of conditioned reflex which will be produced automatically by certain stimuli. On the contrary, attention is now regarded as active rather than reactive: children actively choose to pay attention to television, and the choices they make depend on their efforts to understand what they watch and on the other activities which are available within the viewing environment (see also Salomon, 1983a, 1983b).

Much of the research to be considered in this book derives from this cognitive paradigm, and will be reviewed in more detail in due course. However, some general remarks here will serve to locate my overall argument.

Firstly, there are many ways in which the 'cognitive revolution' has remained incomplete. Despite their apparent rejection of behaviourism, cognitive researchers often continue to rely on behaviourist theories and methodologies. Cognitive processing is widely defined as a 'mediating variable' — in other words, as something that intervenes between stimulus and response. Despite the emphasis on children as active constructors of meaning, meaning is still largely seen as something contained within the text, which can be 'objectively' identified and quantified. Thus, the text itself is typically defined as a 'stimulus': 'formal features' such as camera movements or editing techniques are seen to have a fixed meaning, and their 'effects' are studied in isolation from the contexts in which they occur. This approach would appear to neglect the complexity of even the most apparently simple programmes (Livingstone, 1990). Ambiguity, 'openness' and contradiction, which many analyses of popular television have seen as fundamental to its success (e.g. Fiske, 1987a), are effectively ignored, in favour of statistical content analysis.

Furthermore, cognitive researchers have focused almost exclusively on the intellectual aspects of children's understanding of television. 'Cognitive' and 'affective' elements are typically regarded as separate, and the latter tend to be left aside. Attempts to account for the role of television in children's 'affective development' have generally been quite inadequate (see Dorr, 1982). Perhaps the most striking absence, for example in accounts of the role of television in children's acquisition of gender roles (e.g. Durkin, 1985), is of any reference to psychoanalytic theory. Researchers have tended to concentrate on 'meaning' — and to account for it in rather limited terms — while neglecting the central question of 'pleasure', with which it is inextricably connected.

This problem is compounded by researchers' reliance on a Piagetian model of child development — a reliance which is perhaps surprising given the extensive critiques to which it has been subjected (e.g. Donaldson, 1978; Walkerdine, 1984). In the hands of many researchers in this field, the Piagetian model is interpreted as a rigid series of 'ages and stages', which lead inexorably towards the achievement of adult rationality (e.g. Noble, 1975).

As James Anderson (1981) has argued, much cognitive research tends to regard the child as a 'deficit system' — as more or less 'incompetent' when compared with adults. Using normative developmental models, children at certain ages are defined as being unable to accomplish the 'proper' sequencing of visual images, to recall the 'essential' features of a narrative, or to identify correctly the 'messages' that are being beamed at them. This preoccupation with identifying the 'inadequacies' of children's understanding — as compared with adults — has led to a neglect of children's own perspectives.

Finally, the cognitive emphasis on the individual's internal mental processes makes it difficult to account for the role of social and cultural factors in the formation of consciousness and understanding. While certain cognitive researchers appear to acknowledge this in theory (e.g. Dorr, 1986), much of the research itself tends to ignore social differences in favour of a notion of 'the child' which is abstracted from any social and historical context. Elements such as social class, 'race' and gender tend to be bracketed off, or regarded as influences which only come into play once the already-formed individual enters the social world.

Many of the problems I have identified here apply well beyond the limited field of research on children and television. As James and Prout (1990) indicate, psychological explanations of child development have dominated the study of childhood, and have served both to support and to naturalize existing social relationships between adults and children, for example in child-rearing and in education (cf. Walkerdine, 1984). Yet, as they argue, cognitive psychology is based on notions of the 'naturalness' of childhood and the 'rationality' of adulthood which effectively ignore the way in which cognitive development is inevitably situated within social experiences and relationships (cf. Richards, 1974; Richards and Light, 1986). Here again, it is remarkable that the field of television research has remained largely insulated from broader developments in social psychology and social theory.

Social Readings?

As I have indicated, the relationship between children and television has predominantly been conceived as a psychological phenomenon. Sociological research on media audiences has largely concerned itself with adults, and with the impact of television on attitudes and beliefs. This division of labour reflects a much more general conceptualization of childhood within the human sciences: the 'sociology of childhood' remains an underdeveloped, although emergent, field of study (see James and Prout, 1990).

Insofar as sociologists have concerned themselves with children and television, they have often done so from the perspective of functionalist 'socialization theory'. Broadly speaking, this approach regards children as passive recipients of 'external' social forces, rather than active participants in the construction of their own social lives and identities. As James and Prout (1990) indicate, socialization theory tends to regard childhood as a rehearsal of adult life, a period in which children are gradually made to conform to adult norms. While the rhetoric is different, many of the basic assumptions here in fact have much in common with psychological theories of child development: through the impact of external 'models' and stimuli (such as those provided by television) the child progressively overcomes its inadequacies and enters the social world of adulthood.

From this perspective, analysis of the content of television is often taken as sufficient evidence of its effects. Thus, for example, researchers have consistently pointed to numerical imbalances and 'stereotyping' in the representations of men and women on television — although there is some evidence that this is changing. However, there is much less research on the ways in which children themselves make sense of these representations. Some studies have suggested that 'heavy viewers' may be more likely to adopt stereotyped expectations (Beuf, 1974; McGhee and Frueh, 1980), although as in the case of the violence research, correlation is generally taken as evidence of causality. As Durkin (1985) indicates, these studies rely on a 'direct effects' model, which assumes that the response will be the mirror-image of the stimulus: other variables — such as social class or parental expectations — which might potentially play a part are seen as constants which can be statistically 'accounted for'. Yet, as Durkin suggests, 'heavy viewers' will be more likely to encounter 'counter-stereotyped' material, and if only because of its rarity, this may have more significance for them. Here again, quantitative measures of 'stereotyping' or of viewing behaviour do not provide adequate evidence of the meanings viewers make from what they watch. Ultimately, the notion of 'direct effects' on which this kind of research is based seems to be a particularly inadequate means of accounting for the longer-term ideological role of television.

In fact, mainstream sociological research on media audiences has increasingly moved beyond these behaviourist assumptions (see de Fleur and Ball-Rokeach, 1982; Lowery and de Fleur, 1983; McQuail, 1983). The emphasis on 'intervening variables' such as social class and subculture which developed in the 1950s led to a view of the media as a relatively insignificant influence, whose power was largely confined to reinforcing beliefs which were already in place (e.g. Himmelweit *et al.*, 1958; Klapper, 1960; Schramm *et al.*, 1961).

'Uses and gratifications' research, which is largely a development of this approach, remains the dominant perspective among sociological studies of children and television (see Blumler and Katz, 1974; Brown, 1976; Rubin, 1979). On one level, this approach appears to turn the basic proposition of 'effects' research on its head: in the famous words of Katz and Foulkes (1962), the focus is no longer on 'what the media do to people', but on 'what people do with the media'. Far from regarding the audience as a mass of passive consumers, uses and gratifications research examines the ways in which individuals actively select and use different types of media for their own needs and purposes — for example, for social contact, for information, for escape, as a means of filling time or acquiring a sense of personal identity, or for resolving a whole range of problems.

Much of the British work in this tradition (e.g. Brown, 1976) adopts a more sociological perspective, emphasizing demographic variables such as social class and considering individuals' uses of the media in the context of their membership of broader social groups, such as teenage subcultures (e.g. Howitt and Dembo, 1974; Dembo and McCron, 1976).

By contrast, the more dominant North American approach tends to adopt a psychological perspective. The emphasis here is on individual attributes of 'personality' and 'motivation', and on the ways in which different personality 'types' use the media for different purposes. For example, much of the early research in this field was concerned with the use of television as a means of psychological 'escape' from unsatisfactory relationships or social circumstances, or from the 'stresses' of growing up (e.g. Katz and Foulkes, 1962). As Carmen Luke (1990) argues, this kind of uses and gratifications research tends to 'psychologize' the social: the social context only becomes intelligible in terms of the psychological reactions and experiences of individuals.

While this approach appears to subscribe to the notion of the 'active viewer', and thus to oppose the 'direct effects' approach, the viewer is ultimately seen here merely as a passive respondent to 'behaviour-determining needs' (Luke, 1990). Indeed, critics of this approach (e.g. Elliot, 1974; Morley, 1980a) have pointed to limitations in the central concept of 'needs': the assumption that there are basic human needs which the media satisfy ignores the possibility that the media may themselves create 'needs', and thereby perform an active ideological role. Relying on individuals to state their own needs — for example, in response to a questionnaire — may lead one to neglect the 'unconscious' needs which they are unable or unwilling to acknowledge. Furthermore, this approach fails to recognize the fact that media use may not necessarily reflect explicit 'personal' needs and preferences: the programmes we watch are not necessarily those we say we prefer, partly because we often watch with others, and because at least some viewing may be 'non-purposive'. In this respect, uses and gratifications research runs the risk of defining television viewing as a much more conscious, purposeful activity than it actually is.

As these criticisms suggest, uses and gratifications research largely fails to provide a fully *social* account of children's relationship with television. Like cognitive psychology, it appears to define children as 'active' participants in making sense of television, yet in practice it tends to account for this 'activity' in individualistic terms. Here again, the emphasis on quantitative techniques enables researchers to generate an impressive array of 'hard' scientific data, yet it effectively precludes any more fundamental questioning of basic theoretical assumptions.

Media Studies

While all these traditions of research have had their counterparts in Britain, the history here — and the history from which this book emerges — is rather different. The origins of academic Media Studies in this country may be found primarily in literary criticism, although the field has subsquently embraced a complex and occasionally bewildering series of theoretical approaches, including semiotics, Marxist theory, structuralism, poststructuralism and psychoanalysis (see, for example, Coward and Ellis, 1977; Silverman, 1983). Again, this is not the place for a review of these developments, although some brief remarks will help to situate the study that follows.

The dominant paradigm within academic Media Studies in the 1970s — which has come to be termed '*Screen* theory' — in fact displayed little if any interest in media audiences. This psychoanalytic version of structuralism sought to define the ways in which the film text 'produces' the subjectivity of the spectator, by con-structing 'subject positions' from which it is to be read. The emphasis here was primarily on the psychic dynamics of film spectatorship: the act of viewing was defined in terms of psychoanalytic processes such as scopophilia, voyeurism and fetishism (e.g. Metz, 1982). According to this approach, the language of dominant cinema — for example, 'classical' continuity editing — 'sutured' (or literally 'stitched') the spectator into the text, and thereby into the 'dominant ideology' — a process which the spectator was seen as largely powerless to resist.

During the late 1970s and early 1980s, *Screen* theory came under attack from a number of directions, for its neglect of the political economy of the media (e.g. Garnham, 1979), its reliance on the 'patriarchal' psychoanalytic theories of Freud and Lacan (e.g. Gallop, 1982), and its privileging of the elite avant-garde (e.g. Harvey, 1978; Lovell, 1980). However, perhaps the most damaging limitation of *Screen* theory from the point of view of audience research was its exclusive emphasis on texts. While the analytic methods used here were much more sophisticated than the statistical content analysis favoured by most US researchers, both ap-proaches tended to assume that the meanings identified by critics would be 'swallowed whole' by audiences. As Paul Willemen (1978) argued, *Screen* theory tended to conflate the 'inscribed' reader, constructed by the text, with real readers, living in real social and historical formations.

It was David Morley's study *The 'Nationwide' Audience* (Morley, 1980a), that represented the most significant shift towards an engagement with real — as opposed to 'inscribed' — audiences. Morley's work derived from the more socio-logical tradition of 'British Cultural Studies', developed primarily at the Univer-sity of Birmingham Centre for Contemporary Cultural Studies (see Hall *et al.*, 1980; Fiske, 1987b; Turner, 1990). Drawing on his previous analysis of an early evening news magazine programme (Brunsdon and Morley, 1978), Morley identified some of the ways in which the text sought to promote a 'preferred' reading which was in line with the 'dominant ideology' — for example, in how items were framed and defined, the kinds of people chosen as 'experts' or 'ordinary people', and how studio discussions and interviews were conducted. The readings of viewers drawn from a broad range of social and occupational groups were then classified in terms of the degree to which this preferred reading was accepted, negotiated or rejected.

In retrospect, the significance of this work lies more in its critique of *Screen* theory, rather than in the empirical study itself — which, as Morley and others have acknowledged, suffers several limitations (Morley, 1981; Wren-Lewis, 1983; Jordin and Brunt, 1988). Morley claimed that *Screen* theory amounted to a form of 'textual determinism', in which the audience was 'reduced to the status of an automated puppet pulled by the strings of the text'. He argued that the viewer was 'interpellated', not by a single 'dominant ideology', but by multiple discourses — brought into play by virtue of the subject's other social, cultural and institu-tional experiences — which were diverse and potentially contradictory. The viewer was not only a 'subject of the text', but a social subject with multiple 'subjectivities'.

Morley's work effectively paved the way for a series of empirical studies of television audiences, both in relation to news and other non-fictional genres (e.g. Wren-Lewis, 1985; Richardson and Corner, 1986; Corner *et al.*, 1991), and in-creasingly in relation to television fiction, particularly soap opera (e.g. Hobson, 1982; Ang, 1985; Buckingham, 1987a; Liebes and Katz, 1990). More recently, there has been a growing emphasis on research into the domestic viewing context (e.g. Morley, 1986; Gray, 1987; Lull, 1988; Morley and Silverstone, 1990): here, the focus of study has shifted away from readings of specific texts, towards the nature of television viewing as an activity, and the social relations which surround and constitute it. While some of this research has begun to focus on family groups, children have remained largely neglected — with the significant exception of Bob Hodge and David Tripp's important study *Children and Television* (1986).

Some of the theoretical and methodological problems of this developing area of research will be addressed in subsequent chapters, particularly Chapters 3 and 11. However, in general terms, it would appear to have a number of advantages when compared with the approaches described earlier. At least in principle, it offers an alternative to the psychological notion of television viewers as individual 'cognitive processors', while also avoiding the danger of regarding them merely as representatives of given demographic categories. Viewers are seen here, not as unique and coherent individuals, but as sites of conflict, 'points of intersection' between a variety of potentially conflicting discourses. Different discourses will be mobilized in different ways by different viewers and in different contexts, and it would therefore be mistaken to look for a single, consistent reading.

Similarly, this approach offers a more complex view of meaning, and of the text itself. Rather than regarding meaning as something contained within the text, it draws attention to the possibility of ambiguity and contradiction. While the text might 'prefer' or 'invite' a particular reading, it might also invite multiple readings. Meaning is seen here, not as given by the text, but as constructed in the social process of reading.

Making Interventions

In a challenging article, Ien Ang (1989) asks a basic but important question of audience researchers. Why, she asks, are we so interested in knowing about audiences in the first place? Ang suggests that audience research in Cultural Studies has often adopted an 'academistic' approach, which is apparently 'driven by a disinterested wish to contribute to "scientific progress"'. This approach, she argues, leads to a lack of clarity about the political functions and implications of research.

Audience researchers in this field have often claimed to be 'on the side of the audience' — to be defending 'ordinary viewers' against those who have characterized them as powerless 'dupes' of the media. In the case of research on children and television, this approach has arisen at least partly as a response to the kind of public debates described at the beginning of this chapter. In seeking to challenge the notion of children as 'television zombies', researchers have increasingly sought to represent children as active, sophisticated and discriminating viewers (e.g. Hodge and Tripp, 1986; Palmer, 1986; Buckingham, 1987a).

While this attempt to speak 'on the viewer's behalf' is certainly important, it also has its limitations. There is a real danger that the desire to validate viewers' perspectives can lead to a superficial populism, and even to a kind of political apathy. In rejecting the dominant view of children as passive victims of television, there is a risk of simply adopting an opposite view. In place of the traditional image of the innocent, vulnerable child, we end up with an equally sentimental image of the wise, liberated child. This view of children is as homogeneous and undifferentiated as the one it seeks to replace. It continues to talk about 'the child' as a universal category, rather than specific children living in specific social and historical circumstances.

Ultimately, I would agree with Ang that the aim of research in this field is not merely to accumulate a set of scientific 'facts' about the audience. On the contrary, the aim is 'to open up critical discourse on television audiences, and to sensitize it for the possibility of struggle in the field of television consumption — a struggle whose outcome cannot be known in advance, for the simple reason that encounters between television and audiences are always historically specific and context-bound' (Ang, 1989, p. 99).

The problem with Ang's argument, however, is that it lacks any specific point of reference. Where is this 'struggle' to be fought? It is surely not a purely domestic struggle — an argument, for example, over who gets to use the remote control. Neither is it a struggle which will be fought primarily in the pages of academic journals, or the seminar rooms of colleges and universities.

So where is this research to be used? Who is it for? As I have argued, popular debates about television — and particularly about children and television — have tended to proceed on the basis of much broader moral and political commitments. Research, where it is not wholly rejected (as it was by Prince Charles) is often used extremely selectively. Even on specific questions such as 'violence', where a premium has been placed on hard proof rather than exploration, academic research has had very little impact either on broadcasting policy or on the professional practices of broadcasters themselves.

While it would be wrong to abandon these debates, it would be naive to expect that research is likely to play a significant part in the 'struggles' that are to be fought within them. If one's primary aim is to change broadcasting policy, or to influence the work of broadcasting institutions, audience research — particularly of the more exploratory kind conducted within Cultural Studies — is probably one of the least effective ways of achieving this.

The research reported in this book arises from a rather different context, in which this 'struggle' is indeed being fought — namely, that of compulsory schooling. As I shall argue in Chapter 12, this is far from being a neutral context, in which political interventions can be made unproblematically. Nevertheless, the major aim of this book is to inform the work of teachers who are seeking to develop media education in schools, and to provide a firmer basis on which that work can proceed.

Although this research is not itself concerned with classroom practice or with children's learning, it is intended to complement the work which has recently begun in this area (British Film Institute, 1987, 1988; Buckingham, 1990a). On one level, the research is seeking to address a prior question — about what children *already* know about television — although it is one which classroom research has raised, often in very stark terms (e.g. Sefton-Green, 1990; Buckingham *et al.*, 1990). Yet on another level, the research has inevitably sought to challenge the terms of that question itself, and to ask how we might identify what children 'know'.

The notion of 'television literacy' may enable us to connect these two areas of media education and of audience research on the grounds of a broader concern with language. As I shall argue in the following chapter, it is a highly problematic idea, yet one which may offer considerable potential for both research and educational practice.

Chapter 2

Rethinking Television Literacy

The term 'television literacy' has been widely used in recent years, both by researchers investigating the relationship between children and television and by educationalists arguing for the formal study of the medium in schools.

On one level, the use of the term 'literacy' in this context is relatively neutral: it could be taken simply as a metaphor for competence in a whole range of communicative forms. Thus, television literacy would take its place on the school curriculum alongside print literacy, computer literacy, visual literacy, political and economic literacy, and so on. Clearly, the use of the term in this context is partly pragmatic. It is based on an analogy between the competencies which apply in relatively new or controversial or low-status areas and those which apply in the established, uncontroversial, high-status area of reading and writing. This analogy is used to bolster the implicit claim for the importance, even the respectability, of the 'new' area of study.

Yet the notion of 'television literacy' is also a polemical one. What is often implicit here is a much broader and more rhetorical attempt to redefine literacy itself. Pattison (1982), for example, suggests that the notion of literacy should not be tied to specific technologies or practices such as reading and writing: on the contrary, literacy as he defines it 'denotes consciousness of the questions posed by language coupled with mastery of those skills by which a culture at any given moment manifests this consciousness'. People who are able to read and write, Pattison argues, may lack this critical sensitivity to language; while those who are unable to do so may in fact possess it. The ancient Greeks, for example, had a 'critical and self-conscious' attitude towards language well before the invention of the alphabet: according to Pattison, the advent of writing simply enhanced their 'existing disposition . . . to treat language with critical vigour and wit'.

Like others who have argued for this redefinition of literacy (e.g. Spencer, 1986; Bazalgette, 1988), Pattison regards the literacy of the electronic media as simply another addition to the diversity of literacies available. This emergent popular literacy, which is keyed more to spoken than written language, is seen as a form of vernacular art which explicitly flouts atrophied standards of 'correct English'. Far from seeking to displace older forms of literacy, it blends with them, altering their practice in much the same way as the advent of print changed existing oral literacies at the time of the Renaissance.

However, this almost utopian argument would appear to underestimate the potential resistance to such changes — a resistance in which schools are likely to play a major role. Indeed, the very notion of 'television literacy' is a direct affront to many popular conceptions of the cultural value of different media. Many 'liberal' criticisms of television (e.g. Postman, 1983; Trelease, 1984; Winn, 1985) are based on a fundamental opposition between television and print literacy. Television is seen to have harmful educational and psychological consequences for the developing mind: it is seen as the deadly enemy of literacy and schooling and the values they are assumed to embody.

This opposition between television and print literacy has repeatedly surfaced in the so-called 'literacy crises' which have hit the headlines with increasing frequency in recent years. Along with 'progressive' teaching methods, television has been widely blamed for an alleged decline in children's reading abilities — yet evidence for these assertions has been limited, if not non-existent. Here too, the argument against television serves to deflect attention from other potential causes of decline — not least the reduction in funding for state education.

In this pragmatic respect, then, the use of the term 'literacy' may well give too many hostages to fortune — not least because it implicitly acknowledges the primacy of written language. Many teachers are likely to regard verbal literacy as infinitely more important than television literacy, and might well argue that children already know how to watch television, and certainly don't need to be taught how to do so in schools.

Nevertheless, the use of the term 'literacy' in this context is more than simply a pragmatic choice, or a polemical assertion. It is also based on a number of theoretical assumptions about language and about learning. In this chapter, I want to explore some of these more fundamental theoretical issues which are raised by the notion of 'television literacy'. As I shall argue, the value of the term will depend significantly upon the ways in which it is defined, and on the theories of language and learning which it embodies.

Television Literacy: Curriculum Theory and Practice

As I have indicated, 'moral panics' about the effects of television on children are at least partly motivated by a perceived sense of social crisis: television, like many other new cultural forms which preceded it, can function as a reassuringly simple explanation for a whole range of social ills. The development of television literacy curricula, particularly in the United States, could be seen primarily as a response to this sense of crisis. Most advocates of these curricula begin by assuming that television is 'a serious social problem' (Abelman, 1983): it is 'an illness', and it must be treated (Lull, 1981). Television, it is argued, exerts an extremely powerful and predominantly negative influence, particularly on children: it is held to be 'addictive', harmful to mental health and personal relationships, and a cause of social unrest and disintegration (see, e.g. Singer *et al.*, 1980).

The role of educators in this context is to defend those who are believed to be less capable of defending themselves. Embedded in their recommendations are prescriptions about styles of 'critical viewing' which are highly normative and often implicitly moralistic. The ultimate aim of most television literacy curricula is to encourage children to police their own viewing behaviour — if not by reducing the amount of television they watch, then at least by watching it in ways which are assumed to minimize its influence.

A representative illustration of this approach may be found in a book entitled *The New Literacy: The Language of Film and Television*, by Harold Foster (1979). Like many exponents of television literacy in schools, Foster argues that the media are primarily instruments of propaganda and mass persuasion. According to Foster, the 'power of the viewing experience' derives from the fact that it 'bypasses the intellect', 'hypnotising' viewers and on occasion causing them to commit violent acts. The fundamental aim of teaching about the media is to enable children to exert rational control over this process, and thereby to help them 'protect themselves against this powerful, primary emotional response'. 'Visual literacy', in Foster's terms, involves an understanding of the 'structural devices' which film-makers use to create a 'realistic facade' and thereby to mislead and manipulate audiences.

Foster's argument begs many questions about the relationship between children and television, and the role of education in intervening in it. Foster in fact collapses film and television together, although nearly all his detailed examples are taken from mainstream Hollywood films, and he fails to acknowledge the very different conditions of television viewing, or the differences between the 'languages' of the two media (cf. Ellis, 1982). Yet even if we confine the argument to film, the notion that viewing 'bypasses the intellect' and is primarily 'emotional' is certainly open to question (cf. Bordwell, 1985), as is the underlying opposition between 'emotional' and 'rational' responses.

Likewise, Foster's assertion that a study of the devices used by film-makers will help children 'to protect themselves' and 'to resist media influence and manipulation' also raises questions about the purpose and the effectiveness of such strategies. Can one necessarily assume that viewers are unaware of such 'manipulation', and thus in need of protection? To what extent is the 'rational' awareness of the protective teacher preferable to children's 'spontaneous' emotional responses, even assuming that such a distinction is possible? And does 'rational' control necessarily enable viewers to 'resist media influence'?

Finally, there is the question of how television literacy is defined. Foster consistently refers to television and film as forms of 'visual language', in which single images are seen as discrete units analogous to words. This 'language' is defined in terms of an abstract grammatical model — an approach which implies that images can be lifted out of context and assigned standard 'dictionary' meanings to which all would agree. It is assumed that this analysis of the elements of 'television language' and of the technical processes of television production will serve to 'debunk' the medium, and thereby give children rational control over their viewing behaviour. Ultimately, the outwardly neutral notion of 'literacy' which is being applied here is based on a series of fundamental value judgments about television and its role in children's lives.

James Anderson (1980, 1983), himself a major exponent of television literacy curricula, identifies four major paradigms which have informed the development of television literacy curricula in the United States. Predominant amongst them are what he terms the 'impact mediation' and the 'goal attainment' approaches. The notion of 'impact mediation' derives from the tradition of experimental 'effects' research: it presumes that television exerts direct behavioural effects on viewers, and that intervention can reduce its impact. Curricula based on this approach typically focus on 'problem areas' such as violent content, advertising and 'television addiction', and are designed to counteract television's 'negative' or 'anti-social' influence.

The 'goal attainment' approach derives from the 'uses and gratifications' paradigm: the assumption here is that individuals use the media in purposeful ways in order to achieve specific goals or gratifications. According to Anderson, 'goal attainment' curricula work in three stages: firstly, helping students to analyze their motives for viewing; secondly, encouraging them to evaluate their use of television in terms of its ability to fulfil or gratify those motives; and finally, providing practice in the process of making decisions about media use.

While these two approaches might outwardly appear quite different, they share a number of basic assumptions about the relationship between children and television, which ultimately derive more from the 'effects' paradigm than from 'uses and gratifications'. Both presume that television exerts a direct influence which is fundamentally negative or anti-social, and that children need to be protected from it. The difference is essentially one of strategy, rather than overall aims: while the 'impact mediation' approach seeks to protect children, for example by encouraging them to reduce the amount of television they watch, the 'goal attainment' approach is designed to enable them to protect themselves, by becoming their own 'critical censors' (Ashton, 1981).

As Marsha Jones (1984) has argued, both approaches start from the basic assumption that 'too much' television is 'bad' for children. Children are deemed to be 'unsophisticated' viewers who typically fail to understand or evaluate what they watch, and who are therefore in need of 'adult assistance' (Corder-Bolz, 1980). They are 'passive' viewers who need to be made 'active' (Finn, 1980). They have to be taught to discriminate, to be 'critical' and selective, since they are assumed to be incapable of doing this for themselves. The fundamental aim of most television literacy curricula is thus to disengage students from their unhealthy preoccupation with the medium, and to encourage a sceptical and suspicious approach to the false pleasures which it affords. As Anderson argues, the basic strategy is one of inducing guilt, and thereby seeking to 'save children from television'.

Nevertheless, the solutions offered to the 'problem' of television are fundamentally individualistic: the curricula are more concerned with enabling students to adapt to their environment, rather than encouraging them to change it — and in this sense, they clearly have a 'hidden' political agenda. As James Lull (1981) argues, these curricula tend to presume that it is up to the 'good little citizen' to deal with the problems of television, rather than seeking to upset the *status quo* which is responsible for them. As he indicates, many television literacy curricula fail to address central questions about the economic structure of broadcasting, and the political factors which determine the kinds of programmes which are made.

These curricula generally attempt to identify the characteristics of 'critical viewing' in terms of a taxonomy of 'receivership skills', which are then translated into behavioural objectives (e.g. Dorr *et al.*, 1980; Lloyd-Kolkin *et al.*, 1980). Yet on closer examination, many of the 'skills' which are specified are far from being as neutral as this term would imply. As Corder-Bolz (1982) argues, many of the 'critical evaluation skills' which are identified are more accurately seen as personal dispositions or attitudes: to choose a couple of the examples he cites, it is certainly difficult to regard the 'tendency to find television content fabricated and inaccurate' or to make 'less positive evaluations of television content' as 'skills' in any meaningful sense of the word.

Nevertheless, this emphasis on skills typically leads to highly mechanistic forms of 'instruction' which are very similar to those advocated by the 'back-to-basics' approach to teaching reading and writing. Literacy is regarded here as 'the sum of a set of precisely specifiable subskills' which can be broken down into sequential hierarchies (de Castell *et al.*, 1986). The standardized 'instructional systems' which proceed from this definition focus on the transmission of skills which can be readily and 'objectively' measured: simple, quantitative indices of 'effectiveness' then become an essential part of educational self-justification.

One of the major problems Anderson identifies here is the failure of television literacy curricula to acknowledge the 'pragmatics' of children's television viewing behaviour — that is, the everyday social contexts in which 'critical viewing' is to occur. Thus, most of the curricula which adopt the 'goal attainment' approach seek to encourage students to make 'rational' choices about their viewing behaviour, and to devise 'personal management strategies' to regulate their selection of viewing. In certain instances (e.g. Ploghoft and Anderson, 1982), elaborate monitoring schemes are provided in order to enable students to categorize their motivations for viewing, the reasons for their viewing preferences, and the changes in 'energy level' or 'emotional state' which occur as a result. As with the 'uses and gratifications' research on which it is based, this approach presumes that television viewing is 'normally' a purposive activity, which is essentially a matter of individual choice. Perhaps as a result, evaluations of television literacy curricula have signally failed to demonstrate their effectiveness in promoting 'literate' or 'critical' viewing *outside* the classroom context.

Ultimately, however, the fundamental problem which underlies such work is the definition of literacy which it employs. Despite the vagueness and confusion which surrounds the term, it is clear that literacy is implicitly regarded here as a set of abstract competencies. Each medium is seen to have its own specific grammar or syntax — that is, a set of objective rules which enable it to generate meaning. The extent to which individuals are seen to 'possess' these competencies can thus be measured by their grasp of these rules and meanings. The definition of literacy which obtains here is fundamentally blind to the diverse social contexts in which these competencies are acquired and used, and the diverse forms of social and cultural knowledge which are involved in producing meaning. In short, it is a definition which fails to acknowledge that literacy is inevitably embedded within specific social practices.

Is Television a Language?

The notion of television literacy rests on a prior assumption that television can be regarded as a language — one which is, at least in some significant respects, analogous to written language. Yet while such analogies may appear superficially attractive, they may also lead one to ignore essential differences and distinctions. In this instance, the value of the analogy crucially depends upon what we regard as the 'essential' features of language — and ultimately upon how we define language itself.

Certainly, it is possible to suggest a number of broad similarities between the two media. Both television and written language are forms of communication: they are both methods of conveying or signifying meaning, which are used in different ways by different social agents in different social and cultural contexts.

Both depend upon a degree of shared understanding between their users, which is learned rather than innate. Both are in a constant state of historical change and evolution.

In a sense, these statements are too general to be of much use: and yet they are already contentious. There are no 'facts' about language which are not already derived from theories — despite the recent arguments of right-wing educationalists! Certainly when one seeks to extend the analogy beyond the generalities I have offered here, these difficulties become even more acute.

There have been a number of attempts to develop analogies between verbal language and the 'symbolic systems' of the visual arts, and to use these as a basis for teaching. Advocates of 'iconics', for example, have argued that visual language can be regarded as a kind of 'alphabet', from which basic minimal units ('graph-emes') combine to form larger meaningful ones ('iconemes'), which in turn lead on to visual 'syntagms', or statements (Cossette, 1982). Likewise, the approach to 'visual literacy' pioneered by Dondis (1973) presumes that visual language possesses a 'syntax' which can be reduced to its constituent parts and then taught in sequence.

Work on cognition in the visual arts has also explored this analogy, although from a less mechanistic perspective. Thus, it is argued that while pictorial systems may not possess a formal syntax (Goodman, 1968), the perceptual processes which are involved in 'reading' images and written texts are more similar than conventional wisdom tends to suggest (Kolers, 1977; Luke, 1985). Nevertheless, such theories have also acknowledged basic distinctions between visual and linguistic systems, particularly in terms of their relationship to the reality they seek to represent (e.g. Pierce, 1940; Goodman, 1968).

Perhaps the most sustained and rigorous attempt to develop the analogy between audio-visual and verbal languages is in the field of film theory, and in particular in the work of Christian Metz. Metz's early work (1974a) amply illustrates the difficulties which arise when the film language analogy is pursued in detail. Indeed, Metz begins by refuting the literal use of this analogy which he detects in early theories of 'film grammar', and in the Russian theorists of montage — the notion that films can be constructed and analyzed according to strict correspond-ences between the shot and the word, the sequence and the sentence, and so on (e.g. Pudovkin, 1960). Like Goodman (1968), Metz argues that there are no basic, clearly distinguishable syntactic elements in film which are analogous to pho-nemes or morphemes in language. The language of cinema, Metz argues, is 'flexible, never predetermined': it is 'a rich message with a poor code, or a rich text with poor system', which is closer to speech than written language.

Using the classic Saussurean distinction, Metz ultimately concludes that film is a language (*langage*), but one which does not possess an underlying language system (*langue*) — that is, a 'code' or 'grammar' (cf. Barthes, 1977). Film does not possess what Metz defines as the three central characteristics of language: it is a one-way form of communication, rather than a form of 'intercommunication'; it is only partly a system; and its images are mainly analogical, rather than 'arbitrary, conventional and codified' like 'true signs' (Metz, 1974a). As a result, he suggests, the attempt to base a semiotics of the cinema on its 'small' elements (its phonemes or morphemes) is doomed to failure: these specific units will only be displayed once one reaches the level of fairly 'large' elements — although the question of how one differentiates between 'small' and 'large' elements is not one Metz himself resolves.

Following this logic, Metz went on to pursue the film language analogy on a broader level, attempting to identify the codes which govern the syntactic combination or ordering of images (Metz, 1974a). Yet in several respects, Metz's *'grande syntagmatique'* (large-scale syntagmatics) runs into the same difficulties as the attempts to identify film language on the level of single images. Again using a Saussurean approach, Metz constructs a taxonomy of eight different combinations, which is based on a series of binary oppositions. Yet the distinctions between these different categories are less fixed than Metz would lead us to believe, particularly when one seeks to apply the system to films which fall outside what he arbitrarily designates as 'classical narrative cinema' (Daniel, 1976). Many of the key distinctions on which the system is based are not purely 'formal', but derive from a prior sense of their *meaning*. As Metz himself acknowledges, one understands the syntax because one has understood the film, and not vice versa. On a historical level, 'it is not because the cinema is language that it has told such fine stories, but rather it has become language because it has told such fine stories' (1974a, p. 47).

Critics of Metz's early work (e.g. Abramson, 1976; Nichols, 1976) argue that this approach tends to ignore elements such as 'style' and *mise-en-scène* which are not easily accounted for in terms of digital or linguistic codes. Furthermore, the use of categories derived from structural linguistics is often misleading: film does not possess equivalents to many basic properties of language, such as tenses and negatives. Nichols asserts that there is no such thing as an 'ungrammatical' statement in film, or an abstract standard which can be used to distinguish 'correct' from 'incorrect' utterances — thus effectively refuting the idea that film possesses a syntax, and by implication the notion of film language itself.

In developing the film language analogy, Metz (1974b) acknowledges the fact that cinema uses a diversity of codes, which together constitute the specific qualities of the medium. Thus, as well as 'iconic' codes, there are auditory codes, and codes which govern the combination of images and sounds. Nevertheless, Metz does not fully specify the relationship between these codes. It may be, as Kjorup (1977) argues, that some codes are more 'basic' than others, and thereby serve to 'elucidate' more complex codes, but this process is difficult to formalize.

However, it is at this point that the language analogy — or, more precisely, the application of Saussurean linguistics to film — begins to break down. Metz (1974b) acknowledges that the Saussurean distinction between *'langue'* (the language system) and *'parole'* (speech, or language in use) may itself be artificial, even in the case of verbal language. By abstracting a language system from the diversity of individual utterances, the analyst risks reducing the dynamic complexity of language use to fixed set of grammatical rules. The decision to include or exclude particular elements from consideration as valid components of *'langue'* inevitably depends upon prior judgments as to what is or is not meaningful. To exclude aspects of *'parole'* such as accent or intonation, for example, is to rule out major aspects of the social *pragmatics* of language.

Despite the potential advantages of the model of language which begins to emerge at this point in Metz's work (Metz, 1974b), his subsequent writing largely evades the questions it raises. The shift away from Saussurean linguistics leads not towards a social theory of language, but towards a psychoanalytic model which fails to resolve many of the basic problems of the film language analogy.

One aspect of Metz's later theory which illustrates this is the distinction between 'story' (*histoire*) and 'discourse' which he derives from the work of Benveniste (Metz, 1982). Both story and discourse are forms of linguistic enunciation: but whereas discourse always contains markers of the source of its enunciation (for example, by the use of pronouns such as 'I' and 'you'), the story form attempts to suppress these. According to Metz, 'classical' realist cinema falls into the category of story: specific discourses (for example, those of characters within the film) are present, but they are framed within a narrative 'metalanguage' which offers itself as invisible or 'unspoken' (MacCabe, 1974).

However, as David Bordwell (1985) indicates, it is difficult to see how many of Benveniste's linguistic categories could ever be applied to film — for example, how we would distinguish between first-person and second-person discourse, or between the utterance (*énoncé*) and the act of enunciation (*énonciation*). While it may have a certain metaphorical validity, the linguistic analogy simply does not hold when one attempts to apply it at the 'micro' level of specific textual features. As subsequent critics have shown (e.g. Feuer, 1986; Flitterman-Lewis, 1987), these difficulties are compounded when one attempts to apply Metz's later theory to the very different conditions of television spectatorship.

Ultimately, what is lacking in both psychoanalytic and structuralist versions of the film language analogy is a means of accounting for the social and cultural diversity of language use. Both offer an ahistorical, asocial account of language: language is seen either as an abstract system of codes and rules, or as a monolithic 'symbolic order' which is simply imposed on the subject. Both are essentially determinist theories, which have considerable difficulty in acknowledging contradiction or the potential for historical change.

It is for these reasons that the social theory of language developed by the Soviet theorists Volosinov and Bakhtin, and the related theories of language and consciousness developed by Vygotsky, appear to offer a more productive alternative. Volosinov (1973) takes issue with Saussure's fundamental distinction between '*langue*' and '*parole*': he argues that Saussure's approach is unable to account for the 'individual creative refraction and variation of language forms', and hence for the relationship between language and consciousness. Saussure's 'abstract objectivism' conceives of language as 'a stable, immutable system of normatively identical linguistic forms', and hence cannot acknowledge the historical processes by which languages change, or the social contexts in which they are used. By contrast, Volosinov regards language as constitutive of consciousness, rather than simply its product: 'the individual consciousness', he argues, 'is a social-ideological fact'.

Bakhtin's central concept of 'dialogue' (Bakhtin, 1986) likewise emphasizes the social, communicative functions of language, which he argues have effectively been bracketed off from consideration in structuralist linguistics. For both writers, the sign is a site on which different discourses intersect: and it is for this reason that it retains its dynamism and its capacity for change. At the same time, speech itself is not, as Saussure suggested, merely individual. Bakhtin's theory of 'speech genres' suggests that speech is inevitably subject to social conventions. Any utterance inevitably draws on, and responds to, previous utterances in a given sphere and is thus far from being self-sufficient.

The theory of language I have briefly sketched here has considerable potential for a theory of television literacy. It enables us to move beyond the impasse Metz encountered in attempting to develop literal analogies between the 'basic elements' of verbal language and the 'basic elements' of film. Rather than seeking to break language down into its smallest constituent parts, or to define its syntactic system in abstract terms, its central focus is on the communicative context. From this perspective, the basic unit of speech communication is not the word or the sentence, but the utterance. The boundaries of the utterance are defined by a change in speaking subjects, since every utterance is always part of a dialogue, even if this fact itself may be repressed.

In this way, the theory also refutes simplistic notions of 'passive viewing'. For Volosinov and Bakhtin, 'understanding' is not a passive process, but on the contrary an act of dialogue, 'a response to a sign with signs'. Every utterance implies an addressee, and every response is an active participation in speech communication. The listener, according to Bakhtin (1981), is active because (s)he is always conscious of other 'alien' words, and interprets the text in a way which is 'pregnant with responses and objections'.

Likewise, the theory offers a more satisfactory account of the ambiguous nature of texts and the social diversity of reading practices. For example, Bakhtin (1981) argues that the novel is the site of social 'heteroglossia', or multiple languages. While the literary language of the novel seeks to 'organize' this heteroglossia in different ways, and thereby to suppress contradiction, this is constantly disrupted by the intrusion of 'alien words' deriving from the 'low genres' of popular literature. Similarly, rather than regarding television as the bearer of a unitary, or even a 'preferred' meaning, this approach would lead to a view of the medium as a site of conflict or dialogue between different social and ideological languages (cf. Newcomb, 1984; Barker, 1987). While the medium might attempt to control this by imposing a unitary, institutional 'voice', the success of this attempt can never be guaranteed: as a result, television can always be interpreted and appropriated in widely divergent ways by different audiences.

Finally, by dispensing with Saussure's distinction between '*langue*' and '*parole*', the theory implicitly dispenses with the related distinction between competence and performance. As Hymes (1972) has argued, the danger of abstracting competence from performance is that competence becomes idealized: many of the factors which pertain to linguistic interaction, to the use of language for the purposes of communication, are simply ruled out of court. 'Competence' thus becomes — as it is in certain theories of literacy — a property which individuals somehow 'possess', and which they retain at their disposal until it is used. A social theory of literacy, by contrast, acknowledges that the display of 'competence' will depend upon the social and discursive contexts in which it is required, and the specific purposes of the user. It thus implicitly rejects this idealized, asocial concept of 'competence', and the pedagogic practices which are based upon it.

Does Understanding Television Require a Form of Literacy?

The origin of the word 'literacy' would suggest that it refers explicitly to written language. To employ the term in relation to television therefore implies that the *competencies* which are involved in using the medium are in some sense analogous to those which are involved in reading and writing.

However, there are a number of significant differences between the competencies which are required by the two media. Television and written language use different technologies, which in turn involve different social relationships. While the technologies required for reading and writing (pens, paper, books etc.) and indeed for watching television, are fairly widely available, at least in industrialized countries, those required for *producing* television are much more scarce, and are largely confined to small elites. While most of us are able to read and write, and nearly all of us are able to watch television, few of us will ever get the opportunity to make programmes. One might justifiably argue that television is fundamentally less 'egalitarian' than verbal language for this reason (cf. Olson, 1986a).

Nevertheless, there are dangers in posing this distinction in such absolute terms. There are certainly powerful institutions which control the dissemination of written language, just as there are limits on the access to television. Many of us may write, but comparatively few of us are published. Furthermore, not all situations which involve speakers and listeners, let alone those which involve writers and readers, are necessarily 'egalitarian': there are always rules which limit what it is possible to say, and in certain cases who is allowed to speak. While it would be misguided to imply that these differences are merely illusory, it would be more accurate to regard them as differences of degree rather than of kind, which take specific forms within specific social and historical contexts.

Perhaps the most systematic and rigorous attempt to define the competencies which are involved in 'television literacy' may be found in the work of the psychologist Gavriel Salomon (e.g. 1979a, 1979b). The implications and the problems of his approach are best illustrated by an article in which he specifically seeks to define the term (Salomon, 1982). The central question, Salomon suggests, is whether the skills required for understanding television are specific to the medium: is 'television literacy' a separate set of abilities, or is it merely part of a more general literacy? As a complex symbol system, he argues, television is composed of elements which are not unique to the medium — both 'the literal visual and/ or auditory portrayal of real-life information' and the symbols, such as verbal language, which are used by a variety of media — and those which are specific to it. It is these latter elements, which Salomon argues are primarily 'single, molar elements such as cuts, fades and zooms, as well as more complex molecular ones, that blend the molar ones into a whole plot' (p. 8), which surely require a more specific form of literacy.

Salomon goes on to ask what weight these TV-specific skills have in the overall comprehension of programmes. He proposes that comprehension follows three sequential stages. The first involves the mental recoding (or deciphering) of a coded message into a parallel mental representation; the second entails 'chunking' or integrating these elements into meaningful units; and the third involves making elaborations on that material — drawing inferences, yielding new attributions or questions, and so on. Salomon argues that the processes which take place in earlier stages are more medium-specific, while those in later stages are more general: thus, if there is a literacy which is specific to the medium, it is manifested only in the earlier phases of processing a message.

The relative weight of these stages will therefore depend upon the viewer's competence. For less experienced (that is, less 'literate') viewers, the earlier stages will be more difficult, since the skills they entail are less automatic. For more experienced viewers, who can carry out the earlier stages more easily, it is the later stages — which are less specific to the medium — that are more important. Salomon therefore concludes that television literacy is acquired easily and early in life, and comes to be applied quite automatically: as such, he asserts, it carries little weight, except for younger children.

In many respects, Salomon's argument here would appear to coincide with common sense. If we look at what a 'competent' viewer does, and attempt to break it down into its constituent parts, certain operations do appear to be easier than others, and it would seem logical to infer that they are both the first things we learn, and also the first things we do in actually making sense of programmes. A 'commonsense' account of reading — and thus a methodology for teaching reading — has been developed in the same way: first we learn to decipher letters, then syllables, words, sentences and so on. Salomon would also seem to be correct in arguing that these 'basic' skills are more medium-specific; just as learning to read involves understanding specific principles such as the fact that print goes from left to right, so learning to make sense of television involves understanding the basic principle of editing, for example. Once we have grasped these skills, basic 'decoding' appears to become automatic, and most of our mental effort is expended on activities which apply to a range of media.

If we look at the argument more closely, however, there are a number of questionable assumptions. Firstly, Salomon presumes 'that processing is an orderly activity that begins with the first phase, entailing medium-specific skills, and progresses towards the third phase' (p. 10). Research on reading print, however, would suggest that this is not in fact the case: even beginning readers are actively predicting and making inferences about texts (that is, engaging in 'third phase' activities), and using these as a basis for their 'decoding' of letters and words ('first phase' activities). Expectations and hypotheses about meaning guide our understanding of language, and 'mistakes' (or 'miscues') in reading are often the result of quite logical, if ultimately mistaken, predictions (Smith, 1973). The act of reading does not follow the sequence Salomon outlines, but on the contrary involves a coordination of these stages (or, in the jargon, of 'bottom-up' and 'top-down' processes) (Cole and Griffin, 1986).

Furthermore, the idea that only 'first phase' skills are medium-specific is also questionable. If one takes one of Salomon's 'third phase' skills, the ability to generate inferences, it is clear that this happens in a very different way in television as compared to print. In reading a novel, for example, at least some of the inferences we generate are visual: we use the writer's descriptions of people or places to construct mental images, which are often revised as we read. In watching television, this process of visual inference is more or less redundant: television can show us things in a way that print cannot. On the other hand, television has much greater difficulty in representing characters' motivations or mental states. While novels can provide us with this kind of information fairly easily (although of course they may not always do so), television often leaves us to infer these, for example from facial expressions or gestures. Only by resorting to verbal language — to devices such as voice-over or dialogue, which may appear dangerously 'literal' — can it hope to remove potential ambiguities.

Secondly, Salomon's definition of the 'essential' characteristics of television's symbolic system is rather limited, and is effectively confined to a list of techniques, such as camera movements and editing procedures. There is a danger here of defining this symbolic system as a kind of rigid 'grammar', in which discrete units are seen to possess a fixed, objective meaning. Yet a zoom, for example, may 'mean' very different things at different times; and it may on certain occasions 'mean' effectively the same thing as a tracking shot or an 'irising' movement or a cut to close-up. For this reason, even such apparently 'basic' units of television language cannot be said to be 'processed' automatically. However subliminally or momentarily, choices have to be made about their meaning, even by experienced viewers.

The further problem here is that Salomon's definition effectively ignores the broader levels on which the language of television is organized — the level of narrative structure, of genre, of mode of address, and so on. These phenomena are also conventional, institutionalized forms of language which are equally specific to the medium. For example, while television genres draw upon genres in other media, they are also inflected in specific ways, and are in some cases unique to the medium. Likewise television has its own unique forms of narrative structure and its own modes of address, which are in a constant state of evolution and which cannot simply be reduced to a few characteristic camera movements or conventions of editing. Yet again, it might be argued that, as in the case of reading, our understanding of specific small-scale 'units' is guided by our knowledge of these larger-scale phenomena: we make sense of the freeze frame at the end of *Dallas*, for example, because of what we know about the genre of soap opera, rather than vice versa.

The third problem here centres on Salomon's concept of 'skills'. As I have noted, the skills he regards as specific to the medium are relatively limited, and are acquired at a fairly early age. Yet if, as I have argued, the skill of 'decoding' even the most basic units of television language depends upon the context in which they are found — that is, upon the meanings viewers attribute to them — this can hardly be regarded as something which is achieved once and for all. Even experienced viewers will decode these units in different ways, and may even ignore or fail to register basic cues which are provided, and thus 'misinterpret' what they watch. In this sense, the basic separation between 'skills' and 'knowledge' (or meaning) is highly problematic: 'skills' are not exercised in the abstract, but are always developed in the process of producing meaning. Learning is not simply a matter of an abstract set of skills being applied to an inert object: it depends upon the learner's motivations, the ways in which the learner perceives the task, and indeed his or her own abilities. In this sense, 'skills' are not simply a function of the demands of the medium: they are also a function of the social context in which meaning is produced.

In educational terms, this emphasis on a sequential hierarchy of skills inevitably leads to mechanistic approaches to teaching, and presumes that children will build up understandings in the same way that teachers break them down (Eke, 1986). As critics of remedial reading instruction have argued, the division into 'top-down' and 'bottom-up' skills can work against children learning to read, in that it leads them to subordinate their own search for meaning (Cole and Griffin, 1986; Olson, 1986b).

In this respect, Salomon's definition of 'literate viewing' as viewing which involves 'deeper processing' is particularly problematic (see also Cohen and Salomon, 1979). To begin with, there is the question of how we define and measure 'deeper' processing. In practice, Salomon's approach is essentially that of a recognition or memory test, or a matter of counting the number of 'inferences' children make, which is at least reductive. More crucially, however, his definition is implicitly normative. The major problem with the way children watch television, as far as Salomon is concerned, is not to do with the content of the medium, or its allegedly anti-social effects; nor is it to do with a lack of the skills which are required to make sense of it. On the contrary, the trouble is that most children just don't make enough *effort*. Yet again, what is being offered, under cover of an apparently neutral rhetoric of 'skills' and 'literacy', is an implicit definition of the *attitudes* children should be encouraged to adopt. While this approach does get beyond evaluative notions about the 'inherent' superiority of one medium over another, it replaces these by similarly prescriptive ideas about the *use* of those media (cf. Shannon and Fernie, 1985).

In many respects, these problems are symptomatic of broader limitations in the way cognitive psychologists have tended to define television literacy. In terms of their definitions of the 'language' or 'symbolic systems' which are specific to television, psychologists have typically focused on a limited range of 'formal features', and sought to study these in isolation from questions of 'content' or meaning. Insofar as meanings are addressed, it is presumed that these can simply be extracted and defined objectively.

Yet again, the theory of television literacy which emerges here is fundamentally asocial. Literacy is defined as a very limited range of 'skills' which are somehow 'possessed' by individuals, and which may be identified without regard to the social contexts in which they are exercised, or the meanings they are used to produce. To pose the question in such terms — as a question of the relationship between television and individual cognition — is to ignore the fact that making sense of the medium is inevitably a social practice, which takes place at least partly in and through verbal language. As I shall argue, work on print literacy has increasingly acknowledged these social dimensions of language use.

Towards a Social Theory of Literacy

One significant danger in many discussions of television literacy is the assumption that there is an agreed definition of verbal literacy with which it can be compared. Yet studies of the social and historical dimensions of verbal literacy indicate that this is not the case. On the contrary, the definition of literacy has itself been the focus of considerable ideological debate.

Brian Street (1984) offers a useful distinction here between what he terms 'autonomous' and 'ideological' definitions of literacy. The autonomous model presumes that literacy develops in a single direction, and is associated with notions of social progress, 'civilization', individual liberty and social mobility. Literacy is distinguished from the social and educational institutions in which it is typically acquired. It is seen as an independent variable, which has specific consequences both for societies and for individuals: it brings about economic prosperity, for example, and facilitates the development of logical, objective thought.

Street identifies a number of problems with this model. He argues that the methodologies researchers have used to substantiate such claims for literacy often reveal forms of ethnocentric bias. In many respects, the 'essentialist' distinction between literate and pre-literate societies merely replicates the earlier distinction between 'primitive' and 'modern' societies — a distinction which anthropologists have increasingly acknowledged is based on a misunderstanding of so-called 'primitive' cultures and thought processes. The use of the term 'literacy' here provides an aura of the 'technical', and thereby gives legitimacy to statements which would otherwise be seen as culturally loaded.

By contrast, Street's 'ideological' model of literacy is fundamentally opposed to the determinism of the autonomous model. Literacy is seen here, not as an independent variable whose consequences can be studied in isolation, but as inevitable embedded in specific social practices which are in turn embedded in specific cultural and institutional contexts. The skills and competencies which accompany the acquisition of literacy do not simply follow from the 'inherent' qualities of the written word: they are socially constructed in the practice of that literacy, and hence cannot be seen as neutral or merely 'technical'. What literacy 'means' depends on the processes by which it is learnt, the purposes for which it is used, and the institutions in which this takes place. In effect, the model dispenses with the notion of a *single* literacy, and replaces it with the idea of *plural* literacies, which are defined by the meanings they produce and the social uses they serve.

Street's ideological model of literacy finds support both from work in linguistics (e.g. Bourdieu, 1977; Halliday, 1978; Hodge and Kress, 1988) and from historical research on literacy instruction (Graff, 1979, 1986). Ethnographic research in contemporary societies also suggests that the 'literacies' of different social groups can only be interpreted in relation to broader institutional and sociocultural processes. Heath (1983), for example, points to the different functions which literacy serves for different social classes and ethnic groups: the nature, and indeed the consequences, of literacy vary significantly according to the roles which reading and writing play in the family, the community and the workplace. Likewise, Street's own ethnographic research on different forms of literacy in Iran the 1970s points to the importance of relating practices of reading and writing to the broader social and economic changes of the period (Street, 1984).

Perhaps the clearest illustration of the issue, however, is the debate over 'functional literacy'. The work of many adult literacy campaigns, and of UNESCO in developing countries, has typically been informed by the notion of a minimum level of literacy which is necessary for the individual to 'survive' or to function adequately within a particular social sphere. However, such definitions inevitably depend upon what one means by 'survival' or 'adequate functioning': as Levene (1986) indicates, any notion of functional literacy is inevitably ideological, in that it depends upon prior assumptions about social welfare, rights and responsibilities. As such, it cannot be defined simply by impartial, factual investigation. Indeed, in the case of UNESCO, the debates over functional literacy have been inextricably involved with broader struggles over cultural values and economic resources.

In seeking to define literacy, therefore, we are centrally concerned with the relationships between cognitive and linguistic processes and the specific social practices within which they are situated. As I have argued, literacy cannot be reduced to an abstract set of 'skills', which can be studied in isolation from the meanings which readers (or viewers) produce or the institutional and social structures in which they are embedded. Likewise, language cannot be reduced to an abstract set of grammatical 'rules', which function independently of the meaning and social context of communication.

In terms of the models of literacy outlined here, much of the work on television literacy I have discussed implicitly shares the assumptions of the autonomous model. It presumes that television literacy is a single set of cognitive abilities which individuals 'possess', that meaning is objective and inherent in texts, and that both can be defined irrespective of social or cultural forces. Educationally, it gives rise to a narrow, mechanistic pedagogy which seems designed to produce conformity rather than genuine, open-ended critical enquiry.

By contrast, a social theory of television literacy would begin by acknowledging that children's use of television is an integral part of the texture of their daily lives, and of their relationships with the family and the peer group. It would acknowledge that the competencies which are involved in making sense of television are not equally available, but socially distributed, and that they are intimately connected with the operation of social power. Children would be seen as members of different 'interpretive communities' (Fish, 1980; Luke, 1985), which have different orientations to television, and may use it as a means of negotiating social and cultural identities in quite diverse ways. In this sense, different social groups may employ different 'television literacies', or different modalities of literacy, which have different social and ideological functions and consequences. Finally, like print literacy, television literacy would be seen as subject to historical change and development. As media languages and technologies evolve, so do definitions of what it means to be literate — a process which is arguably accelerating at the present moment, with the proliferation of media sources being made available by 'new' technologies such as video, cable and satellite.

An Outline of the Research

The research reported in this book is offered as a contribution to the development of this broader social theory of television literacy. It concentrates on one aspect of the process, and on a limited age group, and is therefore not intended to be all-encompassing. Nevertheless, my intention here is not merely to 'describe' the development or distribution of children's competencies as viewers — even assuming that such a neutral process were possible. On the contrary, the research seeks to question many of the basic assumptions which might underlie such a description, and which also inform a good deal of educational practice in this area.

The research is centrally concerned with the ways in which children aged between 7 and 12 years of age *talk* about television. This age group was chosen for a variety of reasons. Much of the psychological research considered in the previous chapter is in fact concerned with quite young children, often of pre-school age. There appears to be much less research on children in 'middle childhood' and early adolescence, although it is in this period that children in fact watch most television. Furthermore, it is also with children in this age group that recent developments in media education, at least in Britain, have been particularly concerned.

All the qualitative data to be presented here is taken from discussions with small groups of between two and five children. The core sample of ninety children contained equal numbers of boys and girls, and was divided into three age groups. The youngest children were 7 at the start of the research; the next youngest 9; and the oldest 11. The children were recruited from four schools, chosen to given a balance of ethnic and social class backgrounds: in each case, a secondary school was paired with one of its 'feeder' primary schools. An initial questionnaire was used to exclude children who appeared to watch very little television.

The sample in each of the schools can be characterized briefly as follows, using information gained from a detailed questionnaire sent to parents. The two 'inner-city' schools (one primary, one secondary) were situated in the inner London borough of Hackney, which according to conventional social indices is one of the most deprived areas of the country. A high proportion (27 per cent) of the children came from single-parent families, and the majority (82 per cent) could be described as working-class. These groups were ethnically very diverse, with a comparatively high proportion (62 per cent) of black children of Asian or Afro-Caribbean descent.

The two 'suburban' schools (one primary, one secondary) were situated in the comparatively affluent outer London borough of Enfield. The majority of these children (80 per cent) could be described as middle-class, and a much smaller proportion (8 per cent) came from single-parent families. These groups were also much less ethnically diverse, with only 13 per cent of the children being black, all of Asian descent. The secondary school was a selective, voluntary aided school with a competitive entrance examination — although the class mix here was more or less identical to that of the primary school.

These blunt statistics tend to disguise the complex nature of class and ethnic identity, and this is an issue I shall take up in some detail at various points in the book. Just as feminists have rightly objected to the way in which definitions of women's social class are often derived from their husband's occupational status, there are similar problems with defining children simply in terms of their parents' class position. By default, I have had to designate children in terms of the two broad categories 'working-class' and 'middle-class', according to their parents' occupation, educational level and type of accommodation — although in some cases these indicators are contradictory. Certainly in this case, it would be possible to argue that the culture of the schools concerned and the nature of the peer group played a significant role in defining children's perceptions of their class identity. Being 'middle-class' meant something very different for the minority of middle-class children in the inner-city schools compared with those in the middle-class majority in the suburban schools.

Similar arguments apply in the case of ethnicity, although here it is also important to draw distinctions between 'first' and 'second' or 'third generation' immigrants. The large majority of black children here (and all those of Afro-Caribbean descent) were second or third generation, although there were some Asian children who were first generation, and whose parents often spoke little English at home. I have designated the former group 'British/Afro-Caribbean' or 'British/Asian', the latter simply 'Asian', while recognizing that there are significant problems with these crude labels. Furthermore, there were children in all of the schools whom I have classified as 'white' yet whose parents were Greek Cypriot, Turkish, Polish or Italian — to name but a few. As I hope to demonstrate in my analysis of the group discussions, social identities of this kind are not simply 'given', but at least to some extent determined or achieved in the process of talk.

The children were grouped in different combinations for each of the eight activities undertaken across a period of around fifteen months. In some cases, where this was felt to be relevant, they were placed in single-sex groups, or divided according to social class or ethnic background. In other instances, the groupings were either random, or devised in terms of friendship patterns. The discussions and activities were convened by three different researchers — two female, one male. The researchers 'circulated' twice during the course of the research, so that each group met each of the three researchers on two or three occasions. The aim here was not so much to 'control' for the influence of different groupings or different interviewing styles, as to make it possible to study children's talk in a range of different interpersonal contexts.

The various activities undertaken with these groups will be described in subsequent chapters. While some were comparatively open-ended, others were designed to investigate quite specific conceptual areas. However, it is important to emphasize that the central focus of this book is one the ways in which children *talk* about television. This is, as I shall indicate, not necessarily identical with what they 'think' or 'understand'; nor does it by any means exhaust all the possible parameters of 'television literacy'. Nevertheless, what children say about television, and the ways in which they discuss it with their peers and with adults, is undoubtedly a central aspect of the process by which its meanings are established and circulated.

Conclusion

As I have argued in this chapter, the notion of 'television literacy' is far from straightforward: it begs many complex theoretical questions, and can be defined in some very diverse and contradictory ways. Yet, as I have shown, this is no less true of the term 'literacy' itself. While there are certainly pragmatic and even polemical reasons for continuing to use the term, my main reason for doing so is precisely because of the fact that it is such a contested area. Attempting to define what is at stake in children's use and understanding of television in these terms raises much broader questions about language and learning, and about the relationship between the 'individual' and the 'social' — question which mainstream research has often failed to address. The notion of 'television literacy' is ultimately a metaphor — a metaphor which is undoubtedly problematic, yet in my view extremely powerful.

Part Two

Making Sense of Television Talk

Technically, television is a means of encoding sounds and images into electronic signals. These signals are delivered to receivers, which in turn convert them back into sounds and images. Yet these signals, sounds and images are not inherently meaningful. They have to be invested with meaning by the individuals who see and hear them. In this sense, television does not deliver meaning: on the contrary, viewers construct it.

Yet as I have argued, this process cannot be seen merely as a matter of the individual's isolated encounter with the screen. It is inevitably a social process, which involves a variety of forms of dialogue, both spoken and unspoken. It is principally through talk that the meanings and pleasures of television are defined and circulated.

Critics of television tend to regard viewing as an anti-social pastime which has 'killed the art of conversation'. Yet in fact television viewing is predominantly a social activity, which usually takes place in the company of others. Viewers do not, by and large, sit passively absorbing what they watch: they talk to each other, and may even talk back to the screen. Even when we actually watch alone, we will often talk about what we watch with others. Talk about television is a vital element of our everyday social lives.

The production of meaning from television is thus part of a broader 'oral culture' (Fiske, 1987a). The meanings which circulate within everyday discussion of television are 'read back' into individual responses to the medium, thereby generating a dynamic interplay between 'social' and 'individual' readings — and perhaps ultimately rendering the distinction itself irrelevant. What we 'think' about television and how we use it in our daily lives depend to a great extent on how we talk about it with others, and the contexts in which we do so.

At the same time, talk about television is instrumental in constructing and sustaining our social relationships, and thus our sense of our own social identity. As Hodge and Tripp (1986, p. 143) have argued:

> Discourse about television is itself a considerable social force. It is a major site of the mediation of television meanings, a site where television meanings fuse with other meanings into a new text to form a major interface with the world of action and belief.

As Hodge and Tripp imply, talk inevitably possesses social functions, which are specific to the situation in which it occurs. What we say about the television programmes we watch — and even what we admit to watching in the first place — will depend upon who we are talking to, and the context in which we are doing so. It will vary according to how well we know our listeners, what we would like them to think about us, and what kind of relationship we would like to establish with them.

Thus, there are undoubtedly situations in which talk about television is seen as an extremely useful way of establishing social relationships. Rather like the weather, television can appear to provide safe ground for what linguists term 'phatic speech' — that is, speech which serves simply to establish and maintain communication. Nevertheless, this kind of strategy is likely to be more problematic as the social distance between the speakers increases. While there are some programmes that might be seen to serve as a kind of 'common culture' — particularly highly popular programmes — talk about television can very quickly reveal the speaker's social, political or moral affiliations.

Similarly, different styles of talk may be perceived as more or less appropriate, according to the context. For middle-class adults, and perhaps especially for parents and teachers, talk about television often functions as a kind of indicator of one's 'responsibility'. Proclaiming one's dislike of television, and one's concern about its effects on children, can serve as a powerful guarantee of the speaker's political and moral concern (see Chapter 5; also Fraser, 1990). The regularity with which people will condemn programmes they have never watched, or regale you with stories about how television depraves and corrupts other people's children, indicates how much is at stake in adopting a principled opposition to the medium and all its evil works.

Yet even for children, television can be used to establish and negotiate social relationships in ways which are far from neutral. For the children involved in this research, their everyday social talk about television — which sometimes seemed to take place in the classroom, on the margins of school work — seemed to provide a means of defining friendships, and establishing a kind of social pecking order among the peer group. Certain programmes — the Australian soaps *Neighbours* and *Home and Away* and the comedies *Red Dwarf* and *Desmonds* for example — seemed to have acquired 'cult status', to the extent that they had become compulsory viewing for certain groups. There were anecdotes about children who had been caught out claiming to have watched certain films or programmes which in fact they had not, in a desperate attempt to gain status. This was particularly true in the case of films which had only recently been released, or which had 18 certificates: a number of children who claimed to have watched films like *Nightmare on Elm Street* — and in some cases, offered quite detailed retellings of the most gory parts of the narrative — had in fact only seen trailers, or heard about the film from others.

As these examples suggest, talk about television may carry a significant social charge. It is an arena in which we may — deliberately or inadvertently — display our moral values, our social and political affiliations, and our perceptions of ourselves and of others. Talking about television defines us, and we know it.

Of course, this is also the case in research. Obviously, the context of a research interview is more unusual and perhaps more 'artificial' than everyday social conversation. The context is not a neutral one, and it cannot be 'deducted' or ignored. Yet the relationships between an adult interviewer and the children in a discussion group, and indeed between the children themselves, will inevitably reflect the kinds of social relationships which exist outside this particular context — although they will also *inflect* them in specific ways. Such discussions are undoubtedly a 'special' form of social interaction, but they are nevertheless intelligible in terms of more everyday behaviour.

In the following three chapters, I will explore some of the major parameters of children's talk about television. Chapter 3 draws on data from the pilot stage of the project, and develops some of these questions about the *status* of talk as data. Chapter 4 provides an overview of the more extensive interviews conducted at the start of the project itself, tracing the relationships between children's talk and the social and interpersonal context in which it occurs. Chapter 5 examines the ways in which parents and children talk about the domestic viewing context, and how children's viewing is regulated and defined through discourse.

Chapter 3

What are Words Worth?: Interpreting Children's Talk about Television

Speaking for Themselves?

Research on television audiences within the Cultural Studies tradition has frequently been motivated by a desire to take the viewer's side. Researchers have often sought to speak on behalf of those who are seen to lack a voice — and even to enable them to 'speak for themselves'.

While this attempt to defend the viewer is certainly important, it can also lead to a rather superficial and indeed partial account of what is taking place. I would argue that a good deal of research in this field — including my own previous work (e.g. Buckingham, 1987a, 1990b) — has adopted a fundamentally empiricist approach. Researchers have tended to take data at face value: what people say is generally seen as sufficient evidence of what they think. The influence of the researcher, and that of the act of 'doing research', have largely been neglected. Where researchers have used group discussions or interviews, the role of interpersonal or group dynamics has often been ignored. Furthermore, there has been a tendency to attribute a causal role to social factors such as class, 'race' and gender, in ways which are unduly reductive and deterministic.

In this chapter, I want to raise some questions about the *status* of viewers' talk about television, by considering some extracts from discussions held during the pilot stage of the research. In the process, I want to identify some limitations in previous research in this field, and to indicate the need for a more *analytical* approach to the data, which considers the relationship between talk and the social contexts in which it is produced.

The Social Context of Research

This chapter draws upon data gathered as part of a pilot study for the main research project. The research took place in a small primary school in Hackney, East London, in the spring and summer of 1989. A total of forty-seven children aged between 8 and 11 were interviewed by a white, male interviewer (myself) in mixed groups of four or five, some on a number of occasions, and in a variety of combinations. The topics for discussion and the programmes we viewed together were largely determined by the children themselves.

In the case of the data presented here, we are dealing with children's responses to an unfamiliar researcher's questions, which have been recorded outside the classroom, but nevertheless within a school context. The children knew that I was a friend of their regular class teacher and also that I worked at the University. Beyond this, my motivations were deliberately left vague: the brief explanation that I wanted to 'find out what they thought about television' appeared to suffice. They seemed to accept my right to ask questions of them, without expecting to do so in return. While many of them asked to hear the tapes played back, they rarely enquired about what they would be used for — although on one or two occasions I had to reassure them that their teacher was not going to listen to them!

While I was inevitably to some degree perceived as a 'teacher', there was little evidence that the children regarded the interviews as a primarily 'educational' activity. Most probably saw them simply as an opportunity to get out of lessons. Nevertheless, any adult asking children questions about television within a school context is likely to invite what children themselves would perceive as 'adult' responses. Children know that most teachers disapprove of them watching television, and they are familiar with at least some of the arguments about the harmful effects the medium is supposed to exert upon them.

There is some explicit evidence of this in the transcripts of these discussions. For example, in discussing relatively 'violent' action-adventure cartoons, one group of 10- and 11-year-old boys did consider their potential effects:

Colin: It's because / little children. Like my mate, his little brother, he's two and he watches it [*Thundercats*]. And that's why they don't put nobody getting killed at the end / Because they'll be going about, and if somebody hits them or something they'll be going 'I'm gonna kill you' and everything. It will put hate in their hearts. They put something on, 2-year-olds can't watch it, because they do it, things like that.

Although Colin appears to agree that harmful effects can occur, it is significant that he attempts to displace these onto children much younger than himself — a finding which has been noted in previous research (Cullingford, 1984; Buckingham, 1987a). In addition, he argues that the producers are responsible enough not to put younger children at risk: while he himself finds the 'pro-social' morality of the cartoons tiresome — elsewhere in the discussion, he likened the 'happy ever after' endings to those of children's fairy tales — he implied that this was necessary in order to 'teach children a lesson'.

In other instances, the children were more directly concerned to refute the idea that television exerted any influence upon them. One group of 10-year-olds engaged in an almost competitive display of cynicism about the false claims made by television advertisements:

Robin: Really, I like adverts, 'cause they don't make sense. 'Cause you know Ariel ones. They say they test an ordinary powder. They go off and probably choose the worst powder in history. And then they choose the best powder in history

> and they put an Ariel sign on it / whenever I get Ariel liquid, I washed my coat, and there was this tiny little soup stain on it, and then when I got it out of the wash, the soup stain was still there.
>
> *Interviewer*: So you're saying you don't believe what they're saying, then?
>
> *All*: No!
>
> *Robin*: That's why I like them, 'cause they lie. [*Laughter*]

This was merely the first of a series of instances where the children accused the advertisers of using misleading techniques, or where their own experience of products had led them to doubt the claims being made. They were certainly under no illusions about the persuasive intention of advertising, or about the economic factors involved. In viewing a brief selection of advertisements, they constantly drew attention to continuity mistakes, and mocked them for being 'unrealistic' and for 'showing off'.

While the responses of another group of 8-year-olds were much more enthusiastic — including singing along and dancing to the videotape! — they too were keen to show that they could 'see through' advertising. In their view, the enjoyment of advertisements had little to do with the products themselves:

> *Garry*: Some people think that adverts are to make them / buy it. But the advert is just, like, for watching. Some people love the advert but they never buy it.

Garry's view was perhaps supported by the fact that the children's favourite advertisements were for products they themselves would never have bought, such as pensions or petrol.

As these examples indicate, the children were to some extent already familiar with 'adult' discourses about the harmful effects of television. More crucially, they seemed to perceive the context as one in which a relatively 'critical' response was at least appropriate, and possibly even required. This 'critical' discourse thus serves a dual purpose: it enables the children to present themselves as 'adult', for the benefit of each other and of an adult interviewer; and it provides a means of refuting what they might suspect adults (including the interviewer) to believe about the influence of television upon them.

To this extent, it would seem reasonable to suspect that the children were more 'critical' here than they might have been in another context, for example where they were not so obviously positioned as 'children' in relation to an 'adult', or in a non-educational setting. But this is not to imply that the children were merely dissembling, or seeking to please, and that 'what they really think' can be found elsewhere. It might be more accurate to suggest that children have at their disposal a range of discursive possibilities, or repertoires: even within these interviews, for example, these ranged from singing along to advertisements to accusing them of lies and deception. Yet given the context, there was definitely something to be gained from being seen to employ a 'critical', 'adult' discourse.

This possibility is one which has largely been ignored by previous audience research. It seems to be assumed that the role of the interviewer remains constant, and can therefore simply be effaced. For example, in *The 'Nationwide' Audience*

(Morley, 1980a), David Morley classified the responses of the different groups he interviewed according to their social position. Yet it is clear that, for example, black female working-class further education students and white male middle-class bank managers are likely to respond very differently to a white male middle-class academic, irrespective of what they are discussing. Some groups may perceive the interview situation as requiring a 'critical' response, while others may not: some may choose to play what they perceive to be the game, while others may actively refuse to do so.

Similarly, in *Family Television* (Morley, 1986), the different — and indeed, as Morley admits, unusually highly stereotyped — responses of males and females need to be related to the context of the interview itself. Women, for example, will be likely to say quite different things in the presence of their husbands (as was the case in this research) and to a male interviewer, from the kinds of things they would say if interviewed alone by a female interviewer. Again, this is not to suggest that any one context is inherently more valid than any other, or that we will ever arrive at some uncontaminated 'truth' about what viewers really think. It is simply to argue that we need to see discourse in context, and take account of how subjects themselves perceive that context.

Group Talk

Nevertheless, as I have implied, how individuals perceive the context is not constant or easily predictable. 'Context' cannot be seen, as it often is in traditional social research, as a variable which is of equal weight or significance for all subjects, and which can therefore be 'subtracted' from the findings, or simply ignored.

In the case of these discussions, for example, the children did not consistently adopt the 'adult' or 'critical' discourse I have identified. For example, a number of the children — both boys and girls — took great pleasure in recounting the narratives of horror films which they were legally forbidden to watch, complete with vivid descriptions of dismemberings and graphic sound effects of bodies being torn apart. What their accounts focused on was not the complexity of the narrative or the subtlety of the characterization: on the contrary, it was the explicit violence they were keen to talk about. For many adults, this data would present a disturbing picture of young children traumatized and depraved by video violence.

I shall have more to say about this in due course; but the point here is simply that the children did not consistently adopt a 'critical' discourse. While at least some of what they said might be seen to be for the interviewer's benefit — whatever they may have perceived that to be — much of it was not. In certain contexts, children may indeed seek to please, by telling us what they think we want to hear: but equally, for a whole variety of reasons, they may not.

The crucial additional factor here is obviously that these discussions were held in groups, generally of four or five. The children were thus interacting with their peers as well as with an adult, and would be likely to perceive these two audiences (or in fact multiple audiences) in very different ways. In this context, as Hodge and Tripp (1986) have argued, 'non-television meanings' may be powerful enough to swamp 'television meanings': the existing social relationships between members of the group, and the ways in which these relationships are negoti-ated and redefined in the process of discussion will significantly determine the meanings which are produced. Trying to 'filter out' these social relationships in order to arrive at an account of 'what children really think' may be a futile and indeed misguided activity.

Again, this is a point which has been neglected by previous research in this field. All too often, potential debates and differences within groups are suppressed, and groups are taken to be 'representative' of unified social or ideological positions. In their critique of Morley's *Nationwide* research, Jordin and Brunt (1988) argue that this approach 'compromises the ethnographic, qualitative and contextually specific aspects of the research by radically abstracting from the real material complexity of the groups'. The focus, they suggest, should be on what groups *do*, rather than what they represent. While broad social structural factors such as class are bound to influence the ways in which individuals make sense of television, it is important to regard these not as *external* constraints, but as social relationships which are actualized or brought into play in the specific context of the discussion itself. 'Decoding' television is itself a social process, not merely an effect of other social processes.

I would like to develop these points by examining some extracts from a discussion with a mixed group of 10-year-olds about the US sitcom *The Cosby Show*. The group was all white, with the exception of one black British/Afro-Caribbean girl, Serena, who plays a crucial role in the discussion.

The Cosby Show, which stars the veteran comic Bill Cosby, is a long-running sitcom based on the exploits of an affluent black family, the Huxtables, who live in a large New York brownstone. The show has been top of the ratings in the US, and (at least in Britain) is particularly popular with black children. The show has attracted a considerable amount of criticism, both here and in the States, for its attempt to offer a 'positive image' of black people to a mass audience, both black and white. It has been argued that the programme effaces the 'blackness' of the characters, and thus avoids raising the issue of racism, largely by virtue of its focus on an affluent and generally harmonious black family. While the programme occasionally focuses on 'black' issues, it has been argued (significantly, by many white critics) that the Huxtables 'might as well be white' (see Sefton-Green, 1990).

Much of the discussion in this group centred on the issue of modality — that is, the extent to which the programme can be regarded as 'realistic'. This was, it should be emphasized, an issue which the children raised themselves at the very beginning of the discussion.

Thus, the children were clearly conscious of the fact that the family shown in the programme is fictional. They commented on the quality of the acting, and speculated about how old the actors were in real life. They were also aware that the programme is made in a studio: as Kate said, 'you never get to see them going upstairs, because it's probably a film crew up there'.

Similarly, they were familiar with the recurrent narrative devices characteristic of the programme, and indeed of comedy more generally. Thus, in the episode we saw, they were able to predict that the male characters would meet their downfall: when Theo (the Huxtables' son) is 'trying to act all cool', it is inevitable that 'something happens to him'.

At the same time, the children were concerned with the extent to which the family could be seen as 'representative', primarily in relation to their own experience. Certainly in comparison with their own families, the Huxtables were seen not merely as considerably more wealthy, but also as implausibly harmonious:

Kate: But no parents look after their children in that way. The children wouldn't talk about their problems so much to the grown-ups because / Know what I mean, in that programme they find it so easy just to go and tell their mum and dad, but it's not always that easy. It's really quite hard sometimes. So in some ways it's not realistic.

On the other hand, the children were conscious of, and enjoyed, the ways in which the programme gently subverts the patriarchal 'head of the family', although again this did not necessarily reflect their own experience:

Serena: [*Spoken with relish*] Whatever the woman says, the man listens! My dad tells my mum what to do sometimes, because he's like over her /

Newton: Usually in a house it's the man who's the boss. What I like about this, it's the lady's sort of the boss.

Yet despite their sense of the programme's low modality status — that is, its lack of realism — at least some of the children were prepared to look to it as a source of advice about 'family problems': the programme was 'not exactly the same' as their own families, but showed 'the same problems but in a different way'.

Kate: I liked one where Theo goes and insults someone at a burger bar and gets chucked out. I thought that was good because it's about going and apologizing and things. Sometimes it can really teach kids a lot / What happened, he went on his own somewhere, and if I found myself in a situation like that, I'd remember about all the things I've seen about that, and how much trouble you can get into.

In debating the modality of *The Cosby Show*, these children were employing some quite diverse criteria, which in turn reflect the variety of uses to which the programme is put. We might distinguish here between 'internal' criteria — which emphasize the programme's constructed nature — and 'external' criteria — which seek to compare it directly with real life (see Chapter 9).

In applying 'internal' criteria, the children recognized that the programme is a fictional text, which obeys certain rules and conventions, and which is scripted and acted out in front of cameras in a studio. To this extent, they acknowledged that the programme will never be completely 'realistic', and indeed in certain respects is not intended to be. Yet they were also aware, in using 'external' criteria, that the programme offers representations of the social world which may be partly accurate, and to that extent useful to them in making sense of their own lives.

In both respects, the children were aware of agency — that is, of the fact that the programme is produced by a group of people working for a television company, and that these people have certain intentions or motivations. Throughout the discussion, the children inferred a variety of intentions to the 'authors' of the programme, ranging from a relatively straightforward desire to make people laugh, to the more complex and potentially more ambiguous intention to educate or at least offer advice to their viewers.

Pleasure may also be found in both types of reading. On the one hand, there is a kind of enjoyment which is based on acknowledging the fictional nature of the text, and in particular its status as comedy: thus, the children imitated the 'unrealistic', comic performances of the stars — for example, the way in which Rudy, the youngest member of the family, 'acts like a big woman'. Yet in terms of the comparison with real life, there may also be a pleasure of recognition:

Serena: . . . if they [the parents] are gonna have a good talking to them, I listen to that because it could have happen to me. And I like it, 'cause I start laughing.

To a certain extent, these two elements may be in tension with each other. For example, the requirements of comic narrative were seen to undermine the programme's ability to deal with 'family problems':

Kerry: You know what's really boring, because you know what's gonna happen, you know it's all gonna turn out right in the end. None of the programmes sort of like end with something bad happening. They always have them all getting all right.

Serena: You know the problem is gonna be all right in the end, so you don't need to worry.

Nevertheless, *The Cosby Show* was seen as preferable to the British sitcom *Bread* in the respect:

Kerry: [*Bread*] is just made to make you laugh. It's not made to make you think about what's happening in families. You're just meant to watch it and listen to the jokes.

Throughout their discussion, the children were attempting to balance out these two ways of reading the programme. In effect, they were debating how 'seriously' they — and by implication other viewers — should take the kind of social learning it is seen to provide. To what extent does the programme 'tell the truth' about family life, and about the social world more broadly? How far can its 'advice' be relied upon? One reason for the success of *The Cosby Show* with these children could be seen to derive from the way in which it balances these potentially contradictory demands, 'to make you laugh' *and* 'to make you think about what's happening'.

We might describe these children as very 'skilled' readers of television. Yet these skills are not being exercised in the abstract, but in the context of a concrete search for meaning. The knowledge about television that is brought into play depends upon the function that you want the programme to perform — for example, whether you want to regard it as 'harmless escapism' or as something from which you might learn. Furthermore, this is not simply a 'cognitive' process: it is not just about making rationalistic judgments (is this true or false?) but also about pleasure (even if it is false, do I want it to be true?).

It is also, crucially, a social and interpersonal process. This was particularly apparent in the later part of the discussion, which related to race and ethnicity. Significantly, it was not Serena, but a white boy, Newton, who introduced this issue:

Newton:	You know the programme I was talking about, called *The River*? All the people on that were white people. But on *The Cosby Show* they used mixed people, like they use=
Others [joining in]:	Chinese people, black people, all sorts of people.
Serena:	But that's nice, I think that's all right.
Others:	That's good. All different cultures.
Newton:	But in *The River*, it's sort of stupid really, they only have white characters.
Serena:	I don't watch a lot of television really, only *Cosby Show* and the news [. . .] I think, because they say that there's more white people than black people and Chinese people and everything, and Indians. And I don't like that. I LOVE white people, because I've got a lotta, lotta white people in my family //
Kate:	There's not a lot of comedies which deal with black people. I've noticed that. Some of them just do not have any. No starring or anything.

.
.
.

Kerry:	I don't think they actually LOOK for black people to be in their programmes. I don't think they even try and get them. I don't think they want them either.
Kate:	I think if you've got a good comedy, making you think, making you laugh, with black, white, Chinese, together /
Serena:	Make it mixed.

While the children do not use the term 'racism' here, it was used in other discussions, and it would be reasonable to assume that they were at least to some extent familiar with an anti-racist discourse: the criticisms offered by Kate and Kerry here depend upon notions of 'fair' representation, for example. At this stage in the discussion, the consensus is one which might be termed 'multiculturalist' — and here the use of the word 'cultures' is itself significant. Thus, while the underlying issue (not least in terms of the composition of the group itself) is the difference between 'black' and white', it is notable that they repeatedly broaden this to include 'Chinese' and Indian'. Throughout the discussion, there is a relatively safe common ground in the argument that the races should be 'mixed'.

Nevertheless, Serena's position here is problematic. Her contribution is the longest, and the most personal. She relates the issue of racial representation to her own viewing behaviour, implying that the relative absence of black people is the major reason for her lack of interest in most television. At the same time, she is quick to disavow the impression that she is anti-white, both by exaggerated emphasis ('I LOVE white people') and by her assertion that there are 'a lot of white people' in her family. Since Serena herself is not of mixed race, it is difficult to know whether this latter assertion is true — it is not beyond the bounds of credibility — although it is interesting that it is followed by one of the few long pauses in what is a fairly animated discussion. It may be that the others doubt what she is saying, but are reluctant to question it, or that the personal force of her contribution leads to a momentary silent recognition of the racial differences in the group. It is notable that the discussion shifts immediately afterwards to less personal ground, and to the reassertion of the 'multiculturalist' position.

Serena went on to compare *The Cosby Show* with the black British sitcom *Desmonds*:

Serena:	I watch it [*Desmonds*], but I don't like it. There was too much black people in it. I like having something where there's a nice lot of black people in it, 'cause I'm black. It don't seem like that. But I like white people, as much as I like black people.
Interviewer:	But there's not a lot of white people in *The Cosby Show*, are there?
Others:	No.
Serena:	There's not a lot, but there's a few.
Kerry:	Like next door neighbours and=
Serena:	=Yeah.

The grounds for Serena's criticism of *Desmonds* here are difficult to evaluate. Although white characters do occasionally appear in *The Cosby Show*, they only ever occupy minor roles. In fact, the white characters in *Desmonds* are more central. On the other hand, *Desmonds* is British rather than American, and if only for this reason, the ethnic identities of its characters — as revealed, for example, in their use of Afro-Caribbean dialect — will be much more marked for a British audience. In terms of a head count, *The Cosby Show* is more of a 'black' programme, although its 'blackness' is geographically and culturally much more distant, and thus perhaps less immediately salient for these children.

Whether or not Serena's criticism of *Desmonds* is fair or accurate is beside the point, however: what is important is the rhetorical function it has in the context of this discussion. Serena is still concerned here to reassure the other children that she is not anti-white ('I like white people, as much as I like black people'), and her criticism of *Desmonds* provides some kind of proof of her sincerity.

At the same time, it is notable that Serena explicitly defines herself here as black, and attempts to explain her judgments in these terms. By contrast, none of the white children — or indeed the white interviewer — appear to regard it as necessary to define themselves as white. Serena is implicitly defined, and defines herself, as different from the rest of the group, and from the norm.

This issue becomes more problematic as the discussion proceeds:

Serena:	I think it's right to have a lot of white people AND black people AND Chinese people AND Indian. This is what my grandad said, now, 'cause he's on his own, he says that there should be MORE black people, more / all different colours in films, and whatever. 'Cause that's not right, just putting white people, white people, white people. They think about more white people than black people. But I don't think that.

Newton:	But that [*The Cosby Show?*], it's all black people.
Serena:	But you think about just white *Neighbours*, and like (&)
	[
Others [*interrupting*]:	[No. I don't, Serena. I don't.
Serena:	(&) everything white this, white that. But I don't.
[*Confusion of voices*]	
Kerry:	Not all persons=
Newton:	Most of my friends are black.
Interviewer:	So what you'd like, Serena, is not to have a white programme and a black programme, but to have programmes that have a mixture of people in it?
Others:	Yeah.
Serena:	But we've only got three black girls and two black boys. I don't think that's fair /
Kerry:	That's bad, if you have a programme for black people and [one for] white people. Because the black people would feel a bit ashamed if they got white friends. They should just mix it.
Kate:	But in most programmes they just base it on one colour. Like in *Cosby Show* they just base it on black people.
.	
.	
.	
Serena:	But it makes a change, makes a change.
Kerry:	I know, but they never usually put them together. It'd be nice if they did.
Serena:	But I'm happy about *The Cosby Show*, because they put. There's always white people and never black people, or many black people.

The most notable aspect here is the way in which Serena's position shifts from an attack on racist bias in television to an attack on the rest of the group. In her first contribution here, the criticism is still directed against a generalized 'they' (i.e. the programme makers), as in Kerry's comments above. It is significant that she draws on an outside authority here, in the form of her grandfather — indeed, in the discussion as a whole, she refers to her own home and family circumstances much more frequently than the other children, possibly suggesting a much more directly personal engagement with the issues at stake. Note also that by the end of this contribution the question of race is being posed much more starkly in terms of 'black' and 'white'.

In Serena's second contribution, however, the pronoun shifts decisively from 'they' to 'you', and is accompanied by a repeated emphasis on the word 'white', which recurs seven times in rapid succession. Serena is clearly spreading the blame, and defining the other children in racial terms, as she has chosen (or been led) to do herself. The others evidently perceive themselves to be accused of racism, and respond by attempting to exempt themselves from individual blame — a classically liberal discursive strategy (cf. van Dijk, 1987).

In an attempt to avoid further conflict, the interviewer tries to pull Serena back to her earlier 'multiculturalist' position, although it is notable that she initially refuses this. Here again, the issue is defined by her in much broader terms: her response to the interviewer's question draws attention to the relative isolation of black pupils in the class — and perhaps implicitly, to their under-representation when compared with the local community at large. Kerry and Kate attempt to move the discussion back to television, and return to more impersonal language ('the black people', conveniently ignoring the black person present, and the indefinite 'they'). Interestingly, *The Cosby Show* is now defined as being much more exclusively 'black' than it was earlier in the discussion. Serena's incomplete comment on the programme in her final contribution suggests that her earlier line of defence — that the programme 'mixes' the races — cannot now be sustained: she has to acknowledge that the reason she enjoys the programme is because it is a black show, and that this 'makes a change'. While Serena is thus not wholly placated, there is no way in which she can refuse the 'multiculturalist' consensus which the others attempt to re-establish, unless she is willing to be perceived as anti-white —which in the context of the school as a whole might not be a particularly comfortable option.

This latter hypothesis found some confirmation in another discussion of *The Cosby Show*, also with 10- and 11-year-olds. Here, the issue of race was not raised at all until it was deliberately introduced by the interviewer: the response of Derek, the only black child in the group, was particularly significant.

> *Interviewer*: One other thing you haven't talked about yet is that it's a black family.
>
> *Derek*: That's what I was gonna say, but then I thought it might be /
>
> *Amy*: I was gonna say that.
>
> *Derek*: Because most — I'm not trying to be bad or anything — most, um / There's not a lot of black comedies, there's only white ones.
>
> .
> .
> .
>
> *Interviewer*: Why did you say, Derek, you didn't want to talk about that, or something?
>
> *Derek*: If I said it, it might be racist, kind of.
>
> *Interviewer*: Why would it be racist?
>
> *Derek*: Because when I said that to one of my friends, he said 'that's racist'. And I said 'no'.

As the following discussion demonstrated, this group was aware, and indeed highly critical, of racism in the media and in their daily lives. What was notable, however, was their initial hesitancy in discussing it. In the extract quoted, Derek is concerned that simply introducing the topic will lead to him being seen as anti-white: like Serena, he needs to reassure his listeners — including the white interviewer — that he is not 'trying to be bad'. Both Derek and Serena find support from their white friends, who are often extremely fluent in articulating their opposition to racism, but they remain concerned that the issue will become divisive.

Determinations

While it would certainly be possible to reduce this kind of discussion to a statement of consensus, this would be to ignore the complexity of what is taking place. We obviously need to account for the differences between individuals in the group; yet we also need to acknowledge the inconsistencies and contradictions in what particular individuals say. From the perspective of discourse analysis, this kind of variability is crucial to an understanding of how discourse operates. What people say can no longer be seen simply as evidence of what they think — of their 'attitudes' or 'beliefs'. On the contrary, we need to pay closer attention to the ways in which people use language to perform a variety of functions in the context of specific social interactions (Potter and Wetherell, 1987).

In the case of the above discussion, we might apply this approach in a number of ways. In particular, we might investigate the different ways in which the object of discussion — that is, 'race' — is constructed in the process of the discussion itself. We might trace the shifting permutations of the key terms 'black' and 'white' and the less frequent use of the subsidiary terms 'Chinese', 'Indian', 'colour' and 'culture'. Evidently, there is a process of categorization taking place here, but there is some variation and negotiation in the way in which this is achieved. The longer list of categories — 'black, white, Chinese, Indian' — or the generalized reference to the existence of categories — 'all different colours' — generally serves to maintain a consensual, 'multiculturalist' position, while the emphasis on 'black' and, particularly, 'white' tends to disrupt it. Serena's insistence on difference and on inequality ('fairness') within the group challenges the artificial harmony of the multiculturalist discourse, with its attempts to efface racial difference and inequality (cf. Carby, 1980). This involves Serena in a process of self-definition ('I'm black') and, most crucially, a process of defining others (through her repeated use of the word 'white').

As Potter and Wetherell (1987) argue, categorization is not something fixed, but on the contrary a highly flexible process: categories do not live in individuals' heads, but are actively constructed and reconstructed in discourse, in order to achieve particular goals. Likewise, definitions of self and other are vital discursive moves, particularly in situations of potential conflict (cf. Shotter and Gergen, 1988). These systems of categorization and self-representation need to be judged, not in terms of their degree of 'accuracy', but rather in terms of what they enable speakers to achieve.

This perspective provides a much more complex understanding of the question of 'determination' considered briefly above. As I have indicated, one of the major criticisms of Morley's *Nationwide* research was of its tendency to aggregate individuals into groups, and to treat these groups as homogeneous 'representatives' of broader categories, most notably social class. Towards the end of *The 'Nationwide' Audience*, and in other work of this period (Morley, 1980b, 1981), Morley begins to develop a less mechanistic model of this process, which traces the role of social class in determining 'the structure of access to different discourses'. Yet while this model is certainly preferable to the economic determinism of Morley's earlier approach, it is arguable whether it fully escapes it. As Jordin and Brunt (1988, p. 241) suggest, 'to simply insert the mediating term of subcultural discourse between class and decoding no more changes the mechanistic nature of their relationship than does extending a line of touching snooker balls'. 'Class' continues to be seen as an *external* determining constraint on the ways in which television is 'decoded': determination 'appears as a process acting *on* human beings rather than a human process' (cf. Hogg and Abrams, 1988).

To regard determination as a 'human process' in this way implies a view of individuals as active social agents: children, in particular, would need to be seen as active participants in their own socialization, rather than passively moulded by broader social forces (cf. Steedman, 1982). Definitions of self and other, of the kind described above, will play a vital part in this process. Furthermore, socialization would need to be seen as a process of contestation and struggle, without guarantees of success.

I would like to develop this argument by looking at some further extracts from the data, in this case taken from discussions focusing primarily on US cartoon series. In this instance, the children were grouped according to gender and age (8-year-olds and 10/11-year-olds). In the first interview, they were invited to discuss their viewing preferences in general, and then to consider cartoons in more detail. In the second, we viewed an episode of the US series *Thundercats*, with pauses for discussion.

Of all the programmes we discussed, cartoons were perceived as the most obviously 'gendered' by the children themselves — a fact which may reflect the extreme gender stereotyping of many of the cartoons (see Engelhardt, 1986). Choosing to discuss them in single-sex groups accentuated this: particularly for the girls, gender was the central issue from the very beginning. In all of the groups, there were very clear statements about which cartoons were 'for boys' and which 'for girls'. Nevertheless, the groups negotiated these definitions in rather different ways, with age and to a lesser extent social class emerging as additional factors.

The group of older girls was perhaps the most explicitly critical. The discussion began with them asking the (male) researcher why he wasn't interviewing any boys:

Serena: You should talk to the boys. Because cartoons are for boys. Because they've got most boys in it, and men.

She-Ra, a cartoon featuring a female superhero, He-Man's twin sister, was seen as a possible exception to this tendency, however:

Interviewer: So what is it you like about *She-Ra*?
Sharon: I just like the way she acts, for a girl. Like *He-Man*, they wouldn't let a girl be it, I thought. They wouldn't let a girl be so strong, and she's strong.
Interviewer: So she does all the things He-Man can do?
Girls: Yeah.
Serena: Makes a change. 'Cause most of the boys thinks that girls are a wimp and everything. But I don't think that's right, so let them shut their mouth. The girls should take over the boys so they know that they're wimp.
Sharon: Like they feel like we're feeling now.
[*General agreement*]
Serena: Because they always say that because they play football every single day that girls can't play with a ball. Because the boys just takes over the ball and keep it.

The girls' discussion them turned to the question of boys' and girls' behaviour in the playground, suggesting that their criticism of the cartoons was merely part of a much broader concern. Later in the discussion it emerged that many of the girls (including Sharon) did not actually watch *She-Ra*, yet in the context of this exchange it seemed to be important for them to take a principled, almost militant, stand. Each individual contribution builds on the preceding one, and there is a good deal of mutual support, both spoken and unspoken: the girls are actively constructing a group solidarity on gender lines, in a way that would obviously be much more risky in a mixed group.

The younger girls were rather more ambivalent, however. They had some difficulty in classifying *She-Ra*, claiming at one point that it is a 'girls' programme', but then going on to argue that boys tend to watch it more than girls. They pointed out that *She-Ra* is not in fact equivalent to *He-Man*, in that it rarely features 'real' fighting, and that the character She-Ra is always seen with He-Man, while the reverse is not the case. The presence of a central female character was thus not sufficient to qualify it unambiguously as a 'girls' programme'.

While gender was certainly a major factor here, age was also important. Even the younger girls described the cartoons as 'babyish' and 'boring', although they were also rather negative about their own preference for 'soppy things' like the Australian soap opera *Neighbours*. One of the older girls explicitly rejected the cartoons' apparent (and 'masculine') preoccupation with power and conflict, irrespective of the gender of the characters themselves:

Gaynor:	I don't like the things that show men being strong or women being strong. I think they're a bit boring.
Interviewer:	So you don't like either *He-Man* or *She-Ra*? What don't you like about it?
Gaynor:	I don't know. They're all about power, and getting revenge on one evil man and that. It's all the same / It's always the goodie getting revenge on a baddie.
Sharon:	And the baddies never get the goodies.
Gaynor:	You know the story, that the baddies aren't going to win, and the goodies are always going to win.

The function of these judgments, therefore, is not merely to assess the programmes. The girls are also actively defining their own position, largely but not exclusively *against* the programmes. They are defining themselves as female, in the sense that they have shared preferences and are able to recognize what is 'for them': if the younger girls do this in a rather self-deprecating way (they like 'soppy' things), the older ones are much more assertive. They are also simultaneously defining themselves in terms of age: in rejecting what they describe as 'babyish' (and, coincidentally, 'for boys'), they are implicitly defining themselves as more mature and sophisticated.

While this self-definition is generally a collective process — there is a good deal of 'we' in these discussions, and comparatively little 'I' — there was at least one instance of open conflict. Here, the younger girls were discussing *Ghostbusters*, a cartoon which appears to be less obviously 'gendered' in its appeal. To begin with, there was general agreement that *Ghostbusters* was 'brilliant', although it was felt that the toys associated with the programme were more 'for boys'. At this stage, the interviewer attempted to draw in a more middle-class girl in the group, who had been relatively silent up to this point:

Interviewer: What do you think, Nicola? Do you think they're just for boys?

Nicola: Yeah. / But I remember I've got a book of *Ghostbusters*. [*General mocking laughter*] I don't know why I've got it, though.

Kerry: You bought it!

Natalie: You like *Ghostbusters*!

Interviewer: Did someone give it to you, or something?

Kerry: She bought it herself, because she likes *Ghostbusters*. She's always got it at school.

Nicola: It's boring.

Natalie: This is true. She always brings her *Ghostbusters* bag to school (&) [

Nicola: [I don't

Natalie: (&) her *Ghostbusters* toys and she takes them over the playcentre.

Nicola: I don't. I don't even go to playcentre.

Clearly, Nicola is not too popular with the other girls in this group, and they use her unwary admission about the *Ghostbusters* book as a means to marginalize her still further. Significantly, *Ghostbusters* is associated with the playcentre, and is thus defined as being for younger children. What remains striking, however, is the fact that a preference for *Ghostbusters* is used here almost as an accusation, when not two minutes previously the same girls had been expressing their own preference for the programme. In this instance, it is very clear that the existing interpersonal relationships among the group supercede the judgments they appear to make about television

Gender and to a lesser extent age differences were also addressed explicitly in the boys' discussions of cartoons. The younger boys, for example, simultaneously acknowledged and attempted to disclaim the importance of gender:

Rodney: Have they [the girls] got *My Little Pony* cartoons to watch, same as us, we've got=

Interviewer: No, they're going to watch *Thundercats* as well.

Boys: Oh [. . .]

Richard: They ain't for girls.

Anthony: Anyone can / they can watch it!

Robert: Yeah. It can be for girls and boys.

Rodney: Yeah. Girls can watch it.

Gareth: It's sexist. It can be for girls and boys. Like, a girl / Like, girls are in it. Like, Cheetara's in it. Cheetara's in *Thundercats*. Cheetara's a girl.

Rodney: She's a woman, you idiot.

Interestingly, the boys use an anti-sexist discourse here to question the validity of these distinctions: Gareth's 'it's sexist' refers not to *Thundercats* or the cartoons themselves, but to the assumption, voiced here by Richard, that the cartoons are 'gendered'. Any sense in which the boys themselves might see their own enjoyment of the cartoons as problematic, or even experience guilt, is very neatly circumvented.

The older boys were also aware of potential criticisms of the cartoons, although in some cases their grasp of the discourse was perhaps less secure:

Vinh:	I think that Three Musketeers [*Dogtanian*] is quite racist.
Darren:	Racist, why?
Vinh:	Because it's always boys going on heroes and all that stuff. Why couldn't it be a girl?
Darren:	There is a girl. Milady. And Juliet.
Vinh:	But why isn't Juliet doing all the adventures?
Interviewer:	So what do the girls or women do in *Dogtanian*?
Vinh:	All they do is walk away, like / wiggling their bums.

.
.
.

Vinh:	See, I told you it was quite racist. Why can't it be a man going down the street wiggling his bum instead of a woman? [*Laughter*]
Daniel:	Men do wiggle=
Colin:	=Let's see you do it, then, Daniel, go on! [*Laughter*]
Vinh:	See, why couldn't a man just be captured and a woman capture him?
Interviewer:	Have you ever seen that in a cartoon on TV?
Boys:	Yeah. *She-Ra*. Yeah. Always does. And *Thundercats*.
Colin:	But it's only because *He-Man* was made and people were saying it was sexist. They made *He-Man* first but I reckon that people were saying that it was sexist and everything so they made *She-Ra*.
Vinh:	*She-Ra* is the opposite of *He-Man*.
Interviewer:	So do you watch *She-Ra*? Do you like that?
Vinh:	Yeah! *He-Man*, *She-Ra*, my best programme!
Others:	No.
Colin:	I watch it, but only because there's nothing on the other side.
Vinh:	I don't! *She-Ra*'s my best programme!
Interviewer:	OK, tell me what you like about *She-Ra*.
Vinh:	Me? Because she always goes 'I am She-Ra!' and she hold up her magic power.
Darren:	And then her legs look really sexy! [*Whistles*] [*Laughter*]

While Vinh's contribution at the start of this extract indicates some confusion about the 'politically correct' position, the group as a whole appears to be familiar with the broad outlines of the anti-sexist discourse. While the younger boys in the previous extract define representation primarily in terms of head-counting (and refute the potential objections by pointing to the token female characters), the older boys here are also concerned with comparing male and female roles, and with the emphasis on female sexuality.

Nevertheless, there is a tension within this group, with the older boys (Colin and Darren, who are both 11) effectively policing the younger ones. Thus, Darren questions Vinh's criticism of the cartoons in his first two contributions, and rather deflates his enthusiasm by his final comment, which of course reinforces the view of women as 'objects' of the male gaze. Colin's role here, and throughout these discussions, is rather more complex. He is concerned to make distinctions between himself and the 10-year-olds (at one point saying quite explicitly 'I'm 11, I'm big'), and to appear adult and worldly-wise. Throughout the screening of *Thundercats*, he kept up a constant stream of modality judgments, pointing out continuity mistakes, and questioning the authenticity and probability of the action. Here too, his perspective is relatively distanced, attributing a kind of opportunism to the programme's producers. At the same time, he also undermines Daniel's support for Vinh's argument, reinforcing traditional notions of masculine behaviour. While the anti-sexist discourse is not explicitly rejected, there is an emphasis on maintaining a group solidarity which is essentially masculine, and ensuring that potential deviants are kept in line.

The children's judgments of the cartoons in these discussions were thus heavily overdetermined by questions of gender. The children's perceptions of the texts as strongly gendered brought into play a set of already well-established gender positions. Yet even in this relatively extreme situation — extreme in the sense that none of the other texts or genres we discussed were perceived as gendered to such a degree — there was some uncertainty and flexibility. As I have shown, the children's gender identities were not unitary or fixed, but were on the contrary established and negotiated in the course of the discussion. The children defined themselves, and were defined by others in the group, in different ways for different purposes. Gender identity, we might say, is *achieved* here rather than simply given.

At the same time, the children did acknowledge ambiguities in the texts themselves. Their uncertainties about how to place *She-Ra*, in particular, point to the fact that the 'gender' of a text is not a straightforward attribute of the text itself. In effect, there was an ongoing debate here about the criteria which one might use to establish this. Is it simply a matter of head-counting, or should one make a more qualitative analysis of male and female roles? Does role-reversal turn a 'boys' programme' into a 'girls' programme'? Or is a 'girls' programme' simply a programme that girls watch?

The picture is complicated further by the use of what I have termed an anti-sexist discourse, which probably derives largely from the school. While the discourse was introduced by the children themselves, it was probably partly cued by the 'teacherly' status of the interviewer. Interestingly however, it was *only* the boys who used the word 'sexist' — although, as I have indicated, it tended to serve some rather ambiguous functions here. While it was the older girls who adopted the most 'militant' anti-sexist stand, the consequences of this position in relation to texts were unclear: while some of them claimed to want fantasies of female power, others professed themselves bored with the whole idea.

While it would certainly be reductive to claim that these programmes are a major *cause* of 'sexist attitudes' (as is often argued), it would be equally simplistic to suggest that the children's readings of them are merely a function of their pre-existing social positions. Neither the meaning of the text nor of the children's social positions are wholly given: while there are definitely limitations on both, they are established and negotiated *simultaneously* through talk. Neither determination by the text, nor determination by social position, would appear to explain the complexity of this process.

Conclusion: Some Notes of Caution

In this chapter, I have argued for the importance of social context and social relations in interpreting children's talk about television. In conclusion, I would like to point to some potential dangers in this approach — not so much to qualify it, as to re-state some fundamental emphases. My concern is that in attempting to do justice to the complexity of the process, we may reach a point at which any meaningful generalizations are simply untenable.

In particular, it is crucial to emphasize the *material*, as well as the discursive, nature of social relations. While it is important to avoid more mechanistic notions of social determination, and to acknowledge the complex ways in which subjects define and negotiate their *own* social positions, it is also vital to avoid an approach which is merely individualistic. We need to acknowledge the complexity of the 'micro', but seek to explain it in terms of its articulation within a network of relations, the 'macro' (cf. Silverman, 1985).

My second note of caution here concerns the role of texts. In this chapter, I have discussed children's readings of a range of texts, from cartoons to advertisements to situation comedies. Each of these genres invites a very different kind of engagement on the part of audiences, perhaps particularly in terms of their different modality status. These children were unlikely to take cartoons particularly seriously as a guide to social behaviour, in the way that they seemed more prepared to do in the case of *The Cosby Show*. Furthermore, while they were engaging in a *debate* about representation, it was the programmes themselves that were partly responsible for setting the agenda for that debate. Thus, despite some of the criticisms that are often made of it, it was *absolutely* salient — at least in this context — that *The Cosby Show* is a 'black' programme. Likewise, the exaggerated gender stereotyping in the cartoons undoubtedly set the agenda for discussion in a particular way, and perhaps led to the adoption of more 'extreme' positions than might otherwise have been the case. As I have argued, there are undoubtedly major limitations in the kind of 'textual determinism' which was adopted by 'Screen' theory in the 1970s, yet there is equally an opposite danger of exaggerating the degree of power or freedom audiences possess. While we do need to acknowledge what readers bring to texts, we also need to account for what they find there.

Chapter 4

Talking about Television:
Relations, Subjects and Contents

In this chapter, I want to move on to consider some of the data gathered during the early stages of the research itself. The material here is taken from initial discussions in which the children were asked to identify and talk about aspects of television of their own choosing. As I shall indicate, the form and the content of these discussions were extremely diverse.

In analyzing the talk which took place, I will be drawing on approaches to discourse analysis which have been developed within social psychology, linguistics and poststructuralist theory. In different ways, all these approaches seek to move beyond the 'realist' view of language identified in Chapter 3 — the notion that, in the words of Potter and Wetherell (1987), language offers 'a relatively unambiguous pathway to actions, beliefs or actual events'. From this perspective, language cannot be used simply as evidence of what people think or know or understand. On the contrary, language is already structured in particular ways, which determine what it is possible to think and to say. Furthermore, as I have begun to indicate, individuals use language to construct versions of social reality, and thereby to perform specific social functions or purposes. Using language is, in this sense, an inherently social act.

Recent work in social psychology, for example, has drawn attention to the inconsistencies and contradictions in individuals' accounts of the social world (Potter and Wetherell, 1987; Shotter and Parker, 1989). These contradictions arise, it is argued, not because of the inherent 'inaccuracy' of language, but because of the diverse social functions it is used to perform. Drawing on poststructuralist theory, researchers have studied the ways in which discourse constructs definitions of 'self' and 'other', and thereby sustains relationships of social power (Shotter and Gergen, 1988).

Similarly, the development of 'critical linguistics' or 'social semiotics' has increasingly drawn attention to the social contexts in which language occurs, and the social functions it performs — concerns which have typically been reserved for the field of pragmatics, and isolated from mainstream linguistics (e.g. Fowler *et al.*, 1979; Kress and Hodge, 1979; Kress, 1985; Hodge and Kress, 1988). Much of this work derives from the theories of Michael Halliday (e.g. 1978, 1985), whose functional grammar offers an alternative to the abstract study of syntactic 'rules' associated with traditional grammar: language is defined here, not as a closed system, but in terms of its meaning and social use.

These theories of language as a social practice clearly have a great deal in common with the social theory of literacy discussed towards the end of Chapter 2, and with recent approaches to audience research. Indeed, they have faced similar theoretical problems in attempting to account for and to 'balance out' the power of the text and the power of the reader (or speaker). Thus, while discourse analysis emphasizes the social nature of language, and its power to 'position' individual subjects, it also seeks to emphasize the element of creativity in language use. Language users are seen, neither as wholly subject to a monolithic language system, nor as completely free to create their own meanings: they are socially and linguistically determined, but there are also contradictions and spaces in which they can determine themselves.

In analyzing texts, including spoken texts, discourse analysts have therefore sought to relate the formal properties of the text to the specific social situation in which it is produced, and in turn to the broader social context. Inevitably, this is not a neutral process, or a purely descriptive one: there is no single method which will offer an exhaustive or objective reading — despite the claims which are sometimes made. However, Norman Fairclough (1989) outlines a basic framework which would seem to offer significant possibilities here.

Briefly, Fairclough distinguishes between three sets of constraints which operate in discourse, namely *contents* (what is said or done), *relations* (the social relations people enter into) and *subjects* (the subject positions they can occupy). He argues that the formal features of texts — vocabulary, grammar and larger-scale textual structures — have three types of value, which correspond to these three constraints. Thus, 'experiential' values reflect the way in which the speaker/writer represents his or her experience of the natural or social world. 'Relational' values indicate the social relationships that are being enacted via the text; and 'expressive' values reflect the way in which the speaker/writer evaluates the aspect of reality to which the text refers.

On a theoretical level, it could certainly be argued that these categories do not offer an exhaustive description, and that the relationships between them are somewhat unclear. The distinction between 'relations' and 'subjects' seems to imply that subject positions are somehow independent of social relations; while the distinction between 'experiential' and 'expressive' values appears to suggest that the representation of experience can be considered independently from the evaluation of it. However, Fairclough does emphasize that these categories are not to be regarded as exclusive.

Despite these criticisms, Fairclough's categories do seem to provide a useful means of *organizing* an analysis of the data, and that is how I intend to use them here. They are not neutral tools, nor do they guarantee scientific objectivity. I offer this analysis, therefore, as a reading of the children's talk — one among a number which may be possible. By quoting substantial excerpts from the transcripts of the discussions, I am seeking to give the reader access to at least some 'raw' data, in order that my analysis can be checked and disputed.

Presenting the Data

The material presented here is taken from a series of taped discussions which took place at the very beginning of the project. Apart from a brief introduction some weeks earlier, this was the first time the research team had met the children. The children were in groups of five, selected in order to provide a gender balance, but otherwise at random. They were taken out of their classrooms into a room elsewhere in the school. The discussions lasted on average around forty-five minutes.

The questions which were used to prompt the discussions were as open and straightforward as possible. To begin with, the children were asked to talk about one thing they liked about television: this could include a programme, a person or character, or just something about watching television that they enjoyed. Later in the discussion, they were asked a similar question about dislikes.

The ways in which the children took up this invitation were quite diverse, and the interviewer's role in the discussion varied accordingly. In most cases, they were extremely talkative: many groups were quite competitive, and the interviewer's role in these instances was primarily to ensure that everybody got a chance to speak, and that not everybody talked at once — although these efforts were sometimes in vain. Topics would often be hijacked by other speakers, or derailed by interruptions, with the result that the discussions often appear fragmented. On the other hand, in a few cases, the children were quite intimidated by the situation, and it became an uphill struggle to get them to talk: yet even here, once they got on to topics they found interesting or enjoyable, they visibly relaxed into the discussion.

In principle, the interviewer's main role was to 'chair' the discussion, and to focus the talk around the topics the children themselves had introduced. The primary aim was to enable the children to set their own agendas, to encourage them to develop or explain points they had raised, to ask for other views on a topic, and so on. Nevertheless, there were undoubtedly conscious and unconscious biases in how different interviewers performed this task, and some of these will be illustrated here.

In selecting extracts to present, I have been aware of a number of dangers. What is being offered here is a construction or representation of a series of events, which has gone through a number of transformations. While audio-taping a discussion is essentially a mechanical (or rather an electromagnetic) process, it inevitably fails to register a great deal of what takes place. Although videotape is more satisfactory in this respect, it renders the act of surveillance much more visible. Similarly, transcribing is far from being a neutral process: it involves choice and interpretation, and inevitably reflects broader theoretical assumptions (Stubbs, 1983).

Finally, in selecting extracts to discuss in detail, a whole series of principles may be employed, only some of which may be made explicit. The extracts presented in this chapter have been selected from over six hundred pages of transcript, and represent only a small fraction of the material. However much one may aim to let the data generate new problems and categories, the selection inevitably reflects predetermined theoretical concerns. For the researcher, and to a much greater extent for the reader, this process means that a very great deal is lost.

Nevertheless, my aim in this chapter is to attempt to do justice to the diversity and complexity of the talk which took place, rather than to argue for or against a particular construction of the 'child viewer'. Using Fairclough's categories, I will seek to trace the connections between relations, subjects and contents (in that order), and the ways in which these might determine the kinds of talk children produce. While there are certainly some conclusions to be reached — for example about the distribution of styles of talk in terms of age and social class — these are necessarily tentative.

Relations: Defining the Situation

The Interview as Social Event

I want to begin by focusing on the ways in which the children perceived the interview situation, and how they judged what it would be appropriate to say. Our initial question 'what do you like about television?' itself sets an agenda, although it is one which may be at odds with other, predetermined aspects of the context. As I argued in the previous chapter, any adult asking questions about television in a school context inevitably invites certain kinds of responses. While the interviewers here were at pains to present the aims of the project as neutrally as possible — we were simply 'interested in finding out what children think about television' — the children were bound to speculate about our motives, and to adjust their responses accordingly. We had gained access to them through their teachers, and were interviewing them in an institution which was, by definition, 'public' and 'educational'. More broadly, the subject position we occupy as adults is inevitably pre-defined as one in which we hold power in relation to children — although that is not to say this power cannot be contested.

There is a kind of harmony among these contextual factors, which might lead one to expect children to adopt a deferential stance. Yet the fact that the discussions were about television disrupted this. In a sense, the research was crossing the boundaries between the public and the private, the school and the home, adults and children, education and recreation — to name but a few. There was likely to be considerable variation in terms of how the children were situated here, perhaps particularly in terms of the broader relationship between school and home culture. To invite them to talk about their private, out-of-school pleasures in this context was thus inevitably very ambiguous.

Interestingly, there were a number of groups, especially in the inner-city schools, where the power-relationship between interviewer and interviewees was directly challenged. While most groups seemed to accept the interviewer's right to ask questions without expecting to do so in return, there were some that transgressed the rule and enquired directly about the interviewer's preferences. In one instance, the children leant back in their chairs, saying 'we've said enough now, it's his turn — he's a child!' While there was a certain curiosity here about the programmes adults might watch, there also seemed to be an unstated assumption that we were asking about something that was fundamentally unknown to us. The interviewers' occasional displays of knowledge, for example about characters in *Neighbours*, seemed to disturb this assumption, if again with ambiguous effects.

Thus, in some cases, the children's initial responses were extremely tentative and formal. The interview was defined here, at least to begin with, as an 'educational' event, rather than an opportunity for social chat. The following extract from the beginning of a discussion with 7-year-olds in the suburban primary school illustrates this:

Extract 1

Interviewer:	OK. My first topic, tell me what you / like about television / Nancy?
Nancy:	I like about television because it's nice to watch and I like the programmes on there.
Interviewer:	Right. /
Diana:	I like it 'cause you get / er more ideas about it and you can try them out for yourselves and things like um *Hartbeat.* You can try them out.
Interviewer:	Uh, uh. / Ritta, what one thing, what one thing do you like about television?
Ritta:	It's because when you get bored you can sit down and watch it / television.
Interviewer:	Nathan?
Nathan:	I like it 'cause they can do trick photography. /
Interviewer:	And David?
David:	I like it 'cause you learn=
Interviewer:	=things.
David:	=things.
Interviewer:	OK / What sort of things do you learn, David?
David:	Like how to do tricks / and make things.

This was, clearly, not a good start. The children are evidently intimidated by the situation: their voices are extremely quiet and their contributions very brief. They seem to perceive the question as a kind of test: note the way in which they nearly all repeat the formulation 'I like . . .' in their answers, in a manner which is reminiscent of a comprehension exercise. More significantly, they all respond by referring to general characteristics of television: only Diana refers to a specific programme, and even this is offered as an example of a more general point. In addition, both Diana and David refer to the *educational* qualities of television, suggesting a need to present it as somehow serious and worthy.

This interview became more informal in tone as it developed — particularly when it came to discussing the soaps, as we shall see below — yet the initial hesitancy and formality was characteristic of many of the groups in this school.

By contrast, the younger groups in the inner-city primary school were markedly informal from the very start. In many cases, there was a considerable amount of social chat before the interview proper could commence. One group, for example, constantly interrupted the interviewer's attempts to begin with a series of comments about how one of the children in a previous group was 'in love' with him, how they had expected him to be older, and so on. One girl responded to the statement that he worked at London University by saying that her mum worked near there, and that she liked going down on the bus to see the lions in Trafalgar Square. To say the least, the interviewer did not seem to be perceived here as an intimidating adult. In this group, there was also a considerable amount of attention to the tape recorder, and a kind of play with the interview situation. Another girl expressed the wish that they could 'go on telly and talk about this', suggesting that the interview was seen as an opportunity for stardom — albeit one which had not lived up to expectations.

In this group, as in most others in the inner-city schools, the discussion focused almost exclusively on pleasurable texts. Groups would often start describing and retelling episodes or programmes before the interviewer had the chance to formulate the question fully. In a number of groups here, there was a sense in which the subversive 'child self' was on the rampage: the discussion was punctuated by bizarre sound effects, the singing of theme tunes and shouting of catch phrases, miming and acting out scenes, and on one occasion jumping around the room pretending to be 'Gummi Bears', from the cartoon of the same name. One might almost say that the interview was being constructed here as an 'anti-educational' event, as a chance to get out of lessons and let off some steam.

The second extract, taken from one of the inner-city secondary school groups, provides a clear contrast with the first in this respect. The extract begins approximately ten minutes into the discussion, following an extended account of the Australian soaps, *Neighbours* and *Home and Away*.

Extract 2

Natalie:	I like *Alf*! [*General laughter*]
Carol:	Yeah, that's funny, Saturdays, twelve thirty.
Natalie:	I always watch that.
Gloria:	I like *Catchphrase, Blind Date*.
Natalie:	Yeah, I like all them.
Gloria:	Um, *Beadle's About, Murder She Wrote*, yeah.
Ranjit:	I like *Murder She Wrote* and video films.
Natalie:	Video, I seen loads of videos.
Carol:	So have I, we just sit there, sit there and watch them all.
Ranjit:	*In Sickness and in Health.*
Gloria:	That's good, and *Bread, Bread* is rubbish without Adeline, and what's that other boy called?
Carol:	Without Joey as well.
Gloria:	Yeah, rubbish, man!
Interviewer:	Are you still watching it?
Gloria:	Yeah. [*everyone laughs*]
Natalie:	It's like *East* [*Enders* as well,
Carol:	[I like, er, and *London's Burning*, I like that.
Natalie:	Yeah, I like that.
Ranjit:	And *The Bill*.
Various:	Oh yeah //
Gloria:	Did you watch *Blind Date* with that fat woman?
Carol:	[Yeah!
Gloria:	[Did you see her, man?

This was one of a number of instances in which the children simply ran through a list of programme titles (or in some cases characters) in rapid succession. Here, 'I like' or 'I watch' appear to be a sufficient pretext for the naming of programmes. While this is sometimes quite arbitrary, there is a kind of logic about parts of the sequence: the naming of one soap opera or situation comedy often leads to another, and some other programmes are linked in terms of their position in the schedules (*Beadle's About* and *Murder She Wrote* are both on

Saturday night, for example). Nevertheless, there is generally very little attempt to explain the reasons for their preferences, although evaluative comments — such as Gloria's remark on *Bread* here — may be offered in passing. Typically, the children seem to perceive little point in being equivocal, or offering more nuanced judgments: programmes are either 'boring', 'rubbish' and 'crap' or they are 'brilliant', 'wicked' and 'safe'.

This naming of programmes has a clear function in terms of defining what Fairclough calls 'relations' and 'subjects'. The sequence resembles an auction, with individuals effectively making bids to introduce a new topic. Whether or not a topic will be accepted depends on others taking it up, and it achieving at least a moderate consensus among the group. Where there is uncertainty, further details may be offered in order to help others identify the programme, yet the discussion often goes no further. On occasion, naming may be followed by an attempt at retelling, or at least by a reference to a shared moment — as in Gloria's comment at the end of the extract — although these are not always taken up by other speakers. There is a sense in which this trading of titles has a dynamic, and a pleasure, of its own.

The nominating of preferences is also a way of assuming or claiming a 'subject position'. While in some instances a great deal may be at stake in this process, in this case it seems fairly unthreatening. Natalie's choice of *Alf*, for example, is received with laughter, probably because it is a programme aimed at younger viewers — although in this context, it seems relatively safe for her to admit to liking it. Similarly, the laughter around *Bread* stems from a recognition that — for a variety of reasons — what you watch does not necessarily reflect what you claim to like.

In instances where there was stronger group pressure, individuals were sometimes forced to revise their stated preferences. Children who admitted to liking a programme which was unpopular with others in the group often backtracked hurriedly, saying they watched it 'when there's nothing else on', or that they didn't really watch it all that often. While consensus generally seemed to be at a premium, there were certainly groups in which differences seemed to play a major role — as will be illustrated below.

In many instances, however, the naming of programme titles was followed by more sustained descriptions. 'I like . . .' often led to 'I like the bit when . . .' Identifying and retelling the 'good bits' was a major preoccupation for all the age groups, although again there was considerable variation here.

Particularly among the younger children, most of the talk took this form. Individuals would often launch into extended retellings with very little by way of context or justification. Often the phrase 'I've got one' or 'I've got a good one' seemed sufficient, as if we were engaged in a kind of joke-telling session, rather than any more general reflection on the role of television in our lives.

Retelling will be considered in more detail later in this chapter, and in Chapter 7, but some general observations about its functions in terms of 'relations' and 'subjects' are relevant here. Some retellings took the form of very brief references, as in Gloria's comment about the fat woman in *Blind Date*: if you missed that episode, the reference will probably be meaningless, although if you are familiar with the format of the programme, there is plenty to imagine. In some groups, particular children took on the role of interpreter, offering an explanatory commentary on the discussion in order to provide the interviewer with basic information which might make it comprehensible. Yet in most cases, few concessions were made to the uninitiated — indicating that at least part of the pleasure lay in keeping it confined to the select few.

In many cases, however, retellings were much more sustained. The majority were collective, with one main speaker taking the burden of the narrative and others contributing details. There was often some strong competition for talk space, with the speaker being repeatedly corrected, as if getting the details exactly right was very important — although correction also served to remind the speaker that the right to speak was only granted provisionally, and could be lost at any time.

However, in other cases, there were individuals who would monopolize the space, offering extended monologues with little dispute or interruption. One group of children in the suburban secondary school, who were unusually reticent, produced a sequence of very long and detailed chronological retellings, with comparatively little dialogue: in such circumstances, it would seem that retelling can provide a kind of safety, something to hide behind without having to put oneself on the line.

These differences between collective and individual retellings were also partly a result of how the needs of the listeners were perceived. Retelling texts which were shared among the group — such as the Australian soaps — tended to be a more collective activity, with individuals quoting lines from the programme, supplying missing details, sound effects, and so on. In these instances, there was often very little attempt to provide a narrative context, or to explain the relationships between characters for the benefit of the interviewer: the focus was on isolated 'magic moments'. Texts which were not shared, often videos or films, were generally related in much more conventional storytelling mode, albeit with a strong emphasis on the 'good bits'.

In addition, there was often a strong and self-conscious element of performance here, with a good deal of mime and face-pulling, and often a considerable amount of parody. While retelling provides an opportunity for re-living pleasurable moments, the act itself often takes the form of a *demonstration* for the benefit of others, and thus perhaps inevitably involves a degree of ironic or critical distance.

The Exercise of Critical Judgment

For the younger working-class children, the vast majority of the talk was focused on specific texts, in the manner I have described. Yet the older middle-class children were more likely to range across texts, making comparisons and illustrating more general assertions. In many cases, these children were also keen to display 'expert knowledge' about television — for example about how certain effects were achieved. In general, they tended to offer more abstract observations about the role of television in their lives, and to be more self-reflexive about their own preferences. There was a much stronger sense here that pleasure had to be explained and justified, rather than merely asserted.

This was evident even in the way in which texts were nominated for discussion. Older children were generally more likely to respond to the question about likes and dislikes by nominating a generic category — such as 'comedies' or 'soaps' — before proceeding to provide examples. Similarly, their discussion of characters was more likely to be framed by a general statement about character traits, before offering an illustration. While there was no shortage of retellings, many of the accounts of texts offered here were much more general, identifying broad characteristics of programmes, or describing recurrent features of the narrative.

The following extract, which features one of the middle-class 9-year-olds from the inner-city primary school, illustrates this.

Extract 3

> Adele: I like / mm things like comedies like *Blackadder* and *Dad's Army*, 'cause it tells you about what's going on and what happens. 'Cause if I watch things like *Shelley*, 'cause they're from nowadays, I think they're rather boring 'cause I know all about nowadays and it's not so funny. But I like things like *Blackadder*, and I like it during Queen Elizabeth times, Prince Regent, because it gives me kind of a bit of a view of how it was in the olden days, and it tells me of how they lived and it's very funny as well.

Adele volunteers her preferences in generic terms — 'comedies' — and proceeds to offer two examples. Yet she also seems to perceive a requirement to explain the reasons for her preferences, which she does without prompting. Unlike many of the younger children, for her it is not sufficient to say that the programmes she likes are just 'funny'. She proceeds to compare programmes within this general category in terms of their historical setting, justifying why she likes some and not others.

Her discussion of *Blackadder* also remains at some distance from the text. Rather than retelling a funny episode or incident, she explains her preference in educational terms, rather like the women in Janice Radway's study who explain their preference for romances by describing how they can teach you about life in other countries (Radway, 1984). At this point, early in the discussion, it seems to be a response which is intended to appeal to what she suspects is the interviewer's agenda — rather like those in Extract 1.

While these characteristics may reflect a greater ability to generalize, they may also represent a rather different perception of the requirements of the situation. There was a sense in which the older middle-class children seemed to be offering their preferences in a more self-conscious way, as developed 'tastes' they wished to display.

This was particularly the case in the suburban secondary school, from which the following extract is taken. The main guarantee of 'taste' for these children was the ability to pour scorn on programmes that were seen in one way or another to fail in what they set out to achieve. In contrast with most of the younger groups, they found it much more difficult to talk about what they liked:

Extract 4

> Nigel: Yeah, the comedy at nine o'clock, because the comedy before it isn't that good, [yeah] except for things like *Fawlty Towers* [yeah].
>
> Ruth: [*Fawlty Towers*, that is brilliant that is.

Pradesh: [Oh yeah, that was funny! [*general agreement*]
Nigel: Now, now, that's, that's about the funniest comedy on before
               nine o'clock [. . .] They bring on really crummy comedies like
               Streets Apart, where they have to dub in [oh yeah] the laughter
               and, in, and in, these people are really stupid and there's not
               many good comedies before nine o'clock.

In this discussion, Nigel is very definite about his preference for the 'nine o'clock comedies', which he also refers to as 'satires'. These have a definite aura of being 'adult' and 'alternative' when compared with mainstream comedy, and it is this sense of difference, of being set apart from the common herd, which seems to appeal to him. He is keen to show that he is clever enough to be able to detect the 'dubbed' laughter — which in fact is no less common in 'alternative' comedies than in mainstream ones — and thereby distinguish himself from those who are merely 'stupid'.

Nigel and the other children here also seemed to be concerned to present themselves as 'discriminating consumers'. Thus, there was a lengthy discussion about whether satellite TV is worth the money, how often the movies are repeated, and whether you could get them on video anyway. This led on to complaints about scheduling, how there are too many good films on over Christmas and late at night, and none in the summer or at half-terms. 'Good taste' and the argument for 'consumer choice' seemed to go hand in hand.

This more self-conscious attempt to account for one's own tastes was often accompanied by more detailed critical judgments. In some instances, these judgments were positive, and reflected a kind of 'television appreciation'. For example, Carol praised *Blackadder* for the quality of the acting — 'Rowan Atkinson's got a good sense of humour . . . he makes little things really funny' — and singled out the Christmas episode because 'it added a theme to it'. Yet in most cases here, a substantial proportion of the talk took the form of mocking television for its various shortcomings. This talk was mainly led by the boys — unlike most of the other groups — and often took on the air of a performance, a display of what we know and how clever we are. At the same time, much of the criticism focused on comparatively easy targets such as cartoons, as in the following extract.

Extract 5

Ruth: *Brave Starr*, that is (. .)
Nigel: That is stupid, that is. [*laughter*]
Petros: I like *Brave Starr*.
Pradesh: So do I. [*laughs*] Honest, honest.
Nigel: It might as well be called Superman with the strength of a
               bear, with the speed of a [puma, the ease of a wolf.
Sally: [That's exactly the same as the
               Phantom in, [um *Defenders of the Earth* [yeah, yeah]
Pradesh: [And, and he doesn't use his powers when he
               needs them / he always stands there looking at his enemy
               and goes, and (. .)
Nigel: No, he, he [stands there and the enemy's about (&)
Sally: [His muscles grow every second.

Nigel: (&) five yards away, and he's going 'you'll never get me' and [they shoot him (. .) Piaow, piaow like that.

Pradesh: [Yeah, by the time they (?target) him Piaow /

Sally: Yeah, they always miss. [*laughter*]

Nigel: [I know.

Pradesh: [And he falls over and he gets trapped and then he escapes then he shoots [somebody then [he wins.

Ruth: [And also.

Nigel: [Yeah, [no, no, no, they always win.

Sally: [He never shoots anybody, he wouldn't hurt,[like you never see anybody get hurt.

Ruth: [In these, in those programmes, they always survive at the end.

Pradesh: Same, yes as when somebody gets=

Nigel: =I know, it's about seconds to go, they got to press this vital button, and they go 'Huurh' [*laughter*] and they press it [*laughter*] and then they (. . .)

?:   For about yeah, five minutes watching them go 'Huurh' like that.

Ruth: And then it just misses it, doesn't it, it goes [bonk!

Pradesh: [Somehow they get their strength back and they start walking [/ like say they fall down.

Nigel: [What, no, what happens, in, in things like *The A-Team*, yeah, [what they do, they, they, they, they're locked (&)

Ruth: [Yeugh, don't mention that, yeugh!

Nigel: (&) in a cupboard and then the bloke says to him, he's (?holding) to my plan and then [*laughter*] they get out of the cupboard and, and [spoil it (. .) I, I, I've (&)

?Sally: [Find some tools.

?Ruth: And they always, well.

Nigel: (&) got a *Mad* comic with all the things [Oh yeah!] you need to have for a, for [um, drama, yeah, like ninety (&)

Petros: [To be a (?. . to be)

Nigel: (&) mile an hour road chases down the motorway there's no traffic, and you all got to be bending out with a machine gun firing at the other person while somebody's firing at you, and, altogether at ninety miles an hour, and he, and he says and he says like N.B. the villain's always got to fall off a bridge or something like that.

Interviewer: Yeah, [no, this is very true.

Nigel: [And, and, and, the lady heroes ha, never smudge their make-up [Oh yeah], and things like that.

Sally: [Oh, I know.

Pradesh: [Oh yeah, they fall on fire, they go through loads of things and at the end they've always got their hair done [yeah] and [/ [*laughter*] and they got make-up, without any bruises.

Ruth:	[Yeah, their hair's all perfectly, [yeah] you know, combed [yeah, I know] it's like they've, they got a comb in their back pocket.
?:	Better than Superwoman.
Sally:	[*laughs*] They've been shot to death.

Clearly, taking the mickey out of television is an extremely pleasurable activity for this group, which they are not indulging solely for the benefit of the interviewer: Nigel's reference to his *Mad* comic suggests that it has a much wider cultural purchase. Again, this is largely a collective activity: each contribution builds on the last, sustaining the laughter and excitement. Yet it is also highly competitive: Petros's tastes are roundly mocked — and indeed satirized by Pradesh — which reduces him to silence, while the others struggle frantically for the floor.

Their judgments are largely concerned with modality, and in particular with plausibility. These comments are partly based on technical knowledge about the production process — for example, Nigel's observation on the way in which the dramatic climax of the cartoon is always drawn out through editing — and partly informed by comparisons with the real world — particularly in their observations on the action-adventure series at the end of the extract.

The discussion also ranges across texts, noting similarities in terms of character and narrative form: while there are specific details, these are offered primarily as illustrations of the predictable nature of the generic formula. Indeed, at the end of this extract, the specific programmes being referred to are not identified, suggesting that the target is almost an *idea* of television — and significantly in this case, American television — rather than anything more specific.

In one way or another, nearly all the talk in this group focused on what is wrong with television. The children took great pleasure in recounting 'mistakes' — continuity errors, moments where the announcer has been caught unawares or where the camera moves to the wrong shot — and in pointing out the ways in which TV is 'fixed' — how they rig the 'clapometer' on game shows, or make studio audiences laugh on cue.

Undoubtedly, there is a degree of safety in this position: the more criticisms you can make, the more intelligent and sophisticated you appear. Yet there is also a kind of ambivalence here. On the one hand, there is a lot to be gained from pointing out what is wrong with television; yet on the other hand, you have to watch the programmes in order to be able to condemn them with any degree of authority. This dilemma can be negotiated, however, as it was repeatedly in this group, either by disclaiming — you watch 'because there's nothing else on' — or by saying that you watch explicitly 'to see how stupid it is'.

From this perspective, accounting for pleasure becomes a significant problem. There was much less retelling here than in other groups, and what there was tended to maintain a highly distanced, evaluative stance. Even programmes which were watched on a regular basis — such as the Australian soaps — were discussed with heavy irony.

Thus, while many of these criticisms appear to be motivated by a straightforward sense of the incompetence of the programme-makers, they also serve to demonstrate the speakers' own critical sophistication. In the process, they enable the speakers to distinguish themselves from 'other people' who are somehow incapable of 'seeing through' television. While this discourse is not explicitly phrased in class terms, there is often a thin line between ridiculing popular television and ridiculing its audience. To commit yourself to liking anything — with the exception of documentaries, which were the only programmes to merit any more serious discussion here — would be to run the risk of aligning yourself with the mass of viewers who are stupid enough to watch it and believe it.

Context and Class

My aim in this section has been to illustrate some of the ways in which the children chose to define the interview situation, and the relationships which characterized it. In some instances, the interview was defined — at least to start with — as a distinctly 'educational' event. In others, it was almost an 'anti-educational' event, providing an occasion for kinds of talk and behaviour which would not be sanctioned inside the classroom. Some groups took the opportunity to display their own critical acumen and 'good taste', while others saw it as a chance to re-live past pleasures. These differences to some extent determined the topics which were nominated, pursued or rejected, and the styles of talk which were adopted.

While it might be possible to explain some of these differences in developmental terms — for example, the degree of generalization or concreteness of the discussion — a number of other factors came into play. Existing relationships within the groups were undoubtedly important, and these will be considered in more detail in the following section. Gender differences also played some part here, and again these will be considered below.

Nevertheless, the most striking differences here are between the parallel groups in different schools — and while the groups were not homogeneous, they were broadly differentiated in terms of social class. In general, the mainly middle-class children in the suburban primary school approached the activity much more formally than the mainly working-class children in the inner-city primary school — although this certainly declined as the research progressed. Faced with an unknown adult, it was as though the middle-class children approached the initial interview as an 'educational' event, and took some time to recognize that there were other possibilities here.

Among the older groups, the middle-class children in the suburban secondary school were much more forthcoming than their younger counterparts, and often simply ignored the interviewer; while those in the inner-city secondary school were significantly more wary both of each other, and of the whole situation. In general, the older middle-class children took the interview as an opportunity to display their own confident superiority — with distinct class overtones. For the more socially diverse inner-city groups, by contrast, there seemed to be more risk in venturing an opinion — although there was little sense of deference towards the interviewer here.

Nevertheless, it is important to beware of a deterministic account of the role of social class — for example, to conclude that working-class children tend to talk about television in one way, and middle-class children in another, and that this directly reflects their class position.

This assertion has been made in some previous research, although in my view it remains very questionable. Frederick Williams (1969), for example, found that working-class children were more likely to describe programmes in terms of isolated incidents — particularly the 'high points', which (according to Williams) 'presumably had a major *visual* emphasis' and were often 'violent' — whereas middle-class children tended to describe complete narratives. Drawing on Bernstein's account of social class differences in language use, Williams speculates as follows:

> Here [in relation to action-adventure programmes] the lower status child would be more attuned to the concrete, the direct verbal and physical action level of a program. The higher status child, by contrast, would be capable of responding both to the concrete and to the more abstract — the *verbal* — levels of a program. It is on this higher level that the visual and concrete components of the programs may be combined by the verbal components into the 'reason' for the action, or the 'story-line' of the program. (p. 353)

Apart from Williams's rather *ad hoc* account of the ways in which the verbal and visual aspects of television interact, there are a number of significant problems with this account. Even if Williams's findings about different styles of talk are generally true — and there is certainly evidence from this research which would dispute them — it is surely illegitimate to suggest that the way in which children talk about television necessarily reflects the way in which they watch it.

In effectively arguing for 'elaborated' and 'restricted' codes (cf. Bernstein, 1971), Williams largely neglects the context in which the interviews took place, and the power-relationships between interviewer and interviewee (cf. Labov, 1973). If the working-class children in these discussion groups were less likely to offer general statements, or to elaborate on their preferences, this does not necessarily prove that they were incapable of doing so. It may simply suggest that they perceived the context in a rather different way, and that they were taking the opportunity to do something rather different within it.

In this respect, it would be more accurate to explain these differences not merely in terms of social class, but in terms of the relationship between school and home (or peer group) cultures. Social class will certainly influence what children perceive to be 'educational', and thus what they will be likely to say about a 'non-educational' subject in an 'educational' context, but the relationship is likely to be complex and contradictory. As I shall indicate in Chapter 12, this issue has a major significance for media education.

Subjects: Defining the Self and Others

As I have argued, talk about television can serve as an arena in which the self and its relation to others are defined. In talking about the programmes we like and dislike, we are inevitably 'positioning' ourselves — although these positions are likely to be multiple and contradictory. From this perspective, the 'self' is not a singular entity, whose 'true nature' can be revealed or kept hidden. On the contrary, it is inevitably constructed in and through discourse (Gergen and Davis, 1985).

This process is perhaps less visible where the topics chosen for discussion seem uncontroversial. Most of the groups involved in this research — perhaps partly because they had been chosen at random — tended to work towards a consensus, using talk as a means of building group solidarity. Talk about popular programmes served as a comparatively 'safe area', in which potential tensions or conflicts could partly be effaced. Yet in some cases, differences began to emerge, which often reflected broader social and cultural distinctions, and it is these I want to focus on here.

This was particularly apparent in the inner-city secondary school, where the groups were much less socially homogeneous than in the other schools. The following summary of one group discussion illustrates this.

This group included a white working-class girl (Della), a white middle-class girl (Beatrix), a British/Afro-Caribbean working-class girl (Chanel), a white working-class boy (Danny) and an African working-class boy (Mahad). This was not a friendship group, and like all the secondary school children at this stage in the research, they were new to the school and to each other. They were also extremely wary of the interview situation: they referred to the tape recorder a number of times during the course of the discussion, wanted to know what would happen to the tape, and seemed uncertain about how to 'place' the interviewer, at some points referring to her as 'miss' (i.e. as a teacher), while at another asking her what TV programmes she watched.

In the discussion as a whole, there was very little sustained talk on any one topic. In effect, what was taking place was an extended version of the 'I like . . .' sequence described above (Extract 2) — although this seemed much more fraught than usual. In the process, the children were working out their allegiances, although nobody seemed to have anyone else they could safely team up with. Very often, individuals would volunteer a preference, only to have somebody else laugh or pull a face or say 'that's rubbish!'. On a number of occasions, titles that were volunteered met with the response 'that's for babies' or 'that's for little kids' — for example in the case of Mahad's preference for cartoons.

These allegiances were primarily based on differences of gender, 'race' and class. Thus, early in the discussion, Della and Chanel agreed on a preference for *Prisoner: Cell Block H*, arguing that the boys wouldn't like this because they were too young for it. Beatrix, the middle-class girl, was rather outside this pairing, having nominated *Red Dwarf*, an 'alternative' comedy, which most of the others had not even heard of. Gender differences were also sustained through the discussion of soap operas, where the boys were effectively excluded, with Mahad expressing strong distaste. However, there were differences between the girls here, with Chanel expressing contempt for Charlene in *Neighbours* ('she's gone out of fashion') and praise of Bobby in *Home and Away* ('she's a tomboy and she fights'), while Della owned up to crying when Charlene left.

Danny then attempted to assert a more masculine preference for sport, with Mahad following in his wake, although this was rather undermined when Chanel joined in the talk about favourite football teams. Danny then moved on to Sky TV — a distinct claim for status here — and *Rambo*, but again the initiative was taken away from him by the girls, who proceeded to retell frightening bits of horror films they had seen.

Later in the discussion, Chanel asserted a preference for three comedies all featuring black characters — *A Different World*, *Desmonds* and *The Cosby Show* — and went on to describe the appeal of *Desmonds* in terms of its black cultural references: 'I like when the boy's rapping, man, that is safe'. This assertion of 'blackness' also took place around musical tastes, where Chanel offered a list of exclusively black singers and groups. Mahad, again following in the wake, also claimed to like one of these, Bobby Brown, earning his only positive feedback throughout the discussion from Chanel: 'yeah, you got taste, you got taste'.

Later, Chanel appeared to be claiming a degree of sexual sophistication in mentioning the film *Scandal*, which she then withdrew, saying 'I can't tell you the rest . . . I can't talk about that'. Overall, it was she who emerged most successful from this combat by television, maintaining a consistently 'hard', streetwise persona, and never having anyone successfully undermine her — indeed, she was the only one who seemed to be prepared to fight back, to defend her preferences, on the one occasion when somebody had the nerve to attack them.

Ultimately, there was only one programme, the comedy/game show *Beadle's About*, they could agree to like — and it is notable that this is a programme which is premised on laughing at other people's misfortunes. It seemed much easier to express dislikes, because there was less risk of being caught out: so there was some consensus here around disliked texts such as the sitcoms *Shelley* and *'Allo 'Allo*. Even here, however, when Mahad attempted to follow the grain of the discussion by asserting that 'all comedies are rubbish', he earned the following put-down from Chanel: 'you don't even know, you don't understand what they're saying' — referring to the fact that English is not his first language.

Throughout the discussion, then, talk about television was being used primarily as a means of establishing relationships and asserting 'subject positions'. Largely because of the social differences within the group, this process was unusually fraught: there were few ways of avoiding exposure, except by withdrawing into silence, as the boys eventually did. In this context, there was little to be gained from offering detailed critical judgments or explanations of the reasons for one's preferences. When pressed on this, the children often shrugged it off with comments such as 'I just like it' or 'it's rubbish, I can't explain'. Yet in a sense, this kind of discursive reflection was irrelevant to what was taking place.

As this description suggests, talking about television necessarily involves defining or positioning oneself and others. While this can occur in a variety of ways, the categories of age, social class, gender and 'race' are unavoidably significant, since it is largely in these terms that power and social identity are defined.

Defining the Self and Others: Age

As in the discussion summarized above, the children often categorized television programmes in terms of the extent to which they were 'childish' or 'grown-up'. While these categories partly reflected their perceptions of the target audience — and indeed the actual audience — of programmes, they were often fairly flexible. Thus, this issue took different forms in different age groups, and according to gender. It seemed to be safe for older children, particularly girls, to express a preference for more anarchic cartoons like *Fantastic Max*, and even a kind of nostalgia for cartoons aimed at a pre-school audience. By contrast, while boys were much more likely to express a preference for cartoons than girls, they were often mocked for this, as in the case of Mahad above. The accusation of immaturity was routinely levelled by girls against boys, but never the other way round. Yet there was often some ambivalence here. While cartoons were often condemned for their predictable narratives — as in the discussion of *Brave Starr* (Extract 5) — there were also some extended retellings, even among the 9-year-olds.

Furthermore, there was a considerable amount of negotiation in a number of groups about which programmes were to be defined as 'childish', and which were not. One of the youngest groups in the suburban primary school, for example, spent almost half the time discussing the puppet show *Sooty* — a programme which appeared to enjoy a strange cult status in the school as a whole. Attempts to launch alternative topics, such as the Australian soaps, repeatedly failed, as they returned time and again to 'magic moments' from the programme — which significantly often seemed to involve the adult puppeteer being duped or humiliated by the anarchic child puppets, notably through the agency of Sooty's magic wand. Their account of the programme was also highly 'situated' in the viewing context, in that they seemed to have to struggle to watch it against the very different preferences of adults and older siblings. At the same time, the 'childish' nature of the programme did become problematic, as the following extract illustrates. Here, Michelle has been talking about how she has to look after her younger sister, and often gets into fights about what they are going to watch.

Extract 6

Michelle:	My sister watches baby ones. [*laughs*]
Interviewer:	She watches?
Michelle:	She watches baby ones. [*laughs*]
Interviewer:	What — what — what do you call baby ones?
Michelle:	Oh! Phew! *Sooty*, things like that.
Christina:	Yeah, I used to like them // I used to like *Rainbow*. [*laughter*] I agree with Richard, because if you're bored and there's something like *Playbus* on you er can — you can just sit down and watch it.

.
.
.

Interviewer:	Charlotte?
Charlotte:	I've got the videotape of *Sooty* as well.
Michelle:	[*laughs*]
Interviewer:	Did you get that for a present or?
Charlotte:	Yeah.
Interviewer:	You bought it — [it was bought for you?
Charlotte:	[Um my broth — my brother bought it for me.
Interviewer:	'Cause he knew you were a fan.
Charlotte:	Yes.
Interviewer:	Do you think *Sooty*'s a baby programme / too? // or
Charlotte:	[// Sort of
Boy:	[Urgh!
Interviewer:	Sort of / you're not sure about that.
Charlotte:	I'm only half watching it because it's boring me sometimes.

Despite the pleasure all the children take in describing the programme, Michelle clearly defines it as 'babyish'. This places Charlotte in a rather difficult position:

while the others have been quick to disavow their preference, she seems more reluctant to do so, hence her hesitation. Charlotte is in fact the youngest child in a family with four older brothers, and this struggle over what is 'childish' is probably a depressingly familiar one for her. The interviewer's return to the topic in the second part of this extract effectively shut her up completely, and she played very little part in the remainder of the discussion — although it did not seem to prevent the others returning compulsively to yet more retellings of the antics of Sooty. Interestingly, this was one of the few groups to turn the question round, and to ask the interviewer which programmes she preferred: they seemed particularly intrigued by the fact that she claimed to watch the children's cartoon *Count Duckula*.

On the other hand, there were instances where individuals claimed distinctly 'adult' tastes in an attempt to gain status with others in the group, or to outrage the interviewer. Violent videos seemed to serve this function in a number of groups, as the following extract, taken from one of the 9-year-old groups in the suburban primary school, illustrates. Here, the boys seem intent on disrupting the dynamic established at the start of the interview, in which the female interviewer engaged the girls in an extended discussion of the soaps. Malcolm begins by whispering 'Bruce Lee', eventually saying he likes it 'because there's loads of blood in it' — a debatable observation, perhaps. Steven responds by offering *The Karate Kid*, prompting Malcolm to raise the stakes with *Robocop*.

Extract 7

Malcolm:	*Robocop* [*laughs*].
Interviewer:	Have you, have you got *Robocop*? Have you watched *Robocop*?
Amarjit:	Oh! That's good.
John:	Loads of blood!
Interviewer:	Certainly bloodthirsty, my god!
Amarjit:	Yeah.
Malcolm:	There's this man with this acid and it's eating him up and he's going around [like that [*imitates*].
John:	[Yeah and a car chucks him up.
Malcolm:	Yeah, blood squirts everywhere.

.

.

.

Malcolm:	*Nightmare on Elm Street*.
Interviewer:	Oh, yes.
Amarjit:	That's good.
Interviewer:	Everybody seems to have (&) [
?:	[Freddy [*choking sounds*]
Interviewer:	(&) seen that. You haven't seen that Donna?
[*Various confirmations and exclamations*]	
John:	It's not scary.
Malcolm:	It is.
John:	I've seen one at night time.
Malcolm:	Yes it is. You must be joking. How would you like it if a [man with claws (&)

Amarjit:	[Freddy and he comes out [of this (. . . .)
Malcolm:	[(&) scratches you (. . .) Yeah, he's got these great big claws coming out (&)[
Amarjit:	[yeah, coming out.
Malcolm:	(&) and scratching everyone.
Amarjit:	Yeah. They're like spears, instead of nails.
Interviewer:	Sounds horrific. [*unidentified choking sounds*] I'm afraid I'm not very good at watching scary films.
Donna:	Oh, my sister's scared at all the scary films.
Interviewer:	But you're not?
Donna:	Nah.
Malcolm:	They're lovely.

These children are talking about material which they are legally forbidden to watch, and they know this. Their account offers nothing in the way of narrative context, but goes straight to the 'good bits', the parts that have the greatest power to offend. The interviewer's response here more than confirms Malcolm's success in outraging her — although his subversive intention is perhaps signalled by the laugh with which he introduces *Robocop*.

This parading of violence may possess a gendered dynamic — as I have noted, it effectively disrupts the girls' discussion of the soaps — although it is something to which the girls contribute with enthusiasm. In fact, Malcolm's position is rather ambiguous in this respect: interestingly, he later confessed to watching *Blind Date* specifically 'to see everyone kiss'. Note that it is he who is keen to argue that *Nightmare on Elm Street* is scary — perhaps partly because to argue otherwise would be to undermine its subversive potential — while the others (including the girls) assert that they can handle it, a much more common response.

This focus on 'adult' material occurred in a number of other younger groups. One group of 7-year-olds in the inner-city primary school, for example, barely mentioned children's television at all. Their talk concentrated on the soaps, horror films, sex and swearing, including retellings of films like *Poltergeist* and *The Terminator* and a bizarre incident with inflatable sex dolls from *Only Fools and Horses*. This made a stark contrast with the videotapes they claimed to possess — such as *The Hundred and One Dalmatians*, *Bednobs and Broomsticks* and *Bambi* — which for some reason did not seem so worthy of discussion.

As I have noted, a number of children were keen to retell incidents from 'adult' films they had not seen, either on the basis of hearsay or occasionally the trailers. (This may be the case, for example, with the account of *Nightmare on Elm Street* above.) On the other hand, the News, which was clearly defined as 'adult', was routinely reviled by the large majority: while some children did admit to watching the News, there was very little status attached to this.

Perceptions of what was 'adult' often appeared to be determined by parental regulation — although, as I shall indicate in the following chapter, regulation of children's viewing would appear to be more of a middle-class concern. For example, one of the groups in the suburban secondary school included a number of children who described the ways in which their parents prevented them from watching horror or 'violent' films. Perhaps partly for this reason, there was a considerable degree of status attached to this material — leading one girl to resort to retelling a horror film she had half-watched at a friend's house.

While the working-class children were less likely to describe this kind of regulation, they were occasionally more frank about their perceptions of 'adult' material. As in the above discussion, there was often a certain ambivalence towards horror films: while some children admitted that they were frightened, and that the films give them nightmares, they claimed to watch them nevertheless. Perhaps particularly for boys, watching horror appeared to be seen as a test of strength, in which you had to train yourself not to display your fear.

As in the extracts quoted at the beginning of Chapter 3, a number of the children showed some awareness of discourses about the 'effects' of television, although they largely attempted to distance themselves, either through parody or outright rejection. Here again, the 'effects' of television were often displaced onto 'other people', notably children younger than themselves. While many of the children were aware of censorship 'ratings', they also disputed the system on which these are decided, suggesting that they were merely an arbitrary form of adult authority.

Defining the Self and Others: Class

While age — or perceptions of age — emerged as an issue in a number of groups, class difference was hardly ever raised in such explicit terms. Looking across the groups, certain programmes or genres did emerge as 'class tastes', albeit not very strongly. Middle-class children were more likely to state a preference for 'alternative' comedies and factual programmes, while working-class children were more likely to favour horror, mainstream comedy and 'entertainment' programmes. Nevertheless, much of what was discussed remained consensual, and there were no instances of programmes being dismissed explicitly in class terms.

One possible exception to this was *EastEnders*, a broadly 'social realist' soap opera which regularly emphasizes class differences. *EastEnders* and its British rival *Coronation Street* were largely condemned as 'depressing' and 'boring', as in the following extract, taken from the suburban secondary school.

Extract 8

Nigel:	Yeah, but *East*, *EastEnders* [*laughter*] *East*, *EastEnders* is really dreadful, though.
Petros:	Yeah I know.
Nigel:	It's, it's not colourful, it's all grey houses.
Sally:	[Oh, what's this?
Pradesh:	[Yeah, I mean, with burnt wallpaper and things like that / [*laughter*] [and it's all brown.
Nigel:	[*laughing*] [Yeah, yeah, yeah.
Sally:	People live in places with burnt wallpaper.
Petros:	It's a bit like=
Pradesh:	=and the carpets are all yeugh.
Nigel:	[*laughing*] Yeah, [it's, it's=
Interviewer:	[Is that why you don't watch it?

Nigel:	[It's, it's=
Pradesh:	[No, it's just boring, I mean, [the, the way (&)
Sally:	[Well *Howard's Way* is more your style.
Ruth:	Yeah [*laughs*].
Pradesh:	(&) everything's set out, it's made to not [watch it.
Nigel:	[It looks, it looks like a, it's, it, it just looks, it looks [really horrid, you'd never want to live there (&)
Pradesh:	[With the man with the fish and chip shop.
Nigel:	(&) and they don't seem to put any colour into it.
Petros:	No, but [some people do live there, that's the only thing=
Nigel:	[It just seems to be all grey.
Sally:	=Yeah, I know, but about [*laughs*] half the people in Britain live like that.

One of the problems with *EastEnders* — at least for Nigel and Pradesh — is that it offers an unpleasant reminder of how the other half lives. Nigel's comment 'you'd never want to live there' is particularly interesting, since it implicitly acknowledges that the programme is 'realistic', even if it is showing us something we would rather not see. While Sally and Petros distance themselves from this criticism, and also claim that the programme displays a kind of realism, they do not include themselves among the 'half the people in Britain' who live like that. *EastEnders* is contrasted with *Howard's Way*, which, while not quite aspiring to *Dynasty*-style opulence, is distinctly middle-class — although there is certainly some irony in Sally's remark here. Interestingly, *EastEnders* is condemned here in similar terms to those in which *Neighbours* was often praised: it is 'grey' rather than 'colourful'.

Nevertheless, these observations were exceptional. While social class positions may occasionally be staked out around specific programmes — and particularly those which emphasize class differences — they are more likely be manifested in more generalized attitudes towards television as a whole. As I have argued, using a discourse of 'critical judgment' is at least partly a means of defining class membership — and thereby distinguishing oneself from the 'gullible masses' — although its class basis was not made explicit by the children themselves.

Defining the Self and Others: Gender

Gender differences emerged as a more salient issue in these discussions in a variety of ways. Perhaps one of the most striking points here was simply the dominance of the girls: in more than three-quarters of the groups, irrespective of the gender of the interviewer, it was the girls who dominated, both in terms of the amount of talk and in terms of initiating topics for discussion. While this finding does not necessarily contradict previous linguistic research (e.g. Spender, 1980) — researchers have certainly found that men tend to dominate in 'public' talk, although they are less likely to do so in small groups — it nevertheless remains surprising. It could well be that talking about television — or perhaps talking in certain ways about television — is itself a gendered activity, and that the competencies involved are those which girls are more likely to have acquired as a result of their other social experiences.

There were certainly gendered tastes — for example, for sport or soap operas — which cut across the groups, although there were many exceptions here. Certainly among the older working-class children, there were girls who could more than hold their own in discussing sport, and talked in depth about boxing as well as football. A preference for the Australian soaps would seem to be prevalent for both boys and girls — although girls tended to talk about them at much greater length and in rather different ways, as I shall indicate below.

Despite this, there was a kind of 'common sense' about gendered tastes which the children undoubtedly drew upon. For boys, expressing contempt for soap operas or an enthusiasm for aggressive sport, for example, can be a way of asserting a 'masculine' position. This was often more transparent among the younger children, as the following extract illustrates. Here, Nathan, one of a group of 7-year-olds in the suburban primary school, attempts to disrupt the 'feminine' dialogue about soap operas which has been established between the female interviewer and the girls.

Extract 9

Interviewer:	Jim and Beverly. Oh yes, quite right, yes. I'd forgotten all about that one [wedding]. That's quite a quiet one compared to Scott and Charlene's wasn't it? You don't like it at all Nathan, why?
Nathan:	Nah. I don't like it because I think it's soppy and I don't like (. . . .) where you have all those things about love in it.
Diana:	[*laughs*]
Nathan:	I just really HATE it.
Interviewer:	You hate all that, do you?
Nathan:	Mm.
Interviewer:	// Tell me more, why?
Nathan:	'Cause I never even like that kind of thing (&) [
Nancy:	[*very quietly*] [he doesn't like girls.
Nathan:	(&) I think it's stupid.
Interviewer:	You think it's stupid.
Nathan:	Mm.
Nancy:	Nathan doesn't like girls that's why.
Diana:	[*laughing*] Yeah, I think that's the reason.

Throughout this discussion, Nathan sought to position himself as 'different' from the other children, and to resist the power of the interviewer. He rarely entered into dialogue, and his contributions often took the form of direct refutations of what others had said. His assertion of a strongly 'masculine' position was one aspect of this generally 'resistant' stance, although it was one which under the circumstances seemed to achieve a degree of success: as in this case, nobody seemed to want to contest him. The reaction of the girls here is typical: they talk about him in the third person, implying that his rejection of soaps is almost a form of impression management (note Diana's laughter here).

Later in the discussion, Nathan attempted to reinforce this position by asserting a preference for fact against fiction. He claimed not to like cartoons because they were 'not real', although he made an exception for *Dinoriders*, a cartoon he described as 'scary' and 'horrible'. Nathan was also one of the very few children in these discussions who claimed to like the News, again in opposition to the others in the group. He explained his preference as follows: 'I really really like films when people get killed, especially the News because I was interested in the army a couple of years ago and now I like the army so much that, that I watch the News and I hope . . . to see people getting killed on it and that kind of thing, soldiers on the News.'

Nathan's ability to combine a 'masculine' preference for the News with a taste for violence could be seen as setting new standards in male sensitivity, although again it should be read in context. There is a sense here, as in Extract 7, that the boys are resorting to very stereotyped expressions of masculinity in order to disrupt the complicity between the female interviewer and the girls in the group. In both cases, the interviewer responds much less enthusiastically to the boys' stated preferences than she does to the girls', and her distaste for 'violence' is quite apparent — a position which effectively cues the boys' responses. Significantly, in a subsequent discussion with a male interviewer, Nathan in fact acknowledged that he watched the Australian soaps, and seemed to experience little embarrassment about this.

One weapon available to girls in this context — and one which a number of them used — was to label boys' tastes as immature or 'babyish'. While this was occasionally quite explicit, it could also be accomplished by offering a critique of the programme in question. In the following extract, taken from one of the groups of 9-year-olds in the inner-city primary school, James's taste for *He-Man* — of which he claims to have an extensive collection on videotape — comes under attack.

Extract 10

Elizabeth:	But *He-Man*, that is absolutely / rubbish [. . .] It's just so sick.
Dipesh:	Yeah!
?Sayo:	[Rubbish!
Elizabeth:	[When you're actually looking at it, it's /
Dipesh:	It's always the same people.
Elizabeth:	There's always something wrong with the world.
Dipesh:	Yeah. / Always the same people.
Emily:	[*singing*] 'I who save the world!'
Sayo:	There's Skeletor, there's no peace!
Elizabeth:	[*singing, funny voice*] 'And I have a=
	[*groans*]
Elizabeth:	What I hate is / er the criminals always get a / always get away.
Dipesh:	Get away.
Emily:	Why can't the goodies all die for once?
Others:	[Yeah! Yeah!
Elizabeth:	[No but when / because in programmes (&) [
James:	[Why can't

                he just get in them, and then put another one on, they'll
                have him back [?].

Interviewer: Elizabeth, yeah.

Elizabeth: (&) It's always the goodie winning, [yeah] it's never the
                baddie actually winning [yeah].

Throughout this discussion, James' tastes for cartoons like *He-Man* and *Ghostbusters* were repeatedly attacked, particularly by the girls. What is notable here is the way in which the boys fall in behind them, with Dipesh and Sayo echoing their criticisms, and even James eventually joining in, albeit rather incoherently. There is perhaps also a kind of class deference here, especially in relation to Emily, who is the only middle-class child in this group. In fact, Sayo's tastes appeared to be similar to James', although he tended to suppress this. Thus, he initially expressed enthusiasm for *Ghostbusters*, but later retracted this; and he increasingly fell back on less committal statements like '*Gummi Bears* is quite popular'.

In this instance, the girls use modality judgments as a means of displaying their sophistication: complaints about the predictability and implausibility of the series effectively define it as too simple for their more demanding 'adult' tastes. Here again, the use of a 'critical' discourse about television needs to be situated within the interpersonal context in which it is produced, and the social functions it appears to serve.

Defining the Self and Others: 'Race'

While many of these groups were racially mixed, the issue of racial difference rarely emerged in such clear terms as it did in the discussion of *The Cosby Show* considered in Chapter 3. Particularly in the suburban schools, there was a sense in which racial differences were actively suppressed. One group in the suburban secondary school, for example, included a British/Asian girl (Navin), a British/Greek Cypriot boy (Terry) and a British/Chinese girl (Susan). While Susan expressed some enthusiasm for the Chinese series *Dirt Water Dynasty*, both Navin and Terry were keen to disavow any preference for 'ethnic' videos: Navin described Indian films, for example, as 'boring' and 'exactly the same', again commenting on their implausibility — 'it's so silly, and they jump off twenty foot high cliffs and land on their feet'.

By contrast, in a few groups in the inner-city schools, racial identity was at least implicitly on the agenda. While this partly reflected the greater proportion of black children in these schools, it may also have derived from the greater cultural status or 'street credibility' of black culture. Ultimately, black children may have stood to gain more in this context. Thus, in the discussion summarized at the beginning of this section, Chanel is clearly using her list of preferences as a way of proclaiming a 'black' identity. Similarly, 'black' programmes like *The Cosby Show*, *A Different World* and *Desmonds* were almost exclusively nominated by black (British/Afro-Caribbean) children. Nevertheless, in some instances white children attempted to get in on the act, although their contributions were often ignored, or even, as in the following extract, actively resented. Here, a group of 9-year-olds in the inner-city primary school is discussing the black British sitcom *Desmonds*. Elizabeth and Sayo are black, Emily and James white.

Extract 11

Elizabeth:	I like this film called *Desmonds*.
Various:	Oh yeah!
Elizabeth:	It's really funny. It's like this Jamaican thing with all Jamaican words in it, [it sounds really funny.
Sayo:	[I like this thing, it's all right, he says [*Jamaican voice:*] 'I don't know what to dooo'
James:	[Oh yeah, man.
Elizabeth:	And I like the name Porkpie.
Interviewer:	One at a time, please, please.
Elizabeth:	He's always getting upset, when they, they did this party for him, when he could have been buying a TV licence, and then he goes [*Jamaican voice:*] 'Ya know what I really tink, it's a waste a your money' and then he walked out of the shop in a rage.
Sayo:	It's so funny / and the son goes [*rapping voice:*] 'It's alright sis, I know what to do, a man's gotta do what a man's gotta do'.
Interviewer:	Yeah.
Elizabeth:	It's funny.
Emily:	I liked / what oh, the boy, I've forgotten his name, put in his mum's birthday card.
Sayo:	Oh yeah.
Sayo, Emily, Elizabeth:	'Some mums are good, some mums are bad, but my mum's wicked in the neighbourhood'.
Sayo:	[*to Emily*] You don't know it. Why were you going, whatever you said.

Much of the pleasure for the black children here, as in some other groups, lies in imitating the 'ethnic' voices featured in the programme: indeed, judging from the wild reactions of the studio audience in *Desmonds*, this would seem to be widely shared. This is an activity in which the black children wish to claim some expertise, hence Sayo's firm rejection of Emily's attempt to get in on the act.

Perhaps the most interesting and paradoxical instance of a text focusing broader questions about racial identity occurred in one of the groups of 7-year-olds in the same school. Here, the discussion was dominated by two black girls, Samantha and Hannah, and concerned the film *Imitation of Life*.

Extract 12

Samantha:	I watched this film on Channel Two and it was about this girl=
Hannah:	Oh yeah, it was about this girl=
Sonia:	BBC2 / She's always saying Channel Two.
Samantha:	[It was about this girl=

Hannah:	[And it was about this girl and she didn't have a real mother and she was a black lady and, um, this other (&) [
Samantha:	[boyfriend.
Hannah:	(&) white lady was her real mum. And in the end the black lady died and I didn't watch the bit what Samantha watched when this man threw all the red stuff over some girl.
Samantha:	Yeah, well, um, that, well, she said to the girl, / uh, she had the boyfriend, she said, the man said to the girl 'is your mother a NIGger' [uh] / And then she said, and then she said 'I'm as white as you are, I'm as white as you are'. And then he just threw her in this / red stuff.
Interviewer:	Mmmm. What film was that? What was it called, d'you remember?
Samantha:	I didn't watch it at the beginning, actually.
Hannah:	But, I didn't either, but it came on before, my nan said. And, um, at the end the white lady what was the girl's real mum, the black lady died and she was crying and all that because that was her nan and she was crying ['cause she never wanted her to die.
Samantha:	[And then the end, she, the girl who was the mother, I mean the girl whose mother died, she just came and just said sorry. If she came earlier, the girl, the lady would have felt much happier, but she went off to some place and been dancing [in these PUBS and that.
Hannah:	[Yeah, cause she was in the grave, in the um tub grave, and she was saying sorry and that, but she, the lady wouldn't come back alive.

.
.
.

Samantha:	It was quite interesting, but um when she was little=
Rachel:	Is it a true story?
Hannah:	No.
Samantha:	When she was little, she was at school, she was pretending she's white. And then they went in this snow, / and then they said, the girl said, the one who's grown up now, she said 'I wish I never had a mother' and then she said 'I'm as white as you', and when they got home to the other girl, her friend. And then she went in her bedroom, and then the little girl said this. She said / [*whining US accent:*] 'Mary Ann wouldn't play with me' [*laughter*] That how she went. But it was interesting.

As this account suggests, *Imitation of Life* is explicitly concerned with questions of racial identity, particularly through the character of a black girl who attempts to 'pass as white'. While there is a certain amount of ironic distance in the girls' account of the film — for example in Samantha's use of the American accent — there is a much more 'serious' engagement with the text here than was apparent, for example, in their discussion of the Australian soaps. Samantha's use of the word 'interesting' is striking here: it was a word which was rarely applied to television in these discussions, and one that she used again when briefly returning to the topic at the very end of the discussion.

The key points in Samantha's account seem to be the lines she quotes directly, particularly those she repeats: 'I'm as white as you are' and 'is your mother a NIGger?', also repeated at the end of the discussion. The word 'nigger' is a taboo word — at least in the confines of the school, if not perhaps the playground — and the mere utterance of it carries a distinct shock value: note the brief pause after it first occurs.

At the same time, the girls do seem confused about the basic family relationships in the film: the 'white lady' they refer to is not in fact the black girl's 'real mum' — her 'real mum' is the 'black lady' whom Hannah seems to assume is her 'nan' (grandmother). This may be simply because they missed the beginning of the film, yet it may be a rather more significant 'misreading', which further complicates the issue of racial identity. Within the multicultural context in which these children live, skin colour is not necessarily such a reliable indicator of family membership, and in this respect, their construction of racial difference may be rather different from that proposed by the film itself.

The Social Self

In this section, I have concentrated on the ways in which talk about television serves to define the self in relation to others. While there is obviously a great variety of ways in which this might occur — and which might ultimately be traced to individual biographies — I have emphasized that children's definitions of self are constructed at least partly in terms of their perceptions of broader social categories.

For these children, age emerged as the most salient of these categories, which may partly be a result of the interview situation. In relation to the interviewer, and in the context of the school, they were defined primarily as 'children' — a definition which they could attempt to negotiate and possibly modify during the course of the discussion. If children are predominantly defined as powerless, there is much to be gained by excluding oneself from this category, and claiming 'adult' status — although one can also take the more subversive option of celebrating 'childish' tastes (cf. Hodge and Tripp, 1986).

To some extent, other social differences may have been minimized by the decision to use mixed groups. There was a sense in which many of the groups sought to construct a consensus, and it was only rare individuals who stood out against this: where differences became apparent, they were often not pursued to the point of open confrontation. In this respect, the extracts included in this part of the chapter may be illuminating, but they are not entirely representative.

Of the other factors I have discussed, gender was the most salient, although its role was far from straightforward. Social class and 'race' were less apparent, although perhaps for different reasons. While there were certainly class differences between the groups, they rarely surfaced explicitly within them, although some were distinctly mixed. While children's lives are undoubtedly located in specific social class cultures, they may to some extent be insulated from the sites in which a specific 'class consciousness' is developed. Racial differences were inevitably much more salient for black children, whose identities are partly formed in the context of a dominant white culture. Yet, as I have implied, the extent to which these differences are raised in a mixed group will depend upon what is likely to be gained or lost in doing so.

Of course, the fact that these differences were rarely made explicit is not to imply that they are insignificant. The ways in which individual children account for their experience of television are bound to be partly 'determined' by their social experience, and the language which is available to them. Yet my emphasis here has been rather different: I have sought to identify the ways in which individuals can 'determine' themselves, through adopting positions in discourse. The fact that an individual adopts a particular position — for example, in professing an exaggerated masculinity — should not necessarily be seen to reflect their 'true self', or alternatively as evidence of some all-powerful form of social conditioning. While these positions are not equally available to all, there remains a considerable margin of creativity and choice.

Contents: Texts and Readers

Thus far, I have ranged fairly widely across different programmes and aspects of television which the children chose to discuss. In this section, I want to concentrate on their accounts of one programme which recurred in nearly every discussion group — namely the Australian soap opera *Neighbours*. Although, as I have indicated, the speaker's selection of 'content' is partly determined by the ways in which 'relations' and 'subjects' are defined, it also serves to constrain the kinds of talk which are possible. Speakers may take up different positions in relation to content — in this instance, to the texts they choose to discuss — but these positions are not infinitely variable, nor are they wholly independent of the texts themselves.

At the time these discussions took place, late in 1989, *Neighbours* was the second most popular programme on British television, and amounted to something of a 'cult' among children. Set in a street in an imaginary suburb of Melbourne, it centres on the lives of two interconnected families, the Ramsays and the Robinsons. It features a number of teenage characters, who would appear to have been given greater prominence as the serial has progressed — probably in response to its popularity with the younger audience.

To a greater extent even than *EastEnders*, *Neighbours* has generated an enormous array of 'secondary texts' (see Buckingham, 1987a; Fiske, 1987a). As well as the obligatory magazines, books, board games and other merchandise, there has been a vast amount of press and other media coverage. Much of this material has an added interest for regular viewers, since *Neighbours* is screened in Britain approximately eighteen months after it appears in Australia. Many of the stars of the programme have also used it as a launching pad for a singing career: in particular, Kylie Minogue and Jason Donovan (who played Charlene and Scott) were at this time extraordinarily popular with the younger audience.

Predictably, the television critics of the British press have generally disregarded the programme, or heaped contempt upon it. Like so many popular programmes,

Neighbours has come to be identified as the epitome of trivial, 'lowest common denominator' television.

The fact that children were aware of this negative view was apparent in a number of the discussions. While some talked about their mothers watching the programme, it would seem that in some cases it had become a focus of domestic power struggles, partly on the grounds of its 'triviality' or lack of cultural value and partly on the grounds of morality. In taking up a position on *Neighbours*, the children were thus inevitably defining themselves in terms of age and (to a lesser extent perhaps) social class.

The same is true in relation to gender, although here again there is some ambiguity. Despite Nathan's explicitly 'gendered' rejection of the soaps (Extract 9), there were a number of boys who nominated them as preferences, and even some girls who rejected them in equally strong terms. Nevertheless, the boys did contribute proportionately less to these discussions in comparison to their contributions elsewhere. Furthermore, they tended to focus on rather different aspects of the programmes, such as the elements of mystery and comedy, rather than the romantic storylines — although there were some exceptions to this.

Of course, the way the children chose to talk about these programmes does not necessarily reflect the way in which they read them. For example, Nathan's assertion of his interest in violence, and his rejection of the 'soppy' soaps, represented a claim for power in a context in which he felt marginalized. Boys may feel they have a great deal to lose in 'confessing' to an interest in romance. In this respect, the 'gendered' nature of certain programmes — or indeed of viewing in general — may appear more salient in the context of discussion than it does at the moment of viewing itself.

Inside and Outside the Text

In this section, I want to consider three more extended extracts from discussions of *Neighbours*, in each of the three age groups. As I shall argue, the positions the children took up in talking about the programme varied during the course of the discussion. At certain points, they were very close to the text — effectively 'inside' it — while at others they adopted a much more distanced position.

The first extract is taken from one of the groups of 7-year-olds in the suburban primary school. This was the group containing Nathan, whose 'gendered' rejection of the soaps had preceded the start of the extract.

Extract 13

	Interviewer:	David, you like *Neighbours*. Tell me why you like it?
	David:	'Cause I like the music when Charlene and Scott got married.
	Interviewer:	Do you like the music, yeah?
5	*Nancy*:	[*starts singing:*] 'Suddenly. . . .
	Interviewer:	Did you buy the record? [*David shakes his head*] You didn't.
	David:	But my brother taped it once.
	Interviewer:	Taped the video of the . . no, just the music.
	David:	The music.

10	*Interviewer*:	Right.
	Nancy:	The song goes [*starts singing*]
	Diana:	'Suddenly a part of me needs to know . .'
	Interviewer:	[*Joins in girls' singing*] Yes, my little one [
	Diana:	[I've got the
15		record.
	Interviewer:	You've got the record. Do you have it as well?
	Nancy:	No. I just like the song. They usually play it when Charlene's thinking about things don't they?
	Diana:	Oh yeah, yeah, when she's sad and when Scott was looking
20		at that photo and Charlene had to go (&) [
	Nancy:	[yeah
	Diana:	(&) to Brisbane. And he was going [*sings:*] 'Suddenly' and they showed this lovely photo of her and it was really nice and it was nice and colourful.
25	*Interviewer*:	[When . . . . go on.
	Ritta:	[When Charlene and Scott broke up they play it and like when um when, when like um she fancied a man called Steve (&) [
	Diana:	[Oh it's awful!
30	*Ritta*:	(&) and they broke up cause Steve thought she loved him, but he, she didn't. And when she told Scott, she put his interviews in the bowl of water that cleans all the floors and they ruined them and then she had to tell him and [and that's when they played the tune.
35	*Diana*:	[No what really happened was um Scott, Ch-ch-charlene was going 'Oh come on I want to tell you something, PLEASE I want TO TELL YOU SOMETHING' and he was trying to do his work, you see. And then she accidentally drop, er
40		she was (&) [
	Ritta:	[knocked his interviews=
	Diana:	(&) No, no his tapes into the bucket of um disin, disinfect-ant, and his tape and er he got really cross and she goes 'Oh' she goes, they were in the living room, and he goes
45		'HOW COULD YOU?' and she goes 'I don't want to tell you now'. And he goes 'You wanted to tell me something and now you've knocked it into a bowl of disinfectant. Something really important'. And then she tells him 'I've been seeing a little bit of Steve', and then um she goes 'Oh,
50		he's been hanging around 'uh (&) [
	Ritta:	[well . . (. . .)
	Diana:	(&) And then she goes 'we kissed but that's all' and then he goes 'HOW COULD YOU!' and he never forgives her but um Scott did, cause he kissed Jane once.
55	*Interviewer*:	Oh, yes I saw that, that was a big, big scene wasn't it?
	Diana:	Yeah.
	Ritta:	And Henry saw.
	Diana:	No, I don't think Henry saw.

	Ritta:	Yeah, he was hiding behind a tree, cause he knew
60		something was going on.
	Diana:	Yeah, cause they did maths together and he drew a picture
		and then he put his arm around her and then he [*laughs*]
		kissed her.
	Nancy:	And Jane never ever talked to him again because it [
65	*Diana:*	[yeah
		she goes um
	Ritta:	[re-
		member the time when Mike looked in the diary
		(&) [
70	*Nancy:*	[Oh that was awful.
	Ritta:	(&) Jane's diary and (&) [
	Diana:	[the best man=
	Ritta:	(&) and she found out
	Diana:	[That the best man was Scott Robinson!
75	*Ritta:*	[That the best man was Scott Robinson!
	Interviewer:	Oh, right.
	Nancy:	Instead of Mike Young, cause they had broke up with Mike,
		Jane [had=
	Diana:	[Now they've broken up now.
80	*Ritta:*	Yeah, and yeah because [Jane
	Diana:	[And Bronwen is in it now, Bron-
		wen Davies.
	Interviewer:	Bronwen is the nanny, isn't she, for the little one?
	Diana:	And Jamie, [I love that Jamie.
85	*Nancy:*	[Yes, and her sister came over because her
		daddy and her brother and her auntie were using her as a
		servant.

Nathan's earlier rejection of the soaps appears to leave David, the only other boy, in a rather awkward position here. He manages to get into the discussion by talking about the music, a comparatively 'safe' way in, in the sense that it does not imply any necessary commitment to the programme as a whole — although, as the girls make clear, the appeal of the music derives largely from the way it is used to amplify Scott and Charlene's romantic moments. Despite having nominated the topic, David plays no further part here, leaving the floor to the girls.

The (female) interviewer's role to some extent reinforces the sense of soaps as a female preserve. By displaying her knowledge of the programme — for example, in lines 13, 55 and 83 here — she effectively sanctions the celebration which takes place. Only in her reference to the argument between Scott and Charlene as a 'scene' (line 55) does she imply a more distanced perspective.

While the interviewer sanctions the talk, the extent to which she is being addressed here is difficult to identify. Ritta's first brief retelling concludes by returning to the song (line 34), suggesting that she is still defining her contribution as relevant to the topic which has already been established as the focus of discussion by the interviewer. However, Diana's subsequent version of this incident ('what really happened' — lines 35–54) loses sight of this, and gives rise to further retellings and observations whose relationship with each other is not made explicit, and in which the interviewer plays no part. If Diana's 'you see' in line 38 is still conceivably addressed to the interviewer, Ritta's 'remember' (line 68) is more likely to be addressed to other members of the group.

The girls' account here is fundamentally based on recalling emotional and romantic storylines, some of which took place many months prior to this discussion. Apart from a passing sense of embarrassment in Diana's laugh (line 62), there is little self-consciousness here. In opposition to Nathan, it is definitely the 'love' and the kissing (mentioned three times between lines 52 and 63) that they are interested in discussing.

The retelling is largely a collaborative effort, with each speaker continuing on from the previous one. As in many such retellings, the children interrupt to correct each other, although there is little sense of competition here, more a shared concern to get the details right. In some respects, the girls are constructing themselves as *Neighbours* 'experts', displaying their knowledge and their ability to recall accurately: note the way in which they refer to three of the characters using their last names (lines 74–5, 77 and 82), which rarely occurs in the programme itself.

While the girls do describe their responses to these events — for example in lines 67–68 — and to particular characters — line 84 — there is no explicit evaluation here, except possibly in relation to the photograph (line 23–4). The only sense of the programme as a text, as something which has been deliberately produced, comes in their comments on the use of music, where 'they' are seen to be responsible for playing the song at certain times, and for 'showing' the photograph of Charlene (lines 17–18, 23 and 26) and possibly in the comment on the new character who has appeared 'in it' (lines 81–2). In all other respects, the programme is described as if it were a set of incidents they themselves had witnessed.

For much of this discussion, then, the girls are positioned firmly 'inside' the text. Diana, for example, uses a good deal of direct quotation, complete with emphasis, rather than describing what happens in more general terms, suggesting that she is close to acting out what took place.

The next extract features a group of 9-year-olds in the same school. Here, *Neighbours* was the first topic to generate any substantial discussion.

Extract 14

	Sally:	Well, *Neighbours* is good because there's always new people coming into it. There's always something happening as — something exciting in it, something boring in it, something good in it, something bad in it.
5	.	
	.	
	.	
	Sally:	We're eighteen months behind so they've got time to film it. And so they can just, they can, they can go
10		eighteen months. Well in when we see it, they've gone already eighteen months before / so=
	Hannah:	=they don't know what's happened. And [we don't either when it happens.

15	*Interviewer:*	[Can you pre — how do you think that — is Scott going to join Charlene?
	Hannah, Sally:	Yes she — he is.
	Hannah:	And Jane and Des should get married. [*Girls laugh*]
20	*Interviewer:*	Jane and Des SHOULD get married. Why do you think [Why do you think they should?
	Hannah, Sally:	[Jane and Des.
	Alex:	[Jane and Des.
	Hannah:	[Apparently Amarjit said, Amarjit said, a person she knows in Australia told her.
25	*Interviewer:*	Told her that they do?
	Hannah:	Yeah.
	Interviewer:	Oh so they've seen the programme over there. So this is a bit of a rumour as to what happens. Why do you think they should get married?
30	*Katie:*	I think [(. . . . . .)
	Sally:	[Well, Jane fancies Des and he didn't know it.
	Katie:	And Bronwen let it slip onto him and now they sort of —
	Sally:	They know it now. [But Des doesn't fancy her.
35	*Interviewer:*	[Now — Oh that's a —
	Sally:	Cause they're just friends=
	Hannah:	[I think she's probably the um
	Alex:	[I think Des is about /
	Hannah:	Either Bronwen and Michael or Bronwen and Henry
40		are going to get married as well.
	Interviewer:	[Hold on
	Alex:	[I think Des is about years old. I think Des is years older than Jane.
	Sally:	Yeah, HE IS! Jane is only a teenager.
45	*Hannah:*	No she's [about twenty.
	Sally:	[No she's twenty or twenty-one.
	Interviewer:	Why is that important, Alex?
	Alex:	Erm, [I think its quite silly for an old man say thirty years old to marry a teenager that is seventeen or
50		eighteen.
	Katie:	[*talking underneath about age of characters*]
	Interviewer:	Katie shush a minute. Do you think that's a — bad idea? You don't think that's=
	Alex:	=I think it's silly
55	*Interviewer:*	You think it's silly.
	Sally:	My, my mum's seven years older than my dad.
	?:	Seven! [*laughs*]
	Interviewer:	Is she?
	Hannah:	No, my dad, no, my mum's one year older than my
60		dad.
	Sally:	My dad's older than my mum.
	Alex:	My dad's older than my mum. By two years.

65 .
 .
 .

Hannah: I just — the bit I like — the bit I like best is the way
they've trained Bouncer the dog (&) [

Katie, Sally: [Yeah

Hannah: (&) and they've um got um Jamie and (. . .) and babies

70 in it and they're getting older and older and [they just

Katie: [They get
old —

Hannah: Keep making it (going?) on and on. They don't like skip
a load, so Jamie's a baby and they leave him out of it and

75 when he comes back he's about fifteen.

 .
 .
 .

Hannah: The whole of Ramsey Street, they all get together at one

80 point and they all go out and they're all friends and they
just pop in and pop out (&) [

Sally: [And they're always making casseroles!

[*loud laughter*]

85 Hannah: (&) but yeah —

Interviewer: You're dead right!

Sally: [*mimics:*] 'I'm just going to take this casserole back to
Mrs Mangel.'

Interviewer: I wished I lived in a street [like that.

90 Hannah: ['a nice new casserole'!

Interviewer: [Do you think=

Hannah: [And then Kylie goes — Charlene goes 'Mum what's
cooking?' and she goes ['casserole'!

Sally, Katie: ['Casserole'! [*laughter*]

95 Hannah: And then, when Charlene's grandad was in the programme, they changed it. They made vegetable soup /
instead of casserole! [*laughter*]

Interviewer: Oh that's right, cos he had a bad heart didn't he? or
stomach. Bad stomach, that's right. He needed to be

100 looked after.

Katie: And he, he, he — couldn't eat casserole. [*laughs*]

Hannah: And he goes 'that smells nice, Maggie. What is it?'
And she goes 'Casserole' and he goes 'Oh yeah, let's
have some!'. And she goes 'No, you're having vegetable

105 soup' [*laughter*].

Again, the girls are dominant here, at least partly because of the interviewer's
responses. Immediately prior to Sally's first comment, the boys had begun the
discussion by offering a series of preferences, ranging from *Visionaries* to *Nightmare on Elm Street*, none of which had gained much response from the interviewer. By contrast, as in the previous extract, there are a number of points here

at which she displays her own knowledge of the programme (lines 86, 98–100), and effectively sanctions further talk. The soaps are a major preoccupation for the girls, although the interviewer later sought to reinforce their status as 'girls' texts' by concluding 'the girls tend to watch *Neighbours*' — to which Hannah, interestingly, responded 'everyone watches *Neighbours*'. At the same time, it was the girls who, later in the discussion, expressed considerable enthusiasm for the cartoon and film version of *He-Man*, a quintessentially 'boys' text'.

Nevertheless, this extract makes a striking contrast with the previous one, in a variety of ways. Sally's initial comment is much more general, and more distanced, when compared for example with David's. She is not identifying aspects that she individually likes ('I' does not appear here), but offering a description of the broad characteristics of the programme, in order to support a critical judgment about its value.

In fact, throughout this discussion, Sally appears to be defining herself as a 'critical viewer'. Although she is not the dominant speaker, she tends to play a significant role in initiating lines of discussion, as she does here in relation to the time lag between *Neighbours* in Australia and in Britain (line 8) and the 'casseroles' episode (line 82–3): both interventions also serve to establish an overall tone which is markedly more distanced than that of the previous extract.

The second part of this extract (lines 8–62) illustrates some of the effects of *Neighbours*'s 'secondary texts'. Here, the source of the information is fairly direct, although later in the discussion it emerges that they have also gained some information from magazines like *Behind the Scenes at Neighbours*. As I have argued (Buckingham, 1987a), much of the pleasure of talking about soap opera lies in predicting future developments. In the case of *Neighbours*, information about future storylines is rather more reliable than the more speculative (and often inaccurate) 'leaks' about the British soaps published by the popular press. The children's discussion here is accordingly rather different: in effect, they attempt to fill in the details which will make the predicted events plausible (lines 30–6).

At the same time, they do debate whether or not these events are themselves plausible, or at least appropriate. Alex's comments here (for example, lines 48–50) may partly reflect a sense of social propriety — note the way Jane and Des's difference in age is compared with that of their own parents, and the laugh which greets Sally's comment (line 57). Yet there may also be an underlying concern here about modality, and the extraordinary regularity with which *Neighbours*'s characters seem to change partners. Either way, it is clear that this use of 'inside information' results in a more distanced attitude: knowing the characters' futures inevitably puts their current dilemmas in perspective, and almost reduces them to the status of pawns in the scriptwriters' hands.

The issue of modality, which is perhaps implicit here, emerges more fully in the final two sections of the extract. The judgments here are both positive and negative, although in some respects it is the former — the comments about training the dog, and the babies (lines 66–75) — that reflect the clearest awareness of the programme as a constructed artefact. Here, there is a clear recognition of agency — a 'they' who are making choices and decisions about the text, and attempting to create an illusion of realism. While there is no sense in which the children believe the illusion, they do seem to appreciate the care that has gone into constructing it.

The laughter which greets Sally's mention of 'casseroles' (line 84) suggests that this is a topic the group has discussed before. Here the concern is partly to do with plausibility — how many casseroles can a family eat? — yet it may also reflect an awareness of the way in which narrative devices like returning a casserole are used to generate links between the characters and storylines (for example in lines 87–88). Again, the tone of the retellings here is significantly more distanced than those in the previous extract: while the 7-year-olds were mostly 'inside', almost re-living the text, the 9-year-olds are 'outside', explicitly satirizing it. While both are pleasurable activities, they do position the speakers in very different ways.

The final extract here is taken from a group of 11-year-olds in the suburban secondary school. Here, the issue of modality becomes very much the central concern.

Extract 15

	Nancy:	*Home and Away* and *Neighbours*, though, they [they (&)
	Navin:	[
		Yeah, yeah.
	Nancy:	(&) they go over the top, and *EastEnders*, right, it's good,
5		I always watch them but they, sort of, like with *Home and*
		Away, with *Neighbours*, I mean, right, say something
		happens you can always tell what is going to happen next,
		whereas with *Home and Away* you're always wrong, be-
		cause, I, it's good=
10	Terry:	Like yesterday [in *Neighbours*.
	Sean:	[In in in in *Neighbours*, it's so many, it's one
		street and people die, there's armed robberies there's crashes,
		there's, it's just really unbelievable.
	Nancy:	Yeah and some one was moving and they go look, some-
15		one's moving and we've never even met this person and
		they [live in the street.
	Terry:	[There's only about six houses in the street.
	Nancy:	Yeah.
	Terry:	And we've never known them.
20	Nancy:	Yeah and when someone moves they go yeah some one
		moving and I wonder who'll go in there.
	Sean:	And it's also, when, when, when they open a door on
		Neighbours you can see the scenery behind them's been
		painted, it's pretty obviously been painted. That that, that
25		gets me sometimes.
	Terry:	Yesterday in *Neighbours* um, Mike bought Jamie for his
		birthday a drum and it goes it's uh so stupid like, Des turns
		round and goes 'Who gave Jamie that drum?' and Mike
		goes 'I did, Des' and he goes, 'No the drumstick, there's
30		something loose at the end and then [*smiles:*] they all get on
		their hands and knees trying [to find it and then Des goes
		'Ah, he must have (&)
	Sean:	[if, if
	Terry:	(&) swallowed it, let's take him to a doctor, quick, quick!

35	*Sean:*	If, if he'd swallowed it er, he'd be, he'd be spluttering, he'd be dead if he'd swallowed it 'cause I mean no way [could you=
	?:	[And Jamie is just sitting there going uh, uh, uh! [*General*
40		*laughter*]
	Interviewer:	Yeah, it's funny um, go on, what were you going to say about Jamie?
	Navin:	No I was just going to say, he didn't look as if he'd done anything he was just sort of sitting there wondering what
45		on earth was going on.
	Sean:	The thing that really got me, in the party they had, it shows that, Jamie was just, e, e, e was just [sitting there.
	Navin:	[Yeah, they were all saying how much fun he was having, he was just sitting
50		there looking really grumpy.
	Nancy:	[Yeah.
	Sean:	[And, and, and, and, they, THEM crowding round him going 'hello Jamie' there was about five people all about right round him like that, and it was just, really=
55	*Nancy:*	When he was [born, when he was born, he was about (&)
	Interviewer:	[He's obviously too young to act.
	Nancy:	(&) three weeks old then (&)
	Sean:	[Yeah.
	Nancy:	[(&) and it was a different baby probably.
60	*Sean:*	Yeah, she, e, [an / it, it, I think=
	Nancy:	[cause / but we've missed some episodes in *Neighbours.*
	Sean:	They, they're talking about, they've done a bit of continuity wrong 'cause Jamie's only one year old, right, but
65		Charlene and Scott have been married, um, well, when, he was born there was lots of things and now they're saying, it was two years before when it was, if Jamie's only one, (&)
	Terry:	It's [odd.
70	*Sean:*	[(&) 'cause, they been, they been, it's a [bit (&)
	Nancy:	[Well, they, yeah=
	Sean:	(&) queer in the continuity.
	Nancy:	Yeah, it, one day it was Christmas the next day everyone
75		was taking their decorations down! [laughs]
	Sean:	And, [yeah=
	Terry:	[Yes, they were mentioning about the Olympics 1988, it's so sort of far behind.
80	.
	.
	.
	Sean:	The thing, the thing that really gets me is you know when they, in the houses, right, there's this really titchy houses

85		and when like in, in the Robinsons' house there's the wall there, two open doorways and there's the living room there and the kitchen there, and when you're in the kitchen and you hear the people shouting at their loudest it's just like a whisper it's, it's really, it's it's a bit stupid, and whenever, something's wrong they, they sort of come in, walk in just
90		look around and go 'Huuuh' like that and instead of, I mean, if, if, if you walked in and something was wrong you'd go straight over to it and stop it /
	Interviewer:	Do, do you like *Neighbours*?
	Sean:	Yeah, I, I like it [but there's so many (&)
95	*Nancy:*	[I always watch it, yeah.
	Sean:	(&) things wrong with it and, and=
	Terry:	How about the till, in the coffee shop it's always got the same price, [they press it and always the same price comes up.
100	*Nancy:*	[Yeah!
	Sean:	One fifty, it says one fifty perpetually . . .

These children are clearly adopting an extremely distanced, 'critical' stance towards the programme. The primary motivation of the discussion appears to be the desire to identify what is wrong with *Neighbours*, and the children move rapidly from one incident to another in order to illustrate this, rather than concentrating on a more detailed retelling. While most of their comments are accurate, there is certainly some exaggeration here, as the speakers attempt to outdo each other.

The concern with modality takes a number of forms. On one level, there are complaints about plausibility. Thus, *Neighbours* is condemned as predictable (lines 5–8), by contrast with its rival *Home and Away*. The incidents in the programme are seen as unrepresentative of real life (lines 11–17), and the characters are criticized for not behaving like real people (lines 26–37, 82–92). On another level, the programme's attempt to create an illusion of realism is seen to fail. Thus, there are complaints about the poor scenery (lines 22–25), bad acting (lines 43–50), limited sets (lines 82–83) and inadequate props (lines 97–101).

An awareness of agency — of the constraints of the production process — is also implicit throughout. Thus, the children comment on the fact that we only meet a limited number of the people who 'live' in Ramsay Street (lines 11–16), and reflect on the problems of featuring babies (lines 55–59). Sean's repeated use of the term 'continuity' here is also interesting. He is referring to the fact that the programme is screened later in Britain than in Australia, following Nancy's implicit accusation (lines 61–62) that certain episodes have been missed in an attempt to catch up. 'Continuity' is a technical term, with a rather more specific meaning than Sean seems to imply here, yet it invests his observations with a degree of specialist authority.

At the same time, the children are very familiar with the programme: they recall incidents which took place many months previously, and they notice details which would only be apparent to the keenest observer. As I have argued (Buckingham, 1987a), laughing at television's inadequacies can be an extremely pleasurable activity for viewers in general. Indeed, a great deal of popular television — from occasional remarks on *Wogan* and sketches on *The Lenny Henry Show* through to *Clive James* and *It'll Be All Right On the Night* — is concerned with mocking the ineptitudes and absurdities of television itself.

Yet mockery is not, I would argue, in itself a sufficient reason for viewing. There clearly have to be other pleasures — yet these barely surface in the context of this discussion. At the very beginning of this extract, Nancy does attempt to explain some of the appeal of *Home and Away* (lines 6–9), although this kind of discussion is effectively ruled out by the comments that follow. Interestingly, later in the discussion, Terry talked about how he had cried over the appearance of a paraplegic in *Home and Away* — although he immediately retracted this, to say only that 'it made you feel so sad'. This incident also seemed to have affected the other children in this group, although here again the dominance of this more critical, distanced perspective appeared to preclude any more sustained discussion.

Ultimately, the most urgent priority for these children in this context was to assert their distance from the text. The interviewer's question (line 93) underlines the extent to which talking about pleasure has effectively become impossible. Although Sean and Nancy are keen to assert their enjoyment of *Neighbours*, the discussion itself provides little indication of the reasons for this.

As these three extracts suggest, there is a development with age in terms of the children's ability or willingness to take a more distanced perspective. In the discussions as a whole, the older children were much more likely to talk about the programme as a fictional text — that is, as something which has been deliberately constructed, rather than a window on the world. While the youngest children occasionally indulged in parody — for example, in imitating characters' voices or mannerisms — they were rarely as directly satirical as both groups of older children are here. Criticism of the programme tended to be much more localized and 'internal', directed for example at specific incidents or characters, rather than offering a more general critique of the programme's lack of 'realism', or its cheap production values.

Thus, for example, the older children were more likely to talk spontaneously about the quality of the acting, where the 7-year-olds simply talked about the characters they liked and disliked, without implying that they were constructions who were 'meant to be like that'. The older children were also more likely to talk about the motivations of the programme's producers — for example, how they invent reasons to explain why certain actors have chosen to leave the programme. In general, the older children appeared to have more 'behind the scenes' information about how the programme is produced, or at least to be more interested in sharing it.

Similarly, the 7-year-olds were rarely as self-reflexive, as, for example, Sally and Nancy are here. Comparing *Neighbours* and *Home and Away* did lead to some more general critical judgments, and the recognition of their competition for audiences provoked some discussion of the institutional context. Nevertheless, the younger children's comments were mostly in the form of retellings. By contrast, the 9-year-olds were much more likely to frame their retellings within more general comments, for example about character traits, or about the kinds of incidents they most enjoyed. By the time we get to the 11-year-olds, retellings have largely disappeared in favour of more distanced critical judgments. While the 9-year-olds are still concerned to account for their own pleasure, for the 11-year-olds, any emotional investment they may have in the text is very much suppressed.

Nevertheless, it is important to acknowledge the significance of context here. For example, there is an understanding of the programme as a fictional text among the 7-year-olds: yet this tends to remain marginal, at least partly because their talk is serving rather different social functions. Rather than using the discussion as an opportunity to demonstrate their sophistication, the younger children tend to opt for a more direct, and more emotional, re-living of key incidents. For the 11-year-olds, it is precisely this emotional engagement with the text that is ruled out in this context: while they are obviously model critics, and while they gain considerable pleasure from performing this role, they are effectively prevented from talking about the direct emotional appeal which the programme must undoubtedly hold for them.

Conclusion: Talk, Text and Context

In this chapter, I have largely concentrated on the ways in which 'relations' and 'subjects' appear to determine 'contents'. I have argued that what children choose to talk about, and the ways in which they do so, need to be understood in terms of the context in which the talk occurs. In selecting 'content' — in this case, programmes or aspects of programmes, or indeed aspects of television more broadly — we are inevitably defining ourselves in relation to others, and in relation to broader social forces. While we do not have infinite freedom here, there is certainly an element of creativity in the way in which individuals use and appropriate the limited range of discourses at their disposal. What I have to some extent underestimated here is the opposite side of the coin — the way in which 'contents' can determine 'relations' and 'subjects'. Selecting a given topic can obviously limit the range of things it is possible to say — and indeed, in certain instances, who is able to speak.

This is obviously the case in relation to texts. Choosing to talk about *The Cosby Show* or *Thundercats* — as in the case of the discussions described in Chapter 3 — almost inevitably places certain issues on the agenda, and effectively marginalizes others. There are options, but these are much less than infinite. Likewise, in the case of the discussions considered here, it would be misleading to imply that *Neighbours* can somehow 'stand in' for texts in general. The kind of talk which is possible in relation to soap opera is very different from the kind of talk which is possible in relation to news, for example, or horror films. Indeed, this was reinforced by the kinds of questions the interviewers asked: 'what's been happening in *Neighbours*?' or 'who's your favourite character?' would appear to be comparatively 'obvious' questions, but they are very different from the questions one might ask in relation to *Nightmare on Elm Street*, for example, or even *The Gummi Bears*.

In my previous work on *EastEnders* (Buckingham, 1987a), I indicated some of the ways in which the narrative form of soap operas enables viewers to shift between a variety of 'reading positions', which may be more or less distanced from the text itself. This possibility is enhanced by the way in which some soap operas appear to incorporate and juxtapose elements of different genres — for example, social realism, comedy and melodrama — which invite different kinds of engagement on the part of viewers. These shifts in 'tone' can contribute to a sense of ironic distance from the characters and their dilemmas, which is reinforced by the 'secondary texts' which characteristically surround soap opera — and in particular their extensive coverage in the popular press and other media. The more we know about how programmes are produced, and about the 'private lives' of the actors, for example, the more possible it becomes to read them in a distanced way.

Christine Geraghty (1991) also argues that this 'oscillation between engagement and distance' is characteristic of the relationship between soaps and their audiences. As she indicates, soap operas deliberately invite the viewer to participate in the process of making fiction. By virtue of the familiarity of the narrative form and of the characters, they encourage viewers to predict and speculate about future events, using evidence from both inside and outside the text. Insofar as they move beyond the conventions of social realism, they could well be seen to *invite* parody and even mockery.

This account of the dynamics of soap opera viewing is certainly reflected in the discussions considered here. Yet the balance that is struck between engagement and distance depends to a large extent upon the dynamics of the group, and the social context of the discussion. Particularly for the 9-year olds (Extract 14) there is a self-conscious play with the fictional nature of the text, which moves easily between these two positions — although, as in the case of the 11-year-olds (Extract 15), this can easily slide over into condemnation and cynicism.

Either way, it is important to acknowledge that many of the characteristics of this talk are at least made possible — though not wholly determined — by the nature of the texts themselves, and the secondary texts that surround them. The children's talk about comedy or horror or cartoons also manifests some of these tendencies, although there is less flexibility here. As I shall indicate in Chapter 7, talk about texts is inevitably determined, at least to some extent, by the 'narrative logic' of the texts themselves.

In the case of soap opera, however, one could argue that the variety of 'reading positions' which they make available is not only a primary reason for their popularity; it also possesses, particularly for children, an *educational* value. It may be through this 'oscillation between engagement and distance ' that children become aware of at least some of the range of possible reading strategies that are open to them as viewers, and thus extend their range of viewing competencies. The ambiguous status of soap opera, as simultaneously 'realistic' and yet obviously fictional, may enable children to develop a more complex understanding of the diverse relationships between reality and its representations than is possible with other genres.

Given the contempt in which soap operas are often held, this is a potentially scandalous possibility, although it is one which researchers have increasingly hinted at. Hodge and Tripp (1986) go so far as to argue that the popularity of soap operas with children of this age is a 'healthy sign', which reflects their ability to select genres which are 'the best available for their cognitive development' — although, as they also suggest, this is not to say that there could be no better programmes for children, or indeed for adults.

Similarly, Liebes and Katz (1990) conclude their cross-cultural study of readings of *Dallas* by arguing that the programme might usefully be seen as a kind of 'educational game'. They reject the notion that such programmes can be condemned as merely 'escapist', or that texts which analysts might define as politically 'conservative' are necessarily read as conservative. The educational value, they argue, comes from the negotiation between the culture of the programme and the culture of the viewer, and this should be exploited and developed by teachers themselves. This is an issue to which I will return in my final chapter.

Chapter 5

Family Viewing: Text and Context

Michelle (7): Well, when I come back from school, I have something to eat and drink, and after some food, then I do my homework, then I have a play with my sister and then I watch TV, and then I watch *Home and Away* and *Neighbours*.

Mr B (father of 10-year-old): I mean television is good, in lots and lots of respects, but the goodness of it is in whether or not you are able to control the viewing. It comes into your living room, and it takes over it, the whole process of your life, if you allow it to.

Particularly for children, watching television is not an isolated activity. It takes place in the home, nearly always in the presence of parents or siblings, and is surrounded and accompanied by other activities. While they may occasionally be 'transfixed' by the screen, children will often play, talk, eat and drink, do their school work, get dressed, read, draw, fight and jump on the furniture when they are supposedly — for the purposes of the ratings at least — 'watching TV'.

Yet although it is part of this context, television is often perceived as alien to it: it is an intruder or at best an 'uninvited guest', and one which possesses considerable powers. It 'comes into' your living room, and 'takes over the whole process of your life'. 'If you allow it to', that is: because if you don't control it, then you can be sure that it will control you. And if children cannot 'control themselves', the responsibility for parents is very clear.

As I shall indicate in this chapter, the relationship between parents, children and television is almost invariably characterized by struggles for power and control. For a variety of reasons, parents may seek to restrict and regulate their children's access to television; and children themselves may well resist this. While television is sometimes applauded for its ability to 'bring the family together', family viewing is often a focus of considerable tension and anxiety.

Cause for Concern?

The growth of television and video as domestic media can be related to a number of broader historical developments: the post-war shift from the extended to the bourgeois nuclear family (Poster, 1978); the growth of 'consumerism' — at least in the form of increased expenditure on domestic technology; and the changing role of technology in domestic labour (Cowan, 1976). These and other changes have undoubtedly led to an increasing privatization of leisure — and, according to some critics, the 'colonisation' of domestic life by the media.

For many on the Left, these developments have been seen to result in a growing sense of political apathy (Lodziak, 1986): the 'public sphere' of political debate and action has been reduced in favour of the 'private sphere' of domestic consumption. For many on the Right, the increasing availability of new technologies and the apparent decline of the family have fed into a growing anxiety about the collapse of social control. In both cases, the concern often seems to be informed by a kind of nostalgia for more 'natural', organic forms of social life.

At the same time, the family has increasingly been perceived to be 'in crisis', causing many on the Right to argue for greater state regulation. Thatcherism, both through its moral stance and through its economic policies, sought to return responsibility for the maintenance of social and sexual relations from the public sphere to the so-called 'private family' (David, 1986). Yet the advent of new communication technologies, particularly satellite TV, have been seen to threaten a further invasion of the sanctity of the family by the forces of moral depravity, this time from beyond national boundaries. Both in family policy and in broadcasting policy, there are indications of essential contradictions in Thatcherism, between the 'free-market' ideology (getting rid of the 'nanny State') and the drive towards greater state regulation (maintaining 'standards'). The recurrent public scandals over child abuse in the past decade illustrate the broader political issues at stake (see Campbell, 1988).

The widespread moral panic about video and other new media technologies in the early 1980s and the resulting increase in state censorship exemplify the ways in which these concerns have been combined. The 'problem' of video was precisely that it enabled families and in some cases children to view material that would otherwise have been unavailable to them — material whose effects were seen as undesirable and anti-social. Video changed the site of regulation from the broadcasting institutions to the family itself: rather than relying on the paternalistic good intentions of the broadcasters, we now had to rely on parents to protect children from harm. And this was, in the government's view, a responsibility which some parents — notably working-class parents, single parents and the more 'permissive' middle classes — were not equipped or disposed to exercise (see Barker, 1984).

In this context, the relationship between television and the family is bound to be a focus of much broader moral and political anxieties. Television is not merely part of the mess of family life, or simply an appliance like a dishwasher or a vacuum cleaner. In considering 'family viewing' we are inevitably considering the operation of social power, both within and beyond the family itself.

Researching the Context

Media research has often sought to remove television from its social context, as if this were some unnecessary 'mediating variable' that could be deduced from the process, leaving us with the 'pure' act of viewing itself. Laboratory experiments, for example, are based on precisely this assumption.

In recent years, however, researchers have increasingly begun to direct their attention to the viewing context. Nevertheless, much of the research in this field still regards the role of television in terms of stimulus and response. Many of the questions asked concern the 'effects' of television on the family. Does television prevent meaningful conversation, and replace family rituals? Does it replace 'real' relationships with vicarious ones, and force 'natural' interactions to conform to its rhythms and demands? And how can the family protect children from the harmful effects of the medium? (For a review of mainstream research, see Gunter and Svennevig, 1987.) Television is implicitly seen here, as it is in much popular debate (e.g. Large, 1980; Winn, 1985) as an independent force which is undermining the family from without.

From this perspective, the role of parents is essentially to 'mediate' the negative effects of television. In some instances, the research appears to recommend a form of behaviour modification: parents are encouraged to help their children model 'pro-social' behaviour, and prevent them from modelling 'anti-social' behaviour (Gunter and Svennevig, 1987, pp. 29–31). Similarly, some researchers have focused on the family conflicts which are apparently caused by advertising (Sheikh and Moleski, 1977a), and the ways in which parental 'viewing rules' — for example, not allowing children to interrupt commercials with requests for products — can mitigate these (Reid, 1979).

Despite the disclaimers, much of this research is based on implicit assumptions about 'good parenting', which have a great deal in common with some of the approaches to television literacy described in Chapter 2. By adopting a 'discussion–explanation' style of parenting, rather than relying on 'power–assertion', parents are urged to transform TV viewing into a pedagogy. Talking to your children about television, rather than banning it outright, is seen as the way to protect them from the 'effects' of televised violence and advertising and the other negative consequences of 'heavy viewing' (Singer *et al.*, 1988; Robertson, 1979) and to sensitize them to 'pro-social' content (Abelman, 1986). Parents who fail to live up to these norms are seen to be in line for some remedial training in 'parenting skills' (Christopher *et al.*, 1989). While there has been much less research on this issue in the UK, there is certainly a sense in which it is seen as 'good parenting' by many middle-class people to intervene in your child's viewing, whether for moral or political reasons (Simpson, 1987).

As I shall argue, it is important to relate these ideas about the regulation and mediation of children's viewing to broader ideologies of child-rearing (Feldman *et al.*, 1977; Traudt and Lont, 1987) — for example, general beliefs about 'discipline' and 'permissiveness', or concerns about forces outside the family which might be seen to be 'interfering' in the process of parenting, or indeed undermining the power of parents.

My concern in this chapter, then, is not so much with the actual uses of television in the home — an issue which has been the focus of a growing body of ethnographic research (e.g. Lindlof, 1987; Lull, 1988, 1990; Morley and Silverstone, 1990) — as with the *discourses* which are used to describe and define it. I particularly want to focus here on the question of parents' regulation of their children's viewing, and the ways in which children themselves respond to this.

A Powerful Medium

These issues were raised very clearly by a series of discussions with parents of children in the sample, held on parents' evenings in the schools involved in the project. While the parents who attended were a self-selecting group, they were socially quite diverse. Despite this, however, there was a considerable consensus among the different groups: their position was almost exclusively, and often vehemently, anti-television.

Across the discussions, a range of familiar concerns was expressed. Television was seen as an inherently 'passive' medium, in which everything is 'done for you', in contrast to reading or listening to the radio. It was described as a waste of children's time, and as inherently anti-educational. The negative effects of television were legion: it took children away from other, more worthwhile activities, and in particular their homework; it reduced them to a 'stupor', or made them restless and irritable; it bred disagreements between siblings; and it was a primary cause of violence and aggressive behaviour. For the more middle-class parents, television was also seen as lacking in artistic 'quality' in comparison with earlier cultural forms: a 'well-made film', seen in the cinema, was seen as much more valid, whereas a video was 'not the same'.

These parents saw it as their responsibility to restrict and regulate their children's viewing, although in some cases they admitted that they were not wholly successful in doing so. Only in the case of one middle-class couple did strict rules appear to be applied, in this case limiting their daughter to two programmes daily, and none in the mornings — yet there appeared to be a considerable amount of debate and negotiation here. Whether or not it was successful, limiting television seemed to be regarded as being in the child's best interests, and as 'good discipline'. While it was acknowledged that some television might have 'educational' benefits, moderation and restraint were seen to be essential.

All the parents here appeared to subscribe to the view that television viewing should be a planned activity, and that children should actively select particular programmes, rather than 'putting it on for the sake of it'. Many of them spoke of the need to 'direct' and 'organize' their children's use of time, for fear that if unchecked they would watch television 'all day long'. Nevertheless, most of them acknowledged that their children did watch 'too much', occasionally describing this as a kind of 'compulsion' or 'addiction' akin to alcoholism.

However, it is important to consider the social context of these discussions, and the function of the talk within this. These individuals were positioned here as 'parents', in relation to an academic researcher, and in a school context. For many of them, this would have been an unfamiliar situation, which would inevitably have placed them on the defensive. They were almost bound to present themselves as 'responsible parents', and to do so in highly constrained ways. As Peter Fraser (1990) has observed, employing an anti-television discourse serves as a powerful guarantee of one's 'responsibility' as a parent, or indeed as a teacher: to talk about one's own pleasure may well undermine this position. In this context, talking about the fat woman who appeared on *Blind Date* or speculating about who pushed Gary off the cliff in *Home and Away* would certainly not have been seen as an appropriate response.

Some of the tensions which surround this position become apparent if we consider the discussions in more detail. In one group, interviewed at the inner-city primary school, the discussion was heavily dominated by the father of a 10-year-old, an upwardly-mobile working-class Afro-Caribbean, whom I shall refer to as Mr B. His talk was faltering at times, and yet also ponderous, as if claiming a kind of authority. It was particularly marked by a tendency towards hyper-correction — that is, the suppression of dialect features (see Edwards, 1979). Throughout the discussion, his (white British) wife sat next to him, and despite the (white male) interviewer's attempts to draw her into the conversation, she said nothing. Both seemed threatened by the situation, although they responded in opposite ways: Mr B seemed to be covering his unease by talking a great deal, often without quite knowing where his sentences would lead.

His responses were initially quite hesitant, although he appeared to become more confident as other parents arrived. Mr F, a middle-class African, entered the discussion with a vehement condemnation of television, which seemed to provide Mr B with a stronger cue as to what might be an appropriate position to adopt. Both men argued that television took up too much of their children's time, and argued for the importance of regulating their viewing. Mr B described how he monitored his children's use of television, to ensure that they watched what he and his wife 'consider acceptable'. He went on to offer some more general reflections, responding to Mr F's argument that television is a 'powerful medium':

Extract 1

Mr B: Yes I mean it is, it is a very powerful medium. We can, we can only but think about the various happenings that / er, that have been about in the past couple of, say last year, year before, early parts of this year. Look at the, the, who was that, that *Rambo* thing that came up, the Hungerford er [*others agree*] / massacre. I mean, this chap, he was a television watcher, he saw exactly, he saw *Rambo*, and he thought well, he er, / he thought that he had something to do, he felt that er / people were against him, and he ended up killing even his very mother. And this as a result, not of, not only of the television programme, but of the mass media, TV, the cinema, of which television and cinema [. . .], the producers say anything, they haven't seen the effect on people, and this shows the great, the magnitude of the power of television as a means of er / influencing, directing and causing people to do things that bring magnifying conditions, and making them absolutely real, bringing them into reality, taking them from fiction into reality [yeah]. And this is the great power of television. So if you can see these things happening to people, who are actually taking it up upon themselves, and doing things with similar results, I mean everybody, he's just another person in the society, in the community, and other people of course are looking, are looking on and are seeing, and they're seeing what he's doing as a result of what he saw. These are the children who are looking at something that was happening because something caused him to do what he did. So it's a re-occurring process, it's a re-occurring situation.

Here, Mr B refers to an incident which has entered the popular mytho of television effects, and which the other parents obviously recognize. While evidence that television 'caused' the Hungerford massacre is in fact non-existen, the incident has come to serve as *prima facie* evidence of the power of the medium. Yet the discomfort in his talk is almost palpable, even in this written form. The constraints of the situation are such that he has very little room for manoeuvre. It is as if he is straining to use complex words — 'influencing, directing and causing people to do things that bring magnifying conditions' — and yet as the words and subclauses accumulate, the risk of collapsing into incoherence looms ever larger. At times he adopts an almost oratorical tone — 'we can only but think', 'his very mother' — and successfully manages to cap his longer perorations with short sentences that are intended to clinch the argument — 'and this is the great power of television'. Repetition and the use of multiple synonyms also serve to lend a rhetorical weight to his assertions.

Typically, television is seen here as a kind of impersonal force, which 'does things' to people which are quite beyond their conscious control. Amid the confusions in the syntax, it is difficult to tell whether it is television that 'takes [things] from fiction into reality' or the people who watch it: in effect, the latter have become agents of the all-powerful medium. Even Michael Ryan, the Hungerford killer, emerges from this as a kind of passive victim. This was a theme Mr B expanded upon in a later contribution, although he met with an interesting response from the other parents present:

Extract 2

Mr B: The thing about television, it has been designed to captivate, it's been designed to hold you, it's been designed to organize you, organize that gathering towards it, to watch it, to perceive it, to have, want it, and I would say television has really succeeded in that, that's why it's so powerful, it has succeeded in captivating, we are a captive. /

Mr F: [*smiling*] It's nice to watch it, some of the programmes are interesting

Ms C: Yes, some of the programmes are interesting [*Mr F and Ms C laugh*]

Mr B: Yeah, that is why, I think. We are its captive, that is why, it has to be, it is, it will continue to be, a captive instrument for us

It is only at this point, towards the end of the discussion, that the consensus begins to break down. Mr B's formulation here carries the anti-television argument into the realms of conspiracy theory, which the other parents feel is going too far — although Mr B continued undaunted for some time beyond this extract.

Like most of the parents in these discussions, Mr B was keen to present himself as a viewer of news and documentaries, and of wildlife programmes: apart from this, he condemned television as simply 'childish' — a significant term in this context. Only the women 'owned up' to watching fiction or comedy — although Mr B did admit that he and his wife might occasionally view something with 'a more jovial edge'. Again, it was a woman in another discussion group who questioned what she termed this 'obsession' with news, and implicitly raised the question of pleasure. Nevertheless, most of these parents claimed to watch very little television, and were keen to present their own viewing as a demanding, educational activity, which was almost an exercise in responsible citizenship.

However, interviews with the children of these parents painted a rather different picture. While many complained about their parents watching the news, Mr B's son also bemoaned the fact that his father would watch westerns, and send him out to the back room to watch the black-and-white set. The following anecdote, which he provided, illustrates the way in which arguments about the cultural value of television can be used for rather different social purposes:

Extract 3

Andrew: I go in the front room when I come home from school, I look at the television for a little while, I just got, when I just got interested in something that I really really like, in / colour, my dad comes home from work and he turns it over to a western and when I ask him 'why d'you do that?' he says 'well, it's good, it's better to read a book than look at the television.' So he says 'read a book!' and then I say 'don't want to' [*laughing*]. So he sends me into the back room to look at black-and-white television.

The picture of rational and selective viewing which the parents describe is far from borne out by the children themselves. Mr F's daughter, for example, would appear to watch all the major British and Australian soaps, and also described watching films like *Ghostbusters Two* and *Nightmare on Elm Street*. Very few of the children appeared to plan their viewing, for example by looking at the schedules, and rarely seemed to watch in the company of their parents, or consult with them about what they wanted to see.

Of course, this is not to say that we should necessarily trust the children any more than their parents, or that the parents are effectively hypocrites. Previous research would suggest that however much parents may *claim* to control the amount or the nature of their children's viewing, or otherwise to intervene in it, this happens much less in practice, particularly as children get older (McLeod and Brown, 1976; Bryce and Leichter, 1983). Even with younger children, where regulation is more likely to occur, the time children go to bed is in fact the main determinant of how much they watch (Wober *et al.*, 1986).

Nevertheless, researchers have often noted contradictions between what parents say they do, and what they actually do, in this respect (for example, Hess and Goldman, 1962; Holman and Braithwaite, 1982). This could be explained in two ways: that a regulatory stance is perceived by parents to be more socially acceptable; or that whatever parents may *like* to do, the realities of family life mean that it is not always possible.

Support for the first of these hypotheses comes from an article by Rossiter and Robertson (1975), who found marked discrepancies between parents' and children's accounts of the use of television in the home. Parents reported that their children watched less, and that they regulated and intervened in their viewing much more than the children themselves claimed. The authors found that this discrepancy was greater for more middle-class families, suggesting that a 'social desirability bias' led to a general pattern of idealized reports of parental control. The second hypothesis above is raised briefly by McLeod and Brown (1976), who suggest that although parents do not appear to influence their children's viewing behaviour to any significant degree, the reverse may be true: children are quick to point to contradictions between what parents say and what they do, and may be much more powerful than is often assumed. As Meyrowitz (1985) argues, television may be inherently less controllable as a medium than books, for example: it is difficult for parents to regulate their children's viewing without also limiting their own.

Obviously this material is entirely in the form of 'self-reporting', and as such provides only part of the picture. It would undoubtedly be interesting to sit in Mr B's living room and observe what really goes on around the family TV set, although it is beyond the scope of the present study. Nevertheless, I think it would be a serious mistake to dismiss this material as merely 'unreliable': as I have argued, how individuals account for their social experience and the meanings they attribute to it play a significant part in how that experience is constituted.

Indeed, it could be argued that the activity of parenting is itself constituted in discourse. Parents do care for, feed and clothe their children, but how they do this, and how they plan and understand what they do, are crucially dependent on the discourses which are available to account for it. As Cathy Urwin (1985) has argued, the discourses about child-rearing which circulate in books, pamphlets and magazines (and, one might add, on television itself) serve to construct norms of child development and of 'good parenting'. Parents, and particularly mothers, have increasingly been defined as responsible for ensuring their child's 'normal' development through providing adequate 'stimulation', and in effect by acting as a tutor or pedagogue. For the 'good' parent, everyday activities — of which watching television is one — can be transformed into a series of opportunities for teaching (see Walkerdine and Lucey, 1989). In this competition to ensure that your child reaches the correct developmental norms, mothers who go out to work are seen as neglectful of their fundamental duties (Urwin, 1985) — as are parents who use television as an 'electronic babysitter'.

As Susan Grieshaber (1989) indicates, the discourse surrounding the regulation of children's viewing is part of a much broader range of discourses which are used to normalize and regulate parenting. In this context, limiting and intervening in your child's viewing — or at least claiming that you do — is as much an indicator of being a 'good parent' as ensuring that your child has good table manners, eats and dresses appropriately, and behaves well on trips to the supermarket. As Lull (1982a) observes, successfully regulating children's viewing behaviour 'confirms proper performance of a particular family role', and may thereby confirm the individual as a 'good parent' — whereas the failure to do so can presumably generate feelings of guilt and inadequacy.

Nevertheless, these discourses are likely to be socially and historically variable. As I have noted, anti-television arguments are more likely to be employed by middle-class parents. Part of the discomfort and strain experienced by Mr B in the extracts above derives, I would argue, from his attempts to take on a class discourse with which he is not wholly at ease — although, as I have acknowledged, this is obviously 'cued' by the presence of the white, middle-class academic interviewer.

Regulation may be less than effective, therefore, but it undoubtedly has a considerable discursive force. As I shall argue, the ways in which children themselves account for the regulation of viewing relate to much broader questions about the nature and operation of power in the home.

Talking Contexts

Most previous research on television and the family implicitly adopts a parental perspective. Children are predominantly defined as a 'problem' for which solutions must be sought, or as passive recipients of their parents' attempts at socialization. In other cases — notably Morley's *Family Television* (1986) — children are effectively absent altogether. In the remainder of this chapter, therefore, I want to concentrate on the children's accounts of family viewing, and in particular on the ways in which they account for parental regulation.

Children's talk about television is often inextricably embedded in talk about the context in which it is viewed. Children don't just talk about programmes: they talk about when programmes are on, and where they fit in the schedules; about who they watch them with, and what they talk about; about where they are when they are watching, and what else they are doing at the time.

Judging from the children's talk, much of the pleasure of television lies in this relationship between text and context. The younger children in particular would often introduce their preferences with phrases like 'me and my mum like . . .' or 'my brother always says . . .' In many cases, the pleasure of particular programmes seemed to be intimately connected with the discussions and games that took place around them — guessing the solution of a detective story or the answers in a quiz show, for example. Television was often described as part of a family ritual or routine: coming into your parents' bed on Sunday mornings to eat your breakfast cereal and watch *Dennis*, for example, or watching *Star Trek* with your mum while she does the ironing.

On the other hand, much of the pleasure of watching TV after school or on weekend mornings appeared to derive from the sense of freedom from adult constraints. There were some loving descriptions of the pleasure of coming home from school and flopping down on the sofa to watch TV in the certainty that nobody would bother you; and of getting up early on Saturday morning before your parents are awake so you can lounge around in your dressing-gown watching the box.

Particularly for younger children, watching television appeared to be a focus for play. Some of the younger boys in particular described how they would act out parallel narratives to the cartoons, using their own toys. At the same time, there was often a certain amount of self-mockery in these accounts: Hitesh (aged 9) described how he would disappear behind the curtains with a towel, to emerge as Superman; and Julie (7) talked about how she would take on the role of Scooby Doo's cousin Scrappy, and start fighting the settee.

However, this sense of the viewing context did not emerge consistently in the children's talk. Particular genres — notably horror — appeared to raise the question of 'effect', and with it the viewing context, much more clearly than others. In addition, the younger children and the girls interviewed here were generally much more forthcoming about their domestic circumstances than the older children and the boys, although there were some exceptions to this: to a large extent, this must reflect the different ways in which these groups are situated in relation to the domestic sphere itself.

Nevertheless, it is important to be aware of the context in which this talk occurred. The interviews from which the material in this chapter is mostly drawn took place at an early stage in the research, and focused specifically on the domestic viewing context. The children were interviewed in pairs (and in a few cases groups of three), wherever possible with a close friend — which in practice meant that all the pairs were single-sex. The interviews were more structured than those described in previous chapters, and covered a predetermined set of topics, although not always in the same order. The children were asked about where and when they liked to watch TV; who they liked to watch and talk about it with; whether they ever had arguments about TV, with parents or siblings; how they used video and home computers; and so on. This information was supplemented by a questionnaire completed by parents.

Compared with the more open-ended interviews described in Chapter 4, the approach here was much more direct and obtrusive. The children were being asked a series of questions by an adult whom they had met only once before, questions which could touch on areas — for example, that of domestic conflict — they might well wish to avoid. A boundary between the 'private' and the 'public', between home and school cultures, was undoubtedly being violated here. The fact that, as adult interviewers, we assumed we had the right to violate it, was a reflection of our power in the situation.

Nevertheless, many of the children — particularly the girls — were very forthcoming about their domestic circumstances: they responded to the situation warmly, and with considerable enthusiasm, as if describing the bizarre and comical nature of family life was in itself a considerable pleasure.

Technology and Control

The programmes people watch don't necessarily reflect those they say they prefer (Goodhardt *et al.*, 1975). While this may partly be because of other commitments, and because of scheduling, it is also partly due to the influence of other family members. Although the majority of households now have more than one set, and the majority of families with children have video-recorders, there is still likely to be a considerable amount of negotiation over the best quality set in the house (Gunter and Svennevig, 1987).

This was certainly the case with the children in this sample. While the vast majority (82 per cent) had access to other TV sets, in some cases in their own bedrooms, most of their viewing appeared to be done in the main living room, amid the confusion of family life and the conflicting demands of parents and siblings. For some children, particularly boys, this question of their access to technology became a major focus of rivalry in the discussions themselves. Satellite TV appeared to enjoy high status here, particularly for working-class children, and some of the boys took to boasting about the programmes they watched on Sky TV. Some of the younger boys extended this discussion to computers, describing the brand of computers they had and others they hoped to get, the number of computer games they possessed, and so on.

Despite the availability of technology, and the potential for privatized viewing, there was a distinct ambivalence in the children's accounts of family viewing. As I have noted, many of them described the pleasure of viewing free from adult interference: there often appeared to be a sense of ritual here, with favourite chairs, sitting positions and accompanying snacks being mentioned. Yet while some of the children (particularly the older ones) expressed a definite preference for viewing alone, few appeared to watch TV habitually in their bedrooms, and would only do so when parents or siblings had succeeded in imposing their wishes. This was partly because of the fact that the main TV was often of better quality, although there was an underlying sense that watching TV was 'properly' a collective activity. Debates over viewing seemed to bring into focus a contradiction between the desire to get your own way and the desire to affiliate with others. Privatized viewing was somehow much less pleasurable:

Extract 4

> *Della (11):* I like watching like, when *Carry on Laughing* used to be on, I like, used to watching it with my mum, 'cause when, then you can have a laugh like, and, it's stupid if you laugh to yourself, ain't it? Sometimes when I watch the telly and my mum's sitting there and I'm talking to her and I turn round and she's not there [*laughs*] she's gone in the kitchen.

However, few of the children claimed to watch or talk about TV with their parents. While some middle-class children did appear to do this, the main exceptions were the less 'Westernized' Asian children, for whom family viewing was very much common practice (cf. Gillespie, 1989, forthcoming). One group of 11-year-old boys claimed not to like Indian videos on the grounds that they were 'soppy' and 'all the same', although they remained a staple part of their viewing. Ranjit, for example, claimed to watch between ten and twelve Indian films in an average fortnight, compared with only one 'English' one: these were very much his mother's choice, reflecting her position which he described as 'head of the house'. (Responses to the questionnaire revealed that non-English-speaking parents generally possessed larger collections of videotapes than the average.)

Much of the overt rivalry over TV was in fact between siblings rather than between parents and children. Many of the children offered detailed accounts of fights over and around the TV, with both younger and older siblings. Alan (9) described how he and his brother would do battle with two remote controls, while Sonia and Colette (7), who turned out to be cousins, even displayed mutually-inflicted wounds for the benefit of the interviewer. These rivalries often centred on programmes which were defined in terms of age or gender, such as soap operas and cartoons, as in the following extract.

Extract 5

> *Carol (11):* My brother starts arguing because as soon as I get in he's watching *London's Burning*, I go 'please turn over I want to watch *Home and Away*'. He goes 'No, no, I always watch what you want to watch'. 'Well go upstairs, you've got a

	television of your own' and he sort of, he gives up and I get to watch the television.
Nancy:	Yeah, well, I'm sort of, I come in and I get the channel, I get the TV control 'cause me and my brother have great arguments over this [*laughs*] and I sort of put on what I want to watch and then my brother goes 'oh this is boring, see what else is on', and he wants to watch things like *Brave Starr* [a cartoon] and all that [*laughs*] and I want=
Sally:	He's fourteen by the way.
Nancy:	Yeah, and he wants to watch *Brave Starr* and *Dangermouse* and all this and he sort of goes 'Oh stay on it' and I go 'no' and I switch over and he goes 'Oh why did you switch over?' and I go 'Well, I'm not a baby, I don't watch stupid cartoons!'

While in Carol's case, the availability of an additional TV appeared to resolve the dispute, this was far from always the case, particularly where there was only one colour set. In other cases, parents appeared to serve as a court of appeal, although with ambiguous results. The children often presented themselves as the unjustly wounded party — particularly where the parents were seen to favour younger siblings, who were repeatedly accused of being manipulative. In many cases, the underlying assumption seemed to be that older people should have the right to impose their own tastes, and if it came to a contest between them and a younger brother or sister, they should win out. Yet many of the children appeared to see themselves as caught — too young to take control, but too old to get preferential treatment. As in the above extract, disputes with siblings appeared to play a major role in defining the differences between 'child' and 'adult' — a theme which will be considered in more detail below.

Previous research has suggested that in general male dominates female and older dominates younger in determining the choice of viewing (e.g. Lull, 1982b; Brody and Stoneman, 1983; Morley, 1986) — although the evidence is mixed, and there is some research which suggests that parents will often defer to their children (Gunter and Svennevig, 1987). This obviously also depends upon the time of day, the number of other sets available, and the ways in which families resolve disputes in general. While a few of the children in this sample claimed to resolve disputes through tossing a coin or throwing a dice, the methods used were rarely so impartial.

Research on the use of new media technologies such as video also tends to suggest that it is largely men who are in control (Gray, 1987; Lindlof *et al.*, 1988), although the reverse may be true in non-Western cultures (e.g. Barrios, 1988). Indeed, research on media use in developing countries suggests that television is often linked to an increasing democratization of power-relationships in the family, particularly along the lines of gender and age (Lull and Sen, 1988; Behl, 1988; Yadava and Reddi, 1988).

Interestingly, James Lull (1982b) points to differences in who actually decides (as observed) and who is claimed to decide (in interviews): in his research, fathers in fact made the majority of viewing decisions (followed by children and then mothers), although fathers themselves felt that it was their partners who decided most, and children often saw themselves as the main controllers of the set. On the other hand, Wand (1968) found that while fathers were perceived to be in charge, it was in fact mothers who dominated programme choice.

In the case of this research, the picture is also rather less clear-cut. In response to the question 'who mainly uses the remote control in your house?', a majority (56 per cent) of parents who named one person or group of people in fact nominated their children. While male parents and (to a lesser extent) male children were more likely to be named than female parents or children, the father was only named in one-fifth of cases. The picture is also complicated because of the proportion of single-parent families in the sample (over 20 per cent) — a group largely neglected by previous research in this area. In many cases, fathers featured very rarely in the children's accounts of their family lives — either because they were completely absent, or because they worked long or unsocial hours.

Clearly, this remains a small sample — although it is in fact larger than many of the samples on which the above conclusions appear to have been reached — and the data needs to be interpreted with caution. For example, there might well be a considerable social pressure in response to the above question *not* to name oneself — and since mothers completed the majority of questionnaires, they may well be under-represented.

The key point here, however, and it is one which emerges very strongly from the interviews, is that the regulation and control of television in the home is not accomplished without a considerable struggle. Children or mothers do not blindly consent to adult or male power. As Foucault (e.g. 1980) has argued, power is not a fixed 'possession', but a shifting relationship of force and resistance: it is not 'owned' but developed through interaction. In the context of the family, *both* children and parents attempt to exercise power *and* to resist it.

Discourses of Regulation

In many households, television may be used as a bargaining counter in quite unrelated struggles — as indeed it was in my own childhood. There are a number of instances in these discussions where the threat of withdrawing viewing privileges appeared to be used to encourage children to eat food they disliked, to tidy their bedrooms or to stop quarrelling with their brothers or sisters. In many cases, however, the children's accounts focus on their resistance to these sanctions:

Extract 6

Colette:	Sometimes her mum says to us, sometimes she goes 'if you can't behave yourself, you won't watch telly at all!'
Sonia:	Yeah, and she'll take the aerial to work.
Interviewer:	[*laughs*] She takes the aerial to work!
Sonia:	And I say to her 'I don't care, I can just listen to that stupid noise'.
Colette:	Yeah, and then when they come in she goes um 'don't like this', she turns the telly over to the news, and we go 'oh, that's boring!'

On the other hand, many of the children reported that they had managed to evade domestic duties by claiming that their 'favourite programme' was on — and admitted that the term 'favourite' could be applied to a range of programmes for this purpose.

As I have noted, bedtime probably serves as the major constraint on what children are allowed to watch, although again there is obviously some resistance. David (7), for example, reported that he could manage to stay up past his official bedtime if he bought into watching *Brookside* with the rest of the family, even though he found this 'boring'.

Nevertheless, there are a number of other rationales which parents appear to use in attempting to regulate their children's viewing, which generally derive from broader moral and psychological discourses. These discourses invoke normative definitions of child development and of cultural value which effectively prescribe 'subject positions' for both parents and children.

Thus, 'violence', and particularly horror videos, emerged as a major focus of parental regulation, although the 'forbidden' nature of the material may well have served only to increase the children's fascination with it. Similarly, while the children occasionally condemned material they defined as 'rude' or 'dirty', they generally distanced themselves from the disapproval expressed by their parents, as in the following extract:

Extract 7

Hannah:	My mum doesn't like me watching ['rude' programmes], 'cause she doesn't think it's right. And people wearing like / um / sort of like this, you know with Alexis and=
Interviewer:	*Dynasty?*
Hannah:	Yeah, *Dynasty.* You know when they get into bed and they have a little cuddle and all that, [my mum doesn't think that=
Interviewer:	[[*laughing:*] She's always getting into bed and having little cuddles, in my memory.
Hannah:	Um, my mum doesn't like me watching those things, she doesn't think it's right. She goes 'when you're eighteen, stuff like that, you can start watching that stuff, cause you might be doing it soon'. [*laughs*]
Interviewer:	And what do you think of her?
Hannah:	She's horrible.
Interviewer:	Your mum [*laughs*] not letting you watch it.
Hannah:	I like it, it's funny / Usually if she does send me out of the room, she goes 'go upstairs to your room' and what I usually do is I creep into the front room and watch it / and when I hear her open the door I quickly turn it off and I quickly sort of like, I stand at the door, going, I get out my homework, and I'm sitting on the floor doing my homework.

Like many of the younger girls, Hannah was not unwilling to admit to an interest in 'kissing' and 'little cuddles' — indeed, this was a major focus of interest in the Australian soaps — although, as the laughter indicates, there is a certain amount of mutual embarrassment here. Significantly, the reason for regulation in this case is defined not only in terms of morality ('it's not right'), but also in terms of what is seen as appropriate at a given age. The debate about television thus invokes much broader assumptions about what children at particular ages should know and how they should behave. Hannah explicitly rejects these assumptions, and laughs at her mother's comments. By describing the sex in *Dynasty* as 'funny', she implicitly positions herself as more distanced and mature, and somehow immune from negative moral 'effects'. Finally, like many of the children here, she claims to be quite skilful in resisting her mother's attempts to regulate her viewing — with homework often being employed as the perfect alibi.

There was often a considerable amount of irony and humour in these accounts of the 'effects' of television, as in the following discussion among a group of 9-year-olds:

Extract 8

Obinna:	My mum doesn't like me seeing those rude bits. [*laughter*]
Interviewer:	Rude bits. So what do you mean by rude bits, like language or?
Hitesh:	My mum don't look, you know, when=
Jessica:	All those love films [*laughs*].
Hitesh:	All the love films when they you know= [*Jessica laughs*] My mum don't, when the film starts yeah, my mum says 'do you want to watch TV?' I go 'yeah', and so I sit down yeah and I don't know what the TV, I don't know what the programme is, so I just watch it and I realize it's a dirty film, so when a dirty bit comes my mum goes 'close your eyes' [*laughter*]. And I get a pillow and I just slam it onto my er / face [*laughter*].
Jessica:	And then you peep [*laughs*].
Hitesh:	And then um I feel like peeping (&) [
Obinna:	[That's what I do.
Jessica:	I go like this
Hitesh:	(&) I feel like peeping, but then I, you know when, one block, this side of my head says, it's the devil's bit, it says 'go on, peep, peep, nothing's gonna happen to you' and everybody says 'no, it's dirty, don't look at it, it's naughty'. And then I go, and then um, / and then I go 'I might as well look, yeah, cause it is gonna finish in a little while', so I just move a little bit and I started looking. [*Jessica laughs loudly*] Like, and then this side, um the good part of my brain goes 'oh no!'
Jessica:	What, does it say 'I'm not your friend now, I'm going to tell on you' [*laughs*].
Hitesh:	No, and the devil's bit, you know, I just look at it and then I just remember it, and when I look at it it's two dogs um / and the devil punches the fairy on the nose and he falls down the cloud and he goes ha ha ha ha and I just start looking it.

Hitesh aptly conveys the combination of fascination and moral disapproval with which he watches these programmes. If we take his account literally, we might say that he displays an extraordinary degree of self-awareness about his own mental processes. Yet to describe his comments in these terms is to ignore the considerable degree of humour. Hitesh's description of his moral dilemmas is conveyed in highly exaggerated, stereotypical terms, as a matter of fairies wrestling with devils. It is clearly delivered for an audience, and with a kind of self-deprecating irony, in which Jessica also participates. One might almost say that it satirizes the conventional ways in which mental processes tend to be described, and with them some of the more absurd formulations of the 'effects' discourse.

Particularly among the middle-class children, discourses concerned with cultural value were rather more prominent than those relating to 'effects', although these were often only partially grasped. Many children reported that their parents mocked their tastes in viewing, particularly for the Australian soaps, which were condemned by mothers and fathers alike. Rachel (7), for example, said that her mother had attempted (without success) to stop her watching *Neighbours* because it was 'a popular programme'. Significantly, she also reported that her mother had suggested that the research itself might be motivated by similar concerns: 'she thought you didn't want us watching telly'. Julian (11), one of the few older children to report any degree of successful parental regulation, said that he had been limited to one hour per day, and that his mother didn't want him to watch *EastEnders* 'because they speak cockney', fearing that he would pick up 'bad habits'.

For Amarjit (9), this argument about cultural value was linked to concerns about 'commercialism' — or perhaps to a more straightforward economic logic:

Extract 9

Amarjit: My mum doesn't like me watching *Home and Away*, but I watch it anyway [. . .] She thinks that, you know, if you get too involved with soaps that you'll have to keep, you know, / kind of like lots of things are coming out, and you'll have your wardrobe full of things like the '*Neighbours* Game' and the '*Home and Away* Game', cause there's a new one, '*Home and Away* Game' now, and things like that, and my mum doesn't like me you know having um / cupboards full of things like to do with Kylie and Jason, and you know, lots of soaps.

Here again, Amarjit claims that she effectively evades her mother's restrictions — although she later admitted that a major reason for watching the soaps was that she didn't want to feel 'left out' when her friends were talking about them.

However, as in the parents' discussions considered above, many of the children identified the *amount* of television they watched, rather than any specific content, as the major focus of parental concern. Many of the middle-class parents of the children in the suburban primary school seemed to have filled their children's lives with so many 'improving' or 'purposeful' activities that they had fewer opportunities to watch television in the first place.

A sense of television as anti-educational also surfaced in some cases: Obinna (9), for example, reported that he was not allowed to watch TV immediately on returning from school, and had to read a book or do some work first, apparently because his mother felt that television was 'not good for you, you don't learn anything'. The conflict between television and homework was particularly salient for the older children in the suburban secondary school. While the two activities could be carried on simultaneously, this was not without its disadvantages:

Extract 10

> *Nancy*: Yeah, I'm sort of going like this [*mimes doing homework and watching TV at once*]. And what I'll do like, say they're saying 'oh Bobby!' 'oh Frank!' sort of thing, you sort of write 'Bobby' down [*laughter*] instead of um, saying 'thank-you' you write 'Bobby' or something and then you go 'oh no!' you had to rub it out and had to write it again and then you end up writing the wrong word and then it can't come out 'cause you used the correction pen.

A number of general points emerge from these accounts. Firstly, in the vast majority of cases, it was the mother who was identified as the parent most likely to take responsibility for regulating children's viewing (cf. Rogge and Jensen, 1988). Insofar as fathers made an appearance in these discussions at all, they were almost exclusively seen to be simply imposing their own tastes. In some instances, these happened to coincide with those of their children — for example in the case of Della (11), who claimed to watch horror videos with her father, although her mother had forbidden this. Yet in general, fathers would appear only in order to set the timer on the video, or to kick the kids out of the living room so they could watch the news or the sport. There is certainly some support here for Urwin's argument that it is mothers who are seen as primarily responsible for their children's development (Urwin, 1985).

Secondly, the extent of regulation — at least as described by the children — varied according to a whole number of factors. While younger children's viewing was predictably more strictly regulated, this also depended on the number of other televisions in the house, and indeed the number of other children, and their ages. However, the attempt to impose 'viewing rules' and the banning of particular programmes would appear to be more prevalent in middle-class homes. Likewise, while some of the working-class children were familiar with the arguments about media 'effects', the concern with cultural value and the view of television as anti-educational were more characteristic of middle-class children.

Finally, nearly all the children's accounts focused very strongly on the fact that parental regulation is *resisted*. While they acknowledged the regulatory discourses I have identified, they rarely used them without distancing themselves, either through irony or through outright rejection. Some of their strategies for resisting regulation will be discussed in the following section.

Fighting Back

Attempts to evade parental regulation characterize many areas of children's lives. Throughout these discussions, the children exchanged anecdotes about how they managed to stay up past bedtime, how they tried to avoid domestic duties, and how they traded one parent off against the other. Getting to watch TV when your parents have said you can't is merely one aspect of the ongoing guerrilla war of family life.

Obviously, there can be an element of bravado here. In general, it was boys who were more likely to boast about the degree of licence they were given — for example, that they could watch whatever they liked or go to bed any time they liked. In some cases, interviews with their parents presented a rather different picture. As I have already noted, a number of children claimed to have watched 'adult' material which they clearly had not.

Nevertheless, many of the children described specific strategies and techniques they had used to overcome parental regulation. In some cases, it was a matter of pestering them until they broke down: in recounting these incidents, many of the children adopted a whining, 'child-like' voice, suggesting that this was a particularly effective way of persuading parents to give in to your demands. In other cases, it came down to sneaking around the house to watch another TV set or alternatively creeping downstairs after everyone else had gone to bed. More deviously, James (9) described how his mother would hide the remote control to prevent him watching TV after bedtime, and how he had bought his own without her knowledge.

In other situations, children sought to exploit the differences between their parents — in many cases, using the father's imposition of his own tastes to counter the mother's attempts at regulation. Particularly in the more strictly regulated middle-class households, this war of attrition appeared to be a constant feature of family life. For example, Adele and Jessica (9) exchanged a number of anecdotes about their attempts to evade parental restriction. Adele reported that her mother had limited her to two programmes a day, apparently on the grounds that she was getting overweight, and had been using a viewing diary (which had been provided as part of the research) as a means of checking up on her. She described how she would occasionally sneak up to the lodgers' room, and lie on their bed watching TV and eating their chocolates — although when she was found out, television would be banned outright, which was apparently 'torture'.

Adele's parents also described the ways in which she would attempt to re-negotiate their 'viewing rules'. For example, the 'two programmes a day' rule was interpreted in such a way that children's television (which could consist of as many as six separate programmes) became one programme. Attempting to 'train' her in planned, selective viewing posed similar difficulties:

Extract 11

> Mr S: We say to her, um / say at the weekend, say in the evening or
>   something, we say 'well, look if there is anything specific that,
>   you know, you want to watch, well there's the newspaper, you
>   choose, you tell us what it is you want to watch, if there's any-
>   thing really that you'd like to see. But other than that, you know,
>   you're not just going to go in there and turn it on'. I mean, it's
>   silly. She'll say 'all right, OK well'. Sometimes she won't even
>   bother for a whole day or whatever, and then we'll see her
>   slumped, and say 'excuse me, do you?' you know, or she'll just

turn it on, you say 'what is it you want to watch?' 'Ummm /
THIS!' [*laughter*] You say 'well, no, you're not actually, er, because you don't know what it is, do you, you're just putting it
on for the sake of it, aren't you?' 'Oh!' You know, well I say, 'no
/ When you, if you know what it is you want to watch, fine,
OK, if you've really decided that's what you'd like to see'. Not
much problem with that, as long as it's within certain time
limits, but don't just turn it on.

As this extract suggests, 'viewing rules' can be subject to a process of constant attrition. Here, the notion of planned viewing amounts almost to a kind of
'work ethic': children are expected to have predetermined 'needs' which they will
look to television to fulfil. The only alternative to this model of the rational,
selective viewer is that of the couch potato, watching 'for the sake of it', 'slumped'
in front of the set. In this case, a norm of viewing behaviour is held up which
would not apply to most adults, let alone children, and it is perhaps not surprising
that it meets with resistance.

Power and Resistance: Justine

This relationship between power and resistance was particularly apparent in the
case of Justine (7). She was an only child, of Turkish and Egyptian parents, and
her father was a mini-cab driver, who often worked late shifts. Here, the conflicts
within the household were staked out in terms of both age and gender — although
what is particularly notable is the degree of humour which characterizes Justine's
account of them.

Extract 12

Justine: I've got two televisions, one in the living room and one in
my mum and dad's bedroom, and when my dad's watching
the snooker or the sport, he says 'go in the other room and
watch TV' and I say 'no, why don't you for a change?', and
then we all have a little fight and then [*laughter*] at the end
me and mum say 'no, we don't want to go!' and dad says
'yes, you have to!' and I say 'two against one, we win, go
in the other room!' [*laughs*]. And it's always me and my
mum going in the other room, so we just do a little bet,
and my dad [. . .] goes in the other room sometimes [. . .]
And he says, I say 'dad, I need to go toilet', so I go toilet,
he hides the control, and I have to find the control, if I can't
find it, I go over the telly, I switch the little button in it
over to what I want to watch, and then he turns it with the
control, and that's it, and then I try and get it off him, and
then sometimes he even hits, he hits me by mistake and
then I start cry-ing [*baby voice*].

Interviewer: Owww. [*Justine laughs*] So is it always your dad who has
the remote control then?

Justine: No, sometimes it's me and my mum, we hide his keys and his cigarettes 'cause we don't want him to go out all night [*laughter*]. And then we hide them, and he says 'where's my keys, I want to go work', and he calls on the radio and they say 'OK, I've got a job for you', and we have to give him the keys and then afterwards he goes snooker and that's why we hide the keys from him. And afterwards I say 'go, daddy, go, thanks, I like it when you go, and then we can watch our TV programmes' [*laughs*].

Interviewer: So is it always you and your mum against your dad? Do you have arguments with your mum / about TV? /

Justine: Sometimes. I say 'mum, I want to watch children's ITV!'. 'I want to watch this Cary Grant film!'. And my dad says 'I want to watch my sport!', and then he says, and my mum says 'keep your sport out of it!' He said 'let the child watch her programme then'. I said 'go in the other room'. We have all these arguments about, and I can't even hear myself think. [*laughter*]

Justine takes considerable pleasure in relating these comic anecdotes of family life. Her account is almost a kind of performance, which is realized through a substantial amount of direct speech. Family life is re-lived here as a kind of situation comedy: indeed, particularly when she is quoting herself, she sounds uncannily like Roseanne Barr, in the US sitcom *Roseanne*, imitating her children.

While the tastes of the family members are 'gendered', there are shifting alliances here, in which Justine herself is far from powerless. She resists her father's attempts to impose his own tastes in a variety of ways, ranging from direct manipulation of the TV set to disrupting his viewing by provoking an argument. She appeals to a kind of family democracy — 'two against one' — and also tries resorting to chance — 'a little bet'. Finally, she works on his emotions, expressing pleasure when he leaves to go to work. While she often seeks alliances with her mother, she can also exploit division between her parents, as her final contribution shows.

The crucial point here is that these strategies are quite conscious and deliberate. The picture — which emerges from some recent research in this area — of children and women blindly consenting to adult male domination would seem to ignore the considerable power they possess. Justine and her mother are far from 'duped' or cowed into submission by patriarchal authority. The ironic humour which infuses her account suggests that, on the contrary, she knows the score very well.

At the same time, Justine's viewing is also constrained by her mother's notions of morality and cultural value — notions which she partly accepts, as the following extract indicates. In fact, both girls here report that their mothers dislike the Australian soaps, and try to prevent them from watching.

Extract 13

Interviewer: I'm interested, neither of your mums like *Neighbours* then, no? / Why is that, do you think?

Justine:	'Cause my mum thinks it's not really for children and it's a load of twaddle.
Interviewer:	I see.
Nancy:	That's what my mum thinks.
Justine:	And she says 'you've got to do your piano homework, you've got to give it to your teacher on Saturday'. I say 'but Muuum, I've got a week off, you took it off, I've got to go to Amy's'. She says 'never mind that, just do your homework!' I say 'muuum, he didn't give me no homework', she says 'go and check!' And then I go and check and pretend I don't get no homework. And then on Friday I say 'mum, I've got to do my homework, can you record *Neighbours* for me?', and she said 'I thought you didn't have no homework', I said 'I did'. And I was, and then she comes and hit me, very softly, [*laughter*] and she said 'I thought you had no homework', I said 'I did and I was lying'. She goes 'go and do your homework! I'm not recording *Neighbours*, you can miss it a day', and then my dad comes, and I sulk in my room and my dad says 'what's the matter?' I say [*baby voice:*] 'she won't let me watch *Neighbours*, I have to do my boring old homework'. And then he says 'let her do the homework for a little while'. I said 'I don't want to do homework, it's her that getting me to do the homework, and I want to watch *Neighbours!*' And he gets all, and it gets all quiet in the house and then I say 'what you got to say for yourself, mum?' [*laughs*]

.
.
.

Interviewer:	Why do you say *Home and Away* is not for children?
Justine:	Because / it's like when Bobby lost her mind and um it's sort of things and drugs and sort of [?wine] and everything, and it's going to encourage children to do that when they get older.
Interviewer:	Mm, mm. /
Justine:	And to run away from their parents and everything. [. . .] I think it should be a 15 programme, cause it's got lots of things that children shouldn't see, and it will encourage children to do all that, [so it=
Nancy:	[I think it should be at ten o'clock.
Justine:	Yeah.
Interviewer:	But do you think it encourages you?
Nancy:	No, I don't really watch it. [People just tell / people just=
Justine:	[I don't watch it. / I don't really watch it either. I don't watch it at all. People just tell me what happens in it, and I don't really think it's suitable for children. I think *Neighbours* is all right, a bit of violence in it, but, that's all right, just a bit of arguing.

Here too, parental prohibition meets with resistance, as Justine again attempts to play one parent off against the other. Her dramatic delivery implicitly acknowledges that family life — or at least her part within it — involves a considerable amount of role-playing. In this case, she assumes the role of a whining brat, whose wishes her parents would do well to grant if they want a quiet life — and while this would appear to be a useful weapon in her repertoire of techniques, it proves less than effective here.

At the same time, both mothers' judgments about these programmes serve to reinforce definitions of what is 'suitable' for children to know. Their concerns appear to be motivated partly by notions of cultural value — for example in the word 'twaddle', which Justine's mother apparently also uses to apply to game shows — and partly by concerns about television's effects on behaviour. It is significant that in reinforcing these judgments here, the children display a clear knowledge of censorship categories and (implicitly, in Nancy's comment) of the 'watershed' for family viewing.

There is a certain amount of displacement here, particularly in the way in which the two girls use the word 'children', as if these were somehow other people. Yet despite the fact that they exempt *Neighbours* from these criticisms, they do seem broadly to accept the terms of the argument — and in fact they repeated these views in other discussions, against the opinions of others. While parental regulation may not always be effective, it does carry considerable discursive force, particularly in relation to broader definitions of what is and is not 'for children'.

Defining What's Suitable: Anne

Throughout these discussions, definitions of what was appropriate 'for children' were often ambiguous. The tone of moral condemnation which characterizes Justine's and Nancy's comments here was often mingled with fascination and with humour. There was considerable interest in 'adult' material — and no little social status to be gained from claiming to watch it — yet this was difficult for some of the children to talk about in the presence of an adult. The younger girls occasionally talked about 'kissing' and sex, for example in the soap operas, amid considerable amounts of embarrassed laughter, but the boys would rarely talk about this kind of material at all.

This question of what is 'suitable' becomes more complicated when there are a number of children of different ages in the same family. Anne (9) was the middle of three children, and came from a white middle-class family where parental regulation was much more of a constraint. Here again, the parents' rationale for regulation was partly concerned with cultural value, and partly with morality. Negotiating with this, and with the different tastes of other members of the family, proved a difficult balancing act.

Extract 14

> *Anne:*   Well in my family we haven't got Sky Television because
>   my parents don't approve of it. They say 'you'll only be
>   watching more TV — you watch enough as it is. You

shouldn't be watching those soap operas.' // And // when
/ they don't like *Neighbours* and *Home and Away* but we've
— we've convinced my brother that he understands
Neighbours. He doesn't by=

Interviewer: =[*laughs*] How have you convinced him he understands it
then?

Anne: Hm, we've said 'look, you know what's going on here,
don't you? Henry's making plaster gnomes' and he says
'Yes', and so we say 'Well, [*laughs*] why don't you watch
Neighbours with us?' and so we get our way [*laughs*]. But if
we can't do that and mum doesn't want it, like the news
then we can't watch it and [. . .] it's tough luck! Cause if it's
on a Saturday, my dad'll be watching football results upstairs, which means we've got to all agree on what's on
downstairs but since my brother's younger, he would, he
would get his way. I mean if it was — my brother was
away for some reason then my sister's older so she would
get the — her way. But it never seems to come to me that
I would get my way, because mum doesn't like what I
watch. [. . .] she's very against Australian soap operas.

Interviewer: Why is she against them then?

Anne: She says the — she says they're too grown-up for us and so
we shouldn't be watching them and she says that we are too
young to understand what happens [. . .] and that she just
doesn't approve of them. Like when Gary fell off the cliff
she said [*mimics mother's 'nagging' voice:*] 'This is not suitable
for young minds'.

.
.
.

Anne: My parents say my — my imagination is deteriorating.

Interviewer: Is that what they say?

Anne: Yeah. 'You shouldn't watch these, it'll make your imagination deteriorate'. 'But mum it will make my imagination
grow!' 'No it won't, it'll make it deteriorate dear'.

Interviewer: So — have they got quite strong views about what you're
watching? Are there programmes you're not supposed to
watch?

Anne: Mm. But we watch them all the same.

Anne directly parodies and contradicts her mother's arguments, and claims
to be able to evade regulation. However, getting to watch what she wants also
depends on gaining the consent of others — which accounts for her attempts to
delude her younger brother in relation to *Neighbours*. Here again, the central focus
of debate is the extent to which particular programmes are 'too grown-up', both
in terms of morality and in terms of whether children are seen to be able to
'understand' them — although her mother's argument about Sky TV would suggest
that class-based assumptions about cultural value are at stake here too.

In this family, the parents also monitored the first episodes of new series —

particularly Australian soap operas, which appeared to have distinct 'bad object' status — in order to check that they were 'suitable'. Anne also reported that she was occasionally recruited to monitor programmes on behalf of her younger brother:

Extract 15

Anne:	Sometimes my parents, if they, if I've seen it on my own and they're not sure it's suitable for Tim or Alison they think well maybe if we just show it to her, it's not suitable then
Donna:	It's the middle one. It might not be suitable for the younger one
Anne:	She's the most sensible one, she won't — she won't start swearing if she sees swear words in it or something but she'll tell us [yeah] and there was one stage, they showed, they showed — I watched a video which I wasn't supposed to watch
Donna:	[Which one was that?
Anne:	[And they said 'Would you agree this is unsuitable?' and I said no — 'cause it wasn't.

Throughout this discussion, Anne displays considerable independence from her parents' arguments, presenting herself, for example in her final comment, as able to make her own autonomous judgments. Significantly, her parents' view of her as 'sensible' seems to be based on the assumption that she is somehow less vulnerable to the 'effects' of television. While she claims that her younger brother has preferential treatment when it comes to choosing programmes, she is also recruited by her parents to monitor his viewing. In this case, then, what is seen as 'suitable' is subject to a process of negotiation, in which a certain amount of power has been 'delegated' to the children. In this larger family, 'child' and 'adult' are relative, rather than exclusive, terms.

As these accounts suggest, definitions of 'child' and 'adult' are often flexible and subject to negotiation. They are terms which are often used as bargaining counters or rhetorical devices in the ongoing struggle for control. Thus, parents can use the notion of 'being adult' as a means to gain children's compliance: saying 'grow up!' or 'be a big boy!' implies that if you obey my wishes now, other privileges may be granted to you. Yet these weapons are undoubtedly double-edged: while parents may exclude their children from certain experiences on the grounds that they are 'too young', children may use the same rationale to escape responsibilities they wish to avoid. What it means to be a child, or a child of a certain age, is not a given fact. On the contrary, it is socially and culturally relative, and can be defined and redefined in the constant process of negotiation between parents and children (cf. Solberg, 1990).

The Disappearance of Childhood?

I have argued in this chapter that the context of family viewing is characterized by struggles for power and control. While children are likely to resist their parents' attempts to regulate their viewing, often with considerable success, they are nevertheless inevitably 'positioned' in the process. In some cases, regulation arises from adults' attempts to impose their own tastes, while in others it may derive from broader moral, social or even political commitments. Yet the discourses that are used to justify the regulation of children's viewing typically invoke broader notions of what is appropriate or suitable for children to know and to experience, and notions of 'normal' or 'healthy' child development. These discourses thus embody definitions of 'the child' — and, inevitably, of 'the adult' — which have a much broader social purchase.

In general terms, these discourses serve to position children as passive recipients of their own socialization. Children are at the mercy of the 'powerful medium' and will simply absorb its moral and behavioural messages if their viewing is not regulated and controlled. Where it is not perceived as positively harmful, watching television is seen as a waste of time, and as a distraction from more beneficial activities which, unlike television, involve 'work'.

From this perspective, parents inevitably perceive themselves as powerless by comparison. If their child is 'mesmerized' by the screen, or simply too 'lazy' to do anything more constructive, it is up to the parents to intervene in the interests of healthy development. If the children cannot be weaned off television completely, they can perhaps be turned into self-regulating viewers, whose pleasures are subject to rational control.

This struggle for power between parents and children lies at the heart of recent arguments about the 'disappearance of childhood'. Neil Postman (1983) and Joshua Meyrowitz (1985) argue that the electronic media, and particularly television, have led to a blurring or indeed an abolition of the traditional distinction between children and adults. They argue that while print literacy serves to exclude the child from aspects of the adult world, this is impossible in purely oral cultures or in those based on 'total disclosure' media such as television. Television removes barriers and exposes secrets: as Meyrowitz (1985, p. 242) argues, 'it allows the young child to be "present" at adult interactions . . . at wars and funerals, courtships and seductions, criminal plots and cocktail parties'.

As a social or historical theory, this argument has several significant weaknesses (see Hoikkala *et al.*, 1987). The evidence that these distinctions are in fact being eroded, and that television is the primary cause, remains quite limited. Both writers overestimate the distinctions between oral and literate cultures (cf. Ong, 1982), and attribute a determining role to technology, or the information that it makes available. Furthermore, they implicitly define media audiences as an undifferentiated mass, and as passive and defenceless.

Nevertheless, the argument does set parental anxiety about the regulation of television in a broader context. It suggests that the small-scale 'micro' struggles I have described in this chapter may relate to broader social changes — changes which are not in any simple way 'caused' by television, but of which television is perhaps one element.

While struggles over TV are, on one level, merely part of the many other struggles which characterize family life — and indeed, as I have indicated, television can occasionally be used as a weapon for quite other purposes — they are, on another level, qualitatively different. Debates over which programmes are 'suitable' for children to watch, or whether watching television is 'good for you', are different from debates about whether you should tidy your bedroom or when you should go to bed. They are debates, not just about behaviour, but about knowledge.

Ultimately, then, the relationship between children, parents and television is inherently political. The 'disappearance of childhood' thesis is — certainly in Postman's case — profoundly conservative. It derives from a fear that children may no longer defer to their parents' authority simply on the grounds of age. It seeks to promote a return to the traditional nuclear family, and to hierarchical power-relationships between generations (Hoikkala *et al.*, 1987). Yet in describing parental authority as essentially 'humane', Postman effectively ignores the ways in which it is abused, and has been abused throughout history. In regarding children as passive victims of television, he ignores the diverse competencies that are involved in making sense of the medium. And in asserting the need to keep them ignorant, he denies them the right to develop their own critical perspectives.

Postman urges parents and teachers to 'resist the spirit of the age' by rigorously limiting and monitoring what their children watch. If parents have effectively given up the struggle, he argues that it is the responsibility of the school to serve as a 'last defence' against the disappearance of childhood. Yet if teaching about television, or indeed parental mediation, is just a covert form of regulation, a means of policing the meanings and pleasures children derive from the medium, it is bound to be resisted. On the contrary, any effective form of media education will need to acknowledge and build upon what children already know, and the understandings and competencies they already possess. How we define and identify those competencies will be the major theme of the following chapters.

Part Three

Elements of Television Literacy

Psychological research on the development of print literacy has often made a basic distinction between 'lower order' or functional literacy — which is assumed to be acquired at an early age — and 'higher order' or critical literacy, which may be acquired at later stages of development. 'Lower order' literacy is regarded, if in a somewhat abstract and minimal fashion, as a set of 'skills' which enable basic comprehension. 'Higher order' literacy is seen as qualitatively different: it involves not merely comprehension, but also the evaluation of texts, both in comparison with other texts, and in comparison with the reader's own social experience. 'Higher order' literacy can be seen as more than a set of skills: it involves cognitive or conceptual 'understandings' which enable children to become more self-reflexive about their own use of language.

This kind of distinction may also be found in research on television literacy, for example in the work of Gavriel Salomon (e.g. 1982), Aimee Dorr (1980) and Patricia Greenfield (1984). Thus, a 'lower order' television literacy might include any or all of the following:

- the ability to distinguish between voices on a soundtrack, or between figures and backgrounds;
- an understanding of the principle of editing, and the ability to follow a narrative;
- an ability to relate sound and image tracks;
- a grasp of elements of 'television grammar' such as camera angles and movements.

'Higher order' literacy is potentially more diverse, and may include competencies which, at least according to Salomon (1982), are not specific to the medium. These could include the following:

- a more formal understanding of the codes or 'rhetoric' of television language;
- an ability to categorize programmes, and a knowledge of the conventions of different television genres;
- a set of 'story grammars' or models of narrative structure, and an awareness of the ways in which narrative time is manipulated through editing;

- an ability to infer character traits, and to construct psychologically coherent characters;
- an awareness of the ways in which viewers are invited to 'identify' with characters, and the different kinds of identification;
- an understanding of the production process, and of the circulation and distribution of programmes;
- an ability to infer the motivations and intentions of producers;
- an awareness of the ways in which audiences are addressed and constructed;
- an ability to evaluate the 'reality claims' made by different types of programmes, and to make comparisons between the mediated representations they provide and one's own direct perceptions of the social world.

Similarly, media educators have devised curricula which include detailed 'attainment targets' for children at different ages (e.g. Bazalgette, 1989). Table 1 offers a brief outline of the 'key concepts' of media education which have increasingly featured in British syllabuses, together with relevant 'signpost questions'.

Table 1   'Key concepts' of media education

Media Agencies
Who is communicating what and why?
Who produces a text; roles in the production process; media institutions; economics and ideology; intentions and results.

Media Categories
What type of text is it?
Different media (television, radio, cinema etc.); forms (documentary, advertising, etc.); genres (science fiction, soap opera, etc.); other ways of categorizing texts; how categorization relates to understanding.

Media Technologies
How is it produced?
What kinds of technologies are available to whom; how to use them; the differences they make to the production process as well as the final product.

Media Languages
How do we know what it means?
How the media produce meanings; codes and conventions; narrative structures.

Media Audiences
Who receives it, and what sense do they make of it?
How audiences are identified, constructed, addressed and reached; how audiences find, choose, consume and respond to texts.

Media Representations
How does it present its subject?
The relation between media texts and actual places, people, events, ideas; stereotyping and its consequences.

Source: based on Bazalgette (1989), pp. 8, 20.

While this kind of classification is undoubtedly useful, it also raises several problems. As I argued in Chapter 2, there is a danger in assuming that the 'basic comprehension' of television necessarily precedes any attempt at interpretation or evaluation — in other words, that there are simple 'mechanical' processes which function independently of attempts to produce meaning. As with any developmental model, there is a risk of reducing a complex set of interrelated competencies to a hierarchical set of 'skills' which are acquired in an invariant sequence.

Certainly when it comes to 'higher order' literacy, we are clearly talking about a series of interrelated competencies. For example, children's judgments about the modality of television — that is, about how 'realistic' programmes are perceived to be — will clearly be informed by a whole series of different (and potentially contradictory) criteria. Thus, children may be making quite straightforward comparisons between television and their own experience; they may offer broader judgments about plausibility, about what 'might' or 'could' happen, even if they themselves have not experienced this; they may invoke a knowledge of the generic conventions of television, which mark off particular genres as more or less 'realistic'; and they may also use their knowledge of the ways in which programmes are produced, and hypothesize about the motivations of their producers.

Nevertheless, there is the problem of what we take as *evidence* of children's understanding. As I have argued, what children say cannot be taken simply as a reflection of what they think or believe. Language does not provide us with a direct means of access to what goes on in people's heads: on the contrary, what people say is crucially dependent upon the social and interpersonal context in which they say it. Researchers in this field have traditionally sought to bracket off the context in which language occurs, for example by arguing that it has the same significance for all subjects, or that their own methods are simply neutral in this respect.

To develop the earlier example, judgments about the modality of television will also depend upon the context in which they are made. Thus, for younger children, condemning a cartoon as 'unrealistic' may serve as a means of demonstrating one's own sophistication, and claiming a degree of 'adult' status. For a boy to condemn a soap opera for the same reason may be an effective way of distancing himself from what are often seen as 'feminine' tastes, and thus confirming his masculinity. On the other hand, for black children to praise a 'black' programme like *The Cosby Show* as 'true to life' may represent a much broader claim for the authenticity or status of their own cultural experience. The extent to which any of these judgments are expressed — and the way in which they are expressed — will depend on who else is present at the time, and the assumptions the speaker makes about them.

The five chapters that make up this part of the book are concerned with some of the competencies identified here as constituents of a 'higher order' television literacy. Chapter 6 deals with the ways in which children categorize television texts, and in particular with their use of the notion of genre. Chapter 7 focuses on children's retellings of popular films, and their use and understanding of narrative. Chapter 8 considers children's talk about television characters, and issues of identification and representation which arise from this. Chapter 9 investigates the criteria which inform their judgments about the modality of television, and the functions those judgments serve. Chapter 10 considers children's talk about advertising, as a particular form of persuasive communication, and their judgments about the motivations of its producers.

While the activities undertaken here were specifically focused on 'key concepts', they were designed to be as open-ended as possible. The aim was not to 'test' for the presence or absence of particular understandings, but to provide a context in which the children could discuss and debate the issues in their own terms.

In this respect, therefore, the research does not attempt to construct a definitive statement of what children 'know' at different ages, or to provide a developmental model. As I have argued, television literacy should not be seen as a set of cognitive 'skills' which children either do or do not possess. On the contrary, these different elements of television literacy will be seen here as forms of *communicative* competence which are inherently social in nature, and which are established and negotiated in the process of children's talk. In investigating this process, it is ultimately misguided to separate cognitive understandings from affective responses, and from the social contexts in which these are expressed. In taking this broader view, many of the 'concepts' themselves — and the theories on which they are based — will inevitably come to be questioned.

Chapter 6

Sorting Out TV:
Categorization and Genre

In one of his short stories, Jorge Luis Borges describes the following taxonomy of the animal kingdom, which he attributes to an ancient Chinese encyclopedia entitled *The Celestial Emporium of Benevolent Knowledge*:

> On those remote pages it is written that animals are divided into (a) those that belong to the Emperor, (b) embalmed ones, (c) those that are trained, (d) suckling pigs, (e) mermaids, (f) fabulous ones, (g) stray dogs, (h) those that are included in this classification, (i) those that tremble as if they were mad, (j) innumerable ones, (k) those drawn with a very fine camel hair brush, (l) others, (m) those that have just broken a flower vase, (n) those that resemble flies from a distance. (Borges, 1966, p. 108)

While Borges' taxonomy is clearly fictional, it has a great deal in common with the main taxonomy or system of categorization which is used in relation to film and television — namely, that of genre.

The practice of categorizing film and television texts is often regarded as unproblematic. We often describe programmes in terms of their category membership: *Neighbours*, we would probably agree, is a soap opera. We implicitly assign programmes to categories, and compare them on this basis: we are more likely to compare *Neighbours* with *Home and Away* (both soap operas) than with *World in Action* (current affairs) or *Blackeyes* ('serious' drama). Our discussion rests on the assumption that we all know what a soap opera is — that we have a shared *concept* of 'soap opera' which transcends individual instances of the genre. Over time, this process becomes naturalized, and the basis of our judgments may rarely be made explicit.

On the surface, categorization would seem to be a fairly straightforward, even objective, psychological process. It involves noting the shared features of objects — in this case, film or television texts — and grouping them together on this basis. Insofar as children are able to assign texts to their 'correct' categories, we might judge them to 'understand' the principles of categorization — that is, to 'understand' genre.

My argument in this chapter, however, is that categorization — and genre — cannot be seen as either straightforward and objective, or indeed as merely psychological. On the contrary, in studying the process whereby children categorize television texts, we will be addressing some fundamental questions about the nature of their conceptual understanding of the medium.

Genre: an Epistemological Problem

Theories of genre developed within film studies have increasingly run up against the basic epistemological question of how we identify a genre in the first place. Andrew Tudor (1973) poses this problem most succinctly:

> To take a genre such as a western, analyse it, and list its principal characteristics is to beg the question that we must first isolate the body of films that are westerns. But they can only be isolated on the basis of the 'principal characteristics', which can only be discovered from the films themselves after they have been isolated. (p. 134)

The study of film genres has often attempted to sidestep this problem by working from what Tudor calls 'a common cultural consensus' about the nature of the particular genre. From this perspective, genre becomes, in Tudor's terms, 'what we collectively believe it to be'. This approach usefully shifts attention away from the 'inherent' properties of texts, and towards the relationship between texts and audiences — although it may also assume a greater degree of 'consensus' than actually exists.

Certainly, the principles by which genres are defined are quite diverse and often mutually inconsistent. For example, we might argue that westerns or science fiction films are categorized primarily on the basis of their location or setting; thrillers or comedy films on the basis of their intended effects on the viewer; musicals on the basis of form; film noir on the basis of its visual style; and so on. Yet this is certainly simplistic. Generic categorization may rely on a number of such principles acting in combination — so that, for example, the horror genre would be defined by its characteristic setting, its visual style, its narrative form, its intended effects on the viewer, and so on. Furthermore, it would be difficult to argue for a hierarchical ordering among these different principles of classification — for example, that intended effects on the viewer will always override location as a determining principle. Where seemingly contradictory principles are at work, we have the further possibility of hybrid genres, such as 'comedy horror' (see Neale, 1990).

This process is, it should be emphasized, much more than a matter of assigning terminological labels. Generic categorization does make a significant difference to the way in which we read texts. Texts may invite multiple readings along generic lines, yet they may also be read 'against the grain'. There are undoubtedly elements in many soap operas, for example, which draw upon the generic conventions of situation comedy. We might well choose to read *Neighbours*, for instance, as a situation comedy — a reading which might focus much less on empathizing with the psychological dilemmas of individual characters, and much more on elements of performance which disrupt its generally 'naturalistic' tone. A more oppositional strategy would involve directly subverting the generic reading invited by the text — for example, to read the News as fiction, or even as soap opera (cf. Fiske, 1987a).

The inherent flexibility of this process of generic categorization is often evident in critical debate itself. Recent work on film melodrama, for example, has attempted to salvage the genre from previous neglect, with some considerable success (e.g. Gledhill, 1988). Yet this has required a sustained attempt to define, or redefine, the genre itself, not least by recovering its history in the theatre and the visual arts, and through analysis of its specific address to women. Even more adventurously, there have been attempts to appropriate films previously seen as belonging to other genres: some war films and westerns, for example, have been redefined by critics as 'male melodramas' — implying a recognition of the contradictory nature of dominant representations of masculinity. This critical project of defining melodrama has thus involved an emphasis, not only on the 'inherent' formal characteristics of the films themselves, but also on their historical, social and ideological context.

The key point here is that what might be seen as 'a common cultural consensus' about genre is in fact changing and contradictory. Genre is not objective, nor is it simply 'given' by the culture: rather, it is in a constant process of negotiation and change.

This has been increasingly recognized in film theory, where there has been a shift away from a taxonomic approach to genre study — which is primarily concerned with identifying the 'conventions' of a given genre (e.g. Kitses, 1970; MacArthur, 1972) — towards a more dynamic model. Stephen Neale (1980), for example, defines genre as follows:

> genres are not to be seen as forms of textual codifications, but as systems of orientations, expectations and conventions that circulate between industry, text and subject. (p. 19)

According to Neale, definitions of genre are not merely fixed and imposed by the film industry, but a process in which the participation of the viewer plays a vital role. Genre, Neale argues, is not just about the repetition of a formula, but also requires variation and difference. The pleasure of the cinema depends upon expecting and recognizing what is familiar, but also upon having our expectations played with and on occasion subverted. Genre is thus a form of contract between the industry and the audience: like the star system, it serves an economic function for the industry as a means of regulating the market, while also ensuring that audiences know (more or less) what kind of pleasure they will be getting for their money.

In his more recent work, Neale (1990) has argued for the importance of a historical approach to the evolution of film genres, and of studying the role of institutional discourses — for example, of publicity and marketing — in helping to establish audience expectations. Yet while his theory offers a set of interesting hypotheses about how audiences might read films, these remain unexplored. There has been hardly any empirical research on the ways in which real audiences might understand genre, or use this understanding in making sense of specific texts.

Genre: a Psychological Issue?

By contrast, there is now a considerable body of work in cognitive psychology on the issue of categorization — of which genre is one example. In some respects, a similar shift would seem to have taken place here, away from what Lakoff (1987) terms an 'objectivist' view of cognition. According to the 'classical' or objectivist view of categorization, categories are seen to exist out there in the world (much like the 'principal characteristics' of genre films), and the mind is seen as more or less effective in mirroring or representing them. In this view, categories are defined by their shared properties, and have rigid boundaries and conditions of membership (Smith and Medin, 1981).

While this view came to be challenged from a number of sources — for example in Wittgenstein's theory of 'family resemblances' (Bloor, 1983) and, more recently, in Zadeh's 'fuzzy set theory' (Zadeh, 1965) — it was the work of Eleanor Rosch (e.g. 1978) that most decisively questioned the classical approach, by providing evidence of what she termed 'prototype effects'. In her experiments, Rosch found that some members of a category were consistently perceived as better examples of that category than others — for example, robins and sparrows were perceived as better examples of the category 'bird' than ostriches or penguins. Rosch also found that there was a basic level of categorization, which tends to be acquired first: thus, we are more likely (at least initially) to use the basic-level category 'dog' rather than the superordinate category 'animal' or the subordinate category 'retriever'.

In developing Rosch's work, George Lakoff (1987) draws on evidence from linguistics and anthropology to offer an alternative to the classical view, which he terms 'experiential realism'. According to this view, categorization is not a passive process of 'mental representation', or of the disembodied manipulation of abstract symbols. On the contrary, it involves human experience and imagination, and is embedded within physical and social experience.

Lakoff draws on empirical research which compares the ways in which people in different cultures divide up the world in language — for example, in naming and categorizing animals or colours. He argues that these forms of categorization are socially and historically variable, although not wholly relative. While Lakoff acknowledges that there are some kinds of categories that fit the classical model, he argues that most categories are far less coherent.

Lakoff's work represents an advance on Rosch's prototype theory in two main respects. Firstly, Lakoff pays much more attention to the role of language in categorization and concept formation: while he also considers the central role of non-linguistic symbolic structures, much of his argument is based on a parallel between linguistic and other conceptual categories. Secondly, Lakoff emphasizes the social and cultural functions of categorization, although he is careful to reject cultural relativism. Lakoff would probably concur with Potter and Wetherell (1987) in regarding categorization as a social accomplishment, which is achieved largely through discourse — although he is not primarily concerned (as Potter and Wetherell are) with the ways in which people draw upon, and actively construct, categories as they talk.

In these respects, Lakoff's work manages to avoid many of the broad limitations of cognitive psychology identified in earlier chapters, and may usefully inform the more dynamic model of genre described above. At the same time, it raises some significant questions about what is involved in assigning objects to categories (or texts to genres), and indeed what the nature and function of categories might be. What does it mean to use and 'understand' the concept of genre?

The Activity

There was considerable evidence of children using notions of genre, both explicitly and implicitly, in the initial discussions described in Chapter 4. The older children were more likely to identify their likes and dislikes by referring to a generic category, before offering a specific example. They also appeared to have a broader repertoire of terms here, or at least to use these more regularly. However, there was some evidence even in the youngest age group that genre was being used implicitly, for example as a basis of comparison between programmes or at least as an unspoken rationale for moving from one topic to the next. Thus, discussion of one comedy programme was more likely to be followed by discussion of another comedy programme, rather than of news or soap opera.

The activity described in this chapter was designed to explore this issue more systematically. Groups of three or four children, both mixed and single-sex, were asked to sort a selection of around thirty programme titles, laid out on cards. The titles had been derived primarily from those mentioned in previous discussions, and were therefore slightly different for each group. In selecting thirty titles from a much longer list, the aim was to provide titles which the majority of children would recognize, and within this to cover a range of programmes. Each selection included most or all of the following: cartoons and live action programmes; factual and fictional programmes; British and non-British programmes; programmes featuring mainly black characters; programmes from major genres such as soap operas, game shows, science fiction, situation comedies and other comedy shows; and programmes which might be classified according to their perceived or actual audience, such as 'boys'' and 'girls'' programmes, and 'children's' and 'adults'' programmes.

As this list implies, genre was only one among a number of possible principles that the children might use to categorize the programmes. While one might suspect genre to be more salient for adults, it was not assumed that it would necessarily prove to be so for children, at least in this context. As I shall indicate, the principles the children actually used in carrying out the task were extremely diverse, and included many which were not anticipated.

To begin with, the children were asked to 'sort out' the titles in any way they wished. In many cases, this was sufficient to get them started, although they occasionally required further prompting — for example, by asking them to 'put together the ones that you think go together', or to 'put them into groups'. In a few cases, a further example was given, although this was as 'neutral' as possible: *Neighbours* and *Home and Away*, for example, were selected as a possible combination, although the basis for this was not specified (in this case, it could obviously be because both programmes are soap operas, but it could also be because they are both Australian, because they are scheduled at a similar time, because they are — or were — both very popular, and so on). In effect, the aim was to begin with as open an invitation as possible.

The children were subsequently encouraged to attempt a number of different 'sortings' of the programme titles, until it was clear that their interest in the activity had been exhausted. In some cases, they were asked to develop categories they themselves had introduced, or to generalize these across all the titles. On the very few occasions where genre did not emerge as an organizing principle after a number of attempts, it was then explicitly introduced, by asking the children to sort out the cards according to the 'type of programme'.

In nearly all cases, the groups talked their way through the activity, debating and arguing amongst themselves as they moved the cards around on the table. The groupings they produced were often provisional, and subject to further modification. The children often drew attention to overlaps between groupings, and programmes which might be placed in a number of different groups.

The interest, here as elsewhere in the research, was in *process* rather than product. The aim was not to 'test' the children's level of understanding by comparing their agreed solutions with the 'correct' version, but to analyze the methods they used to solve the problem in their own terms. Yet again, in analyzing what the children did, it is the notion of a 'correct' understanding, and ultimately the nature of 'understanding' itself, that comes to be questioned.

Perceptions of the Activity

The activity described here was one of the most 'artificial' of all those undertaken on the project, in the sense that it required the children to do something they would not otherwise have done — except perhaps (and significantly) in school. Certainly in primary schools, the invitation to 'put together the ones that go together' is a fairly routine teaching strategy, a fact which might itself account for the readiness with which most groups got down to the task.

There was certainly a sense in a few of the groups that the activity was perceived as somewhat of a 'school task', to which there would be right and wrong answers. At least some of the groups ended on an inconclusive note, as if some form of evaluation — or at least the 'correct' version — was expected, but had not been provided.

The converse of this, however, is that a number of the groups chose to resist the activity through 'sending it up'. Some of the categories devised were quite bizarre, and while in some cases this seemed to arise from a sense of mild desperation, in others it was distinctly satirical. Thus, a number of groups came up with categories based on the form of the titles themselves — those that begin with the same letter, those that have an apostrophe — and even in one instance on the way the cards had been cut!

Nevertheless, the most appropriate metaphor here — and one which was voiced by a significant number of groups — was that the activity was a kind of 'game', rather akin to 'Happy Families'. At the end of their session one of the groups of 10-year-olds turned all the cards face down and began to play a kind of memory game, while in another, Sanjay (12) suggested (perhaps sarcastically) that we might use the cards to play 'Snap'.

At the same time, the activity seemed to be perceived as pleasurable simply because it was about television. Particularly for the younger children, the laying out of the cards at the beginning of the session offered an opportunity for more staking out of likes and dislikes, and personal preference was also used in many instances as a principle in the sorting itself. In many cases, the activity was accompanied by the singing of theme tunes from the programmes, and occasional retellings of comic incidents, catch phrases and so on. As I shall indicate, affective preferences also played a significant role in the ways in which categories and groups themselves were constructed.

This was a comparatively 'abstract' activity, in the sense that it sought to isolate generic classification from among the range of processes which constitute 'everyday' talk about television. Yet the social interaction which took place in the groups, and the ways in which the children used the activity as a vehicle for their other concerns, clearly point to the limitations of any notion of 'pure' cognition.

Processes of Categorization: Group Dynamics

As with many of the other activities undertaken here, this exercise often seemed to serve primarily as an arena in which social and interpersonal relationships could be negotiated. However, this activity was unusual in that it explicitly required the children to work as a group, and to arrive at a consensus — a requirement which was handled in very different ways. In some instances, an individual — often a child who appeared to be more familiar with the terminology of television genres, or who was generally more confident — took the lead in directing the others. Yet in other instances, such familiarity appeared to count for little when compared with the ability to impose your will, for example by shouting the loudest or grabbing the cards you wanted in order to prevent others from taking them. On the other hand, some groups were able to resolve conflicts by voting on points of contention, or by agreeing to differ. In this respect, categorization was very clearly a social accomplishment.

Across all the age groups, the children's engagement with the task was heavily informed by their personal preferences. While almost all of them took the opportunity to pass evaluative comments on programmes — often of a very summary and absolute kind — in a number of cases in each age group personal preference emerged as a main organizing principle.

In some instances, this functioned on an individual level, as in the case of the three 8-year-old boys who began by grabbing and fighting over the cards they defined as 'theirs' and leaving an unwanted pile in the middle of the table. Here, pre-existing rivalries and tensions were carried over into the activity itself, which became a vehicle for their ongoing struggle for dominance.

In other cases, the children constructed a consensus based on the assertion of their collective tastes. One group of 10-year-old girls began with a few generic categories, such as quizzes and cartoons, although these tended to overlap with evaluative judgments, as in the case of a 'brilliant'/soap opera group, and a 'boring'/ non-fiction group. The girls eventually abandoned these in favour of a straight-forwardly evaluative scheme — 'brilliant', 'rubbish' and 'medium' — which then carried through into their third sorting, where they introduced the concept of audience, dividing the cards between 'boys' programmes', defined as 'rubbish', and 'girls' programmes', defined as 'brilliant'. The boys' group ended up with many fewer programmes, causing Anne to comment, amongst much laughter, 'that's fair, that's fair, that's what I call fair — equal rights!' While there was a sense in which the girls were beginning to send up the activity, the assertion of preferences was clearly being used to construct a group solidarity which was more than merely a matter of individual 'taste'.

Processes of Categorization: Complexes and Concepts

As I have noted, the process of categorization in the groups was an ongoing activity, which was often subject to renegotiation as groups were formed, broken up and re-formed. In the process, inconsistencies often emerged, only some of which can be seen as accidental. In some instances, children forgot the principles they were using to form a group, and overlooked the presence of titles which were incompatible with their declared principles of categorization. Yet in other cases, particularly among the younger children, there were a number of principles operating simultaneously, often linked together in sequence.

One example illustrates this phenomenon fairly clearly. One of the groups of 8-year-olds began by combining *Lost in Space* and *Land of the Giants*, on grounds which were not made explicit, although both are American science fiction series and were scheduled in the same Sunday lunchtime slot. They then added the BBC costume drama *Chronicles of Narnia* to form a group entitled 'different worlds', noting that they were all programmes in which 'people disappear'. *Wildlife on One*, the BBC natural history series, was then moved from a 'news' group to join this group, on the grounds that 'it's a nature thing', and '*Lost in Space* has got nature in'. These were then joined by four more programmes, *Scooby Doo*, *Chip 'n' Dale* (both cartoons), *Doctor Who* (a live action science fiction serial) and *Blue Peter* (a factual children's magazine programme), to form a group entitled 'finding out things'. This group was subsequently split, according to whether the programmes were concerned with 'finding out things' in the sense of 'adventures' or with 'finding out how to do work in school' — essentially a distinction between fact and fiction.

On one level, this example reflects the fact that programmes can be categorized in a multiplicity of ways: the more inventive you are, the more combinations are possible. Yet the extent to which the children ignored possible distinctions in favour of others, and detected underlying similarities between seemingly disparate texts points to some significant differences between their perceptions and those of adults. For example, the children often ignored the distinction between 'fact' and 'fiction' — in this instance, drawing attention to what in grander terminology might be called the hermeneutic drive of both factual and fictional texts, the fact that they are often organized around the desire to 'find things out'.

However, this example also illustrates the fact that the children were not always applying concepts consistently. As in Vygotsky's experiments on concept formation (Vygotsky, 1962), the children had been given a number of objects (in this case, texts) which could be grouped or linked according to a number of different criteria. Here too, the criteria which children used sometimes appeared to shift from one linking operation to the next, suggesting that they were not in fact fully-formed concepts. In Vygotskyan terms, these children — and indeed some of the older children as well — would appear to be thinking in chains or complexes rather than concepts proper.

Processes of Categorization: Concepts and Labels

One further aspect of Vygotsky's work which is relevant here is his theory of the relationship between language and thought. In the case of this activity, the relationship between the language children used — and in particular, their use of generic terminology (like 'comedy' and 'soap opera') — and the categories they produced was not always direct or straightforward.

For example, in the case of 'soap opera', there were instances of each of four logical permutations of the relationship between word and concept. In some cases, children appeared to use neither the word nor the concept. A group of 8-year-olds, for example, grouped *Neighbours* and *Home and Away* together, but this appeared to be based on their scheduling times (at this time, *Home and Away* preceded *Neighbours*, although on a different channel) and on the fact that they featured characters with similar names. One boy suggested that *EastEnders* might be added to this group on the basis that 'they all feel the same', but there was no consistent logic behind their subsequent grouping of these programmes.

In other cases, children used the term 'soap opera' spontaneously, yet seemed to have an uncertain or inconsistent sense of its meaning, and were unable to define it when asked, either by the interviewer or by others in the group. For example, Justine (8) defined soaps as 'serious' — a word which often seemed to be confused with 'series' — and implicitly as realistic, or at least different in kind from science fiction programmes (the 'different worlds' group described above). Nevertheless, the soap opera group here included *The Bill*, *Doctor Who* and (with some uncertainty) *Blue Peter*. Definitions of the term offered by the 10-year-olds often involved two criteria simultaneously, and included the notion of soaps as 'well-known' (i.e. popular) and 'about families', as being 'on every week', as containing particular character types (such as 'whiny bags'), and as being 'based on real life' — although in each case, there was uncertainty and even dispute about programmes which only partly met these criteria.

Some of the older children gradually evolved a more satisfactory definition (at least for their purposes) as the activity progressed. One group of 10-year-olds began by defining soaps as 'things you see nearly every day', which led them to include the twice-weekly *Blue Peter* as well as *Wildlife on One*, alongside a number of British and Australian serials. This criterion was subsequently disputed, as it was argued that many of the programmes here were not in fact screened every day (in Britain, only the Australian soaps appear five days a week). Eventually, a rather different organizing criterion emerged, namely that certain of these programmes were 'continuations', in the sense that they carried on from episode to episode — in other words, a definition of soap opera in terms of form.

A third possibility here was that children were familiar with the concept, but were unable to supply the label. For example, Ivor (8) produced a group entitled 'the ones what go on for ever', although this included the more episodic science fiction series *Land of the Giants* and *Lost in Space* (whose journeys do admittedly 'go on for ever', in the manner of other 'space operas' such as *Star Trek*), alongside *Neighbours* and *Home and Away*, but excluding the British soaps. Likewise, one of the groups of 10-year-olds collected soaps and described these as programmes which 'all come in a series' — 'none of them are on their own', they are 'not like a whole'. In this case, there was quite a sustained discussion of cliffhangers, generally seen as one of the defining characteristics of the genre (cf. Geraghty, 1981):

Extract 1

Interviewer: Would *The Bill* fit?
Dipesh: No, 'cause it's not like in series. /

Interviewer:	Say a bit more what you mean, it's not in series.
Dipesh:	Say if er // They look / Say if there's somebody that robs somewhere or other and they're looking for him, it takes them most of the series to look for it. Most of the time. [. . .] When it come on another day, it's not detached from the one that comes last week. Something like that.
Interviewer:	Right, right.
Michael:	Neither is this [*pointing to* Home and Away].
Dipesh:	Yeah, that is. *Neighbours* and *Home and Away* are.
Michael:	They always come to a different part though. Don't you think so? Whenever it comes on again, they leave out that bit and go on to a different part, and tell you it later on in the series. Instead of just telling you straight away, just carrying on like / in one of the cartoons.
Andrew:	Yeah.
Michael:	Like in *Chip 'n' Dale*, when the adverts come on [i.e. in the commercial break], then they come back straight to the same place, they're all in the same positions [yeah], but in these they're not, they're just in different positions again.

As this discussion proceeds, the children are gradually defining the nature of a cliffhanger — as opposed to the kind of interruption which occurs at a commercial break, for example — but also distinguishing between the ways in which different soap operas (in this case, *Neighbours* and *Home and Away*) use the convention. This distinction was commented upon in a number of other discussions, where *Neighbours* was generally preferred for 'telling you straight away', rather than postponing the resolution of the cliffhanger by failing to return to it immediately at the beginning of the following episode.

Interestingly, the term 'soap opera' did eventually appear in this group's discussion, although their definition remained imprecise, and did not seem to connect with their discussion of the formal characteristics of the programmes:

Extract 2

Michael:	They're more or less like soap operas, some of them. No, not soap operas, just soaps.
Interviewer:	What's a soap opera, then?
Michael:	It's something with er / It's like *Brookside*, it's something with er / people acting and they're trying to /Do it in a studio. It's not like when you go on *Phantom of the Opera*, that's just an opera, it's more or less like a drama.
Interviewer:	Right.
Michael:	That's the word I was trying to say before, but I forgot.
Interviewer:	Right, OK, so they're dramas then, really?
Michael:	Yeah.

Finally, there were instances where children appeared to use both label and concept clearly and consistently. While this was generally the case among the older groups, it was also true of some of the youngest children. Andy (8), for example, offered a clear definition of soap opera, and supported this with an example of the cliffhanger convention:

Extract 3

> *Andy*: It's a programme that joins on to the next programme [. . .] Like, just when Henry's going to get punched or something, it goes [*sings:*] 'Neighbours, ev'rybody's got good neighbours . . .'

These four possible permutations, which I have laid out somewhat schematically here, occurred to a greater or lesser extent with other genres, such as quizzes and game shows. Throughout the discussions, there were exchanges in which the children were struggling to find a terminology or a discourse which would enable them to do justice to their perceptions of the differences between programmes. Remembering or discovering the word, or at least *a* word — as in the case of Michael's use of the term 'drama' — may have resolved the dilemma, but it often did so only temporarily.

However, the more fundamental question which these examples raise — and it is one I have deliberately avoided thus far — is that of the function of the terminology in the first place. What does it mean to describe a given programme as a soap opera? What is a soap opera anyway?

In the foregoing discussion, I have implicitly assumed that a soap opera is defined according to its form — namely that it is a continuing narrative which is broken into episodes, and that the gaps between episodes often (though not always) serve to maintain suspense, most obviously through the cliffhanger device. In making this assumption, I also presume that the process of identifying a given text as a soap opera involves distinguishing between these determining formal characteristics and others which are not determining. Thus, I might assert that while many soap operas are indeed about families, many are not (for example, *Prisoner: Cell Block H* or *General Hospital*); while many soap operas are 'based on real life', many are rather distant from the everyday lives of most of their viewers (for example, *Dynasty* or *Dallas*). These criteria may apply to many instances of the genre, but they are not necessary or defining ones. In making these assumptions, I can establish an apparently objective basis for judging the children's level of understanding: either they 'understand' what a soap opera is — they 'possess' the concept 'soap opera' — or they do not.

However, these assumptions are problematic, for a number of reasons. They assume a primary defining role for certain characteristics — in this case, narrative form — and a secondary role for others. The problem here is that these characteristics may not be particularly salient for viewers themselves; and even if they are salient for adult viewers, or adult critics, they may not be so for children, for whom other characteristics may be much more important. Here again, by comparing children's perceptions with an adult norm (and possibly an imaginary one), we run the risk of neglecting what children themselves are actually doing.

In fact, as a critical term, 'soap opera' is highly problematic. As Robert Allen (1989) has argued, the definitions of 'soap opera' which are used by critics themselves are diverse and often mutually contradictory. There is a distinct danger here of reifying the term, and of blurring distinctions which it is important to sustain. To discuss *Dynasty* in the same context as *EastEnders*, or *EastEnders* in the same context as *Neighbours,* is to run the risk of ignoring fundamental differences in favour of an almost abstract concern with narrative form.

Furthermore, the historical evolution of television genres may rapidly render such terms redundant. As Jane Feuer (1986) has argued, the contemporary dominance of the continuing serial may lead to a situation in which all other genres aspire to, or take on aspects of, its form. Thus, to choose two examples which the children here often grouped with soap operas: *The Bill* is a twice-weekly police series, which has a significant element of continuing narrative, although many of its storylines are contained within single episodes; while *Bread* is a situation comedy which also contains elements of continuing narrative, often centring on the romantic vicissitudes of the characters' relationships. The children's uncertainties over the placing of these programmes may well reflect their generic ambiguity.

As I have suggested, a term like 'soap opera' does not in fact correspond with something which exists objectively, out there in the world. It is a social judgment, not a neutral description. Here again, it would be a mistake to regard language merely as evidence of what children 'know' or 'understand'.

Principles of Categorization

Genre was one among a number of principles which the children used in categorizing the programme titles. Apart from questions of personal preference, which recurred throughout, many of the children sought to categorize the programmes by locating them, not only geographically (in terms of their country of origin, or the place or country in which they were set), but also in terms of their position in the schedules, and the channel on which they were broadcast — providing further evidence of the recurrent preoccupation with locating texts within the viewing context.

Beyond this, the principles used for grouping the programme titles were often inventive and sometimes bizarre. Examples of the latter would include 'you don't know what you're in for', 'about husbands and their troubles' and (applied to *Challenge Anneka* and *Blue Peter*) 'go out and run around'. In many instances, when faced with titles which proved difficult to categorize, such as magazine programmes, the children would focus on one aspect of content as a basis for forming a group, rather than considering programme format.

Overall, however, three major principles emerged, which will be considered below: namely, genre, modality and audience. While these principles tended to interact, both with each other and with those already identified, they can to some extent be considered separately.

Principles of Categorization: Genre

Generic categories emerged at some point in all the groups, with the exception of one of the youngest. However, while most of the older children were more confident in allocating programmes to such categories, and in most cases possessed a bigger repertoire of genre terms, genre was not necessarily any more salient for them than it was for the younger ones. Table 6.1 illustrates the number of occasions on which genre was used as the principle of categorization on the

Table 6.1 Use of genre as a principle of categorization in first sorting

	Exclusively	**Mainly**	**Not at all**
8-yr-olds: inner-city	1	2	2
8-yr-olds: suburban	1	2	1
10-yr-olds: inner-city	3	2	—
10-yr-olds: suburban	1	3	1
12-yr-olds: inner-city	—	3	2
12-yr-olds: suburban	2	—	2

groups' first attempt at the activity — that is, in response to the open invitation to sort out the cards 'in any way you like'.

On the basis of these figures, it would seem that there are no clear distinctions to be drawn in terms of social class or (perhaps most surprisingly) in terms of age. If anything, it is the 10-year-olds who appear to be more likely to use genre, although like most groups they tend to combine genre with other principles, such as personal preference, audience and modality. Among the groups who failed to use genre on their first attempt, four used personal preference, two used channel and one used audience, while one (a group of 8-year-olds) struggled in vain. Nevertheless, these alternative principles were distributed fairly evenly across the age groups, and in terms of social class.

Of course, these figures do not in themselves prove the salience or otherwise of genre, except perhaps within the specific context of this activity. As some of the older children explicitly recognized, opting for genre would make the activity much more difficult than opting for channels, for example. The two groups of 12-year-olds from the suburban school who opted not to use genre in fact initially suggested this — indicating that genre was perhaps more significant for them than the table would suggest.

Nevertheless, as Table 6.2 indicates, the children's repertoire of generic terms definitely did increase with age.

Table 6.2 Generic categories by age group

Categories used by all age groups

Cartoons, comedies, news, soap operas/'serious' (=series), games/game shows, quizzes, 'space films'/'different worlds', adventure, 'finding out things', 'surprises'

Categories used only by 10-year-olds and 12-year-olds

'Investigations', animals, 'comedies with a sort of story' (=situation comedies), comedies with presenters, police/crime, series, information, drama

Categories used only by 12-year-olds

Documentary, educational programmes, comedies with a studio audience, sitcom, 'comedy clips', interviews/chat shows

Here again, this information needs to be interpreted cautiously. The groups were given different selections of programmes, based on what they had already chosen to discuss on previous occasions, a fact which made certain groupings impossible: only the 12-year-olds were actually given documentary titles, for example. Furthermore, this listing tends to obscure the differences within groups, and the distribution of the terms themselves. It was certainly the case, for example, that while some of the 8-year-olds were familiar with slightly more 'technical' terms such as 'soap opera', 'comedy' or 'game show', they were more likely to categorize programmes in terms of their immediate emotional responses, for example using terms like 'funny', 'scary' and 'exciting'.

Nevertheless, the older children were increasingly making finer distinctions, even within genres. For example, 'comedy' or 'funny' appeared to be a fairly commonsense category, which appeared in all age groups. Yet there were some programmes which fitted ambiguously here, forcing the children to make their principles of categorization more explicit. One of the 8-year-old groups, for example, categorized *Grange Hill* as a comedy, although this was disputed on the grounds that 'people don't laugh' — which I suspect means that the programme does not have a canned laugh track, in practice a very useful indication of whether a programme is at least intended as comedy. Yet while most groups seemed to distinguish fairly easily between 'comedies' and programmes which might occasionally be funny, only some of the older children made distinctions between different types of comedy. Thus, while the younger children tended to group situation comedies together with stand-up/sketch-based comedy, older children offered somewhat hesitant categories such as 'comedies with a sort of story', 'comedies with one special person', 'comedy clips', and in one case 'sitcoms'.

In three instances, there were attempts to group a set of comedies featuring black characters, namely *Desmonds*, *The Cosby Show* and *A Different World*. In the case of an all-white group of 12-year-olds, this was quite unproblematic, although for a mixed group of 8-year-olds, it was much more so. Hannah (8), who is black herself, initially grouped these programmes together, although when this was supported by Justine on the grounds that 'they're black people', she firmly rejected this, and attempted to find a different principle. Similarly, an all-black group of 12-year-olds grouped these programmes, although they attempted to explain this in terms of factors such as scheduling and personal preference: when the fact that these are all 'black' programmes was explicitly raised by the (white) interviewer, they were quite evasive. Here again, there appeared to be a good deal at stake for black children in drawing attention to the question of racial difference when whites were present.

Overall, it was the middle-class 12-year-olds who consistently made the finest distinctions between programmes, for example by subdividing groups as the activity progressed. In some cases, they demonstrated the complexity of the process through the physical arrangement of the cards on the table, to suggest overlaps or partial memberships of particular categories. There were a number of programmes which were acknowledged here as being ambiguous in generic terms — for example, *Bread* and *Grange Hill*, which were both seen to contain elements of the continuing serial, while also fitting into other categories. What was certainly implicit in many of these discussions was a self-reflexive use of the *discourse* of genre — an explicit awareness of the fact that many texts can be categorized in a number of ways, and that categorization is a relative, rather than an absolute, process.

What this image of smooth developmental progression tends to obscure, however, is the considerable differences between groups in any single age bracket, and in some cases within the groups themselves. Some of the younger children developed much more elaborate systems — in the sense of having many more categories — than some of the older ones. Similarly, some of the younger children had a much clearer grasp of genre terminology than many of the older ones. While social class differences did appear to play a part, these were again ambiguous: only in the older age group were there consistent distinctions between middle-class and working-class children.

To return to soap opera, for example, the use of the *term* 'soap opera' definitely increased with age, and may to a limited extent be related to social class, as Table 6.3 indicates. However, the distinction between soap opera and other non-comedy drama — as indicated by the groupings, and in some cases by the use of terms like 'drama' or 'serious' — did not increase in such a neat pattern. The middle-class 10-year-olds, who all used the term 'soap opera', tended to do so in a very inclusive sense, to apply not just to series drama, but also to a number of comedies. If anything, it was the working-class children in the younger groups who used the term more consistently, although ultimately it was the middle-class 12-year-olds who were the most consistent.

Table 6.3 Soap opera and non-comedy drama: distinctions by age

	Number of groups	Occurrence of 'soap [opera]'	Distinction soap/drama
8-yr-olds: inner-city	5	2	2
8-yr-olds: suburban	4	1	—
10-yr-olds: inner-city	5	3	2
10-yr-olds: suburban	5	5	1
12-yr-olds: inner-city	5	3	1
12-yr-olds: suburban	4	4	3

Clearly, there is a great risk in this kind of analysis of reducing the complexity of the data to a set of statistical protocols. Nevertheless, it does point to the problems in accounting for children's use of genre as a principle of categorization in terms of a neat model of cognitive development, or indeed in terms of social class simply determining their access to discourses.

Principles of Categorization: Modality

Modality is one of the major principles by which genres are distinguished. Modality judgments often emerged alongside genre, or indeed within generic categories, as a principle of categorization. This was particularly the case in distinguishing between cartoons and live action programmes, and between fiction and non-fiction.

Cartoons appeared to be one of the most 'commonsense' categories for all groups, in the sense that it was often the earliest to emerge in the activity. While some cartoons were occasionally included within a 'comedy' or 'funny' category, generating some debate about which cartoons were funny and which were not, they almost always emerged as a separate group, suggesting that modality was in this case the overriding criterion.

In some of the younger groups, however, programmes like *Rainbow* and *Sooty* (which feature human actors and puppets) and *The Chronicles of Narnia* (which features human actors, puppets and some animation) were included alongside animated cartoons, suggesting that the category 'cartoons' may in some cases be taken to refer to children's programmes more broadly — although factual children's programmes like *Blue Peter* and *Newsround* were never included here. Even among the youngest children, however, the inclusion of such programmes was usually challenged, and in many cases there were clear distinctions between live action — programmes where 'real people do it' or where there are 'real people acting' — and cartoons.

In a few of the younger groups, there appeared to be a shifting relationship between the terms 'film', 'programme' and 'cartoon', in which modality was possibly at stake. In one group, for example, *Land of the Giants* and *Doctor Who* were initially categorized as films, while *Neighbours* was described as a programme, in order to distinguish it from the cartoons — although later in the discussion, the terms 'film' and 'programme' appeared to have become interchangeable. In other groups, the term 'film' was being used to distinguish between live action and animation — 'it's films, and they use real people' — while in others (including one group of 10-year-olds) it seemed to refer to programmes in general. In general, these terms appeared to have a high degree of elasticity — as, for example, in 8-year-old Nancy's description of *Neighbours* and *Grange Hill* as 'filmy cartoons' — although they were used much more consistently by the older children.

Broader distinctions between fiction and non-fiction also occurred in most groups. News emerged as a basic category in nearly all groups, although it was often combined with other non-fiction programmes, to produce groups entitled 'true life', 'telling you about things' (both 8-year-olds) and 'telling you facts' (10-year-olds). More specific genre terms such as 'documentary' occurred in very few cases among the older groups. In other instances, fictional live action programmes were grouped together as 'not true' and 'made up' (8-year-olds), while one group of 10-year-olds distinguished between 'entertainment' and 'information'.

However, in all age groups, there were groupings that crossed this boundary, often in quite inventive ways and for good reasons. As indicated above, one group of 8-year-olds came up with a category entitled 'finding out things', which included both fictional and non-fictional programmes — although these were later separated. Two of the groups of 10-year-olds included news programmes alongside crime series, on the grounds that they all contained police, and one combined *Chronicles of Narnia* with *Wildlife on One*, although they were clear about the difference between 'real' and 'false' animals.

Overall, however, there was very little evidence in any of the age groups of confusion over the modality status of programmes, and where such confusions arose (mainly among the 8-year-olds), they were nearly always challenged. For most of the children, these basic distinctions were taken for granted, a commonsense element of their competencies as viewers.

Principles of Categorization: Audience

Notions of audience also intersected with those of genre, especially in terms of age. In all age groups, 'children's programmes' emerged as a separate category, and was often included in the initial attempt at the activity, alongside more strictly generic categories. In some cases, groups were invited to extend this principle across all the titles, while in others they did this spontaneously.

In many respects, categorizing programmes in terms of their audience seemed to represent a slightly more distanced approach to categorizing in terms of preferences. In both cases, however, definitions of 'self' and 'other' were seen to be at stake. In many cases, groups simply mapped their preferences onto audience categories, to make categories such as 'hates/grown-ups'. In others, audience was mapped onto modality, with non-fiction programmes (apart from game shows) being categorized as for adults. The fate of children's programmes which were disliked (or for which the expression of dislike was *de rigueur*), such as *Blue Peter* and to a lesser extent *Newsround*, was significant here. Against the evidence (for example, in terms of scheduling), these programmes were often placed with adults' programmes, and on one occasion with babies' — that is, as distinctly 'other'.

In other instances, there were some fine gradations according to age, with a number of groups making what were clearly for them very salient distinctions between 'children', 'young children', 'babies' and 'teenagers'.

Overall, the principles which were used to determine the audience for a programme were quite diverse, and became a focus of discussion in a number of groups. There was considerable debate in many cases about who watched which programmes, although it was acknowledged that most programmes would be watched by both adults and children, and that adults might on occasion watch children's programmes 'when they're waiting for other programmes to start'. Scheduling time — when 'they' put things on — appeared to provide a more objective criterion: a number of groups acknowledged that programmes that were on late were more likely to be 'adults' programmes', although one group of 10-year-olds argued that this would be different at weekends when they were allowed to stay up late.

Morality was also discussed in some groups: it was argued that programmes with 'rude things' in them were more likely to be for adults, and even, in the case of *Home and Away*, that the violence in the programme meant that it 'should' be for adults, even though it was watched by many children. Nevertheless, this principle was perhaps not always applied consistently, in that many programmes which have attracted adult disapproval for this reason, such as *The Bill*, were often classified as children's programmes.

For some of the younger children, parental censorship appeared to play a major role in defining which programmes were perceived as 'adult'. Graham and Robert (10), for example, categorized *Bergerac* as a children's programme on the basis that they were allowed to watch it. Ben (8) came from a more censorious middle-class household, where his parents would not allow him to watch *Neighbours* and *EastEnders*, perhaps partly for moral reasons — 'they have words in them'. This led him to define these programmes as being for 'older children' — although they were certainly watched by most others in his age group — and he went on to construct a group entitled 'things that my mum and dad don't let me watch'.

On the other hand, a group of 10-year-olds explicitly dismissed such views:

Extract 4

Jessica:	My mum says *EastEnders* isn't a children's programme.
Others:	It is, it is now.

Tracey:	Most of the teachers, they say that / um, kids mustn't watch *EastEnders* and *Home and Away*, they should be, 'cause they don't concentrate on their work enough.
Interviewer:	Who says that?
Tracey:	These teachers on TV.

.

.

.

| Interviewer: | So are *EastEnders* and *Home and Away* children's programmes? |
| All: | 'Course they are! |

Here again, this more moralistic perspective is associated with teachers and other middle-class adults, and is firmly rejected. As I have noted in Chapter 5, the distinction between what is 'for children' and 'for adults' is a situated one, not least in terms of social class.

Interestingly, however, this group acknowledges that such distinctions may be open to change: *EastEnders* may not have started out as a children's programme, but 'it is now' — whether as a result of the programme-makers deliberately changing their approach, or because the programme was taken up by a young audience, or both, remains unclear. This possibility was also a focus of speculation in another group of 10-year-olds, where in the case of *Neighbours* a distinction was made between who the programme was 'meant for' (adults) and who actually watches it (children).

As noted above, gender also emerged as a principle in some groups, although this tended to generate more dispute, even in single-sex groups. For example, Justine and Hannah (8) identified *Ghostbusters* and *Transformers* as being 'for boys', on the basis that they feature a good deal of fighting and are 'more dangerous'. The group (which was all girls) returned to this issue at the end of their discussion, although there was much less consensus here, as the following extract demonstrates:

Extract 5

Justine:	Because it [*Ghostbusters*?] has to go with boys, because it's really boys' stuff, because you know girls, they play with My Little Pony and things like that you know.
Julie:	I don't.
Interviewer:	Do you play with those, Justine?
Julie:	They're rubbish.

.

.

Interviewer:	I was asking you, if these ones are mostly for boys, is there anything here that's mostly for girls?
Hannah:	No. This one's mostly for girls as well, I watch that.
Interviewer:	What, *Ghostbusters*?
Julie:	So do I.
Geraldine:	Oh god, you are turning into a boy, Hannah!
Justine:	I think, um *Grange Hill* and *Neighbours* really.

Geraldine:	[and *Home and Away*.
Hannah:	[I watch every single one.
Interviewer:	Wait a minute, wait a minute, Justine you think *Grange Hill* and *Neighbours*, and Geraldine you said *Home and Away* are mostly for girls, yeah?
Justine:	Yeah because um you know /
Hannah:	Boys never watch it, because you say 'I'm gonna watch *Neighbours*' and they say 'boring *Neighbours*, right'. And this boy comes to me, to my house, because his mum finishes work at about five o'clock, Nicholas right, and he comes home with me, and me and my mum are watching this *Home and Away* right and then he says ['girls, girls, girls'
?Justine:	[Boring, boring

.
.
.

Justine:	But boys don't really think it's really serious, because they just think about *He-Man* and stuff like that [yeah]. And um you know um like Danny sort of thinks, he says 'you gonna watch, gonna watch / *Transformers* today or / what is it, / anything like that, and we say 'no', so he says 'what you watching?' and I say 'I'm gonna watch *Neighbours*' and he says 'boring, boring, all girls' stuff'. And I think it's really made for girls, cause, knowing, you know a lot of girls watch it.
Interviewer:	Are there other things like that, that you think are mostly for girls?
Hannah:	*Neighbours* is, *EastEnders* is, um. *Grange Hill* is mostly for boys.
Justine:	I think all the soap opera there is more for girls.

As in the girls' discussion of cartoons described in Chapter 3, there is an ongoing debate here about the 'gendering' of texts, and the methods one might use to establish this. In the discussion as a whole, there were a number of attempts to identify the gender of programmes on the basis of content: thus, it was argued that *Ghostbusters* and *Grange Hill* are for boys because they have a lot of fighting in them, or that *Chronicles of Narnia* is for girls because it features few boys and many girl characters — although in each case, these arguments were disputed on the basis that people of the 'wrong' sex actually watch the programmes. Yet the attempt to define the gender of a text on the basis of who watches it — for example in the case here of *My Little Pony*, *Ghostbusters* or *Grange Hill* — was also disputed.

In practice, as is clear both from the anecdotes provided by Hannah and Justine, and from the girls' discussion itself, the attribution of gender is very much a situated judgment. Evaluative judgments about television are used as a means of asserting difference — as in the dismissive comments of the boys reported here — or of maintaining or policing group solidarity. Geraldine's comment here 'Oh god, you are turning into a boy, Hannah!' is a very clear example of the latter process. At the same time, there is a sense in which the girls are able to step outside these definitions, most overtly in Julie's case (it is notable that in earlier discussions she was one of the few girls to express a negative evaluation of soap operas).

In this respect, Justine's reference to *My Little Pony* is particularly interesting, since this was a programme which was in fact never discussed, and only occurred in the context of this more abstract discussion of gender. *My Little Pony* represents a highly stereotyped example of what is 'appropriate' for girls, although it is one which girls of this age have definitely 'outgrown'. Attempting to attribute gender to programmes which they actually watch is a process they find much more complex. Note also that the 'gendering' of 'girls' programmes' which takes place here comes primarily in the form of quotations from boys. In general, it seemed to be easier for the children to attribute programmes to the opposite sex than to claim them for themselves, suggesting that in this context, the definition of that which is 'other' may be more straightforward than any explicit definition of self. Even here, though, there was often dispute: for example, as in this case, there were a number of girls' groups which claimed that certain programmes were only 'for boys', and then disputed this by claiming to watch them themselves.

In the case of both age and gender, therefore, judgments about audience are distinctly problematic. While they do involve an awareness of the nature of texts themselves, and of the institutional contexts from which they derive — for example, in terms of the presumed intentions of their producers, or of scheduling — they are inevitably bound up with questions of social identity. In making these judgments, the children were not simply applying dominant definitions of what is 'appropriate' for adults or for children, for girls or for boys, but actively and consciously negotiating with them — and, on occasion, rejecting them. Making judgments about audience, like categorization in general, needs to be seen not merely as a cognitive process, but also as a social one.

Conclusion

The activity described in this chapter was a comparatively artificial one for the children concerned, and we need to be cautious about how we interpret what took place. As with many similar methods involving sorting or scaling, we should not assume that this kind of activity provides direct access to children's systems of categorization, or that the processes which take place in this context can be generalized to other situations (cf. Messaris and Sarrett, 1981).

As I have argued, it would be mistaken to regard the data as a demonstration of the children's pre-existing 'cognitive understandings'. However, there is undoubtedly evidence here that children progressively acquire (or at least come to use) a *discourse* of genre as they mature — that is, a set of terms which facilitate the process of categorization, or at least make certain kinds of categorization possible. As their repertoire of terms expands, this enables them to identify finer distinctions between programmes, and to compare them in a greater variety of ways. At least some of the older middle-class children here have begun to acknowledge the limitations of the discourse, such as its tendency to emphasize similarity at the expense of difference. Nevertheless, as I have indicated, this discourse is not necessarily synonymous with 'understanding', nor can we point to a steady incremental growth in either.

Perhaps most significantly, however, the data raises the question of the *function* of this discourse. As many of the older children here explicitly acknowledged, the process of generic classification is inherently problematic — not least on an epistemological level. So what functions does it serve?

A partial answer to this question may be found in research which looks at pre-school children. Jaglom and Gardner (1981), in an ethnographic study, found that young children begin to generate programme categories such as advertisements and cartoons at around the ages of 3 and 4. According to these authors, categorization is part of a broader process whereby children develop consistent tastes and preferences, and begin to sort out the relationship between television and the real world. Making generic distinctions enables them to seek out what they like and avoid what they dislike; and it also assists them in knowing what they should trust and what they should not take too seriously. As in these discussions, the question of genre thus inevitably involves judgments about modality and about audience.

More broadly, the existence of generic categories — or, more accurately, the *discourse of generic classification* — enables us to develop expectations about texts which will inevitably determine the ways in which we read them. Using the discourse is a social process — which is maintained, for example, by the media institutions themselves — yet it also serves to regulate the meanings and pleasures texts afford. It thus serves functions which are simultaneously social, cognitive and affective.

As a result, generic classification cannot be seen in isolation, as a purely cognitive process. We need to 'relocate' genre within the broader context of children's attempts to use and make sense of television. Indeed, this is precisely what the children themselves did in the course of this activity. Their attempts at generic classification were inevitably and inextricably bound up with questions of modality, of preference, and of the viewing context. Far from being abstract, their judgments were highly concrete and socially situated. As I shall argue in the following chapters, these assertions are true of children's judgments about television more broadly.

Chapter 7

(Re)telling Stories:
Versions of Narrative

In November 1990, the Broadcasting Standards Council published the first of a series of Working Papers designed to offer 'a continuing contribution to the debate about broadcasting issues'. The paper, entitled *Children, Television and Morality* (Sheppard, 1990), received wide press coverage, much of which focused on its conclusions about children's apparent inadequacies as viewers. The *Observer*, for example, under the headline 'CHILDREN FAIL TO PICK OUT THE TV "BADDIES"', reported that 'children cannot distinguish between reality and fantasy in television drama and soaps', and that their 'comprehension of TV drama is low, particularly when it comes to following plots'.

These kinds of arguments are familiar enough in the ongoing 'debate about broadcasting issues'. Yet they often appear to be based on questionable assumptions, and on some rather inadequate evidence. Like much of the research in this field, *Children, Television and Morality* is based on elementary comprehension tests. It identifies the 'essential' elements or 'key details' of the story and then tests whether children are able to reproduce these on demand. This approach assumes that meanings are inherent in texts, and that children's level of cognitive development can be assessed in terms of their ability to recover those meanings.

The author of the report, Anne Sheppard, is only slightly circumspect about this. On page 15, she describes how the children's answers to comprehension questions were sorted into four categories: 'answer in accordance with researcher's reading of author's intention', 'answer based on excerpt seen', 'other guess or own interpretation' and 'don't know'. By page 16, however, the first category has become 'the "correct" answer', although by page 17 even the inverted commas have been abandoned. The thorny question of intentionality is clearly not an issue here. Sheppard concludes that:

> The findings from this study suggest that, when understanding fails children may evoke their own distorted scenarios, perhaps embodying quite different values and attitudes from those intended by the programme. (p. 27)

However, Sheppard's account of these children watching *The Bill* suggests some other possible reasons for their 'misunderstandings'. She indicates that the children in her sample '*claimed* to be viewers of *The Bill*, so they should have known the policeman about whom the questions were being asked' (page 19, my emphasis) — although, as I have argued, it would be mistaken to take this kind of claim at face value, particularly with more 'adult' programmes such as this. During the viewing itself, however, their attitude was much less enthusiastic:

> Most of the 6–7 year olds, bored by the programme, fidgeted on their seats, dropped things, looked at books or rolled around on the floor. A dramatic event — such as a fire, which occurred in one episode — caught their attention, but during dialogue or other plot subtleties, the children preferred to focus their attention elsewhere. (p. 5)

In this context, it is difficult to see how the children's inability to recall 'key details' or to identify the motives of characters 'correctly' is in any sense an adequate measure of their 'inferential abilities'.

Perhaps the major problem here, however, is Sheppard's assumption that what is important for adults will also be important for children — or that if it is not, then it certainly should be. *The Bill*, for example, is described as 'padded out with subplots and extraneous material': while the children often failed to recall 'essential plot elements', she notes that they were sometimes 'able to describe extraneous scenes in some detail', and often 'wove their own stories' around aspects of the plot, 'developing some themes and ignoring others'. However, she does not describe the method whereby the 'essential plot elements' and 'key details' she is concerned with were identified, nor does she consider the significance of the 'extraneous scenes' or the alternative 'stories' the children developed.

Sheppard herself reads these programmes primarily in terms of personal morality: the most important aspect for children to understand is that some characters are 'good' and some are 'bad', and that their moral motives should be identified and evaluated. If children cannot understand motivation, she concludes, 'they will not be able to distinguish justified actions from unjustified ones' — and will therefore, by implication, be more at risk.

My concern here is not so much that Sheppard 'underestimates' children's abilities but that, like the vast majority of psychological researchers in this field, she effectively ignores what children do in favour of what they do not do. Predictably, what the children actually said is barely reported here, except in the form of very brief exemplary quotations. Quite what was going on in their detailed recall of 'extraneous scenes' or the 'distorted scenarios' they developed remains an intriguing mystery.

The Limits of 'Comprehension'

Sheppard's report is in many respects typical of psychological research on children's understanding of television narrative — and indeed, of narrative more broadly. One major strand of research in this field is based on the notion of 'story grammars'. Using structuralist approaches, researchers attempt to identify an abstract 'deep structure' underlying all simple stories. This model is based on a view of stories as logical sequences of 'problem-solving episodes', which are linked together in hierarchical, tree-like structures (e.g. Rumelhart, 1975, 1977; Thorndyke, 1977; Mandler and Johnson, 1977).

This approach regards comprehension as 'a process of selecting and verifying conceptual schemata to account for the situation (or text) to be understood' (Rumelhart, 1977). In making sense of a story, readers are assumed to encode incoming information by filling 'slots' in their own internal 'story grammars', thereby distinguishing between 'essential' and 'non-essential' elements (Meadowcroft and Reeves, 1989).

In experimental studies, these abstract story grammars are compared with the summaries produced by individual readers (e.g. Bower, 1976; Glenn, 1978). Thus, for example, it is found that the 'essential' elements, at the lower levels of the tree structure, are more likely to be remembered; and that the more schemata required to make sense of a story — for example, where there is more than one protagonist — the less comprehensible it will be. Children's knowledge and use of story grammars is also seen to increase with age (Stein and Glenn, 1979; Poulsen *et al.*, 1979): children who are not familiar with story grammars are more likely to tell 'fractured stories with various elements missing, unexplained or out of order' (Bower, 1976).

While these studies are significantly more rigorous than the rather *ad hoc* approach of Sheppard's research, they do have several limitations. The stories used are often specifically written to conform to the story grammar, and are mostly very simple fables or folk-tales: indeed, many researchers acknowledge that the approach may be much more difficult to apply to more complex stories (see Garnham, 1983). Furthermore, the research is based on recall in artificial test situations, which may be perceived in different ways by different children: older children, for example, may be more aware of the 'informational needs of a tester' and may therefore provide greater detail (Stein and Glenn, 1979; see also Krendl and Watkins, 1983). Finally, there is little acknowledgment here of the role of social variations — for example, of gender or social class. The texts used are assumed to be socially and culturally neutral, and recall is seen as a purely individual process.

Although research on children's comprehension of television has tended to avoid the mechanistic use of story grammars, it would appear to rest on similar assumptions. The work of W. Andrew Collins and his colleagues, for example, has focused on children's ability to distinguish between 'central' and 'peripheral' content, to make 'correct' inferences about the motivations for characters' behaviour, and to identify the causal connections between different episodes in a narrative (e.g. Collins, 1970, 1975; Collins *et al.*, 1974). Like Sheppard (1990), Collins tends to conclude that younger children are relatively incompetent at performing these 'basic' tasks, and thus potentially more vulnerable to the effects of television.

In his more recent work, however, Collins has partly moved beyond this approach, and has adopted a 'script' model of comprehension (e.g. Collins, 1981; Collins and Wellman, 1982). The emphasis here is on the knowledge and expectations which children bring to television, and which they use for example in making predictions or in evaluating characters' behaviour. This knowledge is seen to derive not only from children's past experience of the medium, but also from their general social experience, in which factors such as gender, ethnicity and social class play a significant role (e.g. Newcomb and Collins, 1979; List *et al.*, 1983; Collins, 1983). However, Collins and other psychological researchers in this field have continued to rely on the notion that texts 'contain' meanings which can be objectively defined and 'comprehended'. While they may pay lip service to arguments about children as active processors of meaning, they nevertheless adopt a highly normative view of the ways in which meaning is produced, which assumes that reading — or at least recalling — narrative is fundamentally a logical, intellectual process. Furthermore, by abstracting individuals from the everyday interpersonal situations in which talk about television — and indeed, remembering television — actually occurs, these researchers neglect the *inherently* social nature of the process.

Retelling as 'Collective Remembering'

The retelling of film and television narratives is not an activity that is confined to psychological laboratories. On the contrary, it is very much an everyday social activity, perhaps particularly for children. Certainly, the more open-ended discussions described in Chapter 4 were often dominated by the collective recall of the 'good bits' from the children's favourite films and TV programmes. The children's recall was often extremely precise and graphic: there was a good deal of direct quotation, and the account was frequently accompanied by gestures and sound effects. There was often a strong element of performance here, and, in some cases, retelling took the form of 'acting out', with individuals being assigned 'parts' in the scenario.

While in some instances, individuals might take the floor to retell a story the others had not seen, this was generally a collaborative activity. Significantly, a great deal of this talk was not addressed to the interviewer — and there were often few concessions to the uninitiated. While the older children were more likely to preface or conclude their retelling with evaluative judgments, almost in order to 'justify' them, in most cases it would seem that the activity was undertaken 'for its own sake' — as a means of re-living and sharing past pleasures.

Recent work in social psychology has begun to acknowledge these aspects of the process of remembering. As Derek Edwards and David Middleton (1986) point out, the requirement to produce 'a dispassionately accurate sequential account' of one's past experiences is comparatively rare, at least outside of psychological experiments, and a few formal settings such as police interrogations and witness stands. If we want to investigate how people use their past experiences, including their experiences of media texts, they suggest, 'we must be prepared for the possibility that people are not just trying, and largely failing, to be accurate'. The social context of remembering is not an incidental aspect of the process, or an 'influence' upon it: remembering, like all forms of thinking, is embedded in cultural and communicative forms, and in interpersonal relationships.

In a series of empirical studies, Edwards and Middleton (1986, 1988) have analyzed the ways in which people construct accounts of their shared experiences in conversation (see also Edwards and Mercer, 1987, 1989). Of particular relevance here is their analysis of a group discussion of the feature film *E. T.* (Edwards and Middleton, 1986). They describe a variety of means whereby the group defines and monitors the process of joint recall and establishes a 'mnemonic consensus', a shared unitary account of the text. In requesting assistance or agreement, or in disputing each other's accounts, the speakers use 'metacognitive formulations' ('I don't remember', 'we haven't mentioned', 'he's trying to explain') which effectively 'represent' — rather than merely 'reflect' — their own and each other's cognitive processes.

Many of these phenomena were apparent in the extracts discussed in Chapter 4. There too, the accounts of the programmes in question were essentially *negotiated* between the members of the group. At some points in the discussion, individual memories were disputed, while at others a joint account was built up by one speaker following directly on from the preceding one. As in Edwards and Middleton's account, the texts were also judged in terms of their plausibility, as the participants sought to make what they call 'human sense' of the narrative — a process which they argue is based not on an abstract understanding of the nature of stories (as in the 'story grammar' approach) but on appeals to the general nature of human relations and experience.

Edwards and Middleton (1987) also point to the affective basis of remembering, which they suggest is equally neglected by mainstream psychological research. Affect, they argue, is 'a prime marker of significance, of why things matter to people, of what makes them memorable or worth talking about'. In the *E.T.* study, this was most apparent when the participants abandoned sequential recall in favour of a description of the 'good bits'. Yet as the authors suggest, this is also a social process, in which individual judgments are validated or disputed as the discussion proceeds. The process of collective remembering is determined *by* our interpersonal relationships (for example, in defining what is worth remembering) and yet it also determines the form they take: talking about shared experiences provides a forum in which relationships are consolidated, negotiated and redefined (Edwards and Middleton, 1988). As Middleton and Edwards (1990b, 1990c) suggest, this account of remembering and forgetting as forms of social action is linked to a broader view of thought as a fundamentally discursive and dialogic process — and in this respect, it has much in common with the theories of Vygotsky, Volosinov and Bakhtin.

Social and Cultural Differences in Retelling

One consequence of this approach is that we should *expect* to find social and cultural — and indeed even historical — differences in retelling. Thus, in their study of retellings of an episode of *Dallas*, Liebes and Katz (1990) found notable differences between ethnic groups. While all the retellings were selective, for example choosing to focus on one narrative strand or one character in preference to others, there were systematic differences in terms of their structure and function. For example, Israeli kibbutzniks and Americans were more likely to produce segmented retellings, focusing on the psychological dimensions of the characters: their relationship with the programme was playful and inventive, emphasising the 'openness' of the narrative, and was often keyed to the 'real lives' of the actors in addition to their fictional selves. By contrast, Russian groups tended to leave aside the detail of the story and provide a more 'oppositional' account of its broader ideological themes: their relationship with the programme was decidedly critical, and they tended to regard the narrative as 'closed' and predictable. Liebes and Katz also note the significance of gender differences — with women being more likely to offer segmented, psychological accounts, focusing on 'emotional arousal', while men tended to offer linear retellings of the action.

Likewise, Deborah Tannen (1980) describes some of the cultural differences she found when asking Greek and North American women to retell the story of a short film. While the Americans tended to discuss the film as a film, the Greeks were more likely to talk directly about the events depicted without mentioning that they had occurred in a film. Furthermore, while the Americans were concerned to report the events as accurately and in as much detail as they could, the Greeks tended to 'interpret' the events, ascribing social roles and motivations to the characters, and judging as well as explaining what took place. While the Americans appeared to regard the activity as a memory test, the Greeks saw it as an invitation to tell a story, and were much more likely to focus on their own emotional responses to the film.

Tannen attempts to explain these differences in terms of the participants' different perceptions of the context and of the task at hand. The Americans, she argues, were concerned to present themselves as 'sophisticated movie viewers and more able recallers', while the Greeks wanted to present themselves as 'acute judges of human behaviour and good storytellers'. As she suggests, being the subject of a psychological experiment was a more familiar role for the Americans than for the Greeks. As a result, the Americans tended to adopt 'elaborated' discourse strategies which had much in common with the literate culture of schools, and indeed with those of film criticism; while the Greeks adopted 'restricted' strategies more associated with interaction in the peer group or the home.

The key point here is that these differences cannot be seen as evidence merely of different 'cognitive strategies'. The fact that the Greeks chose not to refer to the fact that the events had been presented in a film did not mean that they had forgotten that they were talking about a film: it was simply that they did not consider this to be appropriate or salient in this context. The differences, Tannen argues, should be traced to differences in 'the conventionalization of appropriate rhetorical forms' — or, in other words, to expected or habitual ways of talking in certain social contexts. Commenting on a film may 'mean' something quite different for people of different cultures — and, we might add, of different social groups. As these studies suggest, retelling needs to be regarded as a social act, which serves specific functions within a given social context.

Keeping Sight of the Text

In rejecting the notion that texts 'contain' a given meaning, however, it would be simplistic to imply that they can mean anything anybody wants them to mean. Texts may well invite a multiplicity of possible readings — and this may be particularly true of more complex texts, as opposed for example to the folk-tales used in 'story grammar' research — but the possibilities here are much less than infinite. Readers may indeed be 'active', but they are active under conditions which are not entirely of their own choosing.

Most of the psychological research I have described tends to keep the text itself constant: it seems to be assumed that the 'stimulus' is somehow neutral. Yet one text cannot stand in for all. The text, and, in certain cases, the 'secondary texts' that surround it, inevitably invite certain kinds of readings and tend to discourage others. The 'force' of this invitation, and the range of possible readings which are made available, will obviously vary. As I have shown, certain texts will explicitly raise issues such as gender or ethnic difference, which may have ambiguous consequences in terms of the social relationships of the group. Likewise, as I argued at the end of Chapter 4, discussions of soap opera are likely to take a very different form from discussions of comedy or horror films, not least because of their differences in narrative structure.

Despite the limitations of structuralist theories of narrative — and especially the more mechanistic notions of 'story grammar' — they do provide a means of analyzing and comparing the versions of narrative children produce. In the account that follows, I will therefore be drawing indirectly on the work of theorists such as Propp (1968), Todorov (1977) and Lévi-Strauss (1963). In particular, I will be distinguishing between the syntagmatic (or 'horizontal') and paradigmatic (or 'vertical') axes of narrative. Briefly, the syntagmatic structure organizes events into a temporal sequence of causes and effects: it often involves the resolution of an enigma or problem, and can be described as a movement from the disruption of an initial equilibrium, towards the establishment of a new equilibrium. The paradigmatic structure establishes resemblances and oppositions between different elements of the narrative, for example events, locations or characters: the closure of a narrative is often one in which fundamental oppositions are resolved. Different genres — and different retellings of the same narrative — will organize the relationships between these two structures in different ways.

Nevertheless, I will be arguing that the act of retelling narrative is inevitably one of *selection* from among the range of possibilities the text provides, and that this selection constitutes an interpretation, a provisional reading, which is inherently social in nature. While I will be comparing these different versions with my own reading of the texts themselves, it is not my intention to judge these in terms of the 'accuracy' of recall, or to regard them as 'misunderstandings' of what we assume to be 'really there'.

The Activity

The retellings to be considered here were obtained in a rather more systematic way than those discussed in Chapter 4. In groups of three or four — some mixed, some single-sex — the children were offered a selection of popular film titles and initially asked to choose one each to talk about. (A brief questionnaire had been used to identify titles which appeared to be popular across the age range.) The children were subsequently asked to select a film of their own choice, or another from the titles remaining. Films were chosen as the focus here primarily on the grounds that they are self-contained texts.

While this activity was less 'spontaneous' than the more open-ended discussions, it appeared to generate a similar degree of enthusiasm. Although the children were invited simply to 'tell us about' the film they had chosen, most of them launched immediately into retelling the narrative, or at least selected parts of it. Significantly, it was only a few of the older, more middle-class children for whom this did not seem to be an automatic expectation: their discussions were often more explicitly evaluative, and at least some of them seemed to be less interested in retelling 'for its own sake'. Although the retelling generally began with a monologue, it usually developed into a collective activity: other children would interrupt to correct or dispute the main speaker's account, and there was often considerable competition for speaking rights.

My analysis here focuses on retellings of four popular Hollywood films:

Honey, I Shrunk the Kids (1989, directed by Joe Johnston); *Who Framed Roger Rabbit?* (1988, directed by Robert Zemeckis); *Twins* (1988, directed by Ivan Reitman); and *Grease* (1978, directed by Randal Kleiser). With the possible exception of *Honey, I Shrunk the Kids*, the children had mostly seen these films on video rather than at the cinema. *Honey, I Shrunk the Kids* and *Grease* were chosen by fifteen and fourteen groups respectively; the others by eleven groups each.

My account of these retellings is intended to be illustrative rather than exhaustive: in each case, I have chosen to focus on a specific aspect of the process, with a view to identifying characteristics that apply more broadly. In each case, I shall begin with a very brief synopsis of the film (based on those published in the *Monthly Film Bulletin*), followed by some indications of a possible structuralist reading of the narrative.

Joint Accounts: *Honey, I Shrunk the Kids*

Synopsis

Inventor Wayne Szalinski has been neglecting his family while he toils in his attic developing a miniaturization ray. His neighbours, Big Russ and Mae Thompson, see him as a dangerous weirdo, and his wife Diane is on the point of leaving him. While Wayne is away presenting his ideas at a conference, one of the Thompson children knocks a baseball into the attic and triggers the shrinking machine. The children, Amy and Nick Szalinski and Little Russ and Ron Thompson, are miniaturized, before Wayne returns despondent from the conference and vandalizes the machine. He unknowingly sweeps up the children and dumps them in a garbage bag at the bottom of the garden. The children escape, and begin their trek through the jungle-like tangle of the Szalinskis' lawn towards the house. They are helped by an ant, who sacrifices himself in a battle with a scorpion, and Amy and Little Russ develop a tentative romance along the way. The Szalinskis eventually realize what has happened and overcome their differences to search for the children. After a narrow escape from a lawn-mower, the children find their way to the breakfast table, where Wayne discovers them just as he is about to eat his son with a spoonful of cereal. The children are restored to their normal size, and the families reunited.

Analysis

On a syntagmatic level, *Honey* features three main narrative strands, which might be described in terms of Todorov's basic model (Todorov, 1977). Predominant amongst these is the adventure narrative. Here, the 'disequilibrium' is initiated by the shrinking of the children, and their journey is essentially a search for a new equilibrium, in which they are restored to normal size. Likewise, the second narrative strand is concerned with the reconstitution and reunification of the family. Prior to the shrinking, both families are seen as dysfunctional, although in different ways. Wayne Szalinski has become alienated from his children, and his marriage is on the point of breaking up. Russ Thompson bullies his son Little Russ, attempting to make him live up to his macho expectations. The final scene, in which both families are seen sharing a giant turkey enlarged by Wayne's machine, is one in which these tensions — and indeed the tensions between the two families themselves — are seen to have been resolved. The third narrative strand, which concerns the romance between Amy and Little Russ, takes a similar structure: here, the narrative follows the conventional pattern in which the obstacles to their relationship — Amy's low opinion of Little Russ, her desire to go to the dance with her boyfriend — are progressively removed.

These different narrative strands also entail paradigmatic relationships. Perhaps the central one here is the opposition between big and small itself, which relates to broader oppositions between adults and children, the powerful and the powerless, and is obviously accentuated by the shrinking of the children. While Nick Szalinski is presented as a smaller version of his father, Little Russ Thompson is constantly taunted by his father for being too small and for not being interested in masculine sporting pursuits — and here their names are clearly significant. A further binary opposition, although it is perhaps rather less developed, is that between the two families. While the Thompsons could be seen as representative of all-American values, for example through their interest in sports, Wayne Szalinski (note the non-Anglo name) is repeatedly described as 'weird' and 'abnormal'. Nevertheless, the two older children, Amy and Little Russ, are to some extent at odds with the values of their parents, and their romance provides further support for the unification of the two families, and the assertion of normal 'good neighbourly' relationships.

Retellings

Honey, I Shrunk the Kids was the most recently released of the four films to be considered here, and appeared to be particularly popular with the younger children. Perhaps as a result, the retellings were often extremely detailed.

I want to focus here primarily on the *social process* of retelling, by considering an extract from a discussion with four 8-year-old girls in the inner-city primary school. This discussion manifests many of the characteristics of collective remembering identified in Edwards and Middleton's (1986) *E.T.* study, described above. The extract begins a short way into their discussion:

Extract 1

Samantha: Because, because there was this because there was this man OK? and he didn't really like them, that man, and there was this boy and he was playing and he wanted to play baseball and he hit the ball on the machine and then, then that shrunk and he and in and um there was this and there was this boy [*laughing*] and the girl was dancing funny with the mop [*others laughing here*] and she was dancing like this [*mimes*] and it was all funny [*laughing*], and it was so FUNNY! And he was looking at her and staring and because he hit the um // the um, this ball on — it wasn't him that was looking at the girl — it was his brother and he hit the ball in the machine because of that // um um there was this little boy and the one who was er doing the experiment and the machine and he went up there to get the ball OK? and then and then he thought and — this is him to the girl [*imitates 'cool' chat line:*] 'Do you want a dance with me on Friday night?' or something [yeah!]. And then, and they went up the room and something happened and they SHRUNK and then the man mashed up the machine and they were saying and then he swept down and they managed to get a knife and cut it, cut something through the blag — black bag and then they um the grass was HORRIBLE and there was this ANT and it was SLIMY [ergh!] [*laughter*], it was all slimy and it showed really big on the camera and it was HORRIBLE and me and my cousin every time we saw it we would cover our faces cause it was all DISGUSTING [*laughing*] and they were friends with the ant and they were saying [*imitates:*] 'He haw, he haw!'. Cause it was running. [Yeah!] and they found this little piece, little piece of um Lego and because they didn't I mean um there was this man and he was smoking and wasn't supposed to be smoking and he threw it on the grass [*laughter*] and then and then it went BUMPH and then and this — the boy who hit the ball into the thing he — he got this stick and he lit a fire so that they could all see where they were going and they saw this Lego — the little boy's Lego that [and they slept in it.

Justine: [The one that had been left on the grass

Samantha: And then and the and the girl was sleeping in the Lego and the boy said 'Ah, I don't mind'. Cause he fell in love with her [*sentimental tone:*] and then they kissed [*laughs*]. They were kissing and then this SCORPION came [Yeah!] and the ant and the scorpion had a fight and it [died

Justine: [and the ant died cause the scorpion killed it.

Samantha: It was sad.

Justine: But I don't know how the scorpion got there. Because it can only get there because you can only get them like in the jungle.

Samantha: Yeah [*concurring*] in the seaside [and all the mud was on it and the dad was looking for it and then the water

Justine: [[. . .]

Samantha: And then it was all [. . .] and then the girl got drowned in this mud stuff [yeah!] [and the boy saved her!

Justine: [in the mud.

Samantha: And because he saved her that's why they were kissing and but it was good [and at the end they turned into real people.

Justine: [[. . .]

Samantha: And the man who didn't like the other man [it was so FUNNY [*laughing*]

Justine: [and he got the machine=

Samantha:	=and he was sitting on this thing and um the boy pressed this thing and then they [. . .] and they nearly fell off the chair again like this [*laughing*], and then he done it again didn't he?
Justine:	Yeah and there was this machine and they made the chicken go really big [on the table
Colette:	[Yeah, what about the breakfast bit?
Justine:	Yeah.
Samantha:	And, and — oh yeah! And the dog found them so he put them on a tongue alright and then he put them on a table and and and um the little boy went into the cereal the boy was eating and he went=
Justine:	=No, the man saw it

Inevitably, this transcription conveys very little of the breathless excitement of Samantha's delivery. As in many of these discussions, there was considerable competition for speaking rights, although at least to start with the others are content to support her without interrupting. Perhaps as a result, Samantha appears to be caught between the pressure to get straight to the 'good bits' — which are primarily the elements of romance, and the 'disgusting' giant insects — and the need to identify the sequence of events and the characters for the benefit of her listeners. Apart from Justine, the only contribution by the other two girls present here is Colette's reference to 'the breakfast bit', which appears on the film trailer: it would be reasonable to assume they have not seen the film, and that Samantha recognizes this. It is also likely that, like the American students in Tannen's (1980) study, she perceives the interviewer as expecting 'accurate' sequential recall, although this had not been explicitly stated.

In her initial monologue, Samantha is trying hard to follow the chronology of the narrative, and she often marks narrative continuity, for example by using phrases like 'and then' and 'so'. Prior to this extract, she had begun her account of the film with the words 'at the beginning', and there is a point here where she appears to have reached the end, and offers a final evaluation: 'but it was good and at the end they turned into real people'. This framing of the task as a sequential reconstruction of the story was generally more explicit with the older children, who tended to offer a summary and then go back to fill in the 'good bits'. Like Samantha, many of the younger children appeared to be diverted from this, and often failed to reach 'the end'.

Despite her enthusiasm, then, Samantha appears to be monitoring her account in an attempt to make it as explicit as possible. The hesitations and false starts at the beginning of the extract reflect her efforts to convey the events in the correct order, and thus to imply their causal relationships: the boy saw the girl dancing with the mop, and then his brother hit the ball through the window, and then they went to the door, and then he asked if she wanted to come to the dance. Similarly, she occasionally 'backtracks' to explain what she has described, for example imitating the children riding the ant and then explaining what they were doing, or talking about how they found the Lego and then explaining how they did so. Likewise, the motivation for the 'kissing' — which features no less than four times in the discussion as a whole — is only explained retrospectively: 'that's why they were kissing'. While the onward rush of her account is occasionally halted by attempts to identify the characters — 'it wasn't him . . . it was his brother', 'the boy who hit the ball into the thing' — and while she makes occasional attempts to check her listeners' understanding — for example using tags like 'OK?' — much of this account probably remains incomprehensible to those who have not seen the film.

Justine's contributions here seem to serve two purposes. While she is occasionally drowned out, Justine is primarily seeking to validate Samantha's account, and her judgment, of the film: she murmurs agreement, and repeats many of her formulations, and only rarely (as in her final statement) actively disputes what she says. At one point here, Samantha explicitly requests her support — 'he done it again, didn't he?' — which Justine interprets as an invitation to move on to the next scene in the narrative. At the same time, Justine seems to be helping Samantha to make her account more explicit — as in her first two contributions here — for the benefit of the others. At times, she takes the initiative, and the two engage in what Edwards and Middleton (1986) call a 'build-up sequence', in which each speaker's contribution builds on the last as they follow a joint course through the narrative, mutually validating each other's contributions. Particularly towards the end of the extract, the girls seem to be actively reminding each other of events they had earlier omitted.

At the same time, there is little explicit 'meta-cognitive' discourse here, of the kind identified by Edwards and Middleton. As they suggest, these kinds of statements may only come into play when recall is perceived as problematic. For example, in a parallel group, Rachel (8) began by saying 'how does it start again, I've forgotten?' Her account in fact began at the end, and only subsequently returned to the beginning. In this case, Samantha's desire to retain speaking rights may well prevent her from making the way in which she is monitoring her own recall explicit.

Ultimately, however, the retelling here is largely guided by the emotional significance of what is described. In this respect, correspondence between the original experience and the recall of it may be less important than the social relationships among the group. There is a strong element of performance in Samantha's account, in which she is seeking to evoke emotional reactions in her listeners similar to those she experienced while viewing the film itself — note her exaggerated mimicry, her use of repetition and her emphatic use of evaluative terms such as 'funny', 'disgusting', 'horrible' and 'sad' to convey her reactions. However, these judgments are not merely individual: they are validated by Samantha's reference to her cousin's reactions, and by the laughter and exclamations of Justine and the others.

As Edwards and Middleton (1986) suggest, while sequential narrative recall serves as one possible frame for joint remembering, groups may prefer to frame and organize their discussion around affective responses and evaluative judgments — and while this depends upon the context, it was particularly true of the younger children here. Indeed, there were some instances in which the children explicitly framed the activity in these terms: Michael (8), for example, began his account of the film by saying 'I'll just tell you all the really exciting bits'. Furthermore, these accounts are often suffused with evaluative judgments, which serve to explain the reasons why these specific events have been selected (cf. Labov, 1972).

Nevertheless, both Samantha and Justine step outside the narrative at a number of points here: Samantha talks about how the insect 'showed really big on the camera', while both girls question the plausibility of the scorpion appearing. As was often the case in discussions of horror films, Samantha also locates her reactions in the viewing context, describing this as a shared experience with her cousin. Here too, laughter and modality judgments seemed to enable the children to distance themselves from experiences which at the time were clearly disturbing.

In terms of the syntagmatic axis of the narrative, the version related by this group is broadly typical of those offered by the younger children, especially the girls. The girls were much more likely to focus on the romance between Amy and Little Russ — this was only mentioned in passing by one of the boys, in a group with two girls — and on their reactions to the death of the ant. Later in the discussion, Samantha and Justine were quite explicit about their interest in this, when asked by the (female) interviewer — although there was a considerable amount of laughter here. Their account is also narrated from the point of view of the children, with the adults more or less omitted: in general, only the older children mentioned the adults, for example in explaining how Wayne Szalinski realized what had happened to his children.

The paradigmatic opposition between 'big' and 'small' rarely featured in such explicit terms. Nevertheless, the incident towards the end of the film in which Wayne tests the machine by shrinking Big Russ Thompson was recalled by a number of groups, as it is here by Samantha (it is the part where 'he nearly fell off the chair'). This incident could be interpreted as a kind of reversal, even a revenge, in that the character who is so concerned to emphasize his 'bigness' is precisely the one who gets shrunk. In a group of 10-year-olds in the same school, an account of this incident led into a sequence in which the girls fantasized about how they wanted to shrink one of their teachers and enlarge their favourite food, and then bury the teacher in a mound of mashed potato. The significance of the diverse ways in which children select and organize 'content' will be considered in more detail in the following sections.

Telling Logics: *Who Framed Roger Rabbit?*

Synopsis

Hollywood, 1947. The film industry depends upon the 'toons' who appear in cartoon movies, and who inhabit a ghetto known as Toontown. Roger Rabbit, a toon star, suspects his wife, the voluptuous singer Jessica, of being unfaithful. Studio boss R.K. Maroon hires detective Eddie Valiant — a washed-up alcoholic since his brother was murdered by a toon — to get evidence that will convince Roger to divorce her. Using a camera borrowed from his former girlfriend Dolores, Eddie photographs Jessica playing pat-a-cake with Marvin Acme, owner of the land on which Toontown is built. Presented with the evidence, Roger is distressed; and later that evening Marvin is murdered. Judge Doom, who has devised a liquid that will kill toons, sets out to capture Roger, with the aid of his weasel squad. Roger takes refuge with Eddie, who discovers that Acme was killed for his will, which leaves Toontown to the toons themselves. Eddie visits Maroon, but he is shot before he can reveal the guilty party. Eddie sees Jessica leaving the scene, and pursues her into Toontown, where she reveals that Maroon blackmailed her into setting up Acme. At a showdown in the Acme warehouse, the villain is revealed as Doom, who plans to demolish Toontown to exploit a new freeway. Before Doom can destroy Roger and Jessica, Eddie overcomes him: it is revealed that Doom is in fact the toon who killed Eddie's brother. Acme's will appears, Eddie and Dolores are reunited and the toons rejoice.

Analysis

Syntagmatically, *Roger Rabbit* is organized around two main narrative strands, which each have dimensions relating to the two central characters, Roger Rabbit and Eddie Valiant. The main investigation narrative — which focuses on the attempt to answer the question posed by the film's title — is complemented by a secondary investigation, to discover the identity of the toon who killed Eddie Valiant's brother. Both are resolved by the final unmasking of Judge Doom. The other main narrative strand is one of romance and is also two-fold: it is resolved in the reunification of Roger and Jessica, and of Eddie and Dolores, as they walk out into Toontown at the end of the film. Both narratives are complicated by the presence of snares and obstacles, such as Roger's mistaken beliefs about Jessica, the disappearance of Marvin Acme's will and the confusion over the identity of Judge Doom. Incidentally, the characters could also be aligned fairly easily with a number of Propp's key 'functions' (Propp, 1968): there is a hero (Valiant), a helper (Roger), a villain (Doom), a dispatcher (Maroon), a donor (Acme) and a princess (Jessica).

Paradigmatically, the major opposition here is between toons and humans. While there can be alliances here, notably between Roger and Eddie Valiant, it is the killing of humans (Eddie's brother and Marvin Acme) by toons that drives the narrative on. Characters who cross these boundaries — Doom, in pretending to be human, and perhaps Jessica in inciting the human lust of Marvin Acme and indeed Eddie himself — are inherently problematic. There is also a certain element of voyeurism in this relationship — for example, in the humans ogling Jessica's performance, or Eddie spying on her and Marvin Acme — and it is significant that Eddie finally turns the tables on Doom by acting like a toon and making his toon weasels laugh themselves to death. The power-relationship between toons and humans might be seen as a metaphor for other inequalities: it is clear that the studios exist by exploiting toons ('they work for peanuts', says R.K. Maroon), and Eddie Valiant's trip through the tunnel into Toontown has the air of a journey into the ghetto.

Retellings

In general, the children's retellings of this film were shorter and more fragmentary than their accounts of *Honey, I Shrunk the Kids*. To a large extent, this may have derived from the greater syntagmatic complexity of the film itself. For example, while many referred to the killing of Eddie Valiant's brother, none of the children in any age group even attempted to explain Judge Doom's motivation for framing Roger Rabbit or for his desire to destroy the toons — which may well reflect the fact that much of this information is conveyed verbally, and quite briefly, in the film itself. Likewise, many of the children conflated the murders of Eddie Valiant's brother and of Marvin Acme, effectively merging the two investigation narratives. While a few of the girls did refer to the character of Jessica — and seemed to enjoy the sexual power of her singing routine — the romantic narratives were generally absent from the discussions. Many of the children explicitly said they could not remember what had happened, or that it was hard to explain.

Nevertheless, there were some clear differences in terms of the *logic* of the retellings themselves — that is, the ways in which the children's accounts were framed and organized, and the principles which seemed to inform this. In this section, I want to concentrate on this issue by comparing extracts from the very beginning of three retellings of the film, one from each of the three age groups. We begin again with Samantha.

Extract 2

Samantha:	Well in the film, there was this man and he was a little bit scary. OK — at the beginning — I forgot what hap — there was this baby and it's a girl and she smokes a cigar, alright, and he had to look, and Roger Rabbit had to look after the baby [. . .] / And um in the bit there's this man with a black hat, I don't know what his name is and there's this boot and it's squeaking on the floor and he picks it up and he puts it in this red stuff and / and I thought that it was blood and it was all horrible and he tries to to get Roger Rabbit and he writes on the — and he writes on this blackboard and it's really squeaky and everybody hates it and they hate him and there are other cartoon characters in it.
Interviewer:	OK! Great, great! What did you like about it? What did you particularly like about it?
Samantha:	I liked it when he turned all flat, the one with the black hat — [yeah] and the eyes popped out.

Samantha's account here focuses on small details from four separate scenes in the film. The first is taken from the cartoon sequence with which the film begins, and which is barely related to the narrative as a whole. Interestingly, this sequence recurred in many of the younger children's retellings, and on a couple of occasions was described in very great detail, to the exclusion of all else — which would suggest that the children's difficulty in relating the narrative was not primarily a failure of memory. For the younger children — especially the boys — this kind of spectacular cartoon violence would appear to have been their major preoccupation here.

Samantha goes on to describe three further scenes which are linked insofar as they all relate to the character of Judge Doom — the 'man' she refers to in her first sentence. Two of these incidents — Judge Doom putting the toons in the liquid, and the scene in which he is flattened — were also recalled by a number of other groups. These scenes do occur in this order in the film itself, and it is notable that Samantha's account begins 'at the beginning'. Nevertheless, she makes little attempt to explain the connections between these scenes, or the reasons why the character behaves in this way, except to say that he is trying to 'get' Roger Rabbit. As in her account of *Honey, I Shrunk the Kids,* Samantha's emphasis is very much on her immediate emotional reactions at the time of viewing — 'I thought that it was blood' — and in particular on the parts she found 'scary' and 'horrible'.

To some extent, all the incidents Samantha describes could be regarded as 'peripheral' rather than 'central' aspects of the narrative. Her account is not organized around any sense of *causal* logic, nor is she noticeably concerned with the motivations of the characters. In these respects, her account is typical of those provided by the 8-year-olds: she would certainly get very low marks in any psychologist's comprehension test. Nevertheless, this would be to ignore the fact that her account is organized in a very different way, and that it is serving quite different functions. While it does possess a certain amount of *sequential* logic, it is primarily organized around her desire to share her *emotional* reactions to the evil character of Judge Doom — and in this, her choice of details to recall would seem to be both deliberate and extremely precise.

Extract 3

Peter (10):   Right in *Roger Rabbit*, right there's this, um, there's this, man whose brother got killed by a cartoon, and this cartoon, um, is a man, but he's really a cartoon [*laughs*] / He's a man but he's a cartoon, so um, so all the man, all the person, all the other brother remembers about him is that he's horrible red eyes, and his laugh, he was laughing HA HA HA HA [*laughter*] and another bit was when Ro, when this man went and took some pictures of this, Jessica, Roger Rabbit's wife, and this other man playing pat-a-cake [*laughter*] / and um, Roger Rabbit started going upset and he had some drink, had some booze [*laughter*] and he started going mad, he went OOH and he, and everything got smashed, he was going mad cause he had that drink so and another bit was when he was um, he was hiding cause they all want to get him cause they want to kill him, and, and um, this man, this cartoon, finds him and he says um do you want your last request 'cause he's going to dunk him in this stuff, it's deadly, it's the cartoon, that's right so um, so he just, he says, the man, says what's your last request and this other man says you want a drink don't you, and Roger Rabbit says no and he says you want a drink don't you and, and he said alright then and he had a drink and he starts going mad and he goes like this on the edge, Roger Rabbit, just in case and then that man gets his legs and / goes into this car, right and, and, there's this cartoon car, right, and it's really funny cause um, there's a car, there's a little alley way about that big, right, you know in real life, right, there's a car coming this way, police car, and, and a motorcycle coming that way and he says press this switch, and he says what one and he says this one, and he presses it and his car goes up in the air and it gets long legs and starts walking over this car right and then, I don't know what happens next.

As in Samantha's account, Peter's version of the narrative is partly guided by a kind of emotional logic. He tends to focus on the more spectacular scenes, and in particular those where the cartoon and live action elements interact — a point he makes explicitly in his account of the car chase. As in Samantha's case, there is a considerable attention to 'peripheral' detail here — most clearly in his extensive use of direct quotation.

Again, the scenes Peter describes do occur in this order in the film, and there is therefore a certain sequential logic here. However, while he seems to define what he is doing in terms of offering a succession of 'good bits' — for example in the way he uses the phrase 'and another bit' — there is also a much greater emphasis on the *causal* logic of the narrative. On one level, this is apparent in the frequency with which Peter uses the word '[be]cause', and his care to explain why the events are occurring. Yet it is also apparent in the way in which the account as a whole is organized. Thus, his initial references are to the killing of Eddie Valiant's brother and the eventual unmasking of Doom — which in effect takes elements out of sequence, and summarizes one of the major strands of the narrative.

This causal logic is also implicit in the scenes he chooses to describe. For example, it is the photographs of Jessica and Marvin Acme playing pat-a-cake that cause Roger to be upset. Furthermore, the two scenes in which Roger Rabbit 'explodes' after having a drink take place some time apart: in relating them, Peter implicitly acknowledges that what Eddie Valiant learns about Roger's reaction to drink in the first scene provides the means to help him escape from the hands of Judge Doom in the second.

Compared with Samantha, Peter appears to make more concessions to listeners who might be unfamiliar with the film, for example by providing a more extensive narrative context for the details that interest him. Furthermore, his account of his own responses is less prominent, and there are more straightforwardly evaluative comments here, which occasionally seem to be offered in order to justify his selection of events (cf. Labov, 1972): note, for example, the way he prefaces his account of the car chase with the phrase 'it's really funny cause . . .'

Extract 4

> *Sally (12):* Well, there's like toons, which are the cartoons, and people, and this, there's this man, who's really evil and horrible, and hates toons, he's got this liquid and he tries to kill them all. If you put them in the liquid, they like disintegrate or something like that. And um / he kills someone, but when the police are like onto the trail, cause he's like a gangster, and the police are onto the trail of him and he lets this big piano on a person's, the man's head, and then they frame Roger Rabbit. And like, there's a policeman who believes Roger Rabbit. And like, the gangster's trying to kill the policeman, and / um / and he's also trying to kill Roger Rabbit as well. But really, at the end, the gangster's like a reformed toon, so in the end he disintegrates as well, but he's got like a mask on so he looks like a human, but he's like an evil toon. All the others are like fun-loving, but he's a different kind. It's hard to explain.

Sally's account is organized in quite a different way from the others. Instead of a selection of more or less isolated 'good bits', what we have here is a summary of the main narrative strands in which spectacular detail is subordinated to explaining motivation and causality. This is apparent, for example, in the frequency with which she describes the characters in terms of their personal attributes — particularly, in this case, Judge Doom. Similarly, while few of the younger children referred to the main investigative narrative — the attempt to discover who framed Roger Rabbit — Sally does at least identify this, even if she fails to explain it fully. In the process, she appears to be less concerned with offering a sequential account, and more with identifying broad oppositions between the characters. Particularly in her opening and closing remarks, Sally also refers explicitly to the *paradigmatic* dimension of the narrative, and the opposition between toons and humans.

Perhaps in the interests of offering a reasonably concise summary, with clear demarcations between 'goodies' and 'baddies', Sally tends to oversimplify some aspects of the narrative: Valiant, for example, is not in fact a policeman, whereas Judge Doom is. She also omits the romantic narrative which runs in parallel. Like the other children, her account is selective, but the selection here is guided much more by a causal narrative logic, and by the wish to identify paradigmatic oppositions, less by the desire to convey her own emotional responses.

To some extent, these three versions of the film are representative of the different 'logics' — or combinations of them — employed by children in their respective age groups. So how might we explain the differences between them? On one level, we could regard them as evidence of cognitive development, for example in the children's ability to infer motivations and to perceive causal connections between events. The problem with this, of course, is that it assumes that this is what the children were trying (and in this case, largely failing) to do.

Clearly, these differences are also to do with context, and with different perceptions of what is possible or appropriate within it. In this instance, the older children — especially the more middle-class ones — seemed to perceive the activity in more 'educational' terms: they were more likely to offer a brief, even dispassionate, summary of the narrative and then go back to 'fill in' the parts they had enjoyed. The 'emotional logic' of the younger children was much less evident here, and often only emerged (as in Edwards and Middleton's *E.T.* study) once the children felt the summary 'task' had been successfully completed.

The different 'logics' I have described here do not simply reflect different cognitive strategies: on the contrary, they are essentially *discursive* strategies, different ways of accounting for one's experience, which in turn serve different social functions. What we are dealing with here is not a matter of individual cognitive competencies, but rather of *communicative* competencies, which are inherently social in nature.

Genre and Gender: *Twins*

Synopsis

Julius Benedict, the product of a secret experiment to produce a perfect genetic specimen, learns that he has a twin brother, Vincent, who was sent to an orphanage, and sets out to find him. Meanwhile, Vincent, pursued by the Klane brothers to whom he owes gambling debts, is arrested for non-payment of hundreds of parking fines. Julius appears to bail him out, and then saves him from one of the

Klanes. Vincent begins to warm to him, and deceives him into helping him steal a car. They meet Linda, Vincent's girlfriend, and her sister Marnie, who takes an instant liking to Julius. Julius discovers that his mother is alive and living in Texas, and believes that her sons died at birth. Meanwhile, Vincent listens to a cassette of instructions in the stolen car, intended for Webster, who was due to deliver it with a stolen prototype engine in the boot to a man in Houston. Vincent decides to complete delivery himself, and Julius, Linda and Marnie join him in order to find the twins' mother. Having seen off the Klane brothers, they find the Benedict Foundation, an artists' colony, but are told their mother is dead. Vincent delivers the car and collects $5 million, but is pursued by Webster. Julius helps him defeat Webster, but makes him return the engine and the money. The woman they had met at the artists' colony reads of their exploit, and reveals herself as their mother. They marry the Mason sisters, and both couples have twins.

Analysis

Syntagmatically, the narrative of *Twins* combines three major strands, which can be distinguished generically. On one level, the film could be described as a melodrama: it is about the reconstitution of a family, and involves the characters discovering their 'true' identities as mother, brother or son, and in the final scene, ensuring the continuity of that family into another generation. It is also a thriller, involving the discovery of a crime, the pursuit of 'good' characters by villains, and the eventual re-establishment of a moral order. Finally, perhaps less prominently, it contains elements of romance: Marnie overcomes Julius's shyness, while Linda eventually tames the wayward Vincent, and both relationships end in marriage.

At the same time, *Twins* is most obviously a comedy, and while comedy is perhaps incidental to the onward movement of the narrative — it is apparent less in what actually occurs than in *how* it occurs — it is central to the paradigmatic opposition between the two brothers. Julius and Vincent are opposites in almost every respect — not only physically (they are played by Arnold Schwarzenegger and Danny de Vito respectively) but also in terms of the values they embody. Julius is intellectually 'perfect', but he has learnt everything from books; he is sexually innocent; he expects other people to be morally good and 'does not believe in violence'. Vincent is the 'genetic rubbish' left over from the experiment; he has learnt about life at first hand; he is sexually experienced, even voracious; and he is a small-time criminal, albeit a comparatively harmless one. The process whereby the two brothers are reunited, and come to learn from each other, effectively resolves these oppositions: as the film progresses, they increasingly adopt the same gestures and mannerisms, and end up wearing identical clothes, in what amounts to a display of male bonding.

Retellings

The diversity, and something of the uneasiness, of *Twins's* attempt to combine these seemingly incompatible elements was certainly reflected in the children's retellings. The syntagmatic structure of the narrative here is comparatively complex, yet to an even greater extent than with the other films, it seemed to be possible for the children to construct quite different versions of its 'content'.

While there were some gender differences in the retellings of *Honey, I Shrunk the Kids* and *Roger Rabbit*, these were much more marked in the case of *Twins*: broadly speaking, while the girls tended to emphasize the elements of melodrama and romance, the boys focused much more exclusively on the thriller narrative, and on the elements of comedy. These differences were certainly apparent in the key incidents which recurred throughout. For example, the boys were more likely to describe scenes involving displays of Julius's physical strength, such as the fight scenes and the incident in which he helps Vincent to steal a car by lifting it in order to turn off the alarm. By contrast, the girls were more likely to describe scenes such as the one in which the twins search for their mother at the artists' colony, and their final reconciliation.

In a number of instances, the children offered apparently 'complete' accounts of the film — at least ones with clear beginnings and endings — in which one of these two elements was omitted. Luke (aged 10), for example, offered a detailed retelling of the thriller narrative, completely ignoring the twins' search for their mother and their respective girlfriends. By contrast, Carol (12) concentrated exclusively on the reconstitution of the family.

At the same time, the extent to which these differences were manifested also depended upon the composition of the groups themselves. This was particularly the case for boys. Boys were less likely to acknowledge these elements of romance and melodrama in all-male groups — as in Luke's case, for example — than they were in mixed groups. Where they were mentioned, they were often disavowed or rejected. For example, David (8) explicitly named the scene 'where they went to find their mother' as his least favourite part. Another group of 12-year-old boys (with a male interviewer) described the reunification as follows:

Extract 5

> *Peter*: They go to this like artists' thing.
>
> *Sean*: And they're told she's dead by their mum, 'cause their mum doesn't think she had any babies, so they go to the um
>
> *Petros*: 'Cause she was told that both of them died at birth.
>
> *Sean*: So she goes to the person who owns the laboratory and punches him in, and Arnold Schwarzenegger goes to the um
>
> *Peter*: No, that's after they visited, they visit her at her art thing.
>
> *Sean*: They both beat the er / doctor up. And then right at the end, both the brothers are in business, and their mum comes along and / it's really, you know, they go sort of really soppy ending, where they start crying and everything.

Here, and in the discussion that followed, the boys felt much more comfortable discussing the violence — indeed, Sean went on to provide a very detailed account of the injuries inflicted on the Klane brothers. By contrast, none of the girls referred to either of the fight scenes described here. While it is acknowledged, the emotional reunification of the family is also explicitly rejected here as 'soppy' — a word characteristically applied to 'feminine' pleasures.

In mixed groups, however, this negotiation was sometimes more explicit.

For example, Pradesh (12) repeatedly interrupted Celia's account of the twins' search for their mother by reminding her that they also found their father, or at least one of them — a scene which was comparatively fleeting in the film itself. This kind of negotiation is also apparent in the following extract, again featuring 12-year-olds with a male interviewer. Here, Simon's account of the film had focused mainly on the comic elements, the fighting and the lifting of the car described above.

Extract 6

Simon:	. . . and there's a bit when they're in this dancing room, and they're both doing their hair the same [yeah] and then they start dancing, and you just see psh! psh! they both slapped the girls' bums [yeah], and they're dancing, they go [*laughs, miming*]
Angela:	They dance together, yeah.
Simon:	Yeah, it's badly funny.
Angela:	It's wicked.
Simon:	And then um / I've forgotten the rest. Then they go to the, this, the lady's house or whatever, and they say she's died, and then, oh, I've forgotten what happens.
Angela:	It's wicked.
Simon:	They all find the mum, live happily ever after. [*laughter*]
Natalie:	Can I say something about that?
Interviewer:	Yeah, all right, go on.
Natalie:	I like the part, oh 'cause I forgot, yeah I like the part when they both get this girlfriend, yeah.
Simon:	And go psh!
Natalie:	No, they stay at this hotel place, and um [*laughs*] She goes to kiss Arnold Schwarzenegger but he don't know how to kiss.
Angela:	Yeah. [And they sleep on the floor.
Simon:	[Oh, yeah. And there's a part in the dancing room when the one who he threw in the lift, he's got like those things round his neck, a broken arm, and he comes back with all of his brothers. And then Arnold Schwarzenegger duffs some of them up and the other one comes with a baseball bat or something to hit him again [*laughter*], and the little one goes BOOF! right in his face, and he goes pff! and smacks right into him and slides down or something, he just pff. I can't say much more about that.

While Simon does refer to the twins' search for their mother, he also attempts to distance himself, firstly by claiming that he has 'forgotten' this part of the film and then by mocking the ending for its implausibility — 'they . . . live happily ever after'. Similarly, his account of the twins' relationship with their girlfriends focuses on the explicitly sexual elements, whereas Natalie rejects this in favour of describing Julius's innocence in his first sexual encounter. In his final contribution, Simon redirects the discussion back to the comic violence with which he had begun.

At the same time, there were mixed groups in which the boys found it easier to describe the melodramatic and romantic elements of the narrative. In the company of two girls, for example, Obinna (12) offered quite a detailed description of the twins' visit to the artists' colony, and of the final reconciliation, completely neglecting the thriller narrative. Similarly, Derek (12), also in the company of two girls, offered the following account of Julius's first sexual experience:

Extract 7

> Derek: . . . and they go in and they meet this er, little one's girlfriend, and he's got, they've got her sister, like she really likes Julian, right, so they go off to this motel [*suppressed laughter from Nancy*]. She falls asleep on his arm like that, [*laughs*] and he gets so nervous that his t-shirt rips, 'cause his muscles start tensing [*laughter*], his t-shirt rips apart. And he goes into the shop to get another one, and the little one goes 'what are all those bumps all over you?' [*laughter*] And they go in, because he's never slept on a real bed, he finds it much better if she sleeps, he sleeps on the floor, right, and he's sharing this room with the er sister, right and she goes 'this bed is too uncomfortable, can I come and sleep on the floor with you?' and he goes 'all right'. And she's lying there smoking, like this, right, and he's going [*mimes Julius's stunned expression*]. It's really funny.

Interestingly, Derek chooses to focus on moments in the film in which Julius's excessive masculinity — and his grotesquely muscular physique — is parodied or undermined. While most of the other boys celebrated his physical strength and his fighting skills, Derek was the only boy who chose to offer a more comic account of his role — a choice which is supported here by the laughter of the girls.

As these examples suggest, the ways in which children select and reconstruct the 'content' of a text relates to broader social factors such as, in this case, gender — although this is also dependent upon the composition of the group. Here again, boys found talking about the emotional relationships between the characters quite difficult, particularly in an all-male group, where they might feel themselves to be putting more at risk (see Buckingham, forthcoming). However, this should not necessarily sanction the conclusion that boys are inherently 'unemotional', or indeed that they suffer from an unhealthy preoccupation with violence. On the contrary, talking about your emotions and talking about violence — or indeed refusing to talk about them — need to be seen as social acts, which define the 'self' in specific ways for the benefit of others. Here again, retelling should be regarded not as evidence of what goes on in children's heads, but as an inherently *communicative* process.

Gender, Sex and Critical Evaluation: *Grease*

Synopsis

On a summer holiday in California, Australian teenager Sandy Olsson meets Danny Zucco, and they fall in love. When her parents decide not to return to

Australia, she enrols at Rydell High School, where she makes friends with the Pink Ladies and their leader Rizzo. They reveal that Danny is the leader of the T-Birds, the school's tough-guy gang. However, Danny is cool and off-hand towards Sandy when they meet again, and she begins dating Tom, a clean-cut athlete. A jealous Danny invites Sandy to a drive-in and offers his ring, but she repels his advances. Meanwhile Rizzo starts having sex with Danny's friend Kenickie, and fears she is pregnant. Danny secretly starts athletics training in the hope of winning Sandy's respect, and he also wins a hot-rod race against the Scorpions, a rival gang. At the graduation dance, Sandy loses Danny to the Scorpions' girl, Cha-Cha, but Sandy enlists Frenchie, another Pink Lady, to transform her into a sexy temptress for the end-of-term carnival, at which Danny appears dressed as a sober athlete. The two are reunited, while Rizzo and Kenickie decide to marry, even though they discover she is not pregnant.

Analysis

The dominant narrative strand in *Grease* is undoubtedly that of the romance between the two central characters, which is set against the developing romances of secondary characters, notably Rizzo and Kenickie. Here too, the characters 'really' love each other, but obstacles have to be removed before they can show this fully and then be reunited. The other main narrative strand — the rivalry between the T-Birds and the Scorpions — is strictly subordinated to this: even Danny's victory in the hot-rod race is seen primarily through Sandy's eyes, and it is this which seems to motivate her transformation at the end of the film.

At the paradigmatic level, however, these relationships possess a strong ideological dimension. While the girls, and particularly Sandy, are interested in romance, the boys are primarily interested in sex. While Sandy identifies with the school culture, the boys are dismissive of this, preferring the 'cool' counter-culture — although there is a distinction here between the comparatively 'safe' T-Birds and the more explicitly delinquent Scorpions. These binary oppositions are constantly reinforced by the intercutting between the boys and the girls which occurs in the first part of the film. At the same time, there is an important opposition here between the characters of Sandy and Rizzo: Sandy is innocent and virginal (she is blonde and wears white) while Rizzo is sexually experienced (she is brunette and wears black or red). The transformations of Sandy and Danny at the end of the film, and Rizzo's decision to marry, represent the dissolution of these oppositions: maturity, it would seem, involves combining 'male' and 'female', 'school' and 'anti-school' values.

At the same time, it is important to note that *Grease* is a musical: the musical numbers arrest the narrative flow, moving beyond the conventions of realism, and flouting the unities of time and space. In addition, the film is set in the past — even if its references are somewhat blurred — and there is a kind of knowing irony here, which is particularly manifested in John Travolta's performance as Danny.

Retellings

If *Twins* was to some extent perceived as a 'boys' film', *Grease* belonged much more strongly to the girls. Despite the age of the film — it was first released before most of these children were born — it often generated considerable enthusiasm, and some very detailed retellings.

As with *Twins*, there were significant gender differences here. In almost every case, the boys identified the car chase as their 'best bit', although this was mentioned much less frequently by the girls. Apart from this, however, the boys were quite reluctant to talk about the film at all, particularly in all-male groups. Norman (aged 8), for example, expressed some enthusiasm for the film, but his account of it was a model of economy: 'it's this film, right, where there's this man, right, and he's all / he keeps on kissing um / girls and they sing songs and all that'. Particularly among the younger children, there was a tendency for the girls to relate their account from Sandy's perspective — 'it's about this girl . . .' — while the boys were more likely to begin, as Norman does here, with the character of Danny.

If the boys seemed to find it impossible to talk about the romantic elements of the narrative, the girls were much more enthusiastic here. Tracey (10), for example, gave an extraordinarily detailed retelling of the film, and described the video as one she would 'treasure for ever'. The songs appeared to be particularly important here: Hannah and Samantha (8) described how they used to 'go around' singing the song 'Summer Loving'.

Interestingly however, in the light of the film's 'gendered' opposition between romance and sex, it was often the more explicitly sexual scenes that were described. For example, the scene in which Danny finally makes advances to Sandy and is rejected was described by a number of the girls: as Michelle (8) twice noted with some excitement, 'his hand went on her boob!' However, the scene which appeared to preoccupy many of the girls was that of Sandy's final transformation into a 'sexy' vamp. A number of the girls acted out her gestures in this scene — particularly the contemptuous way in which she blows smoke in Danny's face — and described her clothes in some detail. While there was often some hilarity here, the majority of the younger girls clearly relished Sandy's new-found sexuality, and her move from adolescent innocence to adulthood, almost as a kind of fantasy of female power (albeit a highly ambiguous one).

This focus on sex was particularly apparent in 8-year-old Julie's account of the film, which began as follows:

Extract 8

Julie:	Well, it's about this um girl right and these boys start teasing her cause she hasn't got a boyfriend and at the last bit she meets this Danny Zucco cause her name's Sandy and um she's dressing up right cause first of all right she had straight hair she looked really ugly and now she had curly hair — she had this like red thing — red track suit on um but — but yeah, then she had red heels — high heel shoes and then um it's quite rude — it's like um // *Dirty Dancing* but it's ruder [*laughs*].
Interviewer:	Why is it even ruder?
Julie:	Because they were kissing in the car and they were [*laughs*] and then she said — and then the girl said cause her name's Riz and the other — I forgot the other one and he says 'Oh call me baby!' [*laughs*]. And showed her this money and and

then he said — then she — then Riz said 'Look!' [*laughs*] [*she mimes their actions*]

Interviewer: Are there any other good bits?

Julie: Yeah, and then er he showed this money and um he said 'I got this when I was a little girl [*laughs*] a boy!' and then um and then // then Riz said 'What?' cause he looked like this [*mimes*] and he said 'It's broke!'. And then, and then the um woman said 'But how?'. And then he said 'I don't know'. And then she went, 'Ooooh!' [*laughs*], then Riz just went 'Oh!'.

Julie goes straight to the transformation scene at the end of the film, providing minimal narrative context. She refers to Sandy's previous appearance simply as 'ugly' — a rather negative evaluation of what I have described as virginal innocence! Interestingly, she also recalls Sandy's costume inaccurately — she is in fact wearing black, not red, which is the colour worn by the much more overtly sexual character of Cha-Cha.

The remainder of Julie's account is hard to follow, although there may be a number of reasons for this. The second scene she is describing here (from 'because they were kissing in the car' to the end of the extract) is one in which Kenickie's condom breaks as he is making out with Rizzo in the back of his car. Of course, it may be that Julie has forgotten the details of the scene, or doesn't fully understand it — for example, what Kenickie shows her is not in fact money, but the condom. However, she may also be being deliberately evasive, perhaps in order to avoid possible censure from the interviewer.

In the remainder of this discussion, Julie referred to a number of other 'rude' scenes from the film, such as the one in which one of the boys crawls under a bench to look up some girls' dresses, and where a group of the T-Birds 'moon' at the high school dance. She also repeated with great emphasis the line with which Sandy begins the final song — 'tell me about it, STUD!'

This was far from being the only occasion on which Julie engaged in 'sex talk' — in fact, it often seemed to be her major preoccupation. While one might speculate about the causes of this, it does serve specific social functions here. Rather like the younger boys' discussions of horror movies, sex talk of this kind seems to transgress many of the implicit 'rules' of adult–child interaction. It enables Julie to present herself as 'adult', and to challenge what she might perceive as the interviewer's expectations — although there is undoubtedly a degree of hesitancy here. In many respects, it seems to give her considerable power, not least in ensuring that she can hold the floor. While this extract is taken from an all-girls group with a female interviewer, the presence of boys or a male interviewer seemed to make little difference here. Indeed, in one of the early discussions, Julie directly challenged a boy who suggested there was 'too much sex' in *Home and Away* by exclaiming 'you don't know what that means!' and proceeding to humiliate him into revealing the depth of his ignorance.

If Julie's emphasis on the sexual content of the film seems implicitly to challenge the paradigmatic oppositions identified above, many of the older girls were much more forthright in their critique of the film. While some of this criticism centred on the quality of the acting, and indeed the casting — John Travolta was seen as being much too old for his part, for example — these children were also very critical of the 'predictable' nature of the narrative. While the younger children tended to frame their retellings as a series of 'good bits', as Julie does, or alternatively to organize these around their rendering of the songs, the older children were more likely to offer brief summaries of the narrative which emphasized its schematic approach, and were often distinctly ironical. The following extract, featuring 12-year-olds, illustrates this:

Extract 9

Sally:	I didn't like it much either, cause it had this really rubbish story, it's really like predictable.
Interviewer:	So tell me what happens, it's kind of.
Sally:	Well it's about a sort of boring posh girl, and then she sort of gradually changes and becomes all sort of cool dude-ish [*laughter*]. And then um like no-one liked her at the beginning, cause when she was on holiday she fell in love with John Travolta, and she thought like they were going out, and when they got back to school, he ignored her, so she was sort of changing so he'd notice her. And in *Grease 2*, it's the same but like there's a boring boy and the girl is like all cool. It's virtually the same.
Interviewer:	So when you said you thought it was predictable, I mean, what=
Sally:	=Well they just like, they fall in love and sing a couple of songs, and that's it [*laughter*]. I just don't like that kind of thing.

As in most of the older children's discussions, this group begins with a brief summary of the narrative structure of the film, which is subsequently filled in with details. This was reinforced in many cases by comparison with the sequel *Grease 2*, which was often accused of being 'the same' but 'the other way round'. The older children were also much readier to describe the characters in terms of simple attributes — 'innocent', 'plain', 'boring', 'posh' and so on — and in some cases, ironically — for example, Sally's 'cool dude-ish'. In many cases, the happy ending was also described with considerable sarcasm, rather than accorded major emotional significance.

These children clearly perceive the narrative as a kind of formula, and the characters as functions within it. Yet to some extent, this may also reflect a kind of 'knowing' irony which is characteristic of the film itself. For example, Navin (12) explicitly said she liked the film 'because they were all trying to be really cool and they looked really stupid' — which she felt was a deliberate strategy on the part of the film-makers.

Yet among the older girls, there was also an implicit disengagement from — if not an overt rejection of — the values the film appears to embody. While many claimed to enjoy the songs — and in some cases offered approximate renditions of their favourites — the romance between the characters was generally rejected as merely 'corny'. Furthermore, while the children acknowledged that both Danny and Sandy had changed by the end of the film, they placed a greater emphasis on Sandy's much more dramatic transformation. Yet Carol (12) explicitly acknowledged the imbalance here: 'he changes to please her, but they just ended with her pleasing him, innit?' Regardless of the gender of the interviewer, it was usually the girls who led this critique of the film.

While it would be overstating the case to suggest that *Grease* was taken very seriously by any of the children, the girls certainly seemed to have more invested here, both positively and negatively. If the boys may have attempted to deal with the issues of romance and sexuality by ignoring them, the older girls had more at stake in directly confronting the ideology on which they felt the film was based.

Conclusion

In this chapter, I have argued for a view of retelling as a social, discursive activity, rather than a matter of individual cognitive processing. While it could be argued that retelling has cognitive functions — for example in helping us to 'sort out what happened' in a text, or to make inferences which go beyond what is shown — these cannot be separated from its social and affective dimensions. Retelling is primarily about re-living and sharing pleasure, in order to affect others and to define oneself. To judge it simply in terms of its accuracy as a means of recovering 'the researcher's reading of the author's intention' is thus reductive, to say the least.

As I have shown, the nature of a retelling will depend upon a number of interrelated factors. We might identify these in terms of the interaction between relations, subjects and contents, described in Chapter 4. Thus, the existing social relationships between the participants will to some extent determine how the activity itself is perceived and framed. In this case, for example, the older children generally seemed to observe narrative continuity more faithfully then the younger ones, although this may partly have been because they perceived this to be a requirement on the part of the interviewer. Similarly, where a text is unfamiliar to our listeners — for example as it was in the case of Samantha's account of *Honey, I Shrunk the Kids* — we may need to monitor our account quite carefully, taking care to explain the context of events, and to identify a causal logic. Where a text is more familiar — as in the case of most of the versions of *Who Framed Roger Rabbit?* — it may be possible to go straight to the 'good bits' without bothering to construct a complete or sequential story.

In producing a version of a narrative, we are simultaneously defining our own social position, and potentially that of our listeners. For example, there were significant differences here between the boys' and the girls' retellings of *Twins* and *Grease*, but these also varied according to the composition of the groups. Proclaiming an interest in sex or violence, or rejecting or refusing to consider the romantic or melodramatic aspects of a narrative, can be a means of asserting a 'subject position' and thereby of claiming social power.

At the same time, the specific social differences which are perceived as important will depend upon the nature of the 'content' — in this case, the texts themselves. For example, the almost schematic nature of the paradigmatic oppositions in *Grease* effectively embodies an ideology which the girls in particular sought to redefine and in some cases to reject — although the elements of irony which I have detected in the film itself may well have made this more possible. Similarly, *Twins* is a text which at least makes possible the differentiated readings I have identified, through its combination of syntagmatic narrative strands. While popular texts of this kind are more likely to offer 'invitations' to readers, rather than to exert active compulsion, they cannot be seen as socially or culturally neutral.

For all these reasons, therefore, retellings are likely to be extremely diverse. They will not necessarily be sequential or complete; they will not necessarily focus on 'essential' rather than 'peripheral' elements, even assuming we can agree what these are; and they will not necessarily reflect an abstract 'narrative grammar' which emphasizes causality and character motivation. To judge children's retellings in terms of their failure to manifest these characteristics — and to regard this failure as evidence of their cognitive inadequacies — is to ignore the complexity of the process.

Chapter 8

The Self and Others: Reading Television People

COUNT DUCKULA. Children like his mordant wit and psycho-socio-logical subtext . . . adults just laugh at the jokes. (Advertisement for Independent Television children's programmes, 1990)

Critics of television often describe its pleasures as merely 'vicarious'. Television, it is argued, is a substitute for real, personal experience. It enables us to step into other people's shoes, to share their emotions and experiences without having to suffer the consequences. Television can provide a kind of wish-fulfilment, in which we escape temporarily from ourselves and become the kind of person we aspire to be. Alternatively, it may offer us idealized images of our own lives, in which characters like ourselves discover fantasy solutions to our everyday problems and predicaments. It is through this process of 'identification' that television is often seen to exert its influence upon our values and beliefs.

For example, much of the press coverage of the series *thirtysomething* appears to be premised on this assumption. Reviewers often seem to imply that the programme serves as a kind of 'bible' for a generation, a primer on how to behave: by inviting us to recognize and identify with these 'representative' characters and their dilemmas, it encourages us to share their view of the world. An ensemble cast, it is suggested, offers a greater potential for identification, reflecting different aspects of our personalities: one week we can identify with Michael, the following week with Elliott.

As a 'thirtysomething' myself — that is, as a member of the upmarket thirties audience the programme seems to be aimed at, if not perhaps as affluent or as good-looking — I have experienced a deeply ambivalent response. On the one hand, at least some of the dilemmas and experiences of the characters have been very close to my own: the episode which featured the birth of Gary and Susannah's child, and concentrated on the man's feelings of exclusion and inadequacy, was screened only a couple of months after the birth of my own second child. Yet on the other hand, I am repelled by the programme, both on a political level — it seems to me a crude attempt to recuperate the 'sixties generation' into a right-wing view of sexual and family politics — and on the level of 'taste' — I loathe the programme's pretensions to serious drama, its self-consciousness, its lack of irony and its restrained 'good taste'. And yet . . . there was certainly a time when I *had* to watch it.

In offering this account of my reactions, I am obviously giving the reader hostages to fortune. You know a lot more about me now — or you think you do — than I might have revealed through a more academic account. Yet this is precisely my point. Talking about our preferences, talking about the characters we like, seems to say a lot about ourselves, or at least our perception of ourselves; and we know this. I say 'seems to' because I'm not ultimately sure that it does: the crux is surely that it is *perceived* to do so, largely because of the power of the commonsense notion of 'identification'. If I tell you that I like Michael in *thirtysomething*, or alternatively that I like Arnold Schwarzenegger or Sylvester Stallone, you are likely to assume that I 'identify' with those people — that I would like to be like them, or that in some way I think I already am. You are likely to assume that I am offering you a definition of myself, not least in terms of my perception of my own 'masculinity', whether consciously or not: you will read my tastes and position me accordingly.

In the case of my reactions to *thirtysomething*, and I would argue in most cases, this is much more than a 'personal' process. My ambivalence about identification — my uneasy mixture of emotional empathy and distanced critical judgment — may reflect a specifically 'male' style of reading. I also suspect that my reactions reflect my own ambivalence in terms of social class. Recognizing myself as a *thirtysomething* viewer means recognizing myself as middle-class — partly because the characters in the programme are exclusively middle-class, and because the target audience (and, I would suspect, the actual audience, which in Britain is comparatively small) is predominantly so. I find this difficult, not so much because of some sentimental wish to assert a solidarity with 'the people' (although like many socialists, this is certainly something to which I am prone) but mainly because my own class origins are not comfortably middle-class. Recognizing myself as middle-class means acknowledging my own upward mobility, and the feelings of inadequacy which accompany it.

Of course, the fact that somebody claims to watch a given television programme, or that they say they like a specific character, may not necessarily tell us anything about them. Yet the fact is that tastes and preferences are generally *perceived* in this way, as indicators of 'personality' or 'self-image', or alternatively as reflections of the speaker's perception of their own social position, for example in terms of age, race, gender and class. Taste, as Bourdieu (1984) amply demonstrates, is not a reflection of some inner essence: on the contrary, it is about claiming particular social affiliations, whether consciously or not. In implying that we 'identify' with people on television, it would seem, we may also be 'identifying' ourselves for the benefit of others.

Identification

This notion of identification certainly underlies most psychological research on children's reading of television characters. For example, the classic study here, Maccoby and Wilson (1957), rests on three main assertions: that viewers will identify with one main protagonist; that they will identify with characters like themselves, or alternatively with those they aspire to be like; and that they will feel what is happening to the character as if it was happening to them.

Identification is clearly seen by these researchers as the precondition for imitation — and, predictably, it is the imitation of 'aggressive' or 'anti-social' behaviour which is often the primary concern (e.g. Meyer, 1973; Donohue, 1975). This approach derives explicitly from the social learning theory of Albert Bandura (e.g. 1965), in which 'cognitive processing' is seen as a 'mediating variable' in what is otherwise defined as a process of direct stimulus–response.

Thus, according to Byron Reeves (1979):

> The primary rationale for studying perceptions of television characters has been to study the attributes of characters which are related to children's desires to model their behavior. Consequently, most of the research in this area has actually taken as a starting point children's desires to identify with characters and then asked which attributes of the characters are related to that attraction. (pp. 132–3)

Yet what is essentially lacking in this research is any questioning — or even any sustained description — of the central concept of identification itself. As Martin Barker (1989) argues, identification is typically seen as a kind of 'trick process' whereby the media exert their noxious ideological effects: in stepping into the shoes of a character, in playing their role, we also take on their values, often without being conscious of the fact.

Barker traces the use of the concept through nineteenth-century 'moral panics' about the impact of 'Penny Dreadfuls'. He argues that fears about 'identification' arose from a broader anxiety about working-class behaviour: it enabled 'violence' to be interpreted, not as a form of collective resistance to people's conditions of life, but as an individual problem produced by the exposure to 'bad media'. Underlying the notion of identification is the idea that human beings are essentially 'devils constrained by a veneer of civilization': identification bypasses or overcomes these rational controls, and leaves us prey to irrational instincts. The implicit conclusion here would seem to be that access to imaginative media needs to be controlled by those who 'know better'.

Barker argues that these assumptions also underlie the way in which the concept is used in psychological research, and that it tends to result in arbitrary readings both of texts and of readers' responses to them. Yet, as I have implied, 'identification' is a commonsense notion which may play a crucial role in the ways in which we account for our own and others' relationship with television. Even if viewers do not in fact 'identify' with characters in this way, they may well assume that other people do: and this fact alone may significantly determine what they say.

The Activity

The activity to be described in this chapter was based around the discussion of liked and disliked characters (to include 'real people' such as presenters), drawn partly from a selection of photographs which were provided (see Table 8.1).

The children were asked to nominate a 'favourite' character of their own choosing, and subsequently to select one they liked and one they disliked from the pictures provided. In each case, they were asked to say what they liked or disliked about the character and what they did. This implicitly invited a wide range of

Table 8.1   List of characters/people provided

Male	Female
Mitch (*Baywatch*)	Carly (*Home and Away*)
Edd the Duck (presenter)*	Dot Cotton (*EastEnders*)
Todd (*Neighbours*)	Cilla Black (presenter)
Burnside (*The Bill*)	Rudy (*The Cosby Show*)*+
Philip Schofield (presenter)	Bobby (*Home and Away*)
Sooty (*The Sooty Show*)*	Sharon/Tracey (*Birds of a Feather*)*
Baldrick (*Blackadder*)*	Oprah Winfrey (presenter)+
Desmond (*Desmonds*)*+	Roseanne (*Roseanne*)*
Count Duckula (*Count Duckula*)*	Nanny (*Count Duckula*)*

Totals
9 male characters, 9 female characters
9 comic characters (*), 9 non-comic characters
3 black characters (+)

possible responses, including descriptions, retellings, imitations, and straight-forward evaluative comments, as well as more general statements about the characters as representatives of broader social groups. The children were interviewed in both mixed and single-sex groups.

In the following three sections of this chapter, I want to explore a series of issues which have been raised by previous psychological research in this area: I will be using my own quantitative data, although my primary aim is to contest some of the assumptions which often underlie the use of this kind of data in this field. In subsequent sections, I shall offer a qualitative analysis of some of the data, and consider the insights which might be derived from this approach. Here again, the data raises some fundamental questions about what we might mean by the notion of 'understanding' character, and indeed by the concept of 'character' itself.

Gender and 'Identification'

A good deal of previous research has argued that gender is a major factor in 'identification' with television characters. In general, this research suggests that children are more likely to 'identify' with same-sex models — or at least to say that they like them, which is not quite the same thing. However, Reeves and Miller (1978) find that boys are likely to identify more strongly with *all* TV characters, and more strongly with same-sex models than girls. As they indicate, this may partly reflect the more limited range of identification figures available to girls, given the male bias of TV itself — although it may also reflect the more limited range of female characters which the children were actually offered in the research (see also Miller and Reeves, 1976; Lonial and van Auken, 1986). Girls, they suggest, are more likely to identify with male characters than boys with female characters, particularly as they get older, which may reflect the greater rigidity of male gender roles (cf. Durkin, 1985). Reeves and Greenberg (1977) also find that the attributes which tend to be rated highly also reflect established gender roles. Thus, boys rate physical strength and activity highly, while girls rate physical attractiveness highly.

More significantly, Reeves (1979) finds that girls use a greater range of attributes and psychological terms in describing characters than boys, and also appear to comment on and account for conflicting behaviours more. Reeves suggests that this may reflect their greater 'verbal skills', although it also raises the more far-reaching possibility that discourse about character may itself be gendered — that the social experiences of boys and girls make available rather different ways of accounting for characters and their behaviour.

Nevertheless, there are some significant problems in terms of how we measure these kinds of phenomena, let alone how we explain them. For example, the research conducted here could be rendered in statistical terms, in order to identify these differences. Table 8.2 shows the numbers and percentages of characters named by girls and boys in the sample, while Table 8.3 classifies these characters in terms of gender.

Table 8.2   Characters named, by gender

School/Group	Likes/favourites			Dislikes		
	Total	% by boys	% by girls	Total	% by boys	% by girls
Suburban: 8-yr-olds	59	37	63	17	29	61
Suburban: 10-yr-olds	49	61	39	17	47	53
Inner-city: 8-yr-olds	31	42	58	14	36	64
Inner-city: 10-yr-olds	26	50	50	5	40	60
Suburban: 12-yr-olds	43	60	40	18	50	50
Inner-city: 12-yr-olds	72	42	58	26	65	35
Overall total	280			97		
Average %		49	51		45	55

Table 8.3   Characters named as likes/favourites and dislikes, by gender

School/Group	Likes/Favourites		Dislikdes	
	% male	% female	% male	% female
Suburban: 8-yr-old girls	70	30	33	67
Suburban: 10-yr-old girls	63	37	56	44
Inner-city: 8-yr-old girls	61	39	56	44
Inner-city: 10-yr-old girls	54	46	33	67
Suburban: 12-yr- old girls	47	53	56	44
Inner-city: 12-yr-old girls	57	43	56	44
Average: girls	59	41	48	52
Suburban: 8-yr-old boys	73	27	0	100
Suburban: 10-yr-old boys	83	17	38	62
Inner-city: 8-yr-old boys	85	15	0	100
Inner-city: 10-yr-old boys	100	0	50	50
Suburban: 12-yr-old boys	81	19	44	56
Inner-city: 12-yr-old boys	77	23	53	47
Average: boys	83	17	31	69

These figures could be taken to prove a number of points. Table 8.2 shows that boys were as likely as girls to identify likes or favourites, although less likely to identify dislikes. However, boys' tendency to offer dislikes increased with age relative to girls'.

Table 8.3 shows that both girls and boys were more likely to choose male characters as likes or favourites, although this tendency was much more marked among boys. Girls' tendency to make same-sex choices increased with age, although not wholly consistently. In terms of dislikes, girls' choices were equally balanced, although boys were much more likely to name female characters, with some decline as they got older.

These findings can be related to those of previous research, noted above. Table 8.2 would suggest that, at least in terms of the number of choices, these boys were certainly no more 'preoccupied' with TV characters than girls — a finding which contradicts some previous research (e.g. Miller and Reeves, 1976). On the other hand, Table 8.3 would seem to confirm boys' stronger interest in same-sex characters, as compared with girls. This is particularly notable given that the children were presented with equal numbers of male and female characters (cf. Miller and Reeves, 1976). At the same time, the figures would seem to contradict the finding that girls' tendency to make same-sex choices decreases with age (e.g. Lonial and van Auken, 1986). As I shall indicate, a qualitative reading of the data suggests that at least some older girls were consciously opting for female characters, and that this was informed by more or less explicit understandings about gender representation.

Nevertheless, these figures should be interpreted with caution, for a number of reasons. To begin with, the research used a comparatively small sample — although not much smaller than is often used in mainstream psychological research. Untypical reactions on the part of a single group can skew the results, and this is apparent in some cases here. More significantly, the statistics effectively ignore the different meanings which children might attach to the statement 'I like . . .' or 'I dislike . . .' For example, if girls were to say they 'like' Philip Schofield or Mitch from *Baywatch*, this would probably be very different from saying they 'like' Burnside from *The Bill* or Desmond: while there were often quite fierce debates about the physical attractiveness of the former pair, the issue was rarely raised in relation to the latter. Furthermore, saying you 'dislike' Cilla Black is rather different from saying that you 'dislike' Burnside or even Dot Cotton, fictional characters who are to some extent presented as unsympathetic in the first place.

Similarly, the distinction between 'male' and 'female' may carry quite different meanings in different contexts. For example, if boys express a liking for Edd the Duck or Baldrick from *Blackadder*, this is likely to mean something very different from saying they like Charles Bronson or Arnold Schwarzenegger: while they are all 'male', these characters are not all 'masculine' in quite the same way. Finally, to categorize children's responses solely in these terms is to neglect the other reasons which might inform their choices: for example, if black girls opt for black male characters, the 'maleness' of those characters is perhaps not the most significant characteristic for them. In an activity like this, characters may be chosen for a variety of reasons, and often for several reasons simultaneously (cf. Durkin, 1985).

Ultimately, then, these statistics ignore some very fundamental distinctions.

In no way do they sanction conclusions about 'identification' or 'modelling', or about the role of television in forming or indeed subverting sex-role stereotypes. We need to make much finer distinctions between characters, which take account of what characters mean to the children who choose them. Even basic terms such as 'like' and 'dislike' or 'male' and 'female' need to be defined much more closely: again, we cannot assume that these mean the same thing to different people or in different contexts.

Before moving on, I would like to consider two further sets of statistics. The first concerns the 'attributes' children attach to characters: I will have more to say on this in due course, but one specific attribute has particular relevance to this discussion, namely that of 'physical attractiveness'. Table 8.4 shows the number of references to 'physical attractiveness' made by boys and girls in each age group: these include only explicitly evaluative comments, both positive and negative, and exclude non-evaluative descriptions.

The second set of statistics relates not to gender but to 'race'. Three black characters were deliberately included in the selection presented; and further ones were nominated by the children themselves as 'favourites'. Table 8.5 records the percentage of black characters nominated by black and white children in each school: the definition of 'black' here includes Asian, Afro-Caribbean and African children.

Table 8.4   References to physical attractiveness

	Percentages	
	Boys	**Girls**
8-yr-olds		
Positive comments	0	100
Negative comments	0	100
10-yr-olds		
Positive comments	25	75
Negative comments	39	61
12-yr-olds		
Positive comments	19	81
Negative comments	57	43

Table 8.5   Black characters named as likes/favourites

	% black children in group	% of total named by black children	% of total named by white children
Suburban primary school	13	0	7
Inner-city primary school	66	43	15
Suburban secondary school	13	0	19
Inner-city secondary school	53	32	18

Previous research would suggest that girls are more likely to evaluate characters in terms of their 'physical attractiveness': and this was undoubtedly the case here, as Table 8.4 shows. However, there is a considerable disparity here between positive and negative judgments. While boys make very few positive judgments in any age group, they become progressively more likely to make negative judgments, and in the oldest age group here actually make more than the girls.

While there has been little research on black children's perceptions of TV characters, the 'identification' hypothesis which recurs throughout the research on gender would lead us to expect that black children would be more likely to choose black characters (cf. Donohue, 1975). As Table 8.5 shows, this is partly the case here, although there is an interesting anomaly: black children in schools where they represent a minority are in fact *less* likely to choose black characters, even compared with white children in the same schools.

How might we explain these anomalies? Previous researchers have suggested that girls rate 'physical attractiveness' more highly than boys, and that this is a result of their socialization. This is, I would suggest, a rather dubious assumption anyway, but it certainly does not help to explain the significant increase in boys' negative comments here. Note that their positive comments do not increase, only the negative ones: 'physical attractiveness' *is* a salient attribute for them, but their judgments of it are almost entirely negative.

I would argue that we can only explain this anomaly in terms of the context in which these statements are made. Girls may be putting themselves 'at risk' to a much lesser extent than boys, especially when it comes to expressing a positive evaluation of a character's attractiveness. In these discussions, boys never referred to a male character as physically attractive, except where they described this as an opinion held by girls (and from which they generally dissented): on the basis of a qualitative analysis (see below), I would suggest this was largely a result of the fear of being labelled homosexual by other boys in the group. The equivalent anxiety did not seem to arise for girls.

Similarly, it was much easier for girls to describe male characters as attractive than for boys to describe female characters in this way. The very few admissions by boys that they 'fancied' a female character were almost always surrounded with embarrassment or mockery from other boys. There was a sense of 'exposure' about these moments, at which 'authentic' masculinity was somehow strangely at risk (see Buckingham, forthcoming).

The anomaly surrounding black characters can perhaps be explained in a similar way. As I have noted, there may be a great deal at stake for black children in raising questions of 'race' and ethnicity, particularly where they are in a minority. 'Announcing' one's blackness — for example through expressing a preference for a black character — can be a very powerful discursive move when one is in a position of some strength, although in other situations it can prove extremely fraught.

In both instances, therefore, apparent anomalies can only be explained by reference to the context in which these statements are made. Race and gender are not absolute categories, which possess fixed meanings: on the contrary, they can be emphasized or effaced, defined and redefined, in a variety of ways for different purposes.

Modality and Humour

Modality is likely to be a key element in children's judgments of television characters, and one which undermines simple assertions about 'identification'.

Table 8.6 People nominated as favourites, actors versus characters; and explicit references to 'acting'

School/Group	% as actors	% as characters	References to 'acting'
Suburban: 8-yr-olds	67	33	1
Inner-city: 8-yr-olds	50	50	2
Average: 8-yr-olds	59	41	
Suburban: 10-yr-olds	80	20	2
Inner-city: 10-yr-olds	100	0	1
Average: 10-yr-olds	90	10	
Suburban: 12-yr-olds	73	27	19
Inner-city: 12-yr-olds	61	39	15
Average: 12-yr-olds	67	33	

Children are likely to make distinctions between 'realistic' and 'unrealistic' or 'comic' and 'serious' characters, and to judge them accordingly. In this case, the children were deliberately presented with cartoon and puppet characters as well as presenters and 'realistic' characters, and with 'comic' and 'non-comic' characters.

Nevertheless, much of the research on this issue remains premised on the notion of identification. David Fernie (1981), for example, finds that younger children are more likely to 'identify' with characters he defines as 'unrealistic', and will also say that the characters are like them. Older children will still 'identify', but will be aware that these characters are 'unrealistic', indicating that their identification has become, in Fernie's terms, more 'differentiated'.

While this activity did not explicitly address these questions, many of the children here nominated actors rather than characters in response to the initial invitation to name a favourite 'person' on television. As Table 8.6 shows, there were no clear tendencies here in terms of age, although it was certainly the case that older children were more likely to refer to the quality of 'acting' in support of their judgments. Among the younger groups, there were as few as six clear references to 'acting' throughout all the discussions, although the older children engaged in a number of extended debates about this.

Here again, these statistics should be interpreted with some caution. While children may perceive these distinctions, they may be much less significant for them than they are for adults; and they may perceive or (crucially) describe them in a different way, depending upon how they perceive the task or the situation. Furthermore, these distinctions may be less than clear-cut in practice. With more 'realistic' characters, particularly those in long-running series, the distinction between actor and character may be less significant than it is for less 'realistic' characters, or those in one-off dramas or films. Larry Hagman 'is' J.R. Ewing, whereas Eddie Murphy remains Eddie Murphy, irrespective of the role he may happen to be playing.

In accounting for these choices, we need to make finer distinctions between characters, and take the social functions of this kind of talk into account. Talking about actors rather than characters 'positions' the speaker, both in relation to others in the group and in more general social terms. Saying you like Harrison Ford because you think he's a good actor effectively absolves you from any accusation that you 'identify' with him — that you would like to be like him, or that

Table 8.7   Characters nominated, comic versus non-comic

| | Percentages | | | |
| | Likes/Favourites | | Dislikes | |
School/Group	% comic	% non-comic	% comic	% non-comic
Suburban: 8-yr-old girls	51	49	17	83
Suburban: 10-yr-old girls	27	73	33	66
Inner-city: 8-yr-old girls	44	56	22	78
Inner-city: 10-yr-old girls	69	31	33	66
Suburban: 12-yr-old girls	76	24	33	66
Inner-city: 12-yr-old girls	62	38	33	66
Average: girls	55	45	29	71
Suburban: 8-yr-old boys	53	47	0	100
Suburban: 10-yr-old boys	44	56	14	86
Inner-city: 8-yr-old boys	85	15	0	100
Inner-city: 10-yr-old boys	85	15	0	100
Suburban: 12-yr-old boys	81	19	0	100
Inner-city: 12-yr-old boys	47	53	35	65
Average: boys	66	34	8	92

you think you are — or indeed that you 'fancy' him. It may enable you to present yourself as a budding film critic, who relates to the media in an altogether more mature and sophisticated way than the mere 'fan' who has pictures of the characters they like stuck up on their bedroom wall. Modality judgments of this kind serve to distance the speaker from emotional involvement, and thus minimize the possibility of mockery by others.

This is also the case in relation to humour, another significant marker of modality. In the Reeves and Greenberg (1977) study, 'funny' was the attribute most frequently used in differentiating characters, and this was also the case in the discussions reported here. As Table 8.7 shows, the children also tended to favour 'comic' characters in choosing whom to discuss. (For these purposes, I have defined as 'comic' only cartoon and puppet characters, and those appearing in situation comedies. There were nine 'comic' characters, exactly half the total number: see Table 8.1 above.)

Table 8.7 shows a general preference for comic characters, particularly amongst boys, which is true across class and age differences. How might we explain this? Reeves and Greenberg (1977) immediately relate their findings in this area to the question of identification, asking whether children are more likely to imitate humorous role models. However, they note that children were more likely to favour 'unsupported humour' — that is, laughing at people, rather than with them — and that humour in this sense was not seen as a 'positive, desired attribute'. While humour was the primary dimension children used to differentiate TV characters, they can only conclude that it was 'not related to children's application of television to real life' (p. 124).

Here again, I would argue that the significance of humour can be more fully recognized if we take account of the social context in which the discussion of television characters takes place. It is interesting in this respect that the children often applied the term 'funny' to characters I have designated as 'non-comic', such as soap opera characters. If the discussion of television characters is such a highly charged activity, humour may serve as a means of throwing the listener 'off the scent'. In claiming that you like a humorous character, you are not necessarily implying that you 'identify' with that character, as you may be perceived to do in the case of a more serious character. Saying you 'like' Count Duckula or Baldrick from *Blackadder* is very different from saying you 'like' Clint Eastwood or Todd from *Neighbours*: nobody is likely to assume that you regard Baldrick as a desirable role model, or that you would like to be Count Duckula. Choosing humorous characters — or opting to discuss the humorous aspects of essentially non-humorous characters — can serve as a kind of disclaimer, in which the self is no longer placed at such risk. Particularly for boys, whose self-definitions may be more fragile, and who may stand to lose more through such apparent self-exposure, this may present a very useful way out of a potentially humiliating situation.

'Understanding' Character

A further focus of psychological research in this field has been on the ways in which children's understanding of character develops with age. According to traditional developmental theory, one would expect older children to develop an increasing ability to 'decentre' — to infer other people's thoughts and intentions — and thus to develop more abstract, less concrete notions of character and personality. This hypothesis derives primarily from research on 'person perception' (e.g. Hastorf *et al.*, 1970; Berndt and Berndt, 1975), and it is certainly reflected in some research on character perception in written stories (e.g. Sedlak, 1979) and in television.

Thus, for example, Wartella and Alexander (1978) find that older children are more likely to use 'internal descriptors' (for example, of motivation or personality, rather than physical appearance or behaviour) and 'causal descriptions' (that is, to infer motivation for behaviour) in discussing television characters (see also Abelman and Sparks, 1985). Experimental studies (e.g. Hoffner and Cantor, 1985) would appear to support the view that children become less 'perceptually dependent', and more likely to focus on the 'conceptual attributes' of television characters as they mature.

However, Reeves and Greenberg (1977) find no increase with age in the 'complexity' of children's judgments of TV characters — measured in terms of the number of attributes they assign to them. Furthermore, Reeves (1979) finds that children's perceptions of television characters actually become simpler with age. He suggests that 'increasingly complex cognitive abilities may cause increasingly simple perceptions of television content' (p. 139): for example, the judgment as to whether characters are like real people may become less significant for children as they get older.

This raises a number of interesting hypotheses. Much of the research appears to assume that general theories of 'person perception' will apply to the perception of television characters. Yet why should we assume that television characters will be evaluated and categorized in the same way as people in real life? What appears to underlie this approach is an essentially mimetic view of character. Children, in particular, are implicitly seen to suffer from the illusion that television characters are real, and that they can engage in social interaction with them (cf. Horton and Wohl, 1956). This approach effectively abstracts characters from the texts in which they are situated, and assumes that we relate to them as if they were our friends or neighbours (cf. Bradley, 1965). As Rimmon-Kenan (1983) argues, this approach 'legitimizes the transference of ready-made theories [of character] from psychology or psychoanalysis', yet it ignores the *specificity* of fictional characters.

By contrast, a structuralist perspective would regard characters not in terms of their unique psychological attributes, but in terms of their functions within the narrative (e.g. Propp, 1968; Greimas, 1973). Despite its limitations, this perspective points to the dangers of taking a 'realist' conception of character derived from the bourgeois nineteenth-century novel as a norm for characters in general. The notion of complex, multidimensional characters — 'rounded' as opposed to 'flat' (Forster, 1963) — may be inapplicable to television, or at least to *some* television. Character 'attributes' — or indeed the notion of 'personality' itself — may not be either relevant or meaningful.

In this light, the apparently contradictory findings of the studies noted above take on an interesting significance. As Reeves (1979) argues:

> While the perceptual skills of children are developing to the extent where cognition is abstract, inferential and generalized, children may also be learning that television, unlike real life, requires only the most simple evaluations. Consequently, while older children are making complex personality inferences about peers, for example, they may have learned early that television characters need only be evaluated on the basis of whether they are funny or serious. (p. 128)

While this may somewhat overstate the case, it does suggest that children's perceptions of television characters may need to be distinguished from their perceptions of real people, and that counting 'attributes' may be a rather simplistic way of assessing children's 'understanding'.

In evaluating the 'complexity' of children's understanding of character from the discussions considered here, a number of problems arise. For example, the frequency with which children referred to a character's appearance depended much more on the character concerned than it did upon factors such as gender or age. There were numerous references to the physical appearance of Cilla Black and Todd from *Neighbours* (mostly derogatory, it must be said) yet very few to that of Burnside from *The Bill* or Rudy from *The Cosby Show*. In some cases, one could argue that the physical appearance of characters was much more important in the texts from which they were drawn: thus, many of the children noted that Roseanne was fat or that Edd the Duck had green hair — facts which are effectively part of the way in which their 'personalities' are defined.

Separating references to 'personality' from references to 'behaviour' is also difficult: behaviour was often described in order to illustrate assertions about 'personality', although these were often implicit. The vast majority of descriptions of characters in all age groups focused primarily on behaviour — often in the form of celebrating dramatic or amusing incidents in which they had been involved. While the older children occasionally displayed a more sophisticated vocabulary for describing 'personality' — which is hardly surprising — the fact is that they rarely chose to use this. Judgments of 'personality' were, by and large, extremely rudimentary, and served mainly as a pretext for retelling.

Nevertheless, the kinds of accounts of characters which children provide will obviously depend to a significant extent on how they perceive the task at hand.

In this case, for example, some children perceived the activity as more 'educational' than others, and sought to offer more generalized, reflective judgments of 'personality'. In many cases, however, the activity was perceived simply as a chance to laugh at Todd's big ears or Cilla Black's goofy teeth, or to discuss whether or not Philip Schofield was truly a 'hunk'. Indeed, in a number of instances, the children enquired about how the images had been produced (many of them had been photographically enlarged) and in a few cases even asked if they could keep them. At times, it almost seemed as though we were discussing a series of pin-ups which had been found on somebody's bedroom wall, or going through the contents of a TV scrapbook.

Here again, therefore, we need to consider the social function of character judgments. In looking for abstract, nuanced statements about motivation and personality, researchers may be ignoring the fact that judgments about TV characters may have a rather different function, especially in the context of peer group discussion. While a quantitative approach may suggest some interesting hypotheses about this, it may ultimately obscure the complexity of the process.

Talking about TV Characters

In the remainder of this chapter, I want to focus in more detail on extracts from four of the group discussions. I have chosen one group of boys and one group of girls from each of the two secondary schools. At this point in the research, these children were nearly all 12 years old. All of the groups had the same male interviewer. While these groups are not necessarily 'typical', they do illustrate some of the complex social negotiations which characterize children's talk about television characters.

Group 1: High Stakes

This group (from the inner-city secondary school) consisted of two friendship pairs: two black Afro-Caribbean working-class girls, Gloria and Chanel, and two white middle-class girls, Julia and Beatrix. The significance of these differences within the group emerged most clearly in the first part of the discussion, when the children were asked to nominate 'favourite' characters or people. The initiative here was taken by the two black girls, who went on to name a series of black actors: Bill Cosby, Eddie Murphy and Richard Pryor. The following extract is taken from the very beginning of the discussion.

Extract 1

Gloria:	Bill Cosby.
Interviewer:	OK. [*Chanel laughs*] So tell me what you like about him, then.
Gloria:	I like the way he goes on. [*Laughter*]
Interviewer:	So how does he go on, tell me.
Gloria:	He's funny /
Interviewer:	Uhuh. So what sorts of things does he do that you like?
Gloria:	[*laughs*] Can't explain it. /

Interviewer:	I mean, can you remember things, you're talking about in *The Cosby Show* mostly, [yeah?
Gloria:	[Yeah.
Interviewer:	So what sorts of things does he do in *The Cosby Show* that you like?
Gloria:	Just makes jokes.
Chanel:	Plus he does funny dances /
Interviewer:	Yeah, he does funny dances in the titles at the beginning, doesn't he?
Gloria, Chanel:	Yeah.
Julia:	Yeah /
Interviewer:	So you like him as well, Chanel, yeah? I mean, can you say what you like about him?
Chanel:	He's funny / um / mm
Interviewer:	I mean, can you remember a particular bit of *The Cosby Show* where [you thought he was
Chanel:	[I like the children as well though. I like Rudy.
Interviewer:	Yeah.
Julia:	I like Bill Cosby 'cause he acts like a child a lot of the time (&) [
Chanel:	[When he solves problems.
Julia:	(&) I like it when he get the shield, you know when they were throwing snowballs at him. /

Although the fact that Bill Cosby is black is never mentioned (and this is true of the other black actors named here), I would argue that it is implicitly acknowledged by all present. Here, as in the later discussion of Eddie Murphy and Richard Pryor, there is some laughter from the black girls when the name is introduced, perhaps suggesting that it possesses a certain subversive potential. As in this case, Julia often makes some tentative contributions once it is clear that Gloria and Chanel have had their say, although Beatrix is silent in this part of the discussion. Throughout, there is a sense in which Julia is attempting to gain the approval of Gloria and Chanel by participating in the discussion of black characters/actors — for example, she later nominates Lenny Henry — although her right to do this is insecure.

As in the discussion of programme preferences among this group, considered in Chapter 4, there is a sense here in which the act of naming often appears to be enough. Gloria is generally unwilling to say more about her chosen characters, and the interviewer has to work hard in order to get her to do so: in fact, she seems to be very adept at closing off lines of questioning, repeatedly refusing the interviewer's invitations to talk. This was also the case with the other actors named here: Eddie Murphy was commended by Chanel 'because he's got good taste and he makes me laugh' — although she was unwilling to explain what kind of 'taste' she had in mind — and Gloria claimed to like Richard Pryor 'because he's funny'. In both cases, there was some discussion of the films these actors had been in, although this was largely in terms of who in the group had seen them. Rather more reflective comments about 'personality' — for example, Julia's description of Bill Cosby at the end of this extract — were not followed up.

Nevertheless, it would be false to conclude that these girls are merely 'inarticulate'. It is not that Gloria 'can't explain it', but that she doesn't want to, or that she sees no purpose in doing so here. Her purposes would not be served — indeed they might well be undermined — were she to offer an explanation of why Bill Cosby is 'funny', because that is not primarily why she has chosen him.

This kind of uneasy negotiation continued when Julia and Beatrix were explicitly invited to speak.

Extract 2

Interviewer:	Yeah. All right, so why do you like Richard Pryor, then? Can you say any more? Apart from the fact that he's funny? /
Gloria:	No /
Interviewer:	OK. Anybody else? Julia or Beatrix.
Chanel:	Oliver [*Gloria and Chanel laugh loudly*] Only joking, sir. [*more laughter*] /
Gloria:	Oliver, come on Chanel! [*more laughter*]
Interviewer:	You want to suggest anyone?
Gloria:	Come on Chanel, Oliver!
Interviewer:	Who is Oliver?
Chanel:	It's this black comedian, and he tells jokes, and he's got episodes, like um / Mad Mavis /
Interviewer:	What is this, on the telly?
Chanel:	No! It's on video, it's a Jamaican / comedian.
Interviewer:	Right, right / Can you two think of anyone?
Chanel:	Bugs Bunny [*laughs*].
?Julia:	No /
Chanel:	Madonna! Go on!
Beatrix:	No, it's=
Chanel:	=Do 'Who's that girl?'
Interviewer:	You can have Madonna if you want, I mean. She's a singer, but she's also an actress, isn't she?
Chanel:	[*singing loudly:*] 'WHO'S THAT GIRL! YEAH!' You know it.
Interviewer:	You like Madonna, yeah?
Beatrix:	Yeah. But I like horror movies better.
Gloria:	Horror movies? / So you're learning, though. Come on.
Interviewer:	So if you had a favourite character in horror movies, then, who would that be?
Beatrix:	Freddy.
Gloria:	Freddy Kruger.
Chanel:	Innit, he's the best.
Interviewer:	Right. So tell me about Freddy, why do you like Freddy?
Beatrix:	He's funny when he=
Chanel:	=Kills children!

.
.
.

Gloria:	What about you, Julia?
Julia:	Mmm.
Chanel:	She likes Eddie Murphy, innit. [?Ever] he came into the room.
Gloria:	She likes Aswad.
Chanel:	Go on, talk about Aswad. They've got a new film coming out soon.
Julia:	Film? I didn't [know about that.
Chanel:	[But I lied. [*laughter*]

At the start of this extract, Gloria again closes off the discussion of a black character, suggesting that any further elaboration would be unnecessary. The banter around Oliver raises the stakes further, insofar as it takes Gloria and Chanel into specifically 'black' tastes which are probably inaccessible to a white audience (and not least to the interviewer here). Note the laughter which again accompanies the naming of a black character, and the way in which Gloria refers to the interviewer here as 'sir' (that is, as a teacher), reinforcing the social and cultural distance between them. Note also that Oliver is explicitly identified as 'black', the only time the word is used throughout the discussion: perhaps now that Gloria and Chanel have got everybody else on the run — the interviewer, for example, fails to understand what they are talking about — it seems much safer to refer to this.

This staking out of a 'black' identity by Gloria and Chanel effectively leaves Beatrix and Julia with nowhere to go. They have very little of equivalent subcultural status which they can claim as their own. At this point, the black girls have gained the ascendancy, and they exploit it by effectively mocking the others' tastes. Thus, Chanel jokingly nominates Bugs Bunny on their behalf, and goes on to mock Beatrix's taste for Madonna. Despite being a confirmed Madonna fan, Beatrix attempts to disclaim her preference, and instead, in an almost desperate bid for status, opts to talk about horror movies. Gloria's comment 'so you're learning though' acknowledges the partial success of this strategy — although it positions Gloria as the arbiter of taste, and Beatrix as a kind of apprentice.

In the following exchanges, Julia is also positioned in this way. The preferences Gloria and Chanel nominate on her behalf are again black (Aswad is a British reggae group) — thus colluding in her presentation of herself as knowledgeable about 'black' culture — although Chanel's lie about the Aswad film again effectively positions her as the 'expert' and Julia as the ignorant outsider. By positioning the white girls in this way, Gloria and Chanel effectively maintain their dominance: in the discussion as a whole, they made almost three times as many contributions (Chanel made 196, Gloria 189) as Julia (78) and Beatrix (60).

This negotiation became more complex — although less fraught — as the discussion proceeded. From the images provided, Gloria and Chanel both chose to talk about black characters — Oprah Winfrey and Rudy respectively — and repeatedly asked the interviewer if they could be allowed to keep these pictures, as well as that of Desmond, the other black character. Although some common ground emerged around the soaps, there were also differences here. Perhaps unsurprisingly in view of her role here, Gloria expressed a liking for Bobby in *Home and Away* — 'she just beats people up, boy . . . she stands up for herself' — but she was also ready to condemn Julia's liking of Harold — 'he's a vegetarian, man!'

At least some of these differences might also be explained in terms of social class. Thus, Julia distanced herself from the other girls' interest in the Australian soaps, and in *Blind Date*, for which Gloria and Chanel expressed considerable enthusiasm. Similarly, in identifying their favourites, Julia and Beatrix eventually chose to talk about 'alternative' comedians such as Victoria Wood, Rowan Atkinson (*Blackadder*) and Julian Clary (*Sticky Moments*) — who, at least on the basis of this research, would appear to be much more of a middle-class taste. The fact that Gloria had not heard of most of these was probably lucky for them, although lack of knowledge did not necessarily stand in the way of her repeated condemnations of others' tastes. For example, Beatrix selected Baldrick (from *Blackadder*) as a preference, which led to shouts of 'rubbish!' from Gloria. Later in the discussion, she returned to the attack, selecting Baldrick as a dislike.

Extract 3

Interviewer:	All right, Gloria, you've got Baldrick, you don't like him. / We talked [a bit about this before.
Gloria:	[Everything's wrong with him, everything.
Interviewer:	So what's wrong with him?
Chanel:	He ain't funny.
Gloria:	He ain't funny.
Beatrix:	He is!
Gloria:	He ain't funny.
Julia:	He is!
Chanel:	I like *Blackadder* best.
Gloria:	He ain't funny.
Julia:	He is funny.
Gloria:	He's stupid.
Julia:	He's not. Well he's meant to be stupid, he's meant to be stupid in *Blackadder*, that's what makes him funny.
Gloria:	Just like little kids, man. [*laughter*]
Julia:	Shut up!
Chanel:	*Blackadder*'s good, though.
Gloria:	Is this *Blackadder*?
Julia:	No.
Gloria:	Then what you talking about? / We weren't talking about that.
Julia:	Yeah, but the programme, he's in the programme, he's not rubbish.
Chanel:	Innit.
Gloria:	He can't act, boy.
Julia:	He can act.
Interviewer:	So you don't like that programme, basically, Gloria, yeah?
Gloria:	For little children.
Chanel:	No, you're feisty [*Gloria laughs*] Like you, innit?
Gloria:	[No, 'cause I don't watch it.
Julia:	[What is *Neighbours* for, then?
Interviewer:	For little children, right. So everybody who likes it is a little child, then?

Gloria:	Yeah.
Interviewer:	Right, uhuh.
Chanel:	And you're not.
Gloria:	You're a little child.
Julia:	['Course I'm a child.
Chanel:	[I don't like him, I like *Blackadder.*
Gloria:	You're a little child. [You're kids, you're kids.
Chanel:	[So you're a woman? [You're a woman?
Julia:	[You're grown up?

[some laughter]

Gloria: For little kids, man. /

At this point, the attempt which has been led by Gloria to use the discussion as a means of staking out one's tastes (and with them one's social identity) topples over into parody — although this is certainly encouraged by the interviewer. The reasons Gloria gives in support of her judgment are extremely generalized, and for the most part quite fortuitous — indeed, how would she know that he can't act if she does not watch the programme? While Julia attempts to fight back, referring to Gloria's earlier enthusiasm for *Neighbours*, Chanel is also obliged to distance herself from Gloria's attack, perhaps partly because of her own liking of *Blackadder*, which had emerged earlier in the discussion. She describes her, not for the first time in the discussion, as 'feisty' — in effect, as too assertive or 'pushy' — and mocks her implicit claim to be more mature, to quite decisive effect.

Here, and elsewhere in the discussion, Julia's judgments display a degree of ironic distance which seems to be unavailable — or perhaps just irrelevant — to Gloria. In saying she 'likes' Baldrick or Harold in *Neighbours* or even Edd the Duck, she acknowledges that these characters are '*meant* to be stupid', and that liking does not necessarily imply identification. Interestingly, Gloria rejected the others' preference for Edd the Duck as further evidence that they were all 'babies', and sought to 'explain' — and to condemn — Julia's preference for Harold on the basis that both were vegetarians. From Gloria's perspective, irony would render her open to the accusation that she really meant it, and was thus a luxury she could hardly afford.

Group 2: Blaring

This group (also from the inner-city secondary school) consisted of four boys: one middle-class African (Obinna), one white working-class British (Danny) and two working-class Asians (Ranjit and Mohamed). This discussion began very hesitantly, with many pauses, but gradually wound itself up to a pitch of what can almost be described as comic hysteria. If the dynamic of Group 1 was very much about staking out differences within the group, this group was significantly more consensual: the focus of their energies was not so much each other as the shortcomings of the characters they had been asked to discuss.

Here too, the nomination of favourites at the start of the discussion established a clear agenda, indeed almost a set of criteria on which the remaining characters would be judged. Thus, Ranjit opted for Eddie Murphy; Danny for

Arnold Schwarzenegger; and Obinna for the wrestler Hulk Hogan. While the major quality which appeared to be valued here was undoubtedly their masculinity, there was also a distinct sense of irony in their account, and a great deal of laughter.

Thus, Danny offered a very long retelling of the Arnold Schwarzenegger film *Running Man*, focusing on a series of superheroic exploits, and concluded 'I like it how he's all strong and everything, and he beats everyone up'. Nevertheless, he went on to comment on the unrealistic nature of the violence: 'the thing I didn't get though [. . .] these people throw a hand grenade in front of him, and it blows up and all he gets is a little cut on his head.'

Similarly, Obinna's account of Hulk Hogan focused on moments of excess, in which the fighting continues outside the ring, and the wrestlers cannot be restrained: 'the two men ran in and they started fighting where they talk, they were trying to fight, and two men were trying to stop them, and they were chucking them away, the two presenters and everything, "could you please stop!" And they were asking the cameramen to come and help, and they were helping, and there was BEEP! BEEP!' Danny joined in by describing a wrestler called the Earthquake, whose technique appeared to consist of sitting on his opponents.

The sense of absurdity here was capped by Mohamed's choice of the cartoon character Roadrunner as his favourite. On one level, this might be interpreted as an attempt to avoid the issue of identification implicitly raised by the others' choices. While Danny might be mocked for implicitly identifying with Arnold Schwarzenegger, there was no way that anybody could realistically be accused of identifying with Roadrunner. Nevertheless, the increasingly absurd and ironic quality of the discussion meant that this was hardly an issue: the sense of playing for high stakes which appeared to characterize Group 1 was not in evidence here.

Among the images provided, the boys were only able to find two characters they would admit to liking: both, significantly, were comic characters. Thus, Danny opted for Baldrick, offering another long retelling of a recent incident in *Blackadder*, while Mohamed chose Rudy, whom he described as 'silly'. Ranjit, however, was unable to find a character he liked, and when it came to his turn, launched into an attack on Dot Cotton and *EastEnders*:

Extract 4

Interviewer:	What about you, Ranjit?
Ranjit:	I hate her. I don't like her. I don't like *EastEnders* either. [. . .] Too boring and um er, I saw an episode of *EastEnders*, I was forced by my mum to watch it 'cause she was watching it.
Interviewer:	You were forced to watch it?
Ranjit:	Yeah, it was disgusting man, don't know why people like it. And she er, Nick was killing her, and um er Ethel comes in, and she says um er 'but he's killing her' and she doesn't take any notice. /
Interviewer:	Yeah.
Ranjit:	And then she says um er 'it's not my fault you never had no children'. Oh my god, boy!
Interviewer:	[*laughs*] [Tell me more about this.
Obinna:	[It's so dull and boring.

Ranjit:	It's boring.
Interviewer:	It's dull and it's boring. [yeah]
Mohamed:	[*laughing:*] That's what you like about it.
Obinna:	And they all talk in a funny accent, and it always seems to be cold and dirty.
Various:	Yeah.
Interviewer:	What do you mean, it's a funny accent? Don't they talk just ordinary sort of London accents?
Various:	No.
Obinna:	[No they just go=
Ranjit:	[It's funny.
Interviewer:	So tell, tell me why it's funny, it's interesting.
Obinna:	It's not funny, but they just talk funny. They talk [imitates:] 'Owh'.
Ranjit:	They talk a bit over.
Mohamed:	[*imitating exaggerated Cockney:*] 'Allo, allo'.
Obinna:	'Allo'. [*laughter*]
Interviewer:	Right, so it's like you think they're exaggerating it?
Various:	Yeah.

.

.

.

Mohamed:	*Neighbours* is rubbish, *Home and Away* is rubbish.
Obinna:	I don't even watch *Home and Away* now.
Interviewer:	[*laughs*] Yeah, you don't watch these either.
Danny:	*Home and Away* is so boring.
Mohamed:	*Brookside* is rubbish.
Obinna:	And what about *Prisoner: Cell Block H*, that is so dull.
Interviewer:	[*laughs*] / So tell, yeah, OK, right=
?Obinna:	=And *Home and Away* [*imitates:*] 'Morag!' [*laughter*]

This discussion could be seen as a manifestation of the familiar male contempt for soap operas, although the boys' judgments are essentially concerned with the implausibility of the characters' behaviour, and the lack of authenticity of *EastEnders*'s representation of working-class London, rather than, for example, the elements of romance in the programmes. Despite Ranjit's claim that he had been 'forced' to watch *EastEnders*, he is certainly familiar with the characters and their relationships.

Towards the end of this extract, a dynamic begins to develop which is effectively sustained for the remainder of the discussion. Increasingly, the only position which was possible was one of mockery and condemnation. Ranjit was probably the prime mover here, although Obinna and Danny were also enthusiastic participants. Humour played a major role here, with the more comical and original insults gaining most approval from the group. At times, the discussion came to resemble the kind of insulting competition which is common in many subcultural groups, and which effectively constitutes a 'speech genre' of its own. Among some Afro-Caribbeans and working-class people in London, this is sometimes termed 'cussing' or, more recently, 'blaring'. One particularly sexist variant of this style of talk, which has been common among London schoolchildren for some years now — and not only among boys — consists of finding the most obscene and inventive ways of insulting your opponent's mother.

Interestingly, however, the insults here were not directed against other members of the group. Even Mohamed's choice of Roadrunner, or his defence of cartoons like *Count Duckula*, which most of the others condemned, did not seem to reflect upon him. There was a kind of collective safety about the discussion which was quite different from the cut and thrust of Group 1.

The grounds for condemnation were quite diverse, and at times seemed almost arbitrary. Thus, characters were condemned for their physical appearance: Todd because of his 'Prince Charles ears' and his 'hedgehog' hairstyle, Edd the Duck because of his 'flat feet', and Desmond because of his 'goofy teeth' and 'Adolf Hitler' moustache. Some were condemned because of the roles they played: Burnside, for example, was condemned as 'too bossy', and Desmond because 'he drinks too much'. Others came in for more wholesale demolition: Cilla Black, for example, was criticized for her 'goofy teeth', for her singing, 'the way she laughs' and 'the way she acts'. The litany of 'rubbish', 'useless' and 'boring' was sustained throughout.

Perhaps what emerged most consistently, however, was a sense of popular television as lacking in authenticity, as essentially 'fake'. Thus, Philip Schofield was condemned for 'trying to act flash' — he is 'trying to be excited . . . but he's not really, you can tell he's bored stiff'. Cartoons like *Count Duckula* were rejected as unrealistic and even programmes like *The Bill* were seen by some as predictable and repetitive. This concern with modality emerged most clearly around the discussion of the Australian soaps:

Extract 5

Interviewer:	Obinna, who have you got? Bobby from *Home and Away*, yeah? You don't like her?
Mohamed:	[No, she's rubbish!
Obinna:	[No, I don't like her. [*laughter*] She's so rubbish.
Mohamed:	This girl on the TV=
Ranjit:	=I hate her mum as well, Morag. And her dad.
Obinna:	She goes [*imitates:*] 'Morag [*squeaky noises*]'.
Mohamed:	Sounds like a parrot, man.
Ranjit:	'I know what you're up to!'
Obinna:	'Get away, Bobby, you can't be my sister, I want whatever her name is to be my daughter.' [*laughter*] 'You'll get what you get, I'm out.' Alf. I hate their family, you see the atmosphere that they're in, it just looks=
Ranjit:	=It's not real, it's not real.
Obinna:	It doesn't look real, it looks cardboard.
Ranjit:	Yeah!
[*laughter*]	
Ranjit:	Like in *Neighbours*, um er when they show the street, you can see that it's real houses, not like cardboard. Oh yeah, on *Neighbours* um er Scott and um er Henry were just going out the door, you could see cardboard, you could actually see the scenery!

Mohamed:	Yeah, yeah, yeah, it was so thin! [*laughter*]
Interviewer:	How did you know it was cardboard?
Ranjit:	It looked cardboard.
Mohamed:	It looks like it, yeah.
Ranjit:	You think they're drawing, drawing.
Mohamed:	So thin, and the drawing is [. . .] not like a real view, not like this [*pointing out of the window*].

Here too, the condemnation of the programmes is obviously based on a considerable familiarity with them. Both Obinna and Ranjit quote directly from *Home and Away*, and seem to be well-informed about the characters and their relationships. Similarly, being able to notice the painted backdrops in *Neighbours* requires close observation. Nevertheless, the emphasis on the programme as an artefact — on low production values and poor quality acting — places a considerable distance between viewer and text. By precluding the possibility of emotional engagement, and thus any display of vulnerability, it places the speaker in a position of considerable power. Although this strategy was adopted by some of the girls, it was much more common among the boys.

Similarly, this tendency to denigrate the characters was more common among the boys' groups than the girls'. In this case, while the boys did not question or mock each others' tastes to any significant degree, the ongoing dynamic of the discussion made it increasingly clear that any expression of pleasure would be out of place. Thus, towards the end of the session, the discussion became almost frenzied, as the boys hurled insults at the few remaining images:

Extract 6

Ranjit:	I don't know her.
Obinna:	[Oprah Winfrey.
Interviewer:	[Oprah Winfrey. [She does a kind of chat show thing.
Mohamed:	[Cheers. Cheers.
Ranjit:	Oh, her! Oh, I hate her! [*laughter*]
Obinna:	[*imitating*:] 'So, you! So, you!'
Ranjit:	Is she American?
Interviewer:	Yeah, no, she's American.
Obinna:	Sometimes I like watching it.
Ranjit:	I HATE HER, I DO HATE HER, YOU KNOW! (&) [
Obinna:	[
	Sometimes I like watching it.
Ranjit:	(&) And that chat show what she does! Oh my god, man! It's so boring! On Channel Four!
Interviewer:	That's right.
Ranjit:	Oh, it's her, innit! Oh my god, man!

.
.
.

Ranjit:	Look at her. Look at her stuffing her face, man.
Interviewer:	Yeah, Carly.
Ranjit:	Look at that, look at that! Carly, rubbish!

Obinna: No wonder she's got so fat. [*much laughter*] /
Ranjit: That covers everyone. / Oh look at him [Burnside] again, man, look at that! [*more laughter*] [Look at him trying to act all serious.
Obinna: [He looks like a bulldog. [*laughter*]
Interviewer: So who should I have had, then? Who would be better characters to have here?
Ranjit: Oh, you should, Eddie Murphy, you should have had Eddie Murphy.
Interviewer: I mean, apart from Eddie Murphy and Arnold Schwarze- negger and um /
Danny: Roadrunner.
[*huge amounts of laughter*]
.

.

.

Interviewer: So who would be good to have here, then?
Ranjit: No-one.
Interviewer: No-one. I mean, you can't think of TV characters, TV characters that you like.
Obinna: Cause they're all dry. [*laughter*] You need to get Sky TV.
Mohamed: Get a dish!

Whether or not this discussion provides any insight into the motivations of potential subscribers to Sky TV is perhaps debatable, although it does provide some interesting grounds for speculation. There is undoubtedly a group dynamic here which becomes progressively more extreme as the discussion proceeds. Moderate or ambivalent views are largely swept aside, to the extent that Ranjit, for example, feels compelled to express a virulent hatred of Oprah Winfrey even though he does not initially recognize her. His expression 'that covers everyone' implies that the task of demolition they had collectively set themselves is now complete. Nevertheless, it is important to note the irony and humour of the situation: by this point, the laughter had become almost uncontrollable.

However seriously we might wish to take them, shared values do emerge here, and they are mostly directed against the 'safe', bland qualities of 'family viewing'. Obinna's term 'dry' is current slang, suggesting that the characters are seen as dull and unexciting. In the discussion as a whole, mainstream television — soap operas, children's television, and family entertainment — is comprehensively rejected. While there is some enthusiasm for *The Bill* and (on Mohamed's part) for cartoons, the only material which has genuine purchase here is the more 'adult', streetwise, subversive humour of Eddie Murphy or the excessive masculinity of Arnold Schwarzenegger and the wrestlers on Sky TV. While this identification with the gross and the violent is not without irony, it does have a subversive, subcultural appeal, which is to some extent gender- and class-specific. More generally, however, it could be seen to reflect Bakhtin's notion of 'the carnival', with its celebration of laughter, excess and general 'bad taste', and its rejection of restraint and responsibility (Bakhtin, 1968). 'Blaring', and the laughter that ac- companies it, might be seen as at least a sideshow at this carnival.

Group 3: The Film Buffs

This group (from the suburban secondary school) consisted of four boys: two middle-class white British (Nigel and Paul), one working-class British/Greek Cypriot (Terry) and one middle-class British/Asian (Pradesh). The discussion provided an arena for what was obviously an ongoing antagonism between Paul and Nigel, on the one hand, and Terry on the other. Pradesh, in line with his general presentation of himself as serious and 'mature', tended to remain aloof from this conflict.

In this instance, all the people chosen as favourites were actors rather than characters: Alexei Sayle (Nigel), Arnold Schwarzenegger (Terry), Harrison Ford (Paul) and Gene Wilder and Richard Pryor (Pradesh). Again, while masculinity was certainly an issue here, the boys' discussion in fact focused primarily on the question of acting ability. Terry's nomination of Arnold Schwarzenegger began what was to become an ongoing debate:

Extract 7

Terry: He's really good acting.
Paul: He's violent.
Terry: He's violent / he's like / he's massive anyway, he's tall, he's just really sort of, he can play his part good and everything. He plays in *Predator*, like being like a soldier, but he plays in *Twins* as well which is a completely different sort of thing, like a comedy, the other one's serious. He sort of plays both parts good, whatever he's given he's good at it. He's just a good actor.
Paul: I don't reckon he's be really suited to something, to a film like *Fatal Attraction* though. [*Terry gives false laugh*] He just wouldn't fit the part.
Nigel: It's sort of like, he exaggerates, exaggerated one way to be like funny, like in *Twins* he was exaggerated to be a really bad experiment, but like in *Predator* he's exaggerated to be a really good soldier.
Paul: He wouldn't go in a normal everyday sort of drama.
Nigel: He'd never fit in *Neighbours* or *Home and Away*. Never.
Terry: He does do serious films like *Red Heat*, where he's a policeman.
Paul: That wasn't really serious, that's violent!
.
.
.
Nigel: Yeah, but I don't think he'd fit in an everyday sort of=
Terry: =Yeah, I know, it's just that he, it's unusual to see him in an everyday thing. It's like saying um / it's like Philip Schofield being in um=
Nigel: =a horror movie.
Terry: Yeah.
Paul: You can't exactly see that, can you?
Nigel: You wouldn't expect to see him in a horror film or a normal

film. He's the sort of person who's either in, he's either in a
police or soldier film, or just like ordinary film.

Paul: You can't really take him to *Twins* cause he's only ever been in
one movie.

Terry: It's not what he likes, is it?

Paul: No, it is also what he likes, he chooses his roles, he can turn
down roles if he wants.

Terry: Yeah, I know but=

Nigel: =He is the sort of person who fits that position though, like a
police cop.

Terry: Yeah but he's given this, he is sort of given to be a policeman,
he probably doesn't even want to do it, it's not, it's goes to the
film director and say 'have you got any applications for soldiers,
have you?'

Paul: He can turn it down if he wants, [he doesn't have to accept it.

Terry: [Yeah I know, but he must
like doing them . . .

There are a number of interesting distinctions being made here. The boys are
very clear about the difference between the actor and the characters he plays — to
the extent that, towards the end of this extract, they are able to speculate about
the actor's motivations and the possible reasons for his career choices. This concern with acting ability is part of a concern with modality more broadly, for
example with the distinction between what is real and what is 'exaggerated', or
between the comic and the 'serious'. The distinction Paul makes here between
'violent' and 'serious' is also interesting: it points to a sense of distancing from
violent material, which occurs in a rather different way in Group 2 — and which
is the very opposite of the unhealthy preoccupation with violence from which
boys are often assumed to suffer. Interestingly, Paul later criticizes Arnold
Schwarzenegger for being a 'robot': he is 'scared of nothing', whereas Harrison
Ford (in the Indiana Jones films) is more 'human' because he has phobias, such as
a fear of snakes — a fairly token form of vulnerability, it must be said.

The talk here draws on a discourse of 'film appreciation', of the popular
rather than the academic variety. This was manifested in a number of ways, here
and elsewhere in the discussion. On one level, there was status to be gained from
displaying one's familiarity with as many films as possible, particularly those
which children of this age are not legally permitted to see. The discourse of 'film
appreciation' was also apparent in the display of knowledge about how the film
industry works. Thus, in praising Harrison Ford, Paul described how he does his
own stunts, while Terry offered information (also derived from popular film
magazines) about how stunt men were injured in the making of *Superman 5*.
Finally, this discourse was manifested in the use of specialist terminology —
although their grasp of this was occasionally insecure. For example, Paul described Harrison Ford as a 'multiple role person' and his film *Indiana Jones and the
Last Crusade* as 'comedy action–adventure'.

Later in the discussion, this discourse was extended to television. The question
of acting ability recurred throughout: without exception, all the characters chosen
were initially evaluated in these terms. In many cases, there were detailed critical

comparisons, for example between presenters. The broader question of modality also recurred, for example in Terry's praise for the authenticity of *Desmonds*, or Pradesh's criticism of the 'artificial' behaviour of characters in *EastEnders*. When they were not defining themselves as 'film buffs', the boys were busily construct- ing another related identity, as 'TV critics'.

This 'critical' discourse serves a number of social functions here. It offers a comparatively 'safe' arena in which pre-existing interpersonal rivalries can be conducted. The argument between Terry, Paul and Nigel about whether Arnold Schwarzenegger is or is not a good actor is quite probably 'about' something quite different — or perhaps the topic is just a pretext for another good argument. It is merely the first of a number of such disputes, which culminate in a debate towards the end of the discussion about whether Edd the Duck's 'squeaker' is inside the puppet or whether they use duck calls. The triviality of some of these disputes would suggest that there is little at stake in winning or losing particular arguments here — and certainly much less than in the more intense confrontations of Group 1.

Indeed, the discourse might be seen to serve precisely this function, of pre- venting any display or investment of the 'self'. If we are talking about actors rather than characters, the question of identification is much less likely to arise. To indulge in 'appreciation' is to adopt a very distanced position: it implies the possibility of more considered, objective judgments, which do not depend upon individual whim.

As in the case of 'blaring', I would argue that this discourse serves a specific function for boys, in that it avoids any acknowledgment of 'personal' or emotional responses, and thus prevents the possibility of insecurity or vulnerability being 'exposed'. Where this did occur, the boys were quick to condemn each other. Thus, in talking about *Roseanne*, Nigel said that he preferred the character of Darlene (Roseanne's daughter) to Roseanne herself. Terry and Paul immediately mocked him for this — 'we know why you like Darlene' (by implication, because he 'fancies' her) — although Nigel insisted that it was 'because of her jokes'. Something of this is also apparent in the following extract, which begins with a discussion of the children's TV presenter Philip Schofield:

Extract 8

Paul:	He's just a complete and utter prick.
Interviewer:	OK. Things he does that tell you that, then?
Paul:	The way he acts, he's such a=
Nigel:	=Yeah, he's like such a wimp.
Terry:	He's a children's presenter though, what do you want him to be like?
Paul:	Yeah, I know, but he shouldn't be like a=
Pradesh:	=But he can't be according to you, because a majority of young children, I mean not like us, (&)[
Terry:	[He's been voted=
Pradesh:	(&) I mean, many, but all of us, everybody in the=
Paul:	=Hates him.

Pradesh: Hates him. In junior school, you would sort of mingle with the [common sort of people who / sort of watch it.

Nigel: [No, but a lot of people in junior schools don't even like him.

Paul: It's like New Kids on the Block, right.

Nigel: Yeah, they're useless, [they couldn't sing to save their lives.

Paul: [Everyone hates New Kids on the Block except girls, 'cause they've got no taste.

Interviewer: So what are you saying, Pradesh, you think that it's younger people that like him?

Pradesh: Yeah.

Terry: He's been voted for three years in a row top presenter.

Nigel: Yeah, by younger people.

Terry: Yeah, but still. / Cause he's not really like that probably, he only acts like that because the children like him. [He's not supposed to act like / what you want, is he?

Nigel: [Yeah he has, he's paid to act like that, but I mean.

.
.
.

Nigel: It's like New Kids on the Block, the only reason girls like them is because they're good looking. [They're not even good looking!

Paul: [They're not even / They can't sing.

Pradesh: We're not supposed to say that — [*laughter*] as if I know!

Nigel: Most of them are quite=

Paul: =[*mocking Nigel:*] Yeah, you'd know about that!

In discussing the reasons for their dislikes, the boys are also defining themselves, in terms of age, gender and social class. Thus, they distinguish themselves from younger children, and, in Pradesh's phrase, from 'the common sort of people' whom they had the misfortune to encounter at their non-selective junior schools. Yet while Terry and Pradesh attempt to argue for, if not quite defend, the tastes of these other audiences, there appears to be more at stake here for Nigel and Paul. Their rejection of Philip Schofield, like that of Group 2, is partly based on a sense of his insincerity: they later accuse him of being 'camera happy' and a 'poser' — 'he thinks he's so brilliant'. Yet while they attempt to call his masculinity into question — 'he's like such a wimp' — they are also rather disturbed by his popularity with girls. Their attempt to account for this, and for the popularity of New Kids on the Block, causes further difficulties: even to admit that these people might be 'good-looking' leaves one open to criticism, and the implicit accusation that one might 'fancy' them. Similarly, Pradesh's attempt to disclaim any knowledge of men's physical attractiveness — 'we're not supposed to say that — as if I know!' — derives, I would argue, from a fear of being accused of being homosexual. Here again, the discursive maintenance of masculinity requires some heavy policing.

Group 4: Towards 'Representation'

If the issue of representation was certainly implicit in many of the group discussions, it was raised much more explicitly in the final group I would like to discuss here. This group (also from the suburban secondary school) consisted of four girls: two white British (Celia and Sally), one British/Asian (Navin) and one British/Chinese (Susan).

As in many of the other groups of 12-year-olds, the issue of modality was central here. As with the boys in Group 3, acting ability was a central criterion, and in a number of cases there were comparisons between the different roles played by the same actor. Here too, there was a sense of mainstream popular television as being somehow lacking in authenticity. While all the girls were viewers of *Neighbours*, there was general agreement that there were no good actors in the programme; and Cilla Black was again rejected as 'fake' — as Susan argued, in a virulent attack, 'she's got fake face, fake fingernails, fake laugh . . . and she's got a false accent as well'. Celia constantly brought the discussion 'down to earth' by returning to questions of modality: thus, where the others engaged in a heated (albeit ironical) rivalry about the character of Count Duckula, she suggested that it was rather foolish to 'get worked up about a cartoon character'.

In comparison with most of the other groups, there was a distinct bias in the discussion towards female actors and characters. Thus, Celia nominated Bette Midler as her favourite, while Sally chose Victoria Wood and Navin opted for Miss Piggy from *The Muppet Babies* — a case of Roadrunner revisited, perhaps. Celia and Sally's choices run against the grain somewhat: there are few female Hollywood stars and even fewer female TV comedians from whom they might have chosen. While Navin's choice was probably intentionally comical, she also described Miss Piggy as a strong female character: as she pointed out, 'she's always calling [Kermit] her hero, but she's always saving him'.

Furthermore, at least some of their judgments here were informed by explicit concerns about *representation*. In other words, as well as discussing their emotional responses to the characters, and the extent to which they regarded them as 'realistic', they were also evaluating them as more or less 'representative' of specific social groups. This was particularly apparent in their discussion of Bobby from *Home and Away*:

Extract 9

Navin:	Well I like her because she's always sort of stubborn and she's sort of um / I don't know why I like her, she's always she's sort of like, doesn't act so feminine sort of thing, and everyone's always thinking oh you know they're girls, they're all dainty, but she isn't like that and / and sometimes she's wrong and she has, and she does admit it, like thing. I don't know why I like her.
Interviewer:	Can you tell me something that she's done that you thought has been good, then? /
Navin:	Well when um / Ailsa had that baby thing, and Bobby was being firm with her sort of thing, 'cause everyone else was being all nice and everything, and she needed someone to be firm and Bobby was there and she helped.

Interviewer:	Yeah, yeah. So she helped her sort of sort herself out.
Navin:	Yeah. /
Interviewer:	Mm, OK. What do other people think about Bobby?
Sally:	I think she's really bitchy. [*laughter*]
Interviewer:	Bitchy. What, you mean like nasty to [other people, yeah?
Sally:	[Yeah, like=
Susan:	=I think she's really sick actually
Sally:	Yeah, she, I just hate the way she storms in on everything (&) [
Navin:	[That's why I like her, she storms in on everything.
Sally:	(&) and like that she thinks she can get her own way just cause she's Bobby and everyone has to bow down to her.
Susan:	I like, I like how she stands up.
Navin:	Yeah, I like the way [she stands up to herself.
Sally:	[She stands up for anything even though, like just for the sake of an argument, not 'cause she like thinks it's right or anything.
Interviewer:	Right / right / You don't agree with that Navin, no?
Navin:	I like it, I like her because she stands up for herself and things.
Interviewer:	Yeah, yeah. / Whereas Sally, you're saying she's a bit too sort of pushy or something, yeah?
Sally:	I'm not saying she should be all feminine and everything but / well, I don't think it's very lifelike though.
Interviewer:	Yeah / I mean, can you think of something that's happened in *Home and Away* where you've thought that? That she wasn't=
Sally:	=Er, when she first got married to Frank she was always nagging him, and it wasn't like she's young / like you know, like she doesn't act like, I don't know how old she is, about eighteen or whatever [yeah]. In some ways she's really childish, in other ways she's sort of / I don't know.
Navin:	Old.
Sally:	[*laughs*] Yeah.
Interviewer:	Yeah, yeah. / All right.
Sally:	She's not like a real person, so that's, that's like a soap person though, so it's not like the same as Philip Schofield or someone.

The girls are aware that 'Bobby' is a fictional creation — a 'soap person' — although they are also concerned to debate the merits of her behaviour in the terms provided by the text itself. In effect, they are judging her as a representative of the category 'young women', and debating the extent to which she does (and indeed should) conform to the social norms which are prescribed for that group. If she is judged to be unrealistic, this is not merely in the sense that she can't act, but in comparison with general understandings the girls have derived from their own social experience. While none of them condemns her for being 'unfeminine', there is a concern here with the ways in which assertive behaviour (of the kind praised by Navin) can become merely aggressive (in the manner condemned by

Sally). This is a debate which is conducted in quite abstract terms: the character is described in terms of her general attributes, and specific incidents are offered as evidence in support of these more general assertions, rather than being described 'for their own sake'.

While the ability to generalize about a character's 'attributes' is certainly important here, this kind of debate about 'representation' would probably be impossible without a willingness to regard the character as at least analogous to a 'real' person (as well as ultimately being fictional). In many of the other groups, the children were somehow *too* distanced — too ready merely to condemn the characters as fictional or as otherwise unreal — and thus unwilling to 'take them seriously' as *representations*.

Although the discussion here did not always lead on to the issue of representation, there was a sense in which these more general qualities characterized many of their judgments. Thus, their discussion of Sharon and Tracey from *Birds of a Feather* emphasized the contrasts between the two in quite general terms. For example, Susan pointed out that 'Tracey wants everything to be perfect and everything, and then Sharon just does it any old how, kind of / you know, she doesn't care'. At the same time, there was a definite awareness here that the characters were fictional: Sally argued that Tracey was not 'supposed to be funny' and that 'it would be weird if she said the same kind of lines that the fat one did'. Here again, the question of modality — and the awareness that the characters are fictional — did not appear to prevent other concerns being raised.

Similarly, in the case of male characters, there was some quite 'distanced' evaluation of their physical attractiveness, although this was often balanced with other attributes. Thus, there was debate about Philip Schofield's merits in this department, although (as for the boys) he was condemned for his insincerity and vanity — 'he loves himself'. Todd from *Neighbours* was also judged 'good-looking', although his character was described as 'crap' and his acting ability likewise. Burnside was more roundly condemned for his 'thick eyebrows' and 'vampire haircut': as Sally argued, with some understatement, 'he isn't exactly hunk of the year!'

This issue was also raised in the case of Mitch, who was also accused of vanity — 'he thinks he's such a pin-up'. Nevertheless, here too the discussion moved on to broader questions of representation.

Extract 10

Sally:	[*on Mitch:*] He's quite good-looking. But he knows it. When you see him on *Baywatch*, he's sort of walking like this, sort of all chest out.
Navin:	And Eddie, the way he walks [*laughing*] He goes [*laughter*] He always walks like this, when he's walking.
Sally:	They have to be all macho, I suppose, but /
.	
.	
.	
Sally:	Like it's always him, like, with his son, I mean he's spoilt rotten, like if he says 'can I stay out all-night, go to an all-night party?' he'll say 'yeah son, do what you like, and I'm a great father' and ulllgh, like that.

Navin: He always has stuff like conversations and things but you know like it's [meant to be, but it's never really like that.

Sally: [And there's always a moral to what he's saying to his son.

Navin: So it's not lifelike with him and his son.

Interviewer: Yeah, yeah / So how old is his son?

Sally: About my age. He's cute as well [*laughs*].

Susan: [He's spoilt.

Navin: [Yeah, he's cute. [*laughter*]

Interviewer: You thinks he's a bit soft with his son then, yeah? Or it's not, it's [just not realistic?

Navin: [It's just not lifelike, it's just not realistic.

Sally: [I don't think he's a good actor or anything but / 'cause it's not like he's a really good actor or anything, he doesn't really stand or anything / but like *Baywatch* you don't really need a great actor, you just need to have hunks walking up and down the beach [*laughter*].

Interviewer: That's what it's all about, you think that's why it's so popular then?

Sally: Yeah, but it has got good stories.

Navin: It has got good parts in it.

.

.

.

Sally: The nice one, there's this really pretty lifeguard, they're all pretty and everything.

Navin: They always have to be pretty.

Sally: Yeah [*laughter*] and um [she went out to save this boy.

Susan: [She was one of the best.

Navin: Yeah, she went out to save these other boys as well.

Sally: Yeah, well she got bitten by a shark and she was getting all better and everything, she got a blood clot, and she just died like that. And you're thinking, oh, you know, she's going to live and everything, you think this is so rubbish and everything, and she dies [*laughs*] and you're sort of shocked. [*laughter*]

Navin: 'Cause you expected her to get better again [yeah] 'cause she was going to leave the, [she was going to leave but I didn't think she was going to.

Sally: [[. . .] but I didn't think she was going to leave them.

Interviewer: She was going to leave the, you mean the actress was going to leave the=

Sally: =It wasn't, 'cause it's finished, that was the last one, it finished after that.

Celia: Yeah, it's the kind of thing where you always expect a happy ending, it's one of those films where there's always a happy ending.

Navin: [And you expect her to get better again.

Sally:	[But like, like the la, I think about five people have died in it and that's / [I think it's quite exciting in some places.
Susan:	[It's good.
Navin:	Yeah, it is more real than *Neighbours*.
Interviewer:	Yeah. So it's, so you're not quite sure what's going to happen, basically.
Sally:	Yeah, I like it, 'cause it's not like all the same, the different stories, like one of the girls is getting beaten up by her boyfriend, and that it, it's that as well as people saving them and stuff like that.

Here again, Sally takes the discussion through a series of phases, in which different criteria for judging the character and the programme are established and debated. At the very beginning of this extract, his physical attractiveness is acknowledged, although this is balanced by the accusation of vanity, and the view that muscle-bound good looks constitute a rather limited and conventional form of attractiveness. (Note a similar criticism in Navin's later comment about the way in which the female lifeguards 'always have to be pretty'.) Later in the discussion, however, Sally argues that the programme itself may not in fact require more profound qualities of acting (and, by extension, of 'personality') — 'you just need to have hunks walking up and down the beach'.

The discussion of Mitch's role as a father in the programme focuses in a rather different way on the balance between the 'ideal' and the 'real' — it is 'like it's meant to be, but it's not really like that'. In a sense, then, Mitch is being judged here as a representation of both 'masculinity' and 'fatherhood'. While the fictional nature of the programme is acknowledged, the discussion here reveals a more complex investigation of the relationship between representation and reality.

Significantly, however, what might be seen as more critical, rationalistic judgments do not preclude the possibility of acknowledging one's emotional responses. The discussion of pleasure which occurs in the latter half of this extract is remarkably self-reflexive. The girls do not just describe what they felt: they also talk about what they expected to feel, and how those expectations were changed by the experience of viewing. Interestingly, these expectations appear to have derived not merely from the conventions of the programme itself — the general requirement for a happy ending — but also from the 'extra-textual' speculation about whether the actress in question was about to leave the series. The programme's ability to confound these expectations is taken as a significant guarantee of its realism.

Conclusion

The discussions described in the latter half of this chapter point to the complex, situated nature of children's judgments of television characters. Here again, we might summarize the differences between them in terms of the interaction between relations, subjects and contents.

In this case, there were broad differences between the ways in which the working-class children and the middle-class children perceived the purpose of the activity. For the working-class children, the activity was primarily a forum in which interpersonal relationships could be defined and negotiated — although for various reasons, the children in the first group were more interested in differentiating their tastes and identities, while those in the second were more concerned to establish a secure common ground. For the middle-class children, the activity seemed to be perceived in more 'educational' terms, as an opportunity to display their knowledge and sophistication, and as requiring more reflective judgments. As a result, the middle-class children talked in greater detail about the characters themselves: for the working-class children, the characters often seemed to be a pretext for their other purposes.

At the same time, the talk often seemed to provide an opportunity for claiming and negotiating 'subject positions'. This was most spectacularly the case in Group 1, although there were also some striking gender differences throughout. The two boys' groups here adopted quite different strategies for coping with — and ultimately avoiding — the potential risks of this activity. This is not, I would argue, necessarily a reflection of the fact that boys and girls relate to television in different ways. Rather, it reflects what it is possible for them to say in this context, and how they suspect others might respond to this. The display of 'cultural competencies' is largely constrained and determined by the context in which it takes place.

Finally, the judgments children make also depend on the 'contents' — in this case, the nature of the characters themselves. Characters differ in terms of their 'complexity', in terms of their modality status, and indeed in terms of their attributes. While these can obviously be perceived in different ways, the possibilities here are not infinite. It is obviously much easier to define some characters in psychological terms — that is, in terms of their 'personality' — while physical appearance and behaviour may be more applicable in other cases. There is undoubtedly a risk here of adopting a normative, 'realist' definition of character, which is simply irrelevant in many instances.

For all these reasons, it would be an oversimplification to regard the children's talk merely as evidence of their 'cognitive understanding' — or indeed of their tendencies to 'identify' with television characters. As I have suggested, the issue of 'identification' is undoubtedly a very significant 'hidden agenda' in these discussions. Yet to claim that you would like to be like a character — or just to say that you like them — is a *social* act, which it would be mistaken to accept at face value. While the notion of 'identification' may in fact have little scientific validity, it undoubtedly bears a considerable discursive force.

Similar arguments apply to the issue of children's 'understanding' of television characters, and of the concept of representation. While the girls in Group 4 undoubtedly displayed a more explicit concern with issues of representation than the children in the other groups, this was at least partly because of their perceptions of the context and of the others in the group. In different ways, the boys' definitions of themselves, and their unwillingness to place their own masculinity in question, actively prevented this kind of engagement — as did the extreme social differences which prevailed in Group 1. The issue of 'representation' was undoubtedly implicit in these other groups, yet any more explicit discussion was effectively incompatible with their rather different social purposes. The crux, however, is that judgments about 'representation' are not abstract: like all the other judgments here, they implicitly make claims about one's own identity — claims which must be seen as provisional, and as fundamentally social.

Chapter 9

Beyond the Magic Window: Children's Judgments of the Reality of Television

Anxieties about the effects of popular media are often based on a concern about the boundaries between fiction and reality. The Greek philosopher Plato, for example, proposed that the dramatic poets should be banned from his ideal Republic, for fear that their 'allegorical' accounts of the exploits of the gods would be taken for reality, and thus have a damaging effect on the morals of the young. Similarly, television is often seen by its critics to possess an extraordinary power: by making us believe in an 'illusion', the unreal world of television can simply 'blot out' reality.

This concern appears to rest on a fundamental suspicion of popular fictional narratives. It seems to be assumed that it is the purpose of fiction to offer a truthful, accurate representation of the world as it really is, and that viewers will inevitably read it in this way. This, of course, presumes that there is an objective reality with which these representations can be compared and found more or less wanting. The propensity to believe in fiction or fantasy, at whatever level, is seen as evidence of the reader's immaturity, or at least of the limitations of their experience, and even as an unhealthy or pathological weakness.

Yet here again, these anxieties are typically displaced onto 'other people'. While we ourselves are of course much too sophisticated ever to believe that what we watch on television is real, there are always 'others' who are seen as much more easily persuaded. And if women and working-class viewers are often described in this way, it is children who are quintessentially 'other'.

However, there are often fundamental contradictions here. As Hodge and Tripp (1986) have argued, 'reality' in these debates is often equated with what children *ought* to think. The problem with many of the 'fantasies' that seem to provoke concern is precisely that they are seen as violent and 'anti-social', and represent a threat to adult authority. Yet on the other hand, the attempt to disabuse children of their belief in 'fantasy' may in fact derive from a desire to protect them from unpleasant 'realities' they are assumed to be unprepared to face. The question of how reality is to be defined, and by whom, raises much broader questions of power and social control.

Thus, there is a popular folklore concerning the relationship between television and children's play. Everybody seems to know somebody who knows somebody who read a story in the paper once about a child who jumped out of a window pretending to be Superman. Yet anybody who has spent any time observing young children playing together will know that the boundary between fantasy and reality is of central significance for them. Children will consciously adopt particular roles, and often step outside the fantasy scenarios they have created to readjust or renegotiate these. While 'pretend play' may often permit children to try out forbidden roles and behaviours, children understand that it offers this licence precisely because it is not real.

Children's talk about television also displays this recurrent preoccupation with the question of what is real and what is not. In this chapter, I will describe the findings of an activity which was designed to probe these judgments more systematically. As I shall suggest, making judgments about the reality of television is a flexible process, which may involve many, possibly contradictory, criteria. Yet it is also, again, a social process, which can serve a range of social and interpersonal functions — and which may even actively exclude other considerations.

The Dimensions of Perceived Reality

Mainstream research into the 'effects' of television has often been based on the normative assumptions about fiction and reality identified above. As Hodge and Tripp (1986) have argued, the classic experimental approach to studying the effects of television violence adopted by Bandura and his followers largely neglected the 'perceived reality' both of the stimulus (television itself) and the response (aggressive behaviour). This research effectively ignores the differences between play violence (for example, hitting a doll) and 'real-life' violence (hitting a real person). As a result, its value as a means of predicting the effects of television on behaviour outside experimental settings remains extremely limited.

However, subsequent psychological research in this field has increasingly acknowledged the flexible, 'multidimensional' nature of children's perceptions of reality. Robert Hawkins (1977) makes a basic distinction here between what he terms the 'Magic Window' and the 'Social Expectations' dimensions. The 'Magic Window' dimension relates to children's awareness of television as constructed, or as fictional — for example, their understanding that characters are portrayed by actors. The 'Social Expectations' dimension relates to the ways in which children compare television with their own experience and perceptions of the world — for example, in finding characters' behaviour more or less possible or plausible. These two dimensions depend upon different kinds of knowledge: while the former is based upon children's knowledge of television as a medium, the latter is based primarily on their experience of the physical and social world. These two dimensions may function independently of each other, and even appear contradictory. Children may be highly aware that a particular programme is fictional, yet they may also regard it as a very plausible representation of the world.

From his study, Hawkins concludes that these two dimensions may develop in different ways. In line with previous research, he suggests that the 'Magic Window' dimension — children's awareness of the constructed nature of television — increases steadily with age. However, the 'Social Expectations' dimension displays a curvilinear trend: it is the youngest and oldest children in his sample (preschoolers and 11-year-olds) who are most sceptical of the plausibility of television, while those between these ages see it as a relatively useful source of information about the world. However, this also varies according to the subject being represented: for example, older children were more likely to perceive television families as similar to real families, when compared with pre-schoolers.

Subsequent research has sought to develop this basic distinction, although as in this case, the findings are often inconclusive or contradictory (see Morison and Gardner, 1978; Morison *et al.*, 1979, 1981). Aimee Dorr (1983), for example, finds that the 'Magic Window' dimension — as revealed by children's understanding of the economic system of television production, and their awareness of the formal features of programmes — does indeed develop with age. Nevertheless, the fact that this knowledge is available does not necessarily mean it will be used: it may be seen as irrelevant, or alternatively as so obvious that it does not need to be stated. Like Hawkins, Dorr finds fewer age differences in the 'Social Expectations' dimension, although she also argues that this dimension becomes increasingly significant for older children: certainly beyond the age of 6 or 7, the fact that most television content is 'made up' is not the most potent criterion. While Dorr acknowledges that older children are likely to employ more diverse and flexible criteria, she asserts that children generally tend not to display a monolithic view of television reality. On the contrary, their judgments are 'particularistic', based on the specific contexts of characters and their behaviour.

Hodge and Tripp (1986) employ similar distinctions and arrive at similar conclusions, albeit from a different theoretical perspective. As they suggest, judgments about the perceived reality of television — or what in linguistic terms would be called its *modality* — depend both on the characteristics of the text and on the comparison between the text and reality (or, more accurately, what the reader believes about reality). Using semiotics, Hodge and Tripp identify some of the 'modality markers' of a text — that is, the formal and contextual 'cues' which increase the transformational distance between the image and its referent, and thereby indicate that it has been consciously constructed. Nevertheless, they argue that these 'internal' characteristics may not be recognized, and that readers also use 'external' criteria based on their experience or beliefs about the world — which are, by definition, socially and culturally specific and thus likely to be diverse. Modality, therefore, is not a fixed property of the message, or of its relation to reality, but 'a subjective, variable, relative and negotiable judgment' *about* the message. As a result, they argue, 'it is very likely that the modality judgments of children will be systematically different from those of adults, leading to very different responses to the same message compared to what adults assume is necessarily and objectively "there" ' (p. 106).

Hodge and Tripp also suggest that children's judgments are likely to become more complex and flexible as they mature, although they may become more contradictory. In middle childhood, children begin to develop a much broader range of criteria, yet these are not always integrated into a coherent structure, often resulting in 'mistaken' or at least inconsistent judgments.

For all these reasons, interpreting children's judgments about the reality of television is bound to be complex and problematic. The same judgment can be reached by different children for radically different reasons. What it means to say something is 'real' or 'realistic' can mean very different things at different times, and in different contexts. Furthermore, what children say does not necessarily reflect what they 'know', or all of what they know. These judgments are not fixed, once-for-all statements: we should expect inconsistency, flexibility and contradiction. At the same time, making judgments about the reality of television cannot be seen as a purely individual, cognitive process: on the contrary, it depends upon knowledge which is socially shared, and it performs specific social functions.

Passing Judgments

In this chapter, I intend to illustrate and extend this 'multidimensional' approach to studying children's judgments about the modality of television. The data here are taken from an activity in which the children were asked to group or place in order a series of programme titles, according to whether they were perceived as 'realistic'. In groups of three or four, they were initially presented with a set of twelve titles, selected to cover a range of genres. These were followed by smaller groups of four titles, each representing a particular genre (see Table 9.1). While the first group was designed to raise broader distinctions — for example, between fact and fiction, and between cartoons, puppets and live action programmes — the subsequent groups were selected in order to provide opportunities to make finer judgments. In most cases, as we had hoped, the discussion ranged much more widely than this prepared agenda.

Table 9.1 Programme titles presented

Group One
The Cosby Show: US situation comedy
Blockbusters: general knowledge quiz
The News
Knightmare: 'dungeons and dragons' game
Dennis: US cartoon
Only Fools and Horses: British situation comedy
Blue Peter: British children's magazine programme
Land of the Giants: US science fiction series
The Bill: British police series
He-Man: US action cartoon
Sooty: British puppet show
Baywatch: US live action drama

Group Two: Soap operas
EastEnders
Coronation Street
Neighbours
Home and Away

Group Three: Live action children's drama
Grange Hill
Doogie Howser, MD
Children's Ward
Press Gang

Group Four: Family comedies
The Cosby Show
Roseanne
Kate and Allie
Bread

As with the activity described in Chapter 6, this was undoubtedly a comparatively 'artificial' task, yet here again it seemed to be regarded more as a game than as any kind of test. Very few children appeared confused by the research question, and the interviewers' attempts at clarification were often supported by others in the group. We deliberately used a variety of terms here, and others emerged during the group discussions — 'true-to-life', 'real' and (for some of the older children) 'believable' were among them. These terms — and indeed, the word 'realistic' itself — seemed to take on a variety of meanings in different contexts. Here again, the main focus of interest was not so much in the 'product' — that is, the judgments themselves — as in the *processes* by which they were arrived at.

In the following sections, I intend to identify and illustrate the criteria which appeared to inform the children's judgments. In the process, I hope to refine some of the broad distinctions developed in previous research, and in particular the distinction between 'Magic Window' and 'Social Expectations' reality — or what I shall term (following Hodge and Tripp, 1986) 'internal' and 'external' criteria.

Internal Criteria: Identifying the Modality Markers

In general, there seemed to be little doubt even among the youngest children here that fictional television programmes are constructed *representations* of the world, rather than mere reflections of it. All the children 'knew' that live action drama was scripted, that it was often performed in studios, that the characters were played by actors, and that many of the effects were achieved by 'camera tricks' of various kinds. They were also aware that the stories they saw on television tended to follow certain conventions, for example in order to make them amusing or exciting, and that things didn't happen in quite the same way in 'real life'. While there was occasionally confusion about the level at which this construction operated — Rupert (8), for example, speculated about whether cowboys and Indians wear bullet-proof vests — there was hardly any sense here that television was regarded as a 'Magic Window'. This is, I would suggest, hardly surprising for children of this age.

This use of internal criteria appeared to function on two largely complementary levels, which I will consider in turn below. Firstly, there was some explicit discussion of the 'forms and conventions' of television — for example, of narrative and genre; secondly, particularly among the younger children, there was an ongoing speculation and sharing of knowledge about the technical processes of television production.

Forms and Conventions

Distinctions between puppet shows, cartoons and live action drama, and between actors and 'real people' were employed by children in all age groups as a basic modality marker. While there was occasionally some room for debate here — for example, a number of the 8-year-olds argued that puppets were more real than cartoons because they had 'real people' operating them — these distinctions were invariably clear and consistent.

Comedy also emerged as another broad criterion, used by children in all age groups. A number of children argued that in general, as Navin (12) said, 'comedies aren't really that real'. This was partly a reflection of the constructed nature of comedy — the sense, noted by some children, that comedy is often based on 'coincidences', and that comic characters are deliberately constructed to gain laughs. Nevertheless, it also related to external criteria, and the comparison with reality: as Carol (12) put it, in relation to *Only Fools and Horses*, 'it's not that funny, your life'. As Carol's comment implies, this was partly a matter of *frequency*: as Hitesh (10) argued, in relation to *The Cosby Show*, 'you know, you wouldn't be that stupid, like making jokes every ten seconds, twenty-four hours a day, seven days a week like that'.

However, many of the groups made distinctions between comedies according to how 'serious' they were, which were not just to do with how many jokes they contained. Thus, many of the children argued that *Only Fools and Horses* was more 'realistic' than *The Cosby Show* on the grounds that it was closer to their own experience (working-class British, as opposed to middle-class American); yet others suggested that *The Cosby Show* was more realistic on the grounds that it sometimes dealt with 'serious' issues, albeit in a somewhat moralistic fashion. A similar distinction was made by some of the older children between the British and Australian soaps, even though the latter were generally preferred.

Another major dimension here concerns narrative. Again, while the children were generally aware that fictional narratives had been deliberately constructed according to certain formal requirements, they were often critical of programmes where this was too obvious. Thus, there were complaints about the 'predictable' nature of cartoons — as Nancy (8) noted, 'the goodies always win!' — although this extended to programmes which were generally seen as much more realistic: Peter (8), for example, complained about how the police in *The Bill* always 'pop up from nowhere' when a crime has been committed. Furthermore, like comedies, soap operas and police series were occasionally condemned for their excess of narrative incident. Anne and Luke (10), for example, complained about the repetitions and coincidences in *Neighbours* as follows:

Extract 1

> *Luke*: Well all that happens is they fall in love, then they break up and someone else has them [then they=
> *Anne*:   [=have a couple of pregnancies.
> *Luke*: They break up, then they get back together, break up, get back together, break up, get back together.
>
> .
> .
>
> .
> *Anne*: Everything comes in spurts, suddenly everyone all starts having accidents and killing themselves [*laughing:*] then everyone falls in love, then everybody breaks up, then everybody gets married, and then everybody gets pregnant. And they all happen at the same time!

Likewise, there were complaints about the artificiality of the cliffhanger device, and the ways in which *Neighbours's* narratives tend to be so easily and quickly resolved: according to Nancy (12), 'one day, right, someone's just been kidnapped and they're about to die, and the next day they're suddenly all right and someone else is about to die!'. John (10) felt that the way in which the serial places the viewer in a position of knowledge tended to undermine one's belief in the characters: how, he argued, could Henry be so 'thick' as to go to Brisbane without recognizing that Mike would use the opportunity to take Bronwen away from him — 'who would be that stupid?!' Nevertheless, it is possible to detect in all these judgments an implicit acknowledgment that this rather obvious — and possibly inept — use of narrative devices is part of the serial's appeal: as Sean (12) explicitly argued, 'they've got to make it interesting because otherwise it would just be like any other street, really boring'.

On a rather different level, there were also complaints about continuity, often of a rather 'literal' kind. For example, Michelle (8) complained that Dennis 'never grows up', while a number of children complained about the way in which cartoons and other action programmes tend to draw out a narrative in order to maximize suspense:

Extract 2

John:	[In *He-Man*] it's obvious what's gonna happen [. . .] Well, somebody from, like they're in a different planet, and somebody from Earth comes along and they're holding an atomic bomb to destroy this big fat meteorite [*laughter*] I think, which is like a magnet, is sucking up all their satellites and stuff, and they have to destroy it before it hits Earth, and everyone dies.
Karen:	And of course they do it in the nick of time.

.
.
.

Peter:	Like in other shows, when there's a bomb and, like *The A-Team*, say, when there's a bomb or something, they just manage to defuse it in one second, it's one second and then it's gonna blow up.
John:	Like James Bond.
Interviewer:	So why do you think they do that?
Peter:	Dunno.
John:	Make it exciting, probably.

To some extent, this kind of judgment appears rather 'obvious', and even pedantic. The children recognize that the narrative has been constructed in this way in order to achieve certain effects on the viewer, and (implicitly) that its claim to realism is not a strong one. Similarly, when Luke (10) notes that the characters in *He-Man* never blink, or Michelle (8) complains that Dennis's hair always looks the same even when he's been thrown into some water, there is a sense in which they are applying criteria of literal realism which they know to be inappropriate. Rather like complaints about the lack of blood in *Tom and Jerry* or the fact that you never see anybody go to the toilet in *Dallas*, these almost facetious remarks reflect an implicit awareness that empiricist conceptions of realism — the notion that such texts *intend* to provide an accurate representation of reality — provide a rather limited basis for judgment (see Ang, 1985).

The Production Process

These judgments about the forms and conventions of television were often reinforced by references to the ways in which programmes are produced. Even the younger children were well aware that the characters in fictional programmes were played by actors, and there was often some speculation about how particular feats of 'good acting' were achieved. Justine (8), for example, asked how 'they train the baby to cry all the time' in *EastEnders*, while Nancy and Robin (8) speculated about how the patients in *Children's Ward* managed to vomit so convincingly. Some of the older children also considered the economic context of acting, albeit rather inaccurately: for example, Hitesh (10) argued that most actors just 'do it for the money' — 'at least 200 pounds a week', in Ajita's estimation — but that child actors would lose out on their education because of having to 'rehearse seven days a week'.

Particularly in the case of the soaps, much of this information appeared to have been derived from 'secondary texts'. Many of the children knew that the characters didn't really live in those houses, that the babies were often played by a number of different 'actors' and that the actors were really much more wealthy and glamorous than the characters they played. One specific instance of the effect of this knowledge was provided by Justine (8): '*Neighbours* is a bit unreal because they're doing a trick on us, because Charlene is supposed to be gone, she's supposed to be gone to Brisbane but she's really left the show, and now they're just talking to themselves on the telephone'. To a greater degree than with other genres, the children seemed to be aware of agency, of 'the people who done the programme' and who were responsible for the fate of the characters.

The most significant hesitation here arose in relation to some live action drama programmes, such as *The Bill* and *Children's Ward*, which were often judged to be more 'realistic'. Here, a number of the children suggested that at least some of the people in these programmes were 'really' police officers or hospital patients, although they also asserted very confidently that the programmes were scripted, that the injuries were just 'make-up' and that the blood was obviously 'fake'. The uncertainty here seemed to be motivated, not so much by a belief that the programmes were offering an unmediated 'slice of life', but by an appreciation of the *authenticity* of the fiction, and an interest in how this was achieved. Julia (12) for example, suggested that the actors in *The Bill* 'have to be policemen for about a month or something, they have to join it and see what happens'.

Especially among the younger children, there was also a considerable amount of discussion about the more technical aspects of production. As Hodge and Tripp (1986) have noted, a concern — even an obsession — with 'the mechanics of media illusions' is typical of children of this age, and forms an important basis for their modality judgments. In some cases, this knowledge appeared to derive from personal experience — Ritta and Diana (8) for example, described how they had used a zoom lens on a video camera to 'shrink' people — yet 'behind the scenes' programmes like *Cartoon Time* and *The Making of Michael Jackson's Thriller* were also referred to here. While these explanations were occasionally vague, they were often extremely inventive: as Hodge and Tripp argue, while children may lack all the information they need, they will often overcompensate for this, making what little they know do more work.

Thus, the special effects in programmes like *Land of the Giants* and *Knightmare* were the focus of a large amount of speculation, with several competing theories being entertained. For example, one group of 8-year-olds engaged in an extended debate about how 'they' combine the giants and the humans in *Land of the Giants*. Nathan argued that this was achieved through 'clever tricks' with the camera, and possibly through editing — 'they video them, and then make the video of them very small, and then they put the rest of the programme onto it'. Nancy argued that it might be robots or models — noting that when you saw a close-up of the giants' hands, 'you can see his skin isn't real like ours, it's sort of like foamy rubber'. Even among the 8-year-olds, there were a number of children who had some understanding of the effects that could be achieved through editing, back projection, split mattes, chromakey and computer animation — even if they were unaware of the technical terms themselves.

Nevertheless, this speculation extended to programmes which were generally regarded as more 'realistic'. The scene in which Rory had been killed by a shark in *Home and Away*, for example, provoked considerable debate. Some of the children were convinced that it was a 'remote control' or 'mechanical' shark, while others argued that the footage had been taken from 'a wildlife film' and 'sort of clipped in'. It was also noted that the actual attack itself had not been shown, only the aftermath; and that the scene was 'unreal', when compared with *Jaws* — although here too, the shark was recognized as 'plastic'. Other children argued that the attack was too much of a coincidence: as Michelle (8) argued, it was significant that it was not a well-established character who had been killed — 'he's just come in the series, and I thought probably he [i.e. the actor] doesn't like what he was doing'.

In general, as this example suggests, this 'technical' knowledge of television production serves to undermine any belief in the reality of what is shown — and to defend the speaker from any negative emotions which such a belief might make possible. If we know that the more gory injuries in *The Bill* or in horror films are achieved by make-up, or by tricks and face paints you can buy at the local toy shop — as was repeatedly claimed — their ability to provoke disgust or fear is correspondingly reduced. Nevertheless, some of the children did suggest that this kind of knowledge only came into play after the event: as Nancy (8) argued, 'people don't really think about those things when they're watching the TV, they don't think about it until people ask them about it' — although this view was disputed by others. As I shall argue, modality judgments in general can serve as a powerful form of retrospective distancing or rationalization.

In terms of critical judgments, however, this knowledge often seemed to cut both ways. On the one hand, there were many criticisms of bad acting and cheap production values, often delivered with great amusement. Children in all age groups seemed to have noted the 'fake' painted backdrops and wobbly sets in programmes like *Neighbours* and *Kate and Allie*: as Anne (10) noted, 'if they slam the door, the whole house shakes!' Louise (8) mounted an extensive critique of a recent storyline in *EastEnders* in which Ian had been badly injured in a car accident:

Extract 3

> *Louise:* You know that boy I was talking about, when I said he had a
> disgusting face, that looked really realistic, but parts of it just
> looked really stupid, as though you just sort of like mucked it
> up, you were getting so bored, you just do the stupid, just do
> a stupid thing, and stick it on, camera-fy that or whatever [. . .]
> And the man with his crutches um, just say I've got crutches
> [*she gets up and imitates*], and he goes, he was going really fast,
> and it looked nothing like he had a broken leg.

On the other hand, even programmes that were clearly regarded as fictional
were also described as 'realistic', on the grounds that they '*looked* realistic' — as
is partly the case in this extract. Likewise, Sean (12) praised the acting of 'Mo' in
EastEnders, who had recently been afflicted with Alzheimer's disease: 'it's really
realistic, the way she does it, the way she acts [. . .] she portrayed herself really
well'.

Yet this kind of judgment also applied to programmes that were patently
seen as fantasy: Andrew (10) described *Knightmare* as realistic on the grounds that
'it's holograms, and holograms look really real 'cause um they like walk in and
it's like they've got a hologram of a room and it looks like they're really in it'.
In other instances, the children distinguished between cartoon and live action
versions of the same story — for example in the case of *He-Man* — arguing that
the latter were more 'realistic'. Yet as Michael (10) acknowledged, it was easier to
achieve some 'unrealistic' effects in a cartoon than a film: 'cartoons, you can do
anything with them you want'. In these instances, the programme is described as
'realistic', although there is no sense in which it is seen as 'real': in effect, the
judgment is based on an appreciation of the time and effort that had been taken
by the producers or the actors to construct an effective *illusion* of reality.

This kind of 'realism' also seemed to depend upon how much viewers are
shown — in effect, on the physical extent of the programme's fictional world.
Thus, common (and disputed) complaints about *Neighbours* included assertions that
'you never see the bedrooms' and that 'they hardly ever go out'. By contrast,
outside locations appeared to serve as a guarantee of authenticity: *Home and Away*
and *EastEnders*, for example, were praised for 'going outside' and showing 'more
of a town than one street'. These judgments also reflect on production values —
the more we see, the more money has been spent — although this was not made
explicit. Indeed, there was occasionally some confusion here: some of the children
asserted that the sets of *EastEnders* and *Coronation Street* were real places — the
latter, it was argued, was 'somewhere up in Enfield' (North London) — while
continuing to talk about them as fictional programmes.

Ultimately, then, the term 'realistic' used in this way reflects an *aesthetic*
judgment: it refers to the technical or artistic 'quality' of the illusion, while simultaneously acknowledging the fact that it is an illusion. Indeed, in some instances,
there was almost a sense of 'realism' — and in particular, realist drama — as a *genre*
in itself. Thus, a number of children commented on the way in which visual
details seemed to contribute to what might almost be termed a conventionalized
iconography of realism: Malcolm (10), for example, referred to the coffee machine
in *The Bill* and Sylvester Stallone's stubble in *Over the Top* as evidence of their

realism. Yet these judgments repeatedly reflect the fundamental distinction between what *looks* real and what *is* real — between real*ism* and reality — precisely the distinction children are often assumed to be incapable of making.

Possibility, Plausibility and Truth

These judgments based on the constructed nature of television were both supported and qualified by those based on 'external' criteria — that is, on what viewers know or believe to be the truth about the world. If the judgments considered thus far are essentially concerned with form, these judgments are primarily based on a comparison between the *content* of the text and reality.

In these discussions, there was a broad consensus about the kinds of events which were by definition impossible. It was primarily on these grounds that cartoons or fantasy programmes were deemed 'unrealistic'. Here again, it was the younger children who asserted most confidently that there are no such things as giants (*Land of the Giants*), that walls and trees cannot talk (*Knightmare*), that people cannot lift mountains and cats cannot fly (*He-Man*), and so on. For the older children, these things may have been so obvious they hardly needed to be stated: yet it may also be the case that the younger children here had more at stake in distancing themselves from programmes which, as Adrian (10) remarked, seemed to be perceived as 'babyish . . . like in a story book'.

However, these judgments about what was physically possible or impossible were also applied to the more dramatic events in the soap operas, often with the effect of deflating their significance. Thus, John and Peter (10) complained about how Mrs Mangel in *Neighbours* lost her memory simply by falling off a ladder, while Vicky (8) complained about how Daphne had given birth with her tights on. In other instances, the economic status of the characters was seen as incompatible with their apparent affluence: Anne (10) was one of a number of children who questioned how the *Neighbours* characters could afford such large houses and swimming pools while they were only employed as waitresses.

Yet there was also material which at least outwardly appeared to be accepted as truth. Nowhere was there any doubt that the News was the most realistic programme: it 'tells you what's happened', 'tells you real stuffs' and gives you 'the facts'. There was a little more scepticism about *Blue Peter*. Elaine (8), for example, argued that they had faked a scene in which one of the presenters was supposed to be blowing up some buildings, and claimed that she had watched this on another programme. Yet despite the unpopularity of *Blue Peter* — or at least the children's unwillingness to admit to watching it — few of them disputed its claim to be 'telling you what happens'.

The truth status of both programmes appeared to derive partly from a kind of faith on the children's part that the producers would not — or at least could not — make things up. Michael (10), for example, argued that the producers of the News 'wouldn't make up things to upset us' — although this argument was disputed by others in his group; and Hitesh (10) argued that if the News didn't exist, people wouldn't know what was happening — 'there's got to be ONE programme that has to be real and showing real things'. In a couple of instances, a distinction was made between television news and the press, which the children appeared to be less inclined to trust. Perhaps part of the 'claim to truth' which the children perceived in these programmes lay in their direct address: as Diana (8) suggested, *Blue Peter* is 'talking to *you*', whereas in fictional programmes like *The Bill*, 'they're sort of getting on with their thing [. . .] like they're pretending that we're not there'. Yet despite this generalized faith in the truth of these programmes, they were routinely dismissed as 'boring'.

In general, then, there appeared to be considerable agreement about which programmes were completely 'true' and which were not. But between these two extremes, in making judgments about genres such as soap opera and situation comedy, there was more room for debate and disagreement, and a range of criteria which could potentially be employed.

External Criteria: Levels of Reality

Making judgments about plausibility depends upon a comparison with reality, although reality can be invoked in many different ways. In some instances here, this took a more *generalized* form. Programmes were judged in terms of broad assertions about the world, often delivered without supporting evidence. For example, a number of children in all age groups criticized programmes like *The Cosby Show* and *Neighbours* for providing a rosy picture of family life: as Hannah (8) argued, 'families are not always really that happy, are they, at times?' In some instances, this was implicitly based on a recognition of the conventions of narrative: Navin (12) argued that the Cosby family 'always manage to sort everything out' and that the programme always ended on a note of 'happy ever after'. On the other hand, programmes like *The Bill* were praised for showing 'things that could happen in real life', even though it was acknowledged that many of them were outside the children's personal experience.

It is possible to make a broad distinction here between assertions that seem to depend upon *psychological* assumptions or theories about human motivation and behaviour, and those which rely upon beliefs about the likelihood or frequency of events in *social* life. Thus, Hannah (10) questioned the plausibility of Emma in *Home and Away* suddenly changing from being a 'punk' to 'someone really nice that fancies Steven', although Donna responded by arguing that 'it is possible to change overnight'. Here, the debate is essentially about whether the requirements of the narrative have violated general psychological truths about 'human nature'.

These psychological judgments may also reflect social or even moral norms. For example, Toby (12) argued that Henry in *Neighbours* was immature — 'he's not really realistic, you're never going to get people that age making stupid little jokes like that'; while Ranjit (12) questioned the reaction of Nick in *Neighbours* to the discovery that his girlfriend had 'double booked' their date — 'I don't think that's natural, I think Nick would have got angry or something, just show his strength'. As in these two instances, statements about what *is* real may in fact reflect judgments about what we would *like* to be real, or what we think ought to be. Similarly, in the case of *Roseanne*, comments about its psychological plausibility were occasionally tinged with some more explicit moral judgment: Hitesh (10) accused the parents of 'always thinking about themselves' and not caring about their children, while Nancy (12) argued that 'it's a bit overdone . . . they should be a bit more serious when they're with the kids, to give the kids the right attitude'.

Judgments about *social* reality were often expressed in terms of the frequency of particular events occurring, even where the children themselves had little direct experience of them. In some instances, there was praise for the authenticity of programmes on these grounds: Adele (10), for example, praised *Only Fools and Horses* for showing 'what lots of people have to live like, I mean some people live in council flats just the way they do' — although, it should be said, Adele herself was not one of them. On the other hand, while it was acknowledged that certain events did occur in the world, there was often some doubt about whether they would do so as regularly as they do on television. Anne (10), a highly enthusiastic exponent of modality judgments, delivered the following litany about *Grange Hill*:

Extract 4

Interviewer: How do you think secondary school's going to be different from that?

Anne: 'Cause you're not going to go on demonstrations, and you're not going to feel so strongly, and you're not going to fall in love with forty-year-old men, and you're not going to have weird teachers, and your teachers aren't probably going to change into different people, you're not going to suffocate yourself in an unventilated room with spray paint . . .

Simon: Yeah, that's so stupid.

Anne: I mean, would you sit in a room doing this [*mimes spray painting, inhaling, coughing*] 'Oh dear, we've got some toxic fumes, oh well, we'll just kill ourselves waiting here' [*laughs*].

As Anne's catalogue of implausibilities suggests, the major problem here is not so much the events themselves but their frequency: as Donna (10) argued, these things do happen, but they wouldn't happen 'that much'. Here again, these judgments sometimes appeared to be based on a sense of the constructed nature of the narrative, and the ways in which plausibility was often sacrificed to the need to maintain interest and excitement.

For some of the children, direct personal experience seemed to serve as the major touchstone for their observations. For example, a number confirmed the authenticity of *The Bill* by referring to their own observations of the police at work or robberies that had happened in their families, while others argued that *Grange Hill* reflected their own or their friends' experiences of secondary schools. Likewise, for one group of 12-year-old girls, *Only Fools and Horses* seemed to speak to their experience of working-class family life, by contrast with *The Cosby Show*:

Extract 5

Angela: *Fools and Horses*, 'cause there's more common life [. . .]

Carol: East End sort of thing, normal. Like us, sort of thing [. . .] I mean, you never see in *The Cosby Show* a bill come and they can't afford to pay it [*laughs*]. Do you?

Angela: Yeah.

Interviewer: Yeah, they've got plenty of money. Yeah, that's right.

> Della: Like, *Fools and Horses* like, knock off [steal] things, like they
>   sell things cheap.
> Angela: Yeah, that's like life!

In other cases, the children sought to compare the programmes with the reality directly referenced within them. Thus, a number asserted that the events in *EastEnders* were very similar to those that occurred in the real East End of London. Likewise, Robert (10) claimed to have seen the flats in Peckham (South London) where *Only Fools and Horses* was filmed, while (more exotically) Michael (10) claimed to have seen beaches and lifeguards in California exactly like those on *Baywatch*. In other instances, this knowledge was rather more hypothetical: Donna (10) argued that *Neighbours* was 'probably realistic in Australia', where the kinds of things that occurred on the programme 'probably happen quite often'. Elsewhere, however, they were careful to avoid generalizations based on ignorance: Karen (10) argued that she couldn't tell whether *Baywatch* was realistic because she had never been to America, and Nancy (12) argued that she couldn't make judgments about *EastEnders* 'cause we don't know life like that'.

Internal and External: Debating the Criteria

The relationship between these two sets of criteria was inevitably quite variable. Particularly when it came to negative judgments, they appeared to reinforce each other: *Press Gang*, for example, was summarily condemned by one group of 10-year-olds as follows:

Extract 6

> Interviewer: So can you give me one good reason why it's not so
>   much like real life as the other ones?
> Andrew, Michael: Because it doesn't really happen.
> Hamid: And they don't act that good.

Here, Andrew and Michael's assessment of the implausibility of the programme is supported by Hamid's comment about its constructedness, although the two statements use quite different criteria.

Yet in many cases, programmes were found to be stronger on one criterion than another. *He-Man*, for example, was generally seen as weak on both internal and external criteria, while *Dennis* was stronger on external, though equally weak on internal, criteria. Pradesh (12) described *Dennis* as 'realistic, but in cartoon form' — effectively recasting this distinction into the traditional one between form and content.

Here again, however, it was in the area of 'naturalistic' drama like *The Bill* and *Children's Ward* that finer distinctions were required, and this sometimes led to contradictory or inconsistent judgments. For some of the younger children, the claim that these programmes were more realistic often seemed to be based on a simple evaluation of their content: Nathan (8), for example, argued that *The Bill* was true 'because it's about robbers', while Robin (8) agreed, 'because it's all about handcuffing and police and blood'. In some cases, non-fictional programmes were used as a kind of guarantee of the authenticity of fictional ones: Hannah (8), for example, argued that 'real police shows' like *Crimewatch* featured similar incidents to those on *The Bill*. Such programmes were also occasionally described as reliable sources for social learning: *The Bill* was praised by a number of children for warning you 'not to get involved with the wrong things'. In some cases, this information was seen as useful preparation for the future: *The Bill* could inform potential recruits about life in the police, while *Grange Hill* would tell you how to avoid bullying at secondary school.

Yet despite all this apparent faith in the realism of these dramas, many of the children were quick to assert that they were fictional. *The Bill*, for example, was identified by even the youngest children as fictional: the guns were 'cap guns', the injuries were 'make-up' and the police station was obviously 'fake'. Here, as in many other instances, judgments based on internal criteria appeared to contradict those based on external criteria.

The following extracts from a group of 10-year-olds discussing *Children's Ward* illustrate something of the flexibility with which these different criteria were applied:

Extract 7

	Interviewer:	And what about *Children's Ward* then?
	Hannah:	Oh, I hate that, [I just think it's so revolting.
	Malcolm:	[It's disgusting.
	Hannah:	With the operations, I'm not that keen on seeing a lot of
5		blood.
	Andy:	Yeah, that is stupid.
	Hannah:	When someone cuts their hip open, I will just faint myself. I just don't like, it's OK if it's a little bit of bleed, or your knee starts to bleed, but with a lot of blood, I'll just faint.
10	*Interviewer*:	Donna.
	Donna:	Yeah, I don't like that either. But I think it's better because they do have a children's ward, if you go to ordinary hospitals, they do have a children's ward. You go the big hospitals, they've got their own children's ward, and things
15		like, and they've got proper nurses and rooms where there's the telly and all the toys.
	Hannah:	Yeah, but some people they lock themselves in the toilet down there.
	Donna:	Where, in *Children's Ward*?
20	*Hannah*:	I watched it once, and these people um, they had tattoos and they had to have them off, they were like nine, they had tattoos on their arm.
	Andy:	Nine?
	Hannah:	[. . .] And then they went to the toilet and they locked
25		themselves in the toilet and they wouldn't come out. And I don't think that's really realistic, they wouldn't let them do that in hospital.
	Malcolm:	Yeah that's stupid / I've got a tattoo.
	Hannah:	I don't really think someone would, a nine-year-old would
30		have a tattoo put on their arms.

	Malcolm:	How did they get a tattoo anyway?
	Hannah:	They went to a shop and had it done.
	Malcolm:	They wouldn't do it to a nine-year-old.
	Donna:	[You have to be over a certain age.
35	Andy:	[Well they probably got, they probably got fake ones, which they can probably get off.
	Hannah:	Yeah, but if somebody wanted it done, they'd just say I want a tattoo, and they'd just do it.
	Interviewer:	Mm, mm.
40	Donna:	If you showed them money they would.

.
.
.

	Andy:	I hate *Children's Ward*. Once, right, there was this boy right,
45		taken into the hospital right, and he had, he had a really massive cut down here.
	Donna:	Well I had a really big cut there and I had to go to hospital.

.

50 .

	Interviewer:	So how do you think they do that, I mean do you think that's real when they have a cut?
	Donna:	No, I don't think it's real.
	Andy:	They can't just cut somebody round the head, just to make
55		the series.
	Donna:	It's real, if you go to an emergency ward, you're gonna see things like that. I had to have stitches in my chin when I did it in the playground, and when I went there I saw things like that as well. I had to wait in the emergency ward for
60		a while.
	Hannah:	You know they do those little tattoos that you put on with water and then you can take them off.
	Donna:	The transfer ones.
	Interviewer:	Transfers.
65	Hannah:	You could put one on there, and just put fake blood on it, and then when they wash off all the blood, instead of being just plain normal skin, it would look like it had been cut and it's been stitched back up.

The basis for the children's judgments here shifts a number of times as the discussion proceeds. Early on, it would seem that the children are defining the programme as highly realistic: Hannah compares the programme with her own experience of seeing blood (lines 7–9), while Donna draws on her experience of hospitals (12–16), noting the accuracy of the programme's setting and props. Hannah moves on to dispute one of the storylines (line 17 onwards), rejecting it firstly on the grounds of psychological plausibility ('they wouldn't let them do that', lines 26–7). This leads on to a discussion of the legality or plausibility of these events occurring in the real world (29–40) and how the effects were achieved in the programme (35–36). Following a digression (omitted here) into the series

Press Gang, which includes some detailed speculation about how 'they' managed to fake a scene in which somebody's head was split open, the group returns to Hannah's storyline, debating the possibility of the injuries being real (54–55) and how the effects might have been achieved (65–68).

What is especially interesting here is the relationship between these two sets of criteria. On the one hand, the children know that the programme is constructed and that the injuries are not real; and they are quite ready to dispute its psychological and even legal plausibility. Yet on the other hand, they are clearly 'affected' by it, at least in the sense that they admit to finding it 'disgusting' and 'revolting'. The knowledge they bring to the programme is ambiguous, in that it both confirms and disconfirms the authenticity of the illusion: it is *like* a real hospital, even if they know it isn't, and the injuries look convincing even though they know they are 'fake'. Similarly, they know that the tattoos are make-up and therefore not real (internal), but they are also prepared to get into a debate about the conditions under which they might be possible if they were real (external).

However, it is important to note that these judgments take place at different times. At the beginning of the discussion, Hannah is describing her reactions at the time of viewing — or indeed at some point in the future when she might have to witness such things. Yet right at the end, when she returns to the question of how 'they' did the tattoos, it would seem that this is something she has just thought up. Perhaps, as I have suggested above, judgments based on internal criteria are more likely to occur after the event, almost as a form of post-hoc rationalization. Certainly, there is an element of this here: while Hannah is more upfront about her reactions, Donna characteristically adopts a 'mature', worldly-wise persona, as she does here in displaying her superior knowledge of hospitals. Discussion itself becomes a way of distancing oneself from, and thereby learning to 'handle' potentially unwanted reactions.

Social Distribution

My primary aim here has been to demonstrate the diversity of children's modality judgments and of the criteria they employ in making them. Inevitably, many of the examples I have quoted have been taken out of context, as if they were isolated comments made by individuals. Yet as I have argued, discourse about television needs to be regarded as a social act, in which different social groups are likely to participate in quite different ways. Table 9.2 provides one fairly crude indicator of this: it is based on counting the different kinds of modality judgments made in relation to the four soap operas (Group Two above).

Despite the obvious limitations of this kind of statistical analysis, these figures do seem to confirm some of the general observations made here and in previous chapters. The two most striking differences here concern age and social class. As previous researchers have found (e.g. Dorr, 1983), younger children appear to be more preoccupied with internal criteria, while older ones are more likely to use external criteria as the basis for their judgments. While more middle-class children in fact participated in this activity (62%), they nevertheless made a larger proportion of modality judgments, and also appeared to be more concerned with external than internal criteria. In addition, the older children — and particularly the middle-class ones — appeared to employ a more extensive vocabulary here: terms like

Table 9.2 Distribution of modality judgments of soap operas: by age, gender and social class

	Internal %	External %	Total no.
Age			
8-yr-olds	64	36	53
10-yr-olds	46	54	94
12-yr-olds	36	64	56
Gender			
Boys	46	54	94
Girls	50	50	109
Social class			
Middle-class	43	57	139
Working-class	60	40	64

'fantasy', 'illusion', 'exaggerated', 'over the top', 'overdone', 'overdramatize' and 'make-believe' recurred throughout their discussions, yet they were rarely used by younger children.

However, it would be wrong to take these figures at face value. As Dorr (1983) argues, the fact that knowledge is available does not necessarily mean it will be used — and, one might add, the fact that it is not used does not necessarily mean it is not available. For example, the fact that television is constructed may be so obvious for older children that they do not regard it as worth talking about. Younger children may have more at stake in trying to prove to an adult interviewer that they are not fooled by the illusion. Middle-class children may be much more adept at discerning what a middle-class interviewer 'requires', and thus more likely to produce it. Here again, we need to pay closer attention to the social context in which this discourse is produced, and the social functions it might perform.

Context and Function

A good deal of previous research in this field tends to assume that modality judgments are purely a matter of individual cognition, and that they are made on a once-and-for-all basis. Researchers typically use multiple-choice questionnaires, or interrogate children individually, requiring one-off responses to directive questions which can easily be coded and quantified. While this approach tends to level out inconsistencies in the data — indeed, one might well argue that it is *designed* to do this — these may nevertheless remain troubling.

Yet as I have argued, this is precisely what one should expect. As the discussion of *Children's Ward* in Extract 7 suggests, many different and even contradictory criteria may be in play at the same time. The process is one of debate and negotiation, in which individuals often appear to contradict themselves or indeed consciously revise their own judgments.

From the perspective of discourse analysis, we would need to regard modality judgment as a social act. Modality is something we *do* rather than just something we 'know'. Employing the discourse(s) of modality serves specific social functions or purposes within the context of particular social interactions.

Undoubtedly, there is a great amount of pleasure to be gained here: as I hope the preceding account has indicated, much of the discussion was extremely humorous. Mocking the absurdities of television is, I would argue, a very enjoyable everyday practice for the vast majority of children and adults. Much of the humour here derives from the fact that we know it isn't real and yet we are *supposed* to believe that it is. Most fictional television invites us to suspend our disbelief, and rigorously excludes any evidence of its own constructedness: as Diana (8) put it, 'they're pretending that we're not there'. Yet if we refuse to honour our side of the contract, we acquire a considerable degree of autonomy.

Thus, while it is often pleasurable, the modality discourse is also a very powerful one. It entails a claim to knowledge, whether of the real world or of the ways in which television itself is produced. In condemning television as 'unrealistic' — or indeed in praising it on the grounds that it '*looks* realistic' — we are simultaneously distancing ourselves from the 'other people' who know less than we do, and who therefore implicitly believe it to be 'real'.

The power which the discourse offers inevitably relates to broader relationships of social power. For many of the older children, modality judgments provided a means of distancing themselves from programmes which were seen as 'babyish' or 'kids' stuff', and thereby proclaiming their own maturity. Luke (10), for example, persistently equated 'realistic' with 'grown-up'; while Carol (12) argued intriguingly that *Home and Away* was 'like life for children'. Here again, there was a kind of displacement onto younger children: Sean (12) argued that 'little kids' would say that *Sooty* is real — although none of the little kids in this sample were under any such illusion. While modality judgments provide a powerful means of undermining other people's pleasures, the other people concerned were generally condemned, as in this case, in their absence.

I want to move on to consider two more extended examples of this process. The first is taken from one of the earlier pair discussions considered in Chapter 5. Here, Jennifer and Adele, two 9-year-old middle-class children from the inner-city primary school, are discussing *Brave Starr*, a science fiction cartoon.

Extract 8

Adele:	Yeah! It's about, it's really good, I mean it's about these cowboys and they're mechanical, right, most of them are mechanical and there's sort of a mechanical ranch and all that, and Brave Starr's the sheriff, and
Jessica:	He can always, he always wins, he always wins, [it's not really true.
Adele:	[I'd like to see him lose, it'd be much more exciting, I mean if they weren't robots, no it's a cartoon, if they weren't robots then I think I'd like it, but. If there wasn't so much fighting, and they weren't robots.
Jessica:	I hate the way the horse can talk, it's just / unlifelike.
Interviewer:	Mm, mm. / So is it a bit like *Transformers* or something? I mean, that sort of cartoon, yeah?
Adele:	[Yeah, it's boring!

Jessica: [Yeah, because the horse can change to, like when Brave Starr says um / give me a hand or something, the horse like says something, and he sort of jumps up onto his back legs and then all of a sudden his hoofs turn to hands and he's got a gun on his back, with a little strap, but before it was the saddle, wasn't it?

.
.
.

Jessica: Yeah, 'cause it takes so long for him to transfer that he could be killed by then [mm] and he never is.

Adele: Yeah I mean

Jessica: They're always just going [*mimes people in slow motion*] until he's done it.

The criteria on which the girls' judgments of *Brave Starr* are based are both internal — for example, their comments on the predictable nature of the narrative and the lapses in continuity — and external — for example, their rejection of the talking horse that transforms itself into a warrior. There is great enthusiasm here — this extract is only part of a much longer, and generally extremely fluent critique — but there is also a sense in which the programme is a very easy target for these kinds of judgments. Elsewhere in the discussion, the girls proclaim a preference for programmes like *Doctor Who* and *Batman* and films like *Superman* and *Alice in Wonderland*, which would imply that their preferences are not necessarily guided by considerations about what is 'lifelike'.

In fact, it becomes clear from the remainder of their discussion that the motivation for Adele and Jessica's critique of *Brave Starr* derives largely from the social interaction which frames the viewing context. The programme is introduced into the discussion (immediately prior to the above extract) by Jessica's complaint that her older brother insists on watching it when she wants to watch *Blue Peter*. Adele goes on to describe how her younger cousin makes her watch it when she visits their house, despite her attempts to go elsewhere and watch a 'good video'. Both girls claim that they don't like the fighting in the programme, and Jessica suggests that 'it encourages people to fight', a point which Adele develops in the following extract.

Extract 9

Interviewer: But you're saying you think it encourages people to fight, yeah?

Adele: Mmm. 'Cause [it does.

Jessica: ['Cause it is always fighting, like *The A-Team* and that, like we were talking about last time.

Adele: When I was six, / my cousin was quite young, he was only about ten or eleven, and he um / he didn't watch *Brave Starr* and he was rather gentle /

Jessica: I thought *Brave Starr* wasn't on then.

Adele: Yeah. And he was, he didn't have it in Cheshire you see.

	And so, and then *Brave Starr* just started when he was about seven.
Jessica:	It didn't, it only started about a month ago [*laughs*].
Adele:	It started ages ago, I mean. But / it, when he started watching it, when he was sixteen, he always bullies me, because, I think it's because of *Brave Starr* and all the *A-Team* programmes that he watches. 'Cause he just, I mean, when he=
Jessica:	=At sixteen or seventeen, in their teens, they always think they're so big and stuff.
Adele:	I know, like=
Jessica:	=Like my brother.

.

.

.

Interviewer:	So you're thinking he's become a bit of a bully, then because of [the TV?
Adele:	[Yeah, he's also very babyish. 'Cause I thought, I mean, I watched it a long time ago, / I did, I watched it, but then I went off it, cause I thought, this is stupid, it is just so babyish. / 'Cause it is. I mean it's meant to be violent, for all ages, but it's not! It's for little toddlers, cause they think=
Jessica:	=It's not for toddlers, it teaches them bad manners.
Adele:	I know / They think it is for toddlers, you see. So I went out of it / really long time ago now. /

Here, the critique of *Brave Starr* is extended through arguments about 'effects', both of a general nature — for example, Jessica's comment about 'bad manners' — and in the form of Adele's specific 'case study' of her older cousin. Although Jessica questions the detail of Adele's assertions here — the chronology is certainly confused — the girls are united in their attempt to define the programme's audience as 'other' than themselves. Gender may be an issue here, although Adele's younger cousin is in fact a girl, and she later refuted the male interviewer's suggestion that *Brave Starr* is 'for boys'. Age is also at stake, although this involves Adele redefining her older cousin as 'babyish'. While it is possible for her to admit to some previous enthusiasm for the programme, this is situated well in the past, a 'really long time ago'. Finally, although they are omitted from these extracts, there are recurrent references in this discussion which serve to situate the girls in terms of social class: Adele talks about her cousins' 'massive' country house with its 'TV in every room', while Jessica claims that her own house is equally 'massive' — thereby marking their difference from the other children in their class, whose domestic circumstances are much more deprived.

In general, therefore, it would seem that the girls use the modality discourse, combined with related arguments about 'effects', as a means of building a mutually acceptable definition of themselves, in terms of gender, social class and overall 'maturity'. Given the vulnerability of their target, this is an achievement they manage with comparative ease.

My second example here is drawn from a discussion of the American series *Baywatch* — a programme which was undoubtedly popular, but which was often criticized, particularly by the older children, on the, grounds that its characters were implausibly glamorous. One group of 12-year-old boys in the suburban secondary school seemed highly preoccupied with the muscle-bound good looks of the male characters:

Extract 10

Sean:	The people on it are sort of complete hunks and every girl's drooling over them and everything [. . .] They haven't got any sort of middle-size people, all the ladies are immaculate, and all the men are immaculate, there's no sort of middle-size people who aren't so //
Interviewer:	Perfect?
Sean:	[Yeah.
Petros:	[Even the boy that's about thirteen years old, he's got //
Interviewer:	He's got muscles as well? [*laughter*]

.
.
.

Sean:	It's really pathetic, to be honest but
Interviewer:	Why? I mean, because he's not worthy to be fancied or?
Sean:	No — but he's, he's // [all the girls go MAD over it.
Peter:	[They build it up like that especially for the programme.
Interviewer:	What — this character?
Peter:	Yeah. They make him build up his muscles just for the programme to give him an image in the programme. [They need to build him up.
Sean:	[He doesn't look nothing like he is in the programme. You see without all that make-up on, he's probably just the same as / he / probably just the same as someone in school, isn't he? [. . .] He's nothing special, I wouldn't say // [I think he's ugly, to be honest.
Petros:	[Apart from he's rich!
Interviewer:	You think he'd be=
Petros:	=You would, wouldn't you, Sean?
Sean:	No, but I don't=
Petros:	=It's because he's giving you too much competition!
[*Much laughter*]	

In this instance, the boys combine statistical arguments — about the relative representation of 'middle-size people' and 'hunks' — with assertions about the constructed nature of the programme — the use of make-up and bodybuilding — in what amounts to an attempt to cut the male characters down to their own size. What threatens them is perhaps not so much the physical power of the characters as their sexual appeal, the fact that they apparently make girls 'drool': indeed, elsewhere in the discussion, they speak bitterly about the girls who have posters of these characters inside their desks. In this situation, it is the girls who are the absent 'others': Sean seems to consider it 'pathetic' that they can be fooled into fancying characters who are, in his view, patently fake — although discussions with the girls suggested that in fact they too were critical of the 'glamour' of the programme, and talked about the male characters with a considerable degree of irony (see Chapter 8, Extract 10). As in the boys' discussion of male characters in Chapter 8, modality judgments serve as a valuable resource in their attempt to allay their own anxieties.

Nevertheless, compared with the girls in the previous discussion, there is much less mutual support here. While Sean leads the critique of *Baywatch*, he is uncharacteristically hesitant, suggesting that he knows he is putting himself on the line. Indeed, his arguments are questioned by the female interviewer, and directly contradicted at a number of points by the other boys. Immediately prior to this extract, for example, Peter questions his view of the representativeness of the characters by drawing on his 'expert' knowledge of America derived from a holiday in Florida: 'you do get a lot of people like you see in *Baywatch*'. Petros's final contribution here provides an even more effective put-down, which appears to expose something of the motivation of Sean's argument, and manages (if only momentarily) to take some of the wind from his sails. Ultimately, what is at stake here is the boys' rather fragile sense of their own masculinity — which, as I have argued in previous chapters, would seem to depend upon mutual support and, on occasion, mutual policing (see Buckingham, forthcoming).

Here again, therefore, it would seem that modality judgments are being used to perform particular social functions. Yet while modality is potentially a very powerful discursive resource, this power can also be challenged. In questioning Sean's judgments about the accuracy of *Baywatch*, for example, the other boys effectively undermine his attempts to 'win back' some masculine power from the programme. In this instance at least, modality proves to be something of a double-edged sword.

The Limits of a Discourse

While the motivations for modality judgments may thus be quite diverse, they appear to provide a very effective means of undermining the 'power' of the text and thereby reasserting the 'power' of the reader. They enable readers to place the text and their responses to it at arm's length, to question the motivations of its producers and to challenge its claim to provide an accurate representation of the world.

Yet the discourse also provides a means of asserting 'power' in relation to other readers. At least part of the social function of the modality discourse derives from its ability to present the speaker as 'sophisticated' and 'mature' — as a discerning, critical viewer, who is able to 'see through' the illusions television provides. Here again, it is 'other people' who are seen to be at risk.

However, this 'power' is achieved at a price: the discourse — and perhaps particularly the emphasis on internal criteria, on artificiality — may effectively prevent any attempt to 'take television seriously'. What is unspoken — and to a large extent unspeakable — here is the *affective* dimension of children's engagement with the medium, and their emotional involvement in what they watch.

As I have indicated, modality judgments may offer a valuable means of 'handling' potentially negative emotions such as fear and disgust. While many of the children admitted to being terrified by horror films, for example, they were often quick to assert that it was all done by 'camera tricks' and make-up. It is obviously difficult to identify the extent to which modality judgments come into play at the point of viewing: yet the ability of a horror film to generate fear, and thus a great deal of its pleasure, surely depends upon the viewer's suspension of disbelief at some level — although this is precisely what the modality discourse seeks to prevent, or at least disclaim. As I suggested at the end of Chapter 4, much of the pleasure of fictional television may derive from this playful, 'as if' relationship: viewers move into and out of the text, secure in the knowledge that it is not real, yet prepared, temporarily, to pretend that it is. While the modality discourse undoubtedly provides its own pleasures, these may only partly account for the more dynamic pleasures of the viewing process.

In these discussions, there was often an uneasy balance between the emphasis on modality and the children's attempts to proclaim or even defend their preferences. For the younger children in particular, this was often a major source of confusion: 'realistic' was to be seen as a term of approval, and yet they were well aware that much of what they enjoyed could not really be described in this way. A number of the older children addressed this issue explicitly, often by rejecting the notion that being 'realistic' was necessarily a good thing. This was certainly the case when it came to the soap operas. *Coronation Street*, for example, was rated as highly realistic on the basis that nothing 'interesting' or 'exciting' ever happened in it: many of the children seemed to adopt the general principle here that, in the words of Sean (12), 'the more boring it is, the more realistic it is'. While most were critical of the implausibly happy world of the Australian soaps, with their wooden acting and tacky sets, they were nevertheless preferred to the 'gloomy', 'depressing' realism of *EastEnders*. In effect, what seemed to be happening here — most explicitly for the older children — was an attempt to preserve their preferences in the face of the power of the modality discourse.

As Hodge and Tripp (1986) argue, 'calibrating television against reality is a major concern for children throughout this age group'. It is vital that children learn about the processes of television production, and make informed judgments about its representations of the world. Yet in privileging modality judgments, there is a distinct risk of adopting rationalistic notions of 'critical viewing', which do not do justice to the complex meanings and pleasures which television makes possible. While it is certainly important to affirm children's critical abilities, it is vital to acknowledge that this is only part of the story.

Conclusion: Modality and the Spectre of 'Effects'

Much of the social power of the modality discourse derives from the fact that it implicitly distinguishes the speaker from an invisible 'other' — from the gullible masses who are stupid enough to believe that what they watch is real. If adults typically position children in this way, so children tend to do the same to those younger than themselves, and thereby seek to exempt themselves from blame. Yet again, what informs the discourse is a hidden anxiety about the negative effects of television.

This anxiety is certainly apparent in previous research on this issue. Mainstream psychological research has tended to conceive of 'perceived reality' as an *intervening variable* in a relationship which is still predominantly defined in terms of cause-and-effect. It seems to be assumed that the more realistic a programme is perceived to be, the more likely it is to influence viewers (e.g. Greenberg and Reeves, 1976; Hodge and Tripp, 1986). Yet the evidence on this issue is mixed and inconclusive, even where this is precisely what researchers have set out to discover (e.g. Greenberg, 1972, 1974; Reeves, 1978).

This argument would seem to imply that things which are perceived as 'fantasy' will have very little effect on people's attitudes or behaviour. Yet psychoanalytic theory, for example, would suggest that the relationship between fantasy and reality is much more complex, and that the individual's sense of reality in everyday life is rather more precarious. The notion that there is a 'mature' perception of reality which adults consistently manifest would seem to be at least questionable.

Equally, the relationship between information, attitudes and social behaviour may be much more complicated — and ultimately less 'rational' — than this argument tends to suggest. The fact that we may be able to discount certain kinds of representations as 'unrealistic' does not necessarily mean that they do not play a part in our perceptions of the social world. The power of stereotypes, for example, depends upon their complex combination of 'truth' and 'falsehood', and their appeal to what we *want* to believe or to have explained to us (Perkins, 1978).

These arguments about the effects of modality judgments also have educational implications. Hawkins (1977), for example, suggests that instructing children about the processes of television production may serve as a useful means of 'immunizing' them against its effects. Underlying this view is the assumption that any 'suspension of disbelief' in television is inherently dangerous, and that the less real children find it, the better. Yet this is to assume that the 'effects' of television are uniformly negative. As Reeves (1978) argues, teaching children that television is not real may lessen the impact of its 'pro-social' messages: in his study, perceiving television to be real actually *increased* the incidence of pro-social behaviour and *decreased* anti-social behaviour, at least as reported by children themselves. Perhaps more significantly, this argument assumes that 'rational' judgments will be powerful enough to displace other emotional or social investments, and that 'false' beliefs can be cast aside once they are shown to be 'unrealistic'.

Ultimately, I would suggest that the notion of modality or perceived reality as a *mediating variable* tends to oversimplify the process whereby children make judgments about television. As a result, the attempt to 'immunize' them on this basis may well have contradictory consequences. In privileging the modality discourse, we run the risk of confirming limited, rationalistic notions of the 'critical viewer'. As I have argued, this normative view of 'television literacy' is premised on a conception of the effects of television which is both overstated and theoretically simplistic. It is a view which will be encountered more directly in the following chapter, which deals with children's talk about television advertising.

Chapter 10

Hidden Persuaders?:
Advertising, Resistance and Pleasure

My Little Pony
Skinny and bony
Take him to bed
And bite off his head
(sung by Amarjit (10) to the tune of the My Little Pony ad)

If the influence of television violence has largely been the preoccupation of the political Right, advertising would appear to occupy a similar status for many on the Left. Advertising, it is often argued, is the primary source of the materialist ethos of our 'consumer society'. It creates false needs, and promotes inaccurate and demeaning stereotypes of many social groups. It plays on our fears and anxieties, depicting the consumption of goods and services as the solution to our problems, and pervading and distorting our perceptions of human relationships.

Perhaps the best-known condemnation of advertising remains Vance Packard's *The Hidden Persuaders* (1957). Packard alleged that advertisers were attempting, with considerable success, to 'channel our unthinking habits' by using techniques which bypass our conscious awareness — an argument which has led to some quite bizarre research into 'subliminal persuasion' (Key, 1976). Advertising, Packard argues, has the power to manipulate our subconscious, and even to 'hypnotize' us into submission.

While not all critics of advertising have adopted such mystical explanations, many seem to be convinced of its extraordinary power. For many left-wing cultural theorists, the concern here is not just that advertising may persuade us to buy things we do not really want or need: it may also inculcate 'materialist' values, and even persuade us that our identity itself is derived from what we buy and consume. Herbert Marcuse (1964), for example, argues that advertising produces 'false needs . . . which are determined by external powers over which the individual has no control'. Raymond Williams (1980) describes advertising as a 'magic system', which sustains a false 'consumption ideal' and thereby 'obscures the real sources of general satisfaction'. The appeal of advertising is seen here as a consequence of alienation: people, Williams argues, 'now need the system of fantasy to confirm the forms of their immediate satisfaction or to cover the illusion that they are shaping their own lives' (p. 194). John Berger (1972), in similarly apocalyptic terms, argues that advertising has promoted consumption as a substitute for democracy, and thereby sustained capitalism's 'belief in itself'.

However, in the majority of cases, the evidence for these assertions is derived simply from the analysis of advertisements themselves: yet again, texts are assumed to generate automatic and guaranteed effects. Furthermore, the notion of 'false needs' obviously depends upon the assumption that there are 'true needs' which can be identified and agreed upon. Likewise, the generalized condemnation of 'stereotypes' presumes that accurate and objective representations of particular social groups are possible, and can be commonly accepted.

This rejection of the 'false symbolism' of advertising — for example, in Williams's use of terms like 'fantasy' and 'magic' — often seems to reflect a much broader rejection of symbolism *per se*, as inherently 'irrational'. What frequently appears to underlie these critiques is a vague nostalgia for more 'organic', even more 'human', forms of social relationship — and in this respect, there are significant similarities between many of the left-wing critics I have identified and the more conservative critique of advertising provided by defenders of literary 'high culture', such as Leavis and Thompson (1933).

However, the principal danger of these arguments, I would suggest, is that they tend to displace much larger concerns. Just as anxieties about violence appear to focus much more fundamental fears about social and moral decline, so advertising often seems to serve as a scapegoat for the broader shortcomings of capitalism as a whole, and an explanation for the failure of the working class to overthrow it. As Leiss *et al.* (1990) have argued:

> Objections directed at advertisements, the industry and its alleged social impacts are often indirect attacks on the so-called materialistic ethos of industrial society, or on capitalism in general as a social system; these are critiques of society masquerading as critiques of advertising. (p. 33)

As with the violence debates, the problem here is that these rhetorical (and undoubtedly therapeutic) condemnations of advertising may serve to deflect attention from the complexity of the problems at stake, and lead to unduly optimistic expectations about the ease of social change. As Leiss *et al.* (1990) argue, attempts to correct fundamental social problems merely by regulating advertising are bound to prove frustrating and ineffective: advertising, they suggest, is 'a bit player in a much grander drama'.

Furthermore, these criticisms of advertising implicitly define the audience — the 'consumers' of advertising and the products it promotes — as powerless victims of ideological manipulation. Here again, the discourse serves to differentiate its users from those 'other people' who are the passive dupes of the media. In fact, many of these critiques do acknowledge — if only in passing — that audiences may be quite sceptical and even directly critical of advertising. Williams (1980) and Leavis and Thompson (1933) both provide early examples of advertisers' attempts to incorporate this scepticism; while Williamson (1978) discusses more recent instances of the ways in which modern advertising seeks to prevent the potentially alienating consequences of 'hard sell'. Yet although Williamson appears to grant that the audience may be 'active', this activity is only in the terms permitted by the text — a matter of making the connections or discovering the meanings the ad requires. Ultimately, from this perspective, the 'activity' and the scepticism of audiences appears to be quite limited, and is easily incorporated by the cunning wiles of the advertisers.

Here again, it is children who are seen to be most at risk. Even Leiss *et al.* (1990), who are keen to reject 'crass' notions of manipulation and of audiences as 'malleable consumers', appear to share the view of advertising as 'an effective tool of socialization and persuasion' when it comes to children:

> children as viewers have neither the ability to understand the persuasive intent of advertising nor the level of conceptual and experiential maturity needed to evaluate commercial messages rationally. (p. 365)

Seducers and Innocents

To what extent does empirical research substantiate these claims about the magical powers of advertising, particularly in relation to children? Predictably, much of the academic research in this field has been concerned with establishing evidence of negative 'effects' (Adler *et al.*, 1980). As in the violence research, these 'effects' questions have been translated into empirical research which often seems incapable of providing the required degree of proof (see Goldberg and Gorn, 1983). For example, most children are likely to respond positively to a question like 'would you like to have most of the things they show on TV commercials?' (Atkin, 1980), but this can hardly be said to prove that commercials stimulate these desires, or indeed that they are therefore 'false'. Similarly, while it might be proven that 'heavy viewers' are likely to eat more Hershey bars or to use more mouthwash or acne cream than 'light viewers' (Atkin, 1980), this does not necessarily prove that it is television commercials that lead them to do so. Content analyses of television advertisements may well point to a significant under-representation — and indeed to 'stereotyping' — of certain social groups (Barcus, 1980) or to the prevalence or absence of particular behaviours (Schuetz and Sprafkin, 1979), but this obviously cannot serve as sufficient evidence of 'effects'.

In fact, much of the evidence on the 'effects' of advertising remains equivocal. For example, researchers have tended to conclude that advertising has a relatively weak influence on nutritional knowledge (for example, the belief that sugared foods are healthy), and that parental socialization and socio-economic status are more important (Young, 1990). While advertising may influence preference for individual brands, there is little evidence that it causes children to consume more of any given *type* of product (Gorn and Goldberg, 1982). Younger children, who are often assumed to be more 'at risk' from advertising, are generally least able to remember and to understand advertisements (Wartella and Ettema, 1974; Zuckerman *et al.*, 1978): while they tend to remember 'special offers' and unusual effects, they often forget the brand names. Indeed, research here would suggest that for younger children, television is a less significant source of product information than other sources, such as visits to the shops (Wartella, 1980).

Evidence on the more generalized ideological effects of advertising is, perhaps inevitably, even less conclusive. For example, while content analysis provides clear evidence of sexist bias in advertising (Durkin, 1985), the research on effects is very limited: while there is some experimental evidence of short-term effects (Tan, 1979), this research in fact proves very little about the *causal* role of television.

Ultimately, as in the research on the effects of television violence, the major problem here is the underlying theoretical perspective, which remains primarily a behaviourist one. Yet again, children are seen here as passive victims of persuasion. This view is one which has been aptly characterized by Brian Young (1986) as 'child-as-innocent and advertiser-as-seducer': it is a view which, as Young suggests, carries a considerable emotional charge, not least because it condenses many broader anxieties about the relationships between adults and children. As Young argues, children tend to be defined here as inadequate rather than competent, trusting rather than cynical, pure rather than corrupted. In effect, this definition reflects an ideology of childhood whose primary function is to justify adult 'protection', and thereby to keep children in their place.

On the Defensive

As in many other areas of psychological research on children and television, the so-called 'cognitive revolution' began to permeate research on television advertising in the 1970s. Nevertheless, 'cognitive processing' continues to be seen here as a 'mediating variable' which intervenes between stimulus and response. Rather like 'perceived reality', children's judgments about advertising are seen to provide 'cognitive defences' which protect them against the persuasive influence of television (Rossiter and Robertson, 1974).

Thus, there have been a number of studies which have investigated children's ability to distinguish between programmes and advertisements. Estimates of the age at which this develops tend to vary, but Jaglom and Gardner (1981) put it as young as $2\frac{1}{2}$ years old. However, research has suggested that it is only older children who make this distinction on the basis of intentions and meanings. Younger children are more inclined to rely on basic perceptual cues — such as the fact that advertisements are shorter and tend to use more rapid editing techniques (Meringoff and Lesser, 1980) — and it is not until the age of 8 or 9 that they become aware of the *motivations* of advertisers (Dorr, 1986). A number of studies point to the fact that children often express a remarkable degree of scepticism about advertising at around this age, and may reject the claims of advertisements outright — although some researchers have found evidence of this in children as young as 4 (Gaines and Esserman, 1981).

On one level, the research undertaken here would appear to support many of these arguments. As I shall indicate, the children demonstrated a clear awareness of the functions of advertising, and in many cases a profound degree of scepticism. Their 'defences' were very diverse and often extremely forceful. What emerges here is an image of children, not as vulnerable and innocent, but on the contrary as 'streetwise' and highly cynical about advertising — and indeed as more than capable of protecting themselves from its alleged effects. While this is certainly an important corrective to dominant views, I shall argue that it may also require further questioning. Yet again, it is important to be cautious about how we interpret the data, and to take account of the social functions of children's talk.

Defining Intentions

The data to be presented here derive from an activity conducted towards the end of the research project which focused specifically on TV advertising. Of all the activities undertaken, it was probably the most directive, and the one in which the interviewers perceived themselves to be adopting the most 'teacherly' role.

The session began with the interviewer screening a videotape of four advertisements taken from a commercial break during *Home and Away*: the interviewer then asked the children what they would normally do during a commercial break while viewing at home. Subsequent questions asked the children to identify and discuss liked and disliked ads; and there was then a series of more direct questions about the function of advertising — 'Why do you think they have ads on TV?' 'What are ads for?' and 'Have you ever bought or done anything because you saw it in an ad?' The second half of the interview focused on discussion of two groups of four ads, screened on videotape. While spontaneous responses were invited here, in terms of likes and dislikes, there were also some more directive questions: in relation to the first set, 'why do you think they chose to have those people in the ad?'; and in relation to the second, 'who do you think that ad was aimed at?' As in previous activities, however, these questions were treated not as a rigid 'interview schedule', but as an agenda which could be applied flexibly and indeed supplemented if necessary: in addition to gaining responses to specific questions, the aim was also to encourage discussion among the group.

While there were certainly opportunities here for the children to discuss their 'affective' responses, the direct questions were intended to cue a more 'critical' discourse about the functions and motivations of advertisers. The 'key concept' under investigation here was that of *agency* — 'who is communicating what and why?'

In the event, the youngest children (8-year-olds) offered some inventive responses to the question about the purpose of advertising. Many argued that screening advertisements provided an opportunity for the actors to prepare themselves for the next scene, to remind themselves of their lines or 'to get changed'. Caterina (8) even described how she had sat very close to the TV once and seen one of the actors changing her dress. Likewise, it was argued that advertising breaks allowed the producers 'to get all the scenery ready' or 'to change the clip of the film'. Interestingly, these comments reflect a clear awareness of the constructed nature of television, yet (with the exception of the last) they also a betray a belief that it is somehow 'live'. When confronted with the fact that BBC programmes didn't have breaks, Samantha (8) argued that this was 'not fair', although her friend Sonia suggested that 'they've rehearsed a lot and they just want to get things over and done with'.

In addition, there were explanations which focused on the domestic viewing context: here, ads served to 'amuse people while they're waiting for the thing to come back on', to allow them to get a drink of water or go to the toilet, or 'to keep [little babies] occupied whilst their mums are getting the dinner'. Peter (10) argued that having ads during a long film enabled you to have something to eat, and 'get your eyes back to normal'.

While these sorts of explanations were fairly common among the youngest groups, all the groups with the exception of one of the youngest also volunteered statements which defined advertising as a means of selling products. While there were occasional instances of advertising being described as a form of information or 'advice' — 'to show you things, what's in the shops', or to tell you prices — these explanations generally emphasized the *persuasive* functions of advertising. While this kind of response was most salient for the older children — it was invariably the first, and nearly always the only one provided — it was nevertheless available fairly consistently across the age groups.

In a number of cases, these statements were quite matter-of-fact: Ben (8), for example, said 'they're trying to persuade people to buy things or do things'. However, they were often imbued with assumptions about the actual or intended responses of viewers, and with a generalized scepticism. For example:

Extract 1

Nancy (8): Right, I think the adverts come on, they advertise them, because nobody wants them so they advertise it, and they go [*mimics gullible person:*] 'oh yeah, it's really brilliant!' They try and get them to buy it, do you know what I mean?

Interviewer: Right, right.

Nancy: Buy all the things, that's why they advertise it, cause they can't get anyone to buy it, so they just try and get it, make it look really good.

As Nancy's final statement illustrates, there was often an implicit accusation of deception here — that advertisers make things 'look' better than they are. Robin (8), for example, argued that 'some adverts are probably just to show you what to buy, and they make it better than it actually looks, just to show you to buy it, but when you actually turn it out, you always end up taking it back.'

While there were some children who admitted buying products because they had seen them in ads — or at least pestering their mothers to do so — this was generally described as resulting in negative experiences. This was particularly the case where advertising was reinforced by 'premium' offers, as in the case of 'free gifts' in breakfast cereals. Sally (10), for example, described this as follows:

Extract 2

Sally: 'Cause if it's a really brilliant advert, it's got a catchy tune like Honey Nut Loops, we liked that, so we went out and bought them, especially when, and it's got a really brilliant free gift, and it's a really brilliant spinning wheel. And we got this spinning wheel out of the packet, spin it round and it breaks.

Although (as I shall indicate), 'other people' were often seen as being influenced by advertising, the children hardly ever described themselves in this way. In many cases, there were more general rejections of the idea that advertising influenced people: as Emily (10) argued, they advertise 'so people will go out and buy it because they think the advert is brilliant, but only a few people do that with adverts'.

Finally, although references to the persuasive function of advertising were found throughout these discussion groups, it was only in one of the older groups that there was any reference to its economic function for the broadcasting industry. Terry (12) argued that 'the TV company needs it or they wouldn't have any money to buy programmes' — a point which failed to emerge elsewhere, despite some direct questioning about the differences between BBC and the commercial channels.

The Anatomy of Scepticism

As the foregoing quotations indicate, the children's discussions of advertising were characterized by a considerable degree of scepticism, and even cynicism. In some cases, this took the form of a generalized rejection of advertising as a 'con' (confidence trick) or a 'rip-off': as Ivor (8) said, 'I think they just want our money'. Certain disliked ads met with some spectacular responses. During the screening of an ad for Radion — a washing powder whose downmarket 'hard sell' advertising was generally regarded with contempt both by audiences and by advertisers themselves — one group of children turned their chairs to face away from the screen, while another put their fingers in their ears, and yet another made the sign of the cross, as if warding off vampires.

In other instances, the children took the opportunity to vent abuse on the people featured in the ads, as variously 'ugly', 'stupid' and 'prattish'. Far from being filled with glamorous role models, the world of advertising appeared to be populated largely with 'wallies' and 'boring old has-beens' — at least as far as these children were prepared to admit.

One major dimension of this condemnation of advertising was that of modality. Here again, it is possible to distinguish between judgments based on internal and on external criteria. Thus, in the former case, many of the children condemned the 'real people' in the washing powder ads, both for reading off the autocue and for not being 'good actors'. In a number of instances, the children cast doubt on their credibility by suggesting that the people had been paid for being in the ad, and that as Donna (10) said, they would 'just use anything that they're giving them for some money'. Similarly, there were complaints about bad dubbing in ads for children's toys — 'when they're miming, their mouths don't move' — and imitations of the wooden delivery of the pet owners in cat food ads.

In general, there seemed to be little sense in which the children regarded the people in the ads as 'real'. For example, there was speculation about the auditions you had to pass to get to be in a Diet Coke ad, and how the same people were featured in ads for different products. Peter (12) argued that the families in the Daz advertisement 'are picked like that so they look like a family on screen'.

In some instances, these criticisms extended to technical aspects of production. Thus, an ad for Lucozade featuring the footballer John Barnes was criticized for its deceptive editing: a number of children questioned whether he could in fact have drunk the entire can in the prescribed time, and noted how the sequence in which he kicked the empty can into the waste bin had been assembled out of a sequence of shots. Similarly, John (10) discussed the care which went into preparing food for ads, and that when you cooked it yourself, it wasn't the same: 'they exaggerate a bit, they have to take at least one day to prepare everything, like if one little thing happens, like it goes over the plate, the little mustard stuff, they will probably cut it and do another one, because they want everything perfect'.

In terms of external criteria, the washing powder ads were again a focus of condemnation. In many instances, the children questioned whether the dirty clothes would really get that dirty — generally in comparison with their own experience — and some accused them of being faked. However, in a few cases, these criticisms reflected broader concerns about representation, particularly in relation to gender. Donna (10) complained about the prominence given to boys' sporting activities, and went on to construct an alternative scenario around a family of girls playing netball — 'at least it would be more realistic'. Anne (10) also complained about the way in which women were always seen doing the washing and ironing — 'it's sexist' — while Nancy (12) argued that it would be good to see men doing the cooking for once.

While these criticisms were primarily focused on the inadequacies of the ads, there were also many criticisms of the false claims that were made about products. The before-and-after tests shown in washing powder ads were described by many of the children as faked: among the many allegations made here, it was suggested that the clothes were washed many times, that the 'washed' clothes were in fact brand new and that the whole thing was just a 'camera trick'. In some cases, these comments were reinforced with evidence from the children's own experience — or at least, that of their mothers, who despite the above comments were universally identified as the people responsible for the household wash. Thus, it was argued that clothes washed in these powders came out 'mucky' or 'rough', and in one case that they were covered with a thick layer of powder and had to be 'dusted' before they could be worn.

Likewise, there was much criticism of the deceptiveness of toy advertising. A number of children commented on the fact that the accessories shown in the ads had to be purchased separately, as did the batteries, and pointed out that this was not made apparent in the ads themselves. In other cases, the ads were directly accused of making false claims, for example about dolls that were supposed to blink and cars that were supposed to move without being pushed. The experience of discovering that 'it's not as good as it looks' or that 'half the time you get them and they don't even work' — to quote two representative judgments — was one which many of the children seemed to have had at some time or another.

Some Problems with Defences

As these examples suggest, there was a great deal of evidence here of a thorough-going and extensive scepticism about advertising and the claims that it makes. The children appeared to be well aware of the persuasive intentions of advertising, and more than prepared to resist them, drawing on their knowledge of the processes of television production, and their experience with products.

Mainstream psychological research would regard the phenomena I have described as 'cognitive defences'. According to this view, defences are 'dispositional variables' which intervene in the cause–effect relationship and thereby 'moderate the impact of the advertising stimulus on the child's ultimate behavioural response' (Robertson and Rossiter, 1977, p. 102).

More recent research has tended to qualify this view, however. Brucks *et al.* (1988) argue that the fact that children possess 'cognitive defences' does not necessarily mean they will be used, either during viewing or in subsequent purchasing. The fact that children describe advertising as a 'con', and appear to reject many of the claims it makes, does not necessarily mean they are not 'influenced' by it.

Furthermore, psychologists' measures of children's 'cognitive defences' appear to vary widely according to the methods used. Researchers using non-verbal methods claim to have elicited more sophisticated responses (Rossiter, 1980; Zuckerman and Giannino, 1981). In interviews, it would appear that the more direct the questions asked, the more evident the 'defences' are likely to be. Roedder (1981) and Brucks *et al.* (1988) found that they could easily 'cue' critical responses to advertising that would otherwise not appear; while Linn *et al.* (1982) found that adolescents tended to be sceptical of advertising in general, but did not necessarily criticize specific ads unless prompted to do so.

As Young (1990) points out, performance data should not be confused with competence data: a whole range of responses may be available, but in the context of an interview, only some may be regarded as salient. What children say does not necessarily reflect what they 'know', or all of what they know. As Goldberg and Gorn (1983) argue, it may simply be that older children have learned the appropriate 'adult' responses to such questions.

Wise Consumers

In the light of this, it is important to consider the social functions of this 'defensive', anti-advertising discourse. Critical judgments about advertising serve to establish the speaker as a 'wise consumer', who is capable of making rational judgments about product quality and value for money. The wise consumer is the one who shops around, comparing the different products on the market, testing products before buying, and rejecting the deceptions of packaging, publicity and advertising.

This 'subject position' was certainly one claimed by a number of children here. Thus, some reported that they 'tested' toys their friends had bought before purchasing them themselves; or that they might buy chocolate bars once to try them, but 'if you don't like it, you don't buy it again'. Others reported comparing the prices for similar goods in different shops, 'weighing up the pros and cons' before buying. An ad for fruit drinks led to some discussion about the fact that buying a larger bottle was better value for money, while Elizabeth and Dipesh (10) argued that 'you're just paying for the carton . . . they make the carton like that for attraction'. Similarly, Justine (8) argued that despite the different brand names, all potato crisps were 'just the same', while Terry (12) suggested that this was also the case with washing powders: 'the thing is, Lever make them all, they just put different names to them, it's the same powder'. A number of the older children were also critical of the spurious 'scientific' claims about 'biological' washing powders and 'isotonic' drinks.

This scepticism extended to premium offers, for example in breakfast cereals. A number of children reported having begun to collect tokens, only to find that the offer had finished before they had enough. Similarly, it was noted that the 'gifts' which came with McDonalds' hamburgers actually cost extra, and were not worth the money.

Concerns about the nutritional value of food also featured here. A number of the children rejected the notion implied by one of the ads screened that drinking Diet Coke would make you beautiful:

Extract 3

Charlotte (8):	Diet Coke makes you fat. If you sort of like have ten bottles of Diet Coke, cause you think it's absolutely brilliant, you'll walk around like this [*imitates fat person*].
Others:	Yeah! [*laughter*]

.
.
.

Diana:	It makes your teeth go bad.

.
.
.

Nancy:	Beautiful people, they only get [film] them from a distance, because they've got no teeth!

Likewise, Anne (10) argued that Diet Coke was 'bad for your brain' because of the artificial sweeteners it contained; while Sonia (8) argued that sweet drinks were 'not good for you, they haven't got no vitamins in, they make you hyperactive'. Justine (8) described how she studied the ingredients listed on the packets of cereals, yoghurts and fruit drinks, looking for information about sugar and additives. Perhaps the most cynical perspective here was that of Anne (10):

Extract 4

Anne:	Kellogg's Oat Bran isn't good for your heart [no]. Even though it's in a heart-shaped bowl, and it's supposed to be a sensible breakfast, it's got just as much crap in it as Coco Pops [. . .] It's horrible, so you have to put something in it, it's like / you have to cover it with sugar before you can eat it!

As these extracts suggest, there is more going on here than the neutral sharing of information. What appears to be taking place in many of these discussions is a kind of competitive display of cynical wit at the expense of products and advertisements. This was particularly apparent in some of the older middle-class groups, as Nigel (12) explicitly acknowledged:

Extract 5

Nigel:	I think some people make adverts rubbish so that people will think 'oh that's really useless'. Because a lot of people watch adverts 'cause they're rubbish, and they take the p—, they just take the mickey out of them . . .

As Nigel suggests, this display of cynicism was undoubtedly very pleasurable for many of the children here. Although the children expressed a positive liking for many ads, this was often ambiguous: their renditions of advertising jingles and imitations of voices were frequently tinged with mockery.

Nevertheless, this cynicism often seemed to be based on an implicit contempt for the 'other people' who are presumed to take the ads seriously and to be influenced by them. As in Extract 1 above, these 'other people' were often identified as 'stupid' or as simply 'mugs'. Anne (10), one of the most eloquent critics of advertising here, offered the following account of this process:

Extract 6

> Anne: Like, you have a big sunny beach with Sunkist on it, and when everyone goes on holiday for summer and you remember them and go ['*stupid*' *voice:*] 'uuuh, let's have a drink'.
>
> Peter: [*same voice:*] 'Let's have some Sunkist'.
>
> Anne: [*same voice:*] 'Let's have some Sunkist'.

In fact, most of the ads which attracted the most negative comment here were for products that were identified with 'other people', or at least with oneself when younger. For example, a number of boys mocked the advertisements for 'girls'' products, such as My Little Pony and Girl's World; while some of the girls themselves were also critical of the ads for dolls they admitted they would have bought a few years earlier. As I have noted, some children did admit to having been influenced by advertising or premium offers in the past, although this was often at a safe distance:

Extract 7

> Peter (10): I used to when I was little, I said 'oh mum, come on, 'cause they', even if I didn't like the cereal, I'd say 'oh please mum, can I have them?' and if she said I didn't like them, I'd say 'oh yes I do I do I do' but I didn't really, I just wanted the thing inside.

At the same time, a number of the children actually identified adults as the most gullible audience. For example, at least some of the contempt for the washing powder ads appeared to be based on the assumption that 'mums' would believe the results of the tests and switch brands as a result. A number of children quoted examples of their mothers having bought products in response to advertisements they themselves found inept. Michael (8) argued that 'old people' were less informed than children about certain products, such as potato crisps, and thus more likely to be misled:

Extract 8

> Michael: . . . old people don't really know all these strange things about the product, so they just go, so, they're probably sitting back in their armchair, going 'yum, yum, yum, let's go and get it'. They are quite nice I must admit but I definitely think they're going to try to get old people to go and get it.

Hannah (10) also argued that children were more likely to be discriminating consumers:

Extract 9

Hannah: Some of the adverts are made for children, because children are more intelligent than adults. [. . .] It isn't because adults are brainy, it's because children are seeing more in the adverts, they think, 'oh well, that's that, why don't we compare it with Ariel Ultra?', stuff like that. With grown-ups, they just take one look at it and go 'oh no, we'll just settle for Ariel, we'll just settle with ours'. With the children, they actually look at it and compare it, things like that.

Here again, we have the familiar irony of discourses about television effects. The discourse is essentially concerned with the risks to 'other people': yet when these 'other people' are questioned, they are often equally fluent in the discourse, and equally keen to displace the concern onto yet other people.

While this displacement is often in terms of age — onto people who are younger or (more rarely) older than oneself — it also possesses a social class dimension. In general, the middle-class children were much more fluent in this discourse, and much more likely to engage in the kind of competitive display of cynicism I have identified. By contrast, the working-class children appeared to have less invested in demonstrating their scepticism: while they were certainly capable of 'seeing through' advertising, the whole issue appeared to be much less urgent for them.

Purchasing Power

A second issue relating to this question of 'defences' against advertising is that of the social context in which purchasing requests are made. Ultimately, children's power as consumers is very limited: at least at this age, their earned income is generally non-existent or minimal. Their spending power depends primarily on their ability to extract money from their parents — and in this respect, the 'problem' of television advertising is perhaps primarily a problem for *parents*, since it provides one significant pretext or opportunity for children to make requests for products. Indeed, much of the anxiety about the effects of advertising has been concerned with the extent to which it causes conflict within the family (e.g. Sheikh and Moleski, 1977a; Goldberg and Gorn, 1978).

Yet this has interesting implications for the notion of 'cognitive defences'. For example, Rossiter and Robertson (1974) argue that children's defences against persuasion may be gradually 'neutralized' by the concentrated advertising of the pre-Christmas period. They suggest that increases in television viewing during this period may cause a 'defense override', even among children whose defences were initially strong — an explanation which clearly derives from a stimulus–response hypothesis. I would argue that, on the contrary, children may actively *use* advertising as a source of ideas for presents with which they can then pester their parents, and that they may watch more television, or at least pay closer attention to the ads, for this very reason. In other words, the causality may operate in the opposite direction: rather than television causing requests for products, the need to generate requests for products in the run-up to Christmas may lead to more intensive viewing of television advertisements. On the other hand, children may resist the appeals of advertisements when it is in their interests to do so: they tend not to ask their parents for things they know they won't get, and ask for substitutes they know their parents will approve of (Esserman, 1981).

There is some support for these arguments in this data. Peter's description of the way in which he pestered his mother to buy cereal (Extract 7 above) was echoed by a number of children. For the older children, 'nagging mum' was often described as an activity which was more appropriate for those younger than themselves. Yet even for the 8-year-olds, requesting products appeared to be seen as a fairly self-conscious activity, as it was here:

Extract 10

> *Michelle*: Mum, I want this. Mum, I want that. Mum, come from the kitchen, come and look at this, quick, quick, quick!
> *Christina*: I want, I want!
> *Interviewer*: And what does your mum say?
> *Christina*: She says [*imitates:*] 'you, you've got plenty of toys'.
> *Aziz*: My mum or my dad says 'maybe, maybe'.
> *Christina*: And then maybe always turns out to be no.

Certainly, there is a risk for parents — and for researchers — in taking these requests too seriously. One of the earliest things children learn is that they can't always get what they want — or at least what they ask for, which is not always the same thing. Requesting products can become, as it seems to be here, a routine activity which is worth trying on, as long as you have fairly low expectations of success. Many of the children reported that their parents responded to these requests by agreeing to buy the products, but that they often relied on their children forgetting what had been promised.

On the other hand, a few children provided examples of more committed consumer behaviour. Donna (10), for example, argued that looking in the Argos catalogue was a much more reliable and extensive source of product requests than advertisements. As in the case of advertising itself, it would seem to be more accurate to regard purchasing requests as a purposeful activity, rather than a behavioural response.

'Advertising Literacy'

As I have argued, it is important to locate children's judgments about advertising within their social context — both the interpersonal context of discussion, and the context of purchasing itself. Ultimately, the notion of 'cognitive defences' would appear to be a rather inadequate formulation of what is taking place here: children's resistance to persuasion is not just an individual process, nor can it be seen as a kind of cognitive 'filter' which intervenes between the stimulus and the response.

Brian Young (1986, 1990) offers a useful reformulation of this issue based on the notion of 'advertising literacy'. Drawing on research into the development of children's metalinguistic competencies (e.g. Hakes, 1980), Young argues that children's growing awareness of the functions of advertising, and their increasing scepticism about it, can be seen as part of a more general growth in their 'metacommunicative' abilities. In middle childhood, it is suggested, children become much more capable of standing back from language and other forms of communication, and reflecting upon how they work. These metacommunicative abilities involve a kind of Piagetian 'decentring' — a recognition that other people's knowledge, or lack of it, may differ from your own; and that they may have different motivations, and may actively seek to deceive. They also involve an awareness of the specific characteristics of language, and 'a distinction between the propositional of what is being said or communicated and the way in which this content is conveyed' (Young, 1990, p. 254). Thus, children will increasingly recognize that utterances may not be intended literally, and that they may be inconsistent or indeed deliberately ambiguous; they may come to understand metaphor and other non-literal uses of language, such as hyperbole and understatement; and they may be much more sensitive to irony, sarcasm and humorous uses of language generally. As Young argues, these characteristics of language are precisely those which are most prevalent in advertising.

Some of the data here could be seen to illustrate this broader notion of 'advertising literacy'. This was particularly the case where the children were invited to speculate about the producers' intentions, in response to the question 'why do you think they chose to have those people in the ad?' In psychological terms, the children were being explicitly invited to 'decentre', and to engage in 'recursive thinking' — that is, 'thinking about thinking about thinking' (cf. Paget *et al.*, 1984).

For example, one of the advertisements screened — for Radion washing powder — was in the form of a 'home video', apparently shot by the family featured in the ad. While a number of children complained about the wobbly camerawork, others described it as a deliberate strategy — as Nancy (8) said, 'it's supposed to be like someone is filming them'. Indeed, some children directly rejected the pretence that the family themselves had really made the ad: Vanessa (8) argued that 'it looks like someone not professional has done it, but really someone professional has done it'. When they were asked to speculate about why the ad had been made in this way, some very clear explanations were offered, as in this group of 10-year-olds:

Extract 11

Interviewer:	So why have they done it with a home video camera, then?
Donna:	To make it look more realistic. And I mean, you don't want to have like studio cameras at home, because then you'll be thinking like it's all phoney. That's a very good Radion advert, because they make it more realistic and more at home.

.
.
.

Karen:	'Cause if it's a professional filming it, it would just be you know slow and / all steady.
Donna:	And then it would be in a studio, and you'd just like have a picture of a house in the background or something, and they'd be running on the stage or something, that would be stupid.

Another ad which occasioned similar speculation was one for Golden Wonder crisps. Here, there were some complaints that it wasn't immediately clear what was being advertised — a phenomenon which seemed to cause a certain amount of irritation, both here and in response to some other ads. Yet when they were asked to speculate about why the product wasn't named early on in the ad, there were again some very clear explanations, as in the same group:

Extract 12

Donna:	Yeah, they should have, you should be able to see like the crisps in someone's pocket, or something, at least so you had a slight clue what they were advertising.

.

.

.

Interviewer:	But why do you think they do that?
Elaine:	To make it funny.
Karen:	To make you watch it all, the advert.
Donna:	To make it interesting.
Amarjit:	Yeah, I think it's to make you watch it all.
Interviewer:	Whereas you think if they showed you Golden Wonder right at the beginning=
Elaine:	=You'd go 'oh no, I don't like Golden Wonder, turn it over'.
Donna:	Or, 'I know what they're advertising now, I've seen the packet, I can change the station now'.

.

.

.

Elaine:	It's the same as *Home and Away*, they leave the last good bits at the end so you can watch it the next day.

In both cases here, the children appear to be placing themselves in the position of the producers, and rehearsing the choices that were made in devising the ad. Their arguments are informed both by technical knowledge — for example, about the difference between hand-held and fixed cameras — and by reference to familiar narrative conventions — for example, the cliffhanger in *Home and Away*. Most significantly, they seem to be able to speculate about the assumptions that producers make about audiences. In the case of the Radion ad, they imply that the choice of the 'home video' format may have been informed by a desire to get away from the 'phoney' approach of other ads — in fact Donna later compared the Radion ad to the more 'unrealistic' approach of other washing powder ads — and thus to incorporate the audience's potential scepticism. In the case of the Golden Wonder ad, it is suggested that deferring the naming of the product generates a degree of suspense which may be intended to counteract the channel-hopping behaviour of viewers.

There were many further instances of this in response to the question about target audiences — 'who do you think that ad was aimed at?' In some cases, the answers to this question were fairly broad — 'most people' — or based on knowledge of the products rather than any more detailed reference to the ads. Yet even among the youngest groups, there were clear statements about the ways in which adverts appeared to have been targeted to more specific audience groups: the Diet Coke advert, for example, was seen as being primarily for men because of the sexy women in it; the Lucozade advert was for boys who would want to be like John Barnes; the Golden Drummers ad was for parents who would buy the product in order to please their children, just like the mother in the ad. In most cases, these arguments were informed by assumptions about 'identification', although it was also acknowledged that children could be used in ads as a way of 'getting at' parents, 'to make the adults laugh and say that's a good idea'.

Nevertheless, the assumptions the producers were perceived to be making about their audience were often rejected, as in the case of these 10-year-olds' comments on the Diet Coke and Lucozade ads:

Extract 13

Adele: I think they choose those people, 'cause they get actors or very talented people, but they have to be slim and beautiful 'cause it's an advert for Diet Coke, and they think, [*mocking voice:*] 'you can drink this without doing exercises and you'll get to look like her, or drink this, and you won't have to do exercises but you will be able to look like him'.

.
.
.

Tracey: I know why they've got him [John Barnes] to do that advert because he's a famous footballer and they thought, they think that if they drink that drink and play football, they will score something and it will give them more strength.
Interviewer: And do you believe that?
Tracey: No!
Ajita: No! Anybody who believes that, they're really stupid.

While these comments still imply the existence of 'other people' who might believe the advertisement's claims, they are also informed by a sense that the advertisers are somehow 'talking down' to their audience, in assuming that they are more gullible than they really are. In some instances, this led on to a broader rejection of the advertisements, and of the rhetorical links being drawn between the product and the positive values which the advertisers sought to associate with it (cf. Williamson, 1978).

Thus, while many of the children were prepared to grant that John Barnes's endorsement of Lucozade may have been intended to give the product credibility, even the youngest claimed not to be persuaded that it was anything other than a 'normal drink' — as Dipesh (10) said, 'all it is, is flavouring'. Likewise, an ad for Abbey National Building Society aimed at the young/contemporary market appeared to generate some enjoyment, but was criticized on the grounds that, in the words of Nathan (8), 'it didn't really go with the idea of it advertising a bank'.

In different ways, all these judgments could be seen as manifestations of 'meta-linguistic' competencies. While they obviously draw on the children's scepticism about advertising and the claims it makes about products, they also reflect an ability to speculate about the producers' intentions, particularly in relation to their target audiences — and indeed, to criticize these.

Yet it is important to acknowledge that these judgments are also discursive and context-bound. They arose largely in response to quite directive 'teacherly' questions, and do not necessarily provide us with evidence about the ways in which children watch television outside this context. No less than the more straightforwardly cynical comments reported earlier in this chapter, they too serve to define the speakers as more 'sophisticated' and 'critical' than the 'other people' who are victims of advertising. Here again, this claim to a 'critical' subject position was something which appeared to be more prevalent for middle-class children — not least because they appeared to more adept at recognizing the implicit educational agenda which informed this activity.

Recovering Pleasure

There is undoubtedly evidence here for a view of children as rational consumers, who critically evaluate the claims of advertising and are not easily persuaded by it. However, this is only part of the story. Yet again, one of the major problems with privileging the 'critical' discourse is that it neglects the emotional dimension of children's engagement with television. As Ellen Wartella (1984) has shown, research on children and television advertising has manifested a 'cognitive bias': while researchers have often noted children's strong affective responses to the advertisements they are shown, these have rarely been described or analyzed.

Much of the difficulty here arises from the fact that these responses are rarely articulated explicitly. Throughout these discussions, for example, much of the children's enthusiasm about the ads was conveyed through laughter, singing along, and miming or acting out what happened. The younger children in particular seemed to have even more difficulty than usual in remaining in their seats. Many arrived at the session in a state of excited anticipation, having heard about what they would be doing from others in the class. During the screening of the ads, there was a considerable amount of talk and laughter: many groups participated in a game of 'name that product', competing to identify the product before it was named in the ad itself, while others predicted key lines and actions.

While the context was very different, this behaviour must to some extent have replicated their domestic viewing behaviour. Thus, while many children reported that they would use the commercial break as an opportunity to get some food or drink or go to the toilet — or alternatively to beat up their brother or practice their cartwheels — others said they would normally stay and watch the ads. A number of children expressed a general enthusiasm for advertising which seemed strangely at odds with the scepticism described above, although in practice this enthusiasm appeared to be distinctly selective: some reported that they would change channels if a disliked ad appeared, or fast-forward the video to avoid them.

Some children even presented themselves as 'fans' of advertising, and described how they would zap between channels seeking them out. Nancy (12), for example, said 'I just watch the adverts all the time, I sort of turn on the TV, first thing I watch is the adverts, then I watch the programmes'. Nancy expressed enthusiasm for what she called 'advert serials' such as those for Oxo and British Telecom —

'I try and sort of see each one, cause it's sort of like a TV programme' — and also described how she would 'act out' the adverts she liked — 'I just sort of do all the dancing and all the acting, I just sort of follow the advert'.

Nevertheless, as I have noted, this 'acting out' of the adverts — while it was often extremely accurate — was frequently tinged with mockery. Yet again, this was most apparent in the case of the washing powder adverts, where the testimony of 'ordinary people' was mercilessly satirized. In some groups, there was much competition to deliver the most hilarious parodies, especially where these involved regional accents. Again, this was clearly an everyday activity: following a group parody of a milk commercial, Hannah (10) said 'we do impressions of that in class', while Charlotte (8) described how she and her friend would imitate the 'Wash and Go' shampoo advertisements. Key catchphrases were often repeated, although these were frequently parodied. The Prudential 'I want to be' campaign, for example, was parodied by a number of groups, although it appeared to cause great irritation: as Donna (10) said, 'it goes on and on and on'. In some instances, the slogans themselves were directly subverted, as in Amarjit's parody of the My Little Pony song, quoted at the start of this chapter, and her friend Anne's refrain 'a Mars a day makes your teeth rot away'.

Singing along to music appeared to be a major source of pleasure, although again there was often a certain irony here. There were many hilarious group renditions of the songs from Honey Nut Loops, Blockbuster Video, Anchor Butter and Fairy Liquid, to name but a few. Yet again, a number of children described how they would do this at home: Karen (10), for example, reported that when the Coca-Cola ad came on, 'I run into the kitchen and get the hairbrush and start singing'.

Finally, there was an emphasis on comic incidents, often described in isolation: in many cases, children might identify a particular incident — 'I like that one where the baby falls down the toilet' — although the group as a whole was at a loss to identify the product. Nevertheless, there were certain humorous campaigns that were definitely associated with a product — notably Carling Black Label, which was the focus for detailed retellings in a number of groups.

In general, however, the pleasure of the advertisements often appeared to be unconnected with the products themselves. While there was certainly a high degree of 'product awareness' — at least in terms of the number of brand names mentioned — this was not always associated with the ads. In many cases, product names were not mentioned, or proved hard to recall: as Gwen (8) said, 'you remember all the adverts, but you don't remember what they're for'. Indeed, some children even got the name of the product wrong directly after having seen the ad, or attributed it to a different product.

Much of the pleasure of advertising for these children appeared to derive from the characteristics described by Brian Young (1986) in his account of 'advertising literacy' — for example, the use of non-figurative language, of hyperbole and understatement, and particularly of humour. Yet, as I have indicated, this pleasure was often conveyed in tones of parody and mockery. In some instances, this was quite explicit, as in the case of Nigel (12), who asserted that he liked watching the Radion ads 'because they're RUBBISH!' Yet even the most ardent self-declared 'fans' of advertising, such as Nancy (12), appeared to have a comparatively distanced, ironic relationship with their favourite ads. While she argued that a 'good advert' might make her more inclined to buy the product — and a bad one likely to avoid it — she also said that many of her purchasing decisions were made irrespective of this. Interestingly, she was also the most vociferous critic of sexism in the ads.

Ultimately, then, to define the issues here solely in terms of children's resistance or susceptibility to persuasion would seem to ignore much of what is taking place. It is important to avoid setting up an opposition between 'rational' and 'emotional' responses — for example, to argue that although children may appear to be very sceptical about advertising, they may also be persuaded by it at a level which is below their conscious awareness. In this formulation, pleasure becomes the soft underbelly which lies beneath the hard shell of cynicism: if we could only disavow or overcome pleasure, we would be wholly protected.

This is to posit a wholly rationalistic solution to the 'problem' of advertising, which is in my view not merely puritanical but also ultimately impossible. Educational attempts to convert children into 'rational consumers' are bound to fail, not least because they aspire to a norm which even adults are incapable of sustaining. Adults are not always 'rational consumers' — not only because they don't have the time to plough through consumer magazines and evaluate all the alternatives before deciding what to buy, but also because, as Leiss *et al.* (1990) argue, material objects are inevitably invested with symbolic values, and have always been so, even in non-capitalist societies. To imply, as Raymond Williams (1980) does, that the symbolism and 'magic' which infuse our discourse about material objects derive wholly from advertising, and can simply be done away with, is a dangerous form of wishful thinking.

Effects Revisited

The mistrust of advertising among children which has been demonstrated here and in some previous research must represent a significant problem for the industry. As I have noted, critics of advertising have drawn attention to advertisers' attempts to incorporate and thereby neutralize this mistrust (Williams, 1980; Williamson, 1978) — although they have tended to assume that these attempts are automatically successful.

A recent report commissioned by British advertisers (Scorah, 1990) confirms this view of children as generally critical and antagonistic towards advertising: the children sampled here were very aware of the economic function of advertising, and critical of unrealistic 'stereotypes' in ads. Their own stereotypes of the advertisers were almost uniformly negative:

> For children the ad person was always 'old' (over 30), well paid and male. He had no children, or, if he did, never listened to them. He was the kind of father who thought he was very trendy, and showed off to his friends about how well he got on with his kids, when in fact his kids couldn't stand him. He wrote ads for himself and thought they would appeal to young people. He was out of touch with music, fashion and TV, but didn't know it. (p. 13)

Recent research in Cultural Studies has also pointed to advertisers' growing concern about the difficulty of reaching a young audience, which is increasingly acknowledged to be highly 'TV literate'. Drawing on industry research, Mica and Orson Nava (1990) argue that 'young people consume commercials independently of the product which is being marketed' — an assertion which this research would partly support.

Yet Nava and Nava's broadly 'postmodernist' rejection of the notion of advertising effects appears to sanction a view of it as an autonomous cultural form — and indeed as a form of 'art'. While it is certainly possible to find examples of advertising which rework other artistic forms and are knowingly self-referential, and thereby to interrogate the distinction between 'art' and advertising, this argument ultimately evades the question of the economic function of advertising. While the ways in which audiences respond to advertising may be much more complex than is often assumed, its economic effects on other areas of media production are undoubtedly pervasive (Leiss *et al.*, 1990) — and, I would argue, need to be addressed by media educators.

Finally, while I would agree with Nava and Nava's assessment of the sophistication of young people's critical 'decoding skills' in relation to advertising, it is equally clear that advertising represents a 'special case' among media forms, in that its persuasive intent is relatively apparent. The question of whether this scepticism extends to other forms of television — for example, less overtly persuasive, but no less partial, genres such as news or educational television — is one I have not sought to address here, yet it remains extremely pertinent for media researchers and for educators. Children's broader awareness of 'communicator interests' (Boeckmann, 1991) — or, in terms of the 'key concepts' of media education, their understanding of 'agency' — remains an issue in need of further research.

Part Four

Chapter 11

Television, the Audience and the Academy: The Politics and Practice of Audience Research

Much of this book has sought to engage with, and to contest, the dominant assumptions of mainstream research on children and television. In this chapter and the next, however, I want to move away from these arguments, and to return to the contexts from which my own research has emerged. In the final chapter, I will draw out some of the implications of the research for the practice of media education, particularly in schools. In this chapter, I want to 'relocate' the research within the context of recent work on television audiences in Media and Cultural Studies. In the process, I wish to engage with some current debates about the 'power' of television and the politics of audience research.

Research as Context

The research reported here has several fundamental limitations. The sample of children was comparatively small, and one might reasonably raise questions about its representativeness. The age groups studied here were quite limited, and would not support generalizations about the ways in which younger children, or indeed children as a whole, make sense of television. The children were obviously all British, and they all lived in Greater London. One could not, on this basis, make claims about children living in other cultures, or even in rural communities, whose responses would probably be quite different.

There are also fundamental limitations to do with methodology. The data have been gathered in schools, primarily through small-group talk: as I have shown, what individuals say is heavily dependent upon the other children present, and indeed on the role of the interviewer. The data do not necessarily tell us about how children talk about television outside the context of discussions with adult researchers — and indeed, these particular adult researchers. Using audio-tape has meant that non-verbal behaviour and interaction has largely been ignored. Furthermore, the research has not studied the viewing process at first hand, for example through observations in the home: what we have here are individuals' *accounts* of their viewing, rather than direct evidence of that viewing itself.

Yet limitations — or in fact *choices* — of this kind are unavoidable. The research is bound to be socially, culturally and historically specific, and the value of the data inevitably depends upon the context and the methods which were used to collect them. The problems arise, I would argue, when one attempts to render these limitations invisible — for example, when one claims that twenty children in the University kindergarten somehow 'stand for' children in general, or that interviews with eighteen working-class couples in South London somehow provide direct information about how men and women in general watch television. As I shall indicate, this has implications both in terms of theory and methodology. It means making the research process visible, rather than taking refuge in a spurious neutrality; and it should lead to a questioning of the value of general theories about television and its audiences.

This book has mainly been concerned with what John Fiske (1987a) has termed the 'oral culture' which surrounds and defines television. As Fiske argues, it is primarily through talk that the meanings and pleasures of television are defined, negotiated and circulated. Yet the conventions of talk vary widely between different social groups; and the meanings which are produced must inevitably 'resonate with the cultural needs' of particular talk communities. In this way, Fiske suggests, 'mass-produced' culture is appropriated by individuals and social groups, and forms a kind of contemporary 'folk culture', which may serve purposes which run counter to those of its producers (cf. de Certeau, 1984; Silverstone, 1989; Morris, 1990).

Nevertheless, it would be false to claim that this research provides us with direct, unmediated evidence of this 'oral culture'. The reasons for this are partly to do with logistics, partly a result of deliberate choice. If we are interested in finding out about television audiences, we are almost bound to use 'artificial' methods. While I would not underestimate the interest and significance of more strictly 'ethnographic' observational studies, there seems to me to be a limit to what can be discovered by observation alone. Indeed, many studies using such methods have also relied on interviews and discussions, not least in order to gain access to individuals' own explanations and accounts of their viewing behaviour. At least in the case of media research, as Katz and Liebes (1985, p. 10) have argued, 'we do not know how to sample thoughts without provoking them, or how to sample conversations without constructing them.'

Ultimately, then, this research has dealt not so much with this oral culture itself, as with the ways in which it is manifested in the specific context of research, and of small-group discussion. The talk which has been presented here is obviously not identical with that which takes place in less 'artificial', everyday situations — although we might well question the idea that there is any 'natural' context which will provide us with talk which is somehow pure and uncontaminated. Nevertheless, this kind of talk surely does indicate something of the 'discursive repertoires' which are available to children: what they say is inevitably constrained by the context, but it is far from being merely determined by it.

However, the decision to focus on talk within this particular kind of context was also a deliberate choice. The ways in which children talk about television with adults, and in a more or less 'educational' context, are obviously of particular interest in terms of media education. The act of talking about cultural forms which are largely identified with the peer group, with the home and with leisure, in a context which is defined by its difference from and even opposition to all these things, is bound to be paradoxical.

In effect, what we are studying here is the relationship between what children bring to the context — their existing knowledge and experience of television, as this is manifested in talk — and their understanding of the demands and requirements of the context itself. Inevitably, different social groups appear to be positioned here — and to position themselves — in different ways.

For example, as I have indicated, there were some fairly consistent differences between the kinds of talk produced by working-class and middle-class children. If we apply the 'taxonomy' of viewing skills outlined in the introduction to Part Three, for example, we could argue that *in general*, the middle-class children made more reflective, detailed and sophisticated judgments in most, if not all, the areas discussed in Chapters 6–10. Where it has been possible or meaningful to count these judgments, for example in the case of Chapters 6, 8 and 9, the middle-class children have generally come out on top. On this basis, one might conclude that the middle-class children here were 'more televisually literate' than the working-class children.

It would be possible to make similar arguments about gender, although here the differences are perhaps less immediately apparent. Nevertheless, one could argue that in most cases, it was the girls who engaged in the most complex debates about modality or character, for example, or whose judgments were generally the most fluent and elaborate. Even in areas where boys might have been expected to dominate the discussion, for example in terms of their knowledge of TV production, the girls more than held their own. Here again, girls — or perhaps more specifically, middle-class girls — could be seen as 'more televisually literate' than their male counterparts at the same age.

I would resist these conclusions, for a number of reasons. As I have argued, there is a distinct danger here in extracting such judgments from the social contexts in which they are made. Quantifying these judgments removes them still further, reducing them merely to ticks in boxes. Giving children SAT scores for 'TV literacy' — while it has certainly been an aim of some researchers in this field — seems to me not only reductive but also downright dangerous.

For example, as I have argued, the social class differences which obtained here were at least partly a reflection of different perceptions of the interview context. Certainly in the early stages of the research, the middle-class children were more likely to perceive — and indeed actively to construct — the interview as an 'educational' event. The younger children in particular were much more deferent towards the interviewer, and tended to define television at least initially in terms of 'education' rather than 'pleasure'. While the older children were less inhibited, much of their talk seemed to be based on an implicit distinction between themselves and 'other people'. Their definition of themselves as 'critical viewers' partly depended upon the notion of an 'uncritical' mass audience which simply believes and accepts everything it sees.

By contrast, the younger working-class children perceived the interview in much less formal, 'educational' terms; their talk was more straightforwardly concerned with sharing and celebrating pleasure. While the older ones were much less forthcoming, this was mainly a result of the marked social differences within the groups, rather than of any deference towards the interviewer. The major concern here was with establishing and negotiating these differences through the staking out of individual and collective tastes.

Generally speaking, these differences became less acute as the research progressed, not least because the younger middle-class children increasingly abandoned their deference towards the interviewer. Nevertheless, it remained the case that the working-class children often chose to use the opportunities provided by the discussions in a rather different way. Broadly speaking, they were much more interested in negotiating peer group relationships, and much less in displaying their own knowledge and sophistication.

Of course, this is not to imply that these factors are confined to this context, and are not manifested elsewhere; nor is it to suggest that they are just an artefact of the context itself, a 'researcher effect'. It is to argue, however, that the display of 'knowledge' about television and the exercise of 'critical judgment' need to be regarded as *social* acts, which have social functions and purposes. The crucial point here is that we are dealing with a social, communicative *process*, and not with a finite product. What children say about television cannot be regarded simply as evidence of their 'viewing skills', or indeed their lack of them.

The gender differences might be explained in a similar way. Ultimately, the major problem for many of the boys in talking about television was that it involved a degree of 'self-exposure' which they were unwilling to risk. For example, while it was only marginally embarrassing for the girls to talk about male characters they found attractive, the boys found it much more difficult to discuss the merits of female characters in these terms, except insofar as they could heap abuse on them. As I have noted, the boys resorted to some quite extreme strategies in order to avoid talking about their own pleasure: there was often a kind of mutual policing going on, in which boys who stepped out of line were reprimanded or humiliated.

Although there was certainly a premium — particularly for the older boys — on being 'critical', their reluctance to acknowledge and reflect on their own pleasure set definite limits to this. While some of the older boys were extremely adept at mocking the 'unrealistic' aspects of television, and keen to project themselves as knowledgeable 'film buffs', the girls were much more willing to discuss their own emotional investments in the medium, and their judgments were often more complex as a result.

Of course, these are enormous generalizations, and there was a great deal of diversity both within and between these groups. What individual children said or did depended very much on the different groupings. Generally speaking, for example, boys were much more likely to engage in the kind of mutual policing I have described when they were in single-sex groups than when girls were present. Similarly, girls were certainly capable of being extremely dismissive of the soap operas, although this was much more common in mixed groups (or groups in which boys were dominant) than in single-sex groups, where they were often prepared to discuss these programmes more 'seriously'.

What is important to emphasize here, however, is that these differences were not solely determined by the children's social position, or indeed by biology. On the contrary, they can be explained at least partly as responses to the context of educational research and of peer group discussion — or, more accurately, as *constructions* of that context.

Social positions and biological categories are obviously determined by material factors; yet their *meanings* are actively constructed and negotiated, defined and redefined, in the process of talk. What it means to be male or female, working-class or middle-class, black or white, an adult or a child, is not given or pre-determined. These 'subject positions' are, at least to some extent, relative terms:

they define each other, but their mutual relationships are far from fixed and unchangeable. On the contrary, as I have sought to demonstrate, they can be asserted or disclaimed for different purposes in different social contexts.

This approach acknowledges that these differences are social, rather than merely individual. It recognizes the fact that these different subject positions are not equally available to all, and that individual choices are inevitably constrained by broader relations of power, both within and beyond the immediate context of discussion.

Yet at the same time, it should enable us to avoid the kind of demographic determinism which often characterizes audience research — the notion that these people read television in a particular way 'because' they are working-class, or male, or because of some other single fact about their social position. While the competencies which may be used to make sense of television are socially distributed, and reflect much broader social differences, the extent to which they are brought into play and the ways in which they are used will depend upon the context and on the social purposes of viewers. These different ways of talking about and making sense of television are thus not simply a reflection of children's given social relationships and identities: on the contrary, it is at least partly through talking about television that those identities and relationships themselves are constructed and defined.

This process is thus both a material and a discursive one. The range of positions available, and the discourses in which they are manifested are socially and materially determined; but they also offer spaces and contradictions in which individuals can actively determine themselves. The political and ideological consequences of this process are therefore bound to be diverse and socially specific.

The 'Power' of Television

Over the past decade, the relationships between media and their audiences have become a central focus of research and debate in Cultural Studies. Indeed, the attempt to defend and assert the power of audiences has led to a widespread questioning of many articles of faith. The view of the media as agents of 'the dominant ideology', which was generally shared in the 1970s, has increasingly been rejected in favour of an emphasis on the 'contradiction' and 'complexity' of audience readings. Audiences are routinely described as 'active' and 'powerful', and often as 'resisting' or at least 'negotiating with' dominant ideologies.

While I would broadly share many of these emphases, it is important to acknowledge that there are some significant difficulties here. To describe audiences as 'active', or to emphasize the 'complexity' of their readings of the media, may be a useful corrective to previous arguments; yet it often amounts to little more than an empty slogan. There remains a distinct danger of regarding audiences, and indeed the media themselves, as homogeneous. Yet the debate is increasingly conducted in binary terms: to assert the power of audiences is explicitly to contest the power of the media.

In a sense, the history of media research might be regarded not as a steady accumulation of wisdom and refinement of theory, but as a process of action and reaction between these different positions — a process which obviously reflects a broader tension within the social sciences between 'structure' and 'agency' (cf.

Giddens, 1984). Thus, on the one hand, there are theories which regard the individual primarily as an object of socialization, at the hands of social structures or forces; while on the other, there are theories which argue that individuals actively make their own meanings, and shape their own social identities. If the former are often accused of determinism, and of being politically disabling, the latter are frequently condemned as individualistic and utopian.

Similarly, in the case of media research, we have theories which regard the audience as broadly 'active' and as having a considerable power to determine meaning — for example, uses and gratifications, and cognitive psychology. On the other hand, we have theories that regard the audience as largely 'passive', and as tending to accept the meanings which are contained within media texts — for example, behaviourism and 'critical' research, at least of the North American variety. In the case of Cultural Studies, the more recent shift away from structuralism and *Screen* theory towards poststructuralism and audience research could be seen as part of the same dynamic. While the former theories are often accused of determinism, and of overestimating the power of the media, the latter tend to be accused of underestimating or ignoring it.

One of the major problems here is that the study of audiences is often separated from, and indeed opposed to, the study of media texts or the institutions that produce them. Obviously, specialisms of this kind are inevitable, yet the motivations and assumptions which guide these different forms of media research often appear to be quite incompatible. Undoubtedly, there are distinct limitations with forms of textual study that reduce the audience to a mere 'automated puppet pulled by the strings of the text' (Morley, 1980a). Audience readings cannot simply be 'read off' from the analysis of textual or indeed institutional structures. Yet there are also problems with audience studies that ignore the ways in which texts inevitably invite or prefer particular kinds of reading. Texts may invoke 'multiple discourses' and offer a variety of 'subject positions' from which they can be read, but the potential here is much less than infinite.

The recent work of John Fiske (e.g. 1987a, 1989a, 1989b), and the critical responses it has generated, provide a useful illustration of some of the broader tensions and limitations of recent debates about the power of the media within Cultural Studies. As a primary advocate of the power of audiences, Fiske has been widely accused of a kind of superficial populism, and of evacuating 'politics' in favour of a 'celebration' of the subversive potential of popular culture. (For different versions of this critique, see O'Shea (1989), Bee (1989), Donald (1990), Morris (1990) and Barker (1990).)

In fact, Fiske's earlier book *Television Culture* (1987a) is, for the most part, fairly even-handed about these polarities. Fiske directly rejects at least some of the arguments with which he is charged — for example, he cautions against an 'idealised notion of the people as an oppositional force whose culture and experience are in some way authentic' (p. 310). Nevertheless, as the book proceeds, the equation between popular culture and 'resistance' or 'opposition' to the dominant ideology becomes increasingly paramount. The success of television, Fiske concludes,

> depends upon its ability to serve and promote the diverse and often oppositional interests of its audiences. . . . Far from being the agent of the dominant classes, it is the prime site where the dominant have to recognize the insecurity of their power, and where they have to encourage cultural

difference with all the threat to their own position that this implies. (Fiske, 1987a, p. 326)

It is not hard to see why these arguments have generated so much criticism. Although Fiske's work is rooted in Marxist theories of ideology and social power — and particularly Gramscian notions of 'hegemony' — it increasingly appears to move beyond these. The notion that television might promote consensual or reactionary values, or that it might seek to suppress or contain cultural difference and opposition tends to disappear from view. As the above quotation suggests, Fiske ends up celebrating the pleasures of popular culture on the grounds that they 'escape' or indeed automatically 'resist' ideological control.

Fiske's many critics have not been slow to point out the problems with this argument. Alan O'Shea (1989), for example, rejects the notion that there is a more 'authentic' consciousness which is formed outside ideology. He points out that 'resistance' to the 'dominant ideology' may not always be politically progressive, and indeed in some cases is directly reactionary. Jim Bee (1989) accuses Fiske of a kind of complacency about television itself: in celebrating the 'resistance' of audiences, he effectively obviates the need for struggle and intervention to reform the broadcasting institutions. Meaghan Morris (1990) is much less polite: while she values the 'enabling theses' of recent work on media audiences, she accuses Fiske of an almost narcissistic identification with 'the people', who become 'the textually delegated, allegorical emblem of the critic's own activity'.

While I would agree with these criticisms, I would also argue that they are symptomatic of broader limitations in the debate. There are two major issues here. Firstly, as I have noted above, there is a distinct danger of conceiving of the issues in terms of mutually exclusive oppositions. As his critics have noted, Fiske's arguments appear to be based on a series of binary distinctions: on the one hand, we have 'the people' — identified with 'pleasure', 'openness' and 'resistance' — and on the other we have 'the dominant classes' — identified with 'ideology', 'closure' and 'control'.

Likewise, Fiske erects an opposition between what he terms the 'cultural' and 'financial' economies of television. While the financial economy regards texts as economic commodities, the cultural (or 'popular') economy considers them as 'provokers of meaning and pleasure' (p. 313). It is on this basis that Fiske condemns the sociological study of media institutions, arguing — in my view quite unfairly — that it is incapable of conceiving of the audience as socially diverse, and ignores the 'cultural use-value' of texts (see also Fiske, 1989c).

These oppositions are, I would argue, not unique to Fiske. Ang's (1985) study of audience readings of *Dallas*, for example, appears to be based on similar distinctions. On the side of 'popular culture' and 'the people', we have pleasure, emotion, fantasy and 'common sense'; while the elitist critics of popular culture are aligned with ideology, reason, reality and 'theory'. Despite Ang's claim to be investigating the relationships *between* ideology and pleasure, she increasingly defines these as mutually exclusive categories: it's OK for feminists to enjoy *Dallas* despite its 'fantasies of powerlessness', because fantasy has nothing to do with political action.

The problem here is not just that the categories themselves are regarded as mutually exclusive. It is also that, as a result, they come to be seen as unitary and homogeneous. One particular problem here is that research in Cultural Studies has often been confined to audience groups who have already selected and defined themselves as 'fans'. In the process, the 'pleasure' of audiences often comes to be seen as sacred and beyond criticism or analysis. The genuine desire to defend audiences against the elitist and patronizing assumptions that are often made about them spills over into a defence of television itself, which comes close to the populist argument that the medium 'gives the public what it wants'.

In the process, viewers' own criticisms of television have to be discounted as somehow illegitimate or irrelevant. Yet as I have indicated, this ability to criticize is not necessarily incompatible with pleasure, and indeed can often be pleasurable in itself. To oppose 'pleasure' and 'ideology', or 'emotion' and 'reason', is to oversimplify the complexity of this process.

In this context, the attempt to make political distinctions between different kinds of 'pleasure' or 'resistance' — or indeed any grounds for making critical judgments about television itself — are effectively impossible to sustain. Indeed, in Fiske's case, the terms themselves are barely defined: they come to be used as rhetorical counters, which are increasingly detached from any reference to the concrete experiences of real audiences. As Bee (1989) points out, Fiske fails to specify what he means by 'resistance' and 'empowerment' — although it would seem that he too regards these as primarily 'interior' or psychological processes, which have no necessary relationship with actual political or social activity. The possibility that such individual 'resistance' might function as a kind of safety valve that allows more material forms of oppression to be sustained does not appear to enter the equation.

This leads on to my second point here, which concerns the imbalance between theory and empirical evidence. While the 'turn to the audience' in Cultural Studies has generated a significant amount of theoretical debate, there is still a paucity of empirical research. There remains a considerable unease about the relationship between the 'micro' and the 'macro' — between the accounts and responses of particular viewers, and broader questions of social power. Very grand conclusions often appear to be reached on the basis of quite impoverished evidence. Differences between viewers are often explained in terms of a single cause, while difficult anomalies are ignored or explained away.

Furthermore, while these conclusions are often qualified and tentative in the original texts (e.g. Ang, 1985; Morley, 1986), this necessary caution is sometimes neglected as the research is taken up by other scholars. Cultural Studies very quickly develops its own commonsense assumptions — for example about the different ways in which men and women watch television — which in many cases require much more sustained research.

More damagingly, the influence of postmodernist theory appears to have encouraged a return to totalizing theories of the 'mass audience' which have very little empirical basis. As Meaghan Morris (1990) argues, what often emerges here is a view of the experience of popular culture as *essentially* a matter of 'distraction', of scanning the surface. Some recent research on the domestic viewing context, for example, seems to have sanctioned the idea that 'distracted' viewing — wandering in and out of the room, zapping between channels — is somehow the *only* mode of viewing. Indeed, this is sometimes held up as evidence of the 'intransigence' of audiences (Ang, 1991), and as tantamount to another form of 'resistance'. As Morris argues, this view appears to return to the notion of viewers as 'cultural dopes', albeit in a different form. Yet again, it is necessary to assert that viewing is not a singular activity, or a homogeneous one.

Ultimately, despite its commitment to empirical research, and its rejection of the grander claims of *Screen* theory, Cultural Studies also suffers from the need to reach broad theoretical generalizations about the power of television. In the process, both television and its audiences tend to be defined as unitary and undifferentiated. As both Bee (1989) and O'Shea (1989) conclude, the problem here is that *general* theories of pleasure or power may be inappropriate, and even politically naive.

The relationship between the power of television and the power of its audience is not an abstract equation which can be 'balanced out' once and for all. Clearly, the power of television *depends* upon the power of the audience, and vice versa: structure works through agency, and agency through structure. But the particular ways in which this relationship functions, and its political and cultural consequences, cannot be specified or indeed predicted in general terms. At the very least, we need to define in a much more concrete manner precisely what is meant by 'power', and to acknowledge the distinctions between different *kinds* of power.

Thus, watching *some* forms of television may involve 'resistance' to dominant ideologies — at least for *some* people in *some* contexts. Equally, watching *some* forms of television may involve the reinforcement or imposition of dominant ideologies — again, for particular people in particular contexts. What is clear from this research is that, even for children, there may also be considerable resistance to television itself. Yet the meaning and the political consequences of these various forms of resistance are, it seems to me, matters for further empirical investigation.

Knowing 'the Audience'

In arguing for further empirical work in this field, I am implicitly assuming that there are real audiences out there, and that they can in some way be known. Yet this assumption itself may need to be questioned. In a challenging article, John Hartley (1987) directly contests the idea that there are 'real' audiences that exist independently either of television or of television research. On the contrary, he argues, the audience is merely an 'invisible fiction', which is constructed in discourse.

Hartley suggests that the television industry and its regulatory bodies construct representations of the audience which serve their needs and purposes. In order to maximize its profitability and ensure its survival, the industry has to 'paedocratize' its audience — in effect, to address it as children, with child-like preoccupations and qualities. By ignoring the diversity of audiences, and constituting them as a unified whole, the industry seeks to produce 'regimented, docile, eager audiences, willing to recognize what they like in what they get' (cf. Ang, 1991).

Similarly, researchers also constitute audiences in the practice of research. This is no less true, Hartley argues, in the case of empirical audience research than it is in the case of textual analysis. The audience here is not an independent entity, but a product of 'academic/critical institutional discourses'. In a subsequent article, Hartley (1988) argues that the audience is merely 'a creation of criticism', and that 'audiences are objects of knowledge, not people'. 'Real' audiences are, he asserts, ultimately 'unknowable'.

Hartley's fundamental questioning of the notion of audience has been echoed by a number of recent authors (e.g. Chang, 1987; Allor, 1988; Anderson, 1990;

Ang, 1991), although his argument is certainly the most polemical. In effect, it would appear to lead to a rejection of empirical audience research *per se*. If audiences are just constituted in discourse, there would seem to be little point in bothering to find out about them. We would do much better to stay at home imagining what audiences might do, or at least analyzing other people's discourses about them.

As I have argued, there are substantial problems in the notion that audience research is a means of giving 'other people' a voice, or enabling them to 'speak for themselves'. Yet Hartley's argument would seem to lead to audiences being silenced yet further, in favour of the truly 'critical' voice of the analyst. Indeed, Hartley (1988) defines the major purpose of academic work as being to '*persuade* audiences to take up . . . those positions that our critical analysis suggests are *better* than others' (p. 238, his emphasis). This is, in my view, simply a justification for sustaining the privilege of academic discourse.

While I would reject these conclusions, Hartley's argument does seem to me to have some important implications in terms of the practice of audience research. Firstly, it should caution us against the tendency to identify 'audiences' with 'people', or to conceive of 'people' in unitary terms. As Hartley (1988) argues, 'being an audience is an *act* among others for individuals; a learnt, specialist, critical, discursive *practice*' (p. 238, my emphasis). Likewise, Briankle Chang (1987) argues that we need to regard audiences as 'bundles of practices', which will be combined in different ways according to the context of reading. Audiences, he argues, do not have 'fixed identities', and they cannot be completely defined in terms of 'prescriptive characteristics' such as 'race', gender or social class: readings may well be contradictory or inconsistent, according to the 'reading relations' or practices which are brought into play in the specific context of reading. Audiences, in this sense, do not exist outside of the practices in which they are constituted, and which they themselves constitute.

At the same time, I would argue that these practices may be defined in terms of such social characteristics by those who engage in them. For example, men may well have ideas about what a 'female' reading practice is, and vice versa, and this will partly determine how they read or talk about what they read. As I have indicated, talk inevitably involves definitions of self and other, of 'relations' and 'subjects': while these definitions are not wholly determined prior to the talk itself, neither are they totally free. Reading and talking about what we read are undoubtedly discursive practices, but the discourses which define and constitute them will inevitably have material social origins and consequences. Choosing (or indeed being forced) to adopt a 'masculine' subject position as a reader or speaker is more than an arbitrary subjective process, and it is not a possibility which is equally open to all. While discourse may indeed be central to social relations, the two are not synonymous.

Nevertheless, this approach may enable us to move beyond the rather sterile opposition between 'structure' and 'agency' which has characterized debates about the power of the media. It privileges neither the determining power of the text nor that of the individual reader (cf. Grossberg, 1988). Rather, the discourses readers employ, and the meanings they make, will depend upon the institutional and social contexts in which the activity of reading is itself defined. This emphasis on reading or 'being an audience' as a social *practice* is aligned with the social theory of literacy outlined in Chapter 2.

The second implication of this questioning of 'the audience' relates to the need for self-reflexivity in research. As Hartley and others suggest, the relationship between researchers and audiences is inevitably an unequal one. Audiences rarely 'represent' themselves: on the contrary, they are nearly always represented by others who claim to speak on their behalf. Representations of the audience — whether they are produced by the industry or by researchers — are inevitably representations of 'other people': they are a means whereby 'we' continue to exert our power over 'them'.

These problems are particularly pertinent to research with children. Perhaps to a greater extent than in other forms of social research, the relationship between adult researchers and their child subjects is bound to be unequal. As Matthew Speier (1976) argues:

> [traditionally] sociologists have been going about their study of children mainly like colonial administrators who might be expected to write scientifically objective reports of the local populace in order to increase their understanding of native culture, and who do so by ideologically formulating only those research problems that pertain to native behaviours coming under the regulation of colonial authority. (p. 99)

While we may seek to reduce this power differential — as we did here, for example, by avoiding judgmental or disciplinary responses and by attempting to appear familiar with 'children's culture' — it can never be completely eliminated (Fine and Glassner, 1979). Children are inevitably 'other', and any attempt to identify oneself with them or to speak on their behalf is bound to be highly problematic.

Recent work in ethnography has increasingly acknowledged the power-relationships between researchers and their 'subjects', and the limitations of this attempt to speak on behalf of others (e.g. Clifford and Marcus, 1986). This has led to a more explicit emphasis on the process of writing ethnography and on the institutional contexts in which this takes place. Yet this move towards self-reflexivity also has its limitations. Ultimately, I do not believe that this power can easily be abdicated, or that identifying it is the same as doing away with it. Furthermore, there is a real danger that self-reflexivity can degenerate into self-regard, and even self-indulgence.

Two recent studies of television audiences illustrate these problems quite clearly. Ellen Seiter (1990) offers an account of an interview conducted as part of her research on soap opera viewers, which centres on the social class differences between herself and her two middle-aged male subjects. She suggests that the two men regarded her and her fellow interviewer with a considerable amount of deference, and that this led them to attempt to display their own knowledge and to manifest a critical distance from the programmes they were discussing:

> Throughout the interview, it was uppermost in these men's minds that we were academics. For them, it was an honour to talk to us and an opportunity to be heard by persons of authority and standing. . . . This interview exemplifies the defensiveness that men and women *unprotected by academic credentials* may feel in admitting to television viewing in part because of its connotations of feminine passivity, laziness, and vulgarity. (p. 62, my emphasis)

In my view, this account actually reveals much more about the author's class prejudices and estimation of her own social status than it does about her subjects. For example, Seiter manifests contempt for one of the men's 'autodidacticism', and laments that 'it is difficult for academics involved in television studies to imagine the frustration and anger provoked by a dependency on television for education and a lifelong exclusion from elite forms of higher education' (p. 65). Recognizing these social differences, she suggests, 'will be difficult for academics, Marxists or not, because of our highly homogeneous work environment, and our intensive professional socialization' (p. 69).

Seiter's class prejudices lead her, in my view, to ignore much of what is taking place in the interview itself. She assumes that the two men's comments are offered primarily for her benefit, whereas it is entirely possible to read their remarks as a kind of performance conducted for each other. The fact that the two men are relatively indifferent to her is manifested in their sexist remarks, which clearly succeed in irritating her. She appears to assume that her contempt for them, which she displays so fully in the article, was somehow not revealed in the interview, whereas it is quite apparent even from the written text. Furthermore, she displays frustration with their unwillingness to make their 'critical categories' explicit — in effect, to play the game of talking about television in a middle-class way.

There are significant differences between the context of Seiter's research and the work reported here. While there was certainly evidence of adults deferring to the interviewers as *academics* in the context of the interviews with parents (Chapter 5), there was very little sense of this with the children. If we were to some extent perceived as 'teachers' in the early stages of this research (and primarily by the younger middle-class children), this was much less the case as the project developed. If anything, our problem was one of 'controlling' the children, at least to the extent that they would remain seated, without appearing disciplinarian. Of course, this is not to suggest that our presence as adult researchers (and indeed as individuals located in terms of class, 'race', gender and so on) made no difference. But it is to suggest that the difference it made was not consistent or the same for all the children who were involved. As I have indicated, there were some children who resisted or refused to play what they perceived as our game, and many others who sought to negotiate it on their own terms. Certainly in this instance, the power of the researcher was not something to which the children blindly consented.

On a personal level, I also have difficulties with Seiter's attempt to speak on behalf of 'academics'. As an academic working in the field of teacher education, my work environment is not 'highly homogeneous'. I do not experience what Seiter elsewhere describes as 'the *Angst* of leaving the secure academic context to listen and talk to social groups different from ourselves' (Seiter *et al.*, 1989, p. 10), because this is something I do very frequently in visiting schools. My own background is not comfortably middle-class, and my 'professional socialization', while it has at times been 'intensive', has also been something I have sought to resist and negotiate.

In the second study I want to consider here, Valerie Walkerdine (1986) also discusses the power-relationships between researcher and subject in terms of social class — although she seeks to problematize her own class position. Walkerdine's account centres on her experience of watching the video of *Rocky II* with a working-class family in the living room of their council house. Throughout her analysis, she seeks to draw parallels between her experiences, those of the family and those of Rocky himself. Seeing the film evokes memories of her own painful struggle for upward class mobility; the father's fascination with the fighting reflects his struggle against class oppression, and his desire to be a 'big man'; and the father's nickname for his little girl is compared with her own father's nickname for her, which reflect both a 'terror of femininity' and the father's attempt to claim the role of 'protector'.

Perhaps most significant however, in terms of my concerns here, is Walkerdine's questioning of the researcher's role. As she argues, we need to take account of 'the psychic reality' of both the observed and the observer — and in this instance, her own dual position as a middle-class academic and a working-class child. Research of this kind, she argues, constitutes a form of 'perverse voyeurism', in which the theorist's desire for knowledge disguises a latent terror of 'the other who is watched'. Walkerdine goes on to question the 'will to truth' she detects in analyses of popular culture and its audiences:

> What is disavowed in such approaches is the complex relation of 'intellectuals' to 'the masses': 'our' project of analysing 'them' is itself one of the regulative practices which produce *our* subjectivity as well as theirs. . . . Our fantasy investment often seems to consist in believing that we can 'make them see' or that we can see or speak *for* them. If we do assume that, then we continue to dismiss fantasy and the Imaginary as snares and delusions. We fail to acknowledge how the insistent demand to see through ideology colludes in the process of intellectualizing bodily and other pleasures. (p. 195)

While I would broadly agree with this argument, Walkerdine's study as a whole does raise some significant problems. This is partly a matter, as James Lull (1990) puts it, of sufficiency of evidence. Walkerdine makes a number of claims, for example about the significance of the father's nickname for his daughter and about his reading of the film, which are not fully substantiated with reference to the data. Despite her criticisms, Walkerdine runs the risk of presenting the theorist's voice as though it were the audience's voice. As in Seiter's article, the study tells us a great deal about the researcher, but much less about the researched. While this is undoubtedly valuable — particularly in Walkerdine's case — it can end up, paradoxically perhaps, privileging the experiences of the analyst, and disempowering the subjects of the research still further (cf. Grossberg, 1988).

Future Directions

Recent debates in Cultural Studies appear to indicate two possible directions for future research on television audiences — directions which in some respects are quite opposed. On the one hand, there is an increasing emphasis on the ethnographic study of audiences, in which media use is situated in the wider context of everyday life. On the other hand, there have been calls for a 'return' to the text, or at least for a reintegration of audience research with the study of media texts and institutions. While the former approach appears to challenge the disciplinary boundaries of media research, the latter would seem to end up reasserting them.

Audience research in this field has in fact increasingly defined itself — or has been defined — as a form of 'ethnography'. This is, I would argue, potentially quite misleading. While audience research of this kind may use ethnographic *techniques* — such as long, 'open-ended' interviews — it tends to do so in quite limited ways, and has rather different aims (Radway, 1988; Nightingale, 1989). Within anthropology, the central aim of ethnography is to generate detailed accounts of the daily lives of particular cultures or social groups, primarily through the use of participant observation. Audience research based on one-off interviews — or even (as in this case) on multiple interviews — in which particular aspects of television are specifically identified as topics of discussion is a fundamentally different matter.

However, many researchers in this field are increasingly defining audience research as part of a broader and more inclusive 'ethnography of everyday life' (e.g. Radway, 1988; Silverstone, 1989) — an approach which is partly informed by the work of the French social theorist Michel de Certeau (1984). The rationale for this approach is certainly a powerful one. As Radway (1988) argues, the attempt to understand how audiences read particular genres or media inevitably leads to a neglect of other cultural determinants. Yet any single leisure practice — such as watching television — inevitably intersects with other practices and with subjects' domestic and working lives. As Herman Bausinger (1984) has indicated, television cannot be seen as an independent variable whose 'effects' can be extracted from other aspects of daily life.

Thus, there is a growing body of work based on long-term participant observation of audience groups, particularly in the domestic context (e.g. Lull, 1988, 1990; Morley and Silverstone, 1990). For example, there have been studies of the ways in which TV is physically integrated into the home (Leichter *et al.*, 1985; Lindlof *et al.*, 1988), and of its role in families' organization of time (Bryce, 1987). Observational research, occasionally using video, has documented the wide range of activities that may take place while the set is on (Collett, 1986) and the different forms of children's interaction with TV, ranging from rapt concentration to 'monitoring' during the course of another activity (Palmer, 1986).

While this research is certainly valuable, it has tended to suffer from a familiar tension between the 'micro' and the 'macro'. As James Anderson (1987) has observed, there is often a sense of strain as researchers attempt to force detailed qualitative data into more general theoretical frameworks, for example in the form of a 'taxonomy' of media uses. Yet at the same time, there is undoubtedly a risk that this kind of research will remain purely descriptive, and prove incapable of explaining the phenomena it seeks to identify. As Morley (1991) has argued, there is a need to devise approaches which will trace the relationships between 'local' or domestic practices and the national and indeed global aspects of modern communications.

On the other hand, there has been a growing anxiety that this emphasis on the diversity of audiences may result in a neglect of the more traditional interests of media research. Charlotte Brunsdon (1989), for example, expresses some anxiety that questions about the nature of television texts are increasingly being displaced onto the study of audiences. While this anxiety may be premature, it derives from a valid concern about the quality and social responsibility of television itself — a concern which is often swept aside in more populist approaches:

The recognition of the creativity of the audience must, I think, be mobilized back into relation to the television text, and the demands that are
made on program makers for a diverse and plural programming which
is adequate to the needs, desires and pleasures of those audiences.
(Brunsdon, 1989, p. 126)

Likewise, Graham Murdock (1989) reasserts the fact that many identities, experiences and forms of knowledge are consistently marginalized by mainstream
television, and argues that they should be more fully represented. Like Brunsdon,
Murdock calls for the integration of audience research with the more traditional
concerns of Media Studies, which include the political economy of media production and circulation. As he argues, 'we need to conceptualise the relations between
the material and discursive organization of culture without reducing one to the
other' (p. 45).

In terms of these arguments, the present study has inevitable limitations, and
will need to be extended by future work. The political economy of mass-produced
culture for children has barely been addressed by previous research. Likewise, the
television programmes and other popular cultural texts which are aimed at children
have generally been ignored by academic critics. Popular debates about these
issues have, as I have suggested, often been based on questionable assumptions
about childhood and about cultural value. Here again, those who have sought
to argue 'on behalf of children' have often neglected children's own perspectives
and concerns. Future research in this field will need to take fuller account of
the dynamic and often contradictory relationships between institution, text and
audience.

Nevertheless, these arguments do raise significant problems about the position of the academic 'critic'. Brunsdon (1990) argues for the need to salvage a
notion of 'quality' television that is not simply a matter of imposing fixed class
values. She argues, as I have done here, that ordinary viewers are constantly
making judgments about the quality of what they watch, and that these judgments
may vary from situation to situation. Yet how are we to engage with these perceptions? Who is to speak on behalf of the audience, and in what context?

The central issue which needs to be addressed here is that of the political
purposes of research, and of the contexts in which those purposes might be
achieved. As Lawrence Grossberg (1987) has argued, 'ethnographic' or qualitative
research methods are not necessarily any more 'critical' — whatever we take that
to mean — than more traditional approaches. The political positions and consequences of research are not inscribed within specific methods: rather, they depend
upon the social contexts and relationships in which the research is produced and
used.

The major problem, I would argue, is that Cultural Studies has become
increasingly content to remain within the boundaries of the academy, and has
largely failed to engage with social practices which lie beyond it. While our
perspectives remain confined within this context, the audience will necessarily
remain 'other', a mere figment of our discursive imagination. Yet if we are seeking
to persuade audiences to adopt 'better' positions, or indeed to argue for 'better'
television, it is unlikely that we will get very far just by writing articles in obscure
academic journals, or indeed books such as this one. Ultimately, the most damaging

limitation of academic media research has been its failure to think through the *educational* implications of its own practice — not only in terms of the elite institutions of higher education, but much more urgently in terms of the educational experiences of the majority of the population in schools. It is to this issue that I return in my final chapter.

Chapter 12

Television, Language and Learning: Implications for Media Education

The research described in this book has emerged from a particularly crucial period in the development of media education in Britain. While media education in this country has a long history, stretching back over fifty years (see Alvarado *et al.*, 1987), it has recently begun to expand at a remarkable rate. The advent of new examinations in the upper years of the secondary school has enabled Media Studies courses to attract growing numbers of students, thereby consolidating its position as a separate subject discipline. Yet there have also been significant developments in areas of the curriculum which have hitherto remained largely untouched. In the primary sector, there has been an increasing interest in the possibilities of media education with much younger children, particularly within the language curriculum (Bazalgette, 1989); and there has also been a remarkable growth in the provision of media education in vocational and pre-vocational courses (Buckingham, forthcoming). Perhaps most significantly, the National Curriculum has allotted a major role for media education within the core subject of English (National Curriculum Council, 1990), which ensures that the study of the media is now part of the entitlement of every student. Media education is no longer a 'vanguard' movement, or the preserve of a small band of committed enthusiasts. For better or worse, it is now much closer to the educational mainstream.

Yet at the same time, many of the orthodoxies which were developed in previous decades have begun to be challenged and revised. Historically, media education in British schools has been very much the poor relation of academic theory (see Buckingham, 1990c). In the 1970s, the establishment of Film Studies — and subsequently Media Studies — as academic disciplines in higher education was the major priority of key institutions in the field. Many advocates of media education appeared to subscribe to a 'top-down' model of educational change — a model which was arguably quite inappropriate to the British system, at least at that time. In effect, it was assumed that academics would generate the knowledge, and would then pass it on to teachers, who in turn would hand it down to students (Lusted, 1986).

One consequence of this situation has been that questions of learning and classroom practice — not merely in schools, but also in higher education itself — have largely been ignored. Even today, most books about media education tend to take the form of potted summaries of academic research, with 'suggestions for teaching' appended (or not): yet there is little acknowledgment here of what actually happens when these suggestions are carried out. As a result, there are many fundamental questions which have been neglected, and which now require urgent attention. What do children already know about the media, and how do they know it? What do they need to learn, and what difference do we hope this will make? How might they learn, and what would seem to be the most effective teaching strategies? How can we identify what children know and learn, and enable them to identify this for themselves? These questions are not just to do with *how* we teach, or with the most efficient ways of making academic knowledge 'accessible': they are also to do with *what* we teach, and they raise some significant questions about the nature and the value of that academic knowledge itself.

The recent development of classroom-based research in media education (Buckingham, 1990a) reflects a growing acknowledgment of the difficulty and complexity of these issues, and the need to move beyond the abstract rhetoric which has often characterized the area. The research described in this book is intended to complement this work, and, while it is not directly concerned with classroom practice, it certainly does have implications for media education, as I hope to indicate in this chapter.

Television Literacy Revisited

Mainstream research on children and television has tended to define children as more or less 'incompetent' viewers. What children do with television is typically compared with adult norms, and thereby found wanting. Children, it is argued, are unselective, uncritical and unsophisticated viewers. They lack many of the 'skills' which are required to make sense of television and to use it in a responsible and sensible way. Thus, it is argued that children are incapable of distinguishing between television fantasy and reality; that they are unable to identify the essential elements of a narrative or the motivations of characters; that they do not understand the persuasive functions of advertising; and that they are ignorant about how television is produced.

The application of Piagetian theories of child development has tended to support this definition of the child in terms of what it lacks — namely, adult rationality. Similarly, socialization theory has tended to regard children as passive recipients of external models and norms: childhood is seen here merely as a kind of preparation for adult life. In each case, this emphasis on their apparent inadequacies has led to a neglect of children's own perspectives, and of the complex ways in which they construct their own meanings and pleasures. In concentrating on what children are *not* doing, researchers have inevitably neglected what they actually *are* doing.

Certainly, there is considerable evidence from this research that would contest this view of children as incompetent or uncritical viewers. Even the youngest children in this sample displayed a high degree of critical sophistication in their judgments about television. Their debates about the relationship between television and reality were complex and often extremely lucid. They knew a good deal about how television is produced, and offered some very intelligent hypotheses in areas where they were less certain about this. They were well aware of the persuasive functions of advertising, and often sceptical about many of its claims. Their discussions of their favourite comedies and soap operas displayed a complex awareness of the development of narrative, and of the constructed, fictional nature of the text.

At the same time, there were undoubtedly significant gaps in their know-ledge. Inevitably, their judgments about their favourite programmes were much more complex and sophisticated than their readings of those with which they were less familiar. News, and indeed non-fictional programmes generally, appeared to be of little interest except to some of the older middle-class children: yet even here, there was little discussion of the ways in which television deals with explicitly political issues, and no real questioning of the partiality or 'bias' of news. Similarly, there was very little evidence here that the children understood much about the economic structure of broadcasting, or the operation of broadcasting institutions. And while many were certainly interested in the complexities of television pro-duction, their knowledge here was patchy.

Nevertheless, in many of the areas considered in Part Three, there were clear (if predictable) developmental gains. Broadly speaking, the older children tended to be more reflective, and to offer more informed and considered judgments. They had a wider repertoire of generic categories, and a growing awareness of the difficulties of categorization. Their accounts of film narratives were generally more coherent and well-organized. Their judgments about the relationship between television and reality were more complex, involving a more extensive range of criteria.

On the basis of these findings, it would certainly be possible to outline a developmental model, which could be used in constructing a media education curriculum. For example, it would be possible to identify a series of steps by which children might begin to acquire an understanding of representation, building on their developing judgments about modality. Similarly, it might be suggested that children of around 8 or 9 are 'ready' to learn about the processes of television production — or at least much more interested in this than they are often assumed to be. On the other hand, it could be suggested that much of the effort which is often expended in encouraging children to 'resist' advertising is misplaced, and that at least in this area it might be more productive for them to study the economic functions of the industry.

It might be possible to extend this by identifying ways in which these existing understandings might be 'transferred' to other areas of the curriculum, such as English. For example, children's existing awareness of modality or nar-rative could be extended to the study of books, or indeed to developing their own writing. From this perspective, children's understanding of television would come to be seen, not as an area in which they need remedial instruction, but on the contrary as a very valuable resource which, if given status by teachers, could be of great educational potential.

While these are certainly important tasks, they also seem to me to raise significant problems. This image of a smooth developmental progression inevit-ably ignores the considerable diversity which occurs within age groups. General-ized statements about what children of particular ages understand or do not understand are inevitably reductive, and ultimately of very limited value. Indeed, they may be positively dangerous in the sense that they may lead us to neglect what children are actually capable of doing.

As educators, we need to do more than simply celebrate the diversity and complexity of what children already know — or indeed wait until they are 'ready' to learn more. We need to identify the gaps in their knowledge, and enable them to extend their existing competencies and understandings. In the process, we have to make judgments about what we think children *should* understand, and indeed about what they are capable of understanding. But these judgments are constantly revised and changed in the process of teaching. A developmental model, or indeed a set of attainment targets, ultimately says very little about the *social process* of teaching and learning. The fact that such statements may be required for the purposes of state bureaucracy — for example, for the implementation of a centralized National Curriculum — should not blind us to their dangers and inadequacies.

Furthermore, this definition of children's competencies as a set of 'cognitive skills' inevitably neglects the social and interpersonal contexts in which they are developed and used. Children's 'understandings' about television are almost inevitably embedded and expressed in language, and language itself is bound to serve social functions and purposes. 'Viewing skills' are not exercised in the abstract, and they cannot be separated from the social and affective dimensions of children's relationship with television. 'Television literacy', as I have defined it here, is not a single set of disembodied skills, but a set of social practices which are inevitably plural and diverse.

This broader view of 'television literacy' raises some very significant questions about the overall aims and purposes of media education. In particular, it should lead us to question the normative idea of 'critical viewing' on which most media education is based. It is not merely that children are already much more capable of being critical than they are often assumed to be — although it is certainly important to acknowledge this. It is also that we need to consider the social and affective functions of critical discourse — and ultimately to question what it means, both for students and for teachers, to 'be critical'.

Media Education and the Dilemmas of 'Critical Pedagogy'

Media education in Britain has generally adopted a much more explicitly *political* stance than the outwardly neutral approach of 'television literacy' curricula in the United States — although it is often no less defensive in its approach. Indeed, media education has frequently been regarded by its advocates as a means of bringing about radical political changes, both in the consciousness of students and in the education system itself. Some very grand claims have been made about the ability of media teaching to subvert dominant ideologies, to empower the oppressed, and to revolutionize the school curriculum.

Nevertheless, there has been much less attention to the question of how these changes might practically be achieved. Given the dominance of academic media theory, debates about the practice of media education in schools have inevitably been somewhat limited, although they have often been extremely polarized (see Alvarado, 1981 and Masterman, 1981/2; Buckingham, 1986 and Masterman, 1986; Williamson, 1981/2, 1985). At the risk of caricature, it is possible to identify two contrasting positions here — positions which I would argue are far from unique to media education.

The first of these — which was dominant in the 1970s — is based on a belief in the inherent radicalism of Media Studies as a body of academic knowledge.

Media education is seen as a process of 'demystification', which works in two main ways. Firstly, it involves making previously 'hidden' information available to students. Thus, telling students about the ways in which media institutions operate — for example, about patterns of ownership and control — is seen as a means of 'opening their eyes' to the covert operations of capitalism. Secondly, media education is seen to involve a training in critical analysis, for example using methods derived from structuralism and semiotics. Here too, this is assumed to have an inevitably radical effect. The 'objective' analysis of racist or sexist stereotypes in the media will, it is argued, liberate us from the false ideologies these representations are seen to support and promote.

Theoretically, this approach relies on a view of the media as extremely powerful agents of the 'dominant ideology', and of audiences as passive victims. The media are seen here as 'engineering consent' to a repressive social order, although in ways which are invisible to those who 'consume' them. This approach is often accompanied by an almost puritanical distrust of the pleasures afforded by popular media — the view that, in the words of one advocate of critical pedagogy, the media are 'the major addictive lure to the flesh-pots of our culture' (Sullivan, 1987).

In terms of educational theory, this approach finds its clearest expression in Harold Entwistle's (1979) account of the work of Gramsci. Entwistle rejects as merely patronizing the notion that the school curriculum should be based on what is immediately 'relevant' to students. Children from subordinate classes, it is argued, need to be given access to formal academic knowledge if they are to participate in and to change the dominant culture. This approach is, at least according to Entwistle, bound to involve traditional teaching methods: it represents a form of 'conservative schooling for radical politics'.

By contrast, the second — and more recent — position seeks to validate, even to celebrate, aspects of students' culture which are traditionally excluded from the school curriculum. Thus, it is argued that media education, with its focus on 'popular' rather than 'high' culture, is situated in a very different position in terms of the relation between school culture and the culture of the home or peer group. Primarily by virtue of its *content*, media education has the potential to challenge traditional notions of what counts as valid knowledge and culture. In the process, it is argued, it makes for much more egalitarian relationships between teachers and students: the students are now the 'experts', while the teacher is no longer the main source of authority.

Advocates of this position have increasingly drawn on the celebratory approach to popular culture described in the previous chapter (e.g. Fiske, 1989a). Here, popular texts are seen not as bearers of reactionary ideologies, but as sources of subversive pleasures which challenge and disrupt the educational and political *status quo*. While this approach provides a valuable corrective to the view of the media as mere propagators of 'false consciousness', it has often been criticized as a form of superficial populism.

In terms of educational theory, this approach tends to draw upon the 'progressivist' tradition of English teaching and of creative arts subjects. The rhetoric is one of 'active learning', open-ended investigation, collaborative group work, discussion and practical production. Far from emphasizing 'objectivity' and a received body of academic knowledge, this approach insists on the necessity of students arriving at their own answers, and exploring their own 'subjective' responses.

While both these positions would claim to be politically 'progressive', both would seem to overestimate the possibilities of radical change. The notion of media education as a form of 'demystification' assumes that students will agree that they are 'mystified' and will automatically accept the teacher's attempts to remove the veils of illusion from before their eyes (Buckingham, 1986). Yet in this context, media education is likely to be perceived as an attack on students' pleasures and preferences, and is almost bound to be resisted. As a number of studies have shown, working-class students are likely to reject what they regard as the efforts of middle-class teachers to impose their values and beliefs, however 'politically correct' these might claim to be (cf. Cohen, 1988; Dewdney and Lister, 1988).

Furthermore, to assume that ideologies such as racism and sexism are primarily derived from the media, and can be overthrown by a good dose of critical analysis is, to say the least, wishful thinking (Richards, 1990). As Judith Williamson (1981/2) has argued, students can easily learn to 'do' critical analysis in the same way they might 'do' medieval poetry or the history of the Tudors. Learning to say 'politically correct' things about images of women in the media can easily become just another way of telling teachers what they want to hear. As Williamson suggests, unless the analysis of ideology in the media is related to students' own experience, it will remain a purely academic exercise — and may even lead to the view that ideology is simply 'what *other* people think'.

On the other hand, the 'progressivist' version of media education appears to assume that the power-relations of the classroom can easily be abolished, just by virtue of changing the content of the curriculum. Again, this would seem to be a highly utopian view, which concrete studies of classroom practice have seriously questioned (e.g. Hudak, 1987; Buckingham, 1990a). As these studies make clear, there is no *inherent* reason why studying game shows should make for less hierarchical relations between teachers and students than studying the Metaphysical poets. Indeed, there is a distinct danger here of extending an academic analysis of popular culture into the very different context of schools. While showing Madonna videos may be faintly subversive in the context of an academic seminar, its meaning in a school classroom is likely to be quite different.

Furthermore, if the 'demystification' position can easily end up reinforcing existing power-relationships between teachers and students, the 'progressivist' version of media education runs the risk of simply leaving students where they are. In my experience, the study of popular media often produces the response 'so what?' While they may find the activity enjoyable, students often complain that they are not actually 'learning' anything from it. The desire merely to celebrate or validate students' existing knowledge can easily result in a form of institutionalized underachievement.

My account of these two positions has been brief, and thus inevitably oversimplified. In practice, most British advocates of media education in schools have sought a negotiated position between them — although, in many cases, this has led to a degree of incoherence and contradiction.

For example, the work of Len Masterman (1980, 1985), undoubtedly the most influential advocate of media education over the past decade, is marked by an uneasy alliance between the emphasis on a received body of academic knowledge and an argument for 'progressive' teaching strategies. On the one hand, Masterman argues that the aim of teachers should be to 'demystify' students, and thereby to 'liberate' them from false consciousness. Yet on the other, he argues for a 'non-hierarchical' pedagogy, in which the teacher is merely a 'senior colleague', rather than an expert whose perspective should automatically be privileged. This clearly places the teacher in a contradictory position — on the one hand, as the bearer of a 'truth' which is not available to the students, yet on the other as an equal partner in dialogue.

Similarly, on the level of classroom practice, and in syllabuses and teaching materials, there are often tensions between the insistence on an 'objective' body of academic knowledge and the need to adopt more open-ended teaching strategies. While students are often encouraged to reach their own conclusions, in practice there is often little opportunity for them to generate their own readings, or to explore the contradictory pleasures which media texts might afford. Media teachers are often careful to assert that 'there are no right answers', while clearly believing that there are (Buckingham *et al.*, 1990).

Ultimately, the problem with both approaches outlined here is their failure to acknowledge the complexity of what children *already* know about the media, and hence to develop an adequate theory of learning. Either learning is something that 'just happens' through a process of osmosis, or it is something which follows inevitably as a result of teaching. If it is to be effective, media education will require a more complex understanding of the relationship between students' existing 'commonsense' knowledge about the media and the more formal academic knowledge made available in schools.

Rethinking Conceptual Understanding

As I have noted, media education in Britain has increasingly been defined in terms of a series of 'key concepts'. While there are minor variations here, the concepts identified in the Introduction to Part Three of this book would appear to inform media education syllabuses from the primary school right through to higher degree level. Media education is predominantly defined and organized in terms of notions such as 'media language', 'genre', 'representation', 'audience' and 'institution'.

This definition of media education in terms of concepts — rather than, for example, 'facts' or 'skills' — has significant advantages. It does not specify a given content, thereby enabling the curriculum to remain contemporary and responsive to students' interests and enthusiasms. It makes it possible to compare and contrast different media, and to recognize the connections between them. And it renders the theoretical basis of the subject explicit, for both teachers and students.

At the same time, there are potential dangers here. There is a risk of teaching concepts in isolation from each other, and thus making it difficult for students to recognize the connections between them. Concepts cannot be meaningfully taught without reference to 'facts': any understanding of the structure and operation of media institutions, for example, will be superficial if it is not informed by a certain amount of factual knowledge. Furthermore, it is possible to reduce a set of concepts to a series of abstract definitions — in effect, to a body of 'content' — which can be transmitted and then tested.

Furthermore, this emphasis on conceptual learning raises some fundamental epistemological problems. Many of the difficulties which have been encountered in evaluating and assessing students' learning in media education derive from a basic uncertainty about how we might identify 'conceptual understanding' in the first place (Buckingham *et al.*, 1990; Buckingham and Sefton-Green, 1992). For example, one recent GCSE examination paper in Media Studies required students to provide a definition of the term 'representation' — although apparently only one candidate was awarded the full three marks. This is, certainly, one kind of evidence of conceptual understanding — although it is one which most teachers would probably regard as pretty inadequate. While it certainly serves as a useful measure of students' ability to regurgitate what teachers have fed them, the ability to use an academic discourse in itself tells us very little about 'understanding'.

The work of the Soviet psychologist Vygotsky may offer a more productive approach to the question of conceptual learning in media education (see Buckingham, 1990d). According to Vygotsky (1962, 1978), the development of 'higher mental functions' depends upon the child's access to signs, and thus has *social* origins. Language provides the means whereby the child mediates its own thought, and thereby gains conscious, voluntary control over its own mental processes. Furthermore, the intellectual and communicative functions of language cannot be separated: and in this respect, thought itself can be seen to have a primarily social basis. Vygotsky's work has a great deal in common with the theories of language developed by Bakhtin and Volosinov, considered in Chapter 2 — not least in its explicit basis in historical materialism.

In his work on the development of conceptual understanding, Vygotsky (1962) makes an important distinction between what he calls 'spontaneous' and 'scientific' concepts. Spontaneous concepts are those developed through the child's own mental efforts, while scientific concepts are decisively influenced by adults, and arise from the process of teaching. Scientific concepts — which include social scientific concepts — are distinct from spontaneous concepts in two major respects. Firstly, they are characterized by a degree of distance from immediate experience: they involve an ability to generalize in systematic ways. Secondly, they involve self-reflection, or what Bruner (1986) terms 'metacognition' — that is, attention not merely to the object to which the concept refers, but also to the thought process itself (cf. Desmond, 1985).

To a certain extent, we might consider children's existing understanding of the media as a body of spontaneous concepts. While these concepts will become more systematic and generalized as the children mature, media education might be seen to provide a body of scientific concepts which will enable them to think, and to use language (including 'media language'), in a much more conscious and deliberate way. The aim of media education, then, is not merely to enable children to 'read' — or make sense of — media texts, or to enable them to 'write' their own. It must also enable them to reflect systematically on the processes of reading and writing themselves, to understand and to analyze their own experience as readers and writers.

There were certainly some instances in this research, particularly among the older, more middle-class children, where this kind of self-reflection was already under way — although this was a process which the research itself inevitably encouraged. For example, in the case of the categorization activity (Chapter 6), these children were not just more fluent in their use of generic categories, but were also beginning to question the epistemological basis of genre itself. They explicitly acknowledged that categorization was not an objective process, and that diverse criteria might be employed, with contradictory effects. Likewise, there were a number of instances in the discussions of modality (Chapter 9) where the children began to reflect on the process of modality judgment itself, drawing attention to its contradictions and limitations. In effect, the children were beginning to monitor their own thought processes — although this was, crucially, a *social* activity which took place in dialogue with others.

From this perspective, reflection and self-evaluation would appear to be crucial aspects of learning in media education. It is through shared reflection that students will be able to make their implicit 'spontaneous' knowledge about the media explicit, and then — with the aid of the teacher and of peers — to reformulate it in terms of broader 'scientific' concepts. Significantly, Vygotsky (1962) argues against the 'direct teaching' of concepts — which he suggests will result in 'nothing but empty verbalism, a parrotlike repetition of words by the child'. Nevertheless, he does argue that children need to be introduced to the terminology of scientific concepts — in effect, to the academic discourse of the subject — and that they will only gradually take this on and come to use it as their own.

Bruner's (1986) notions of 'scaffolding' and 'handover' are both attempts to describe the way in which teachers can enable students to connect spontaneous and scientific concepts. Significantly, dialogue with teachers (along with more competent peers) plays a crucial role here. Children do not 'discover' scientific concepts, but are aided in doing so by the systematic interventions of teachers. While Vygotsky certainly emphasizes the importance of 'active learning', he also stresses the importance of teachers enabling children to take on, and participate in, the dominant culture. In this respect, his approach could be seen to transcend the limitations of both 'conservative' and 'progressive' positions (see Edwards and Mercer, 1987).

Nevertheless, there are several unresolved issues here. In particular, there is the question of the relationship between conceptual learning and discourse. From a Vygotskyan perspective, the relationship between language and thought is dialectical. Acquiring or using a specific discourse — for example, the academic discourse of Media Studies — is seen to serve particular *cognitive* functions. Thus, Vygotsky argues that learning the language of scientific concepts enables one to think more systematically and self-reflexively: it serves as a tool which aids understanding.

For example, in the case of modality, the aim of media education would be to encourage children to make explicit the criteria on which their own judgments are based, and to enable them to acquire a discourse in which to analyse their differences and contradictions — and thereby to relate these to broader debates about representation, stereotyping, 'positive images' and so on. The end result of this process would not be a fixed 'position' on questions of representation but an understanding of the social and cultural debates which are at stake, and an ability to intervene in them, both through criticism and through practice.

However, in its emphasis on the *cognitive* benefits of literacy, Vygotsky's work has much in common with the 'autonomous' theory of literacy discussed in Chapter 2. In acquiring literacy, he argues, individuals learn to use signs in less context-bound ways, and thereby develop their capacity for logical thought and abstract reasoning. Yet, as James Wertsch (1985) points out, Vygotsky does not distinguish between literacy itself and the contexts (notably schooling) in which it is acquired. As I have indicated, recent research on literacy questions this view. From the perspective of an 'ideological' theory of literacy (Street, 1984), the relationships between literacy, schooling and mental functioning are much more complex. The consequences of literacy are not automatic or unitary, but depend upon the *uses* to which it is put, and the social contexts in which it is exercised.

Furthermore, as Wertsch (1985) indicates, Vygotsky's theory mainly confines itself to individual or small-group processes, and ultimately fails to account for the relationship between psychological and social or institutional phenomena. Vygotsky does not acknowledge the ways in which the implicit assumptions of 'activity settings' can determine individual mental and communicative processes; and he fails to explore the ways in which the properties of discourse will depend upon the socio-historical situation and position of the speaker — an issue which is much more fully developed in the work of Bakhtin (e.g. 1981). Ultimately, Vygotsky appears to privilege 'decontextualized', abstract reasoning as if this were somehow independent of its linguistic expression, and thus beyond social and historical processes. In these respects at least, Vygotsky's theory remains insufficiently social.

In drawing on Bakhtin's theory, and on recent work in discourse analysis, I have argued against the notion that language merely 'reflects' cognitive processes such as attitudes or beliefs. From this perspective, acquiring or using a discourse has pre-eminently *social* functions: it serves to define the 'self' in relation to others, and is at least partly determined by the social and interpersonal context in which it occurs.

As I have argued, these definitions are flexible, and often contradictory. Yet they depend, crucially, on the power-relationships which obtain within the discussion group and between the group and the interviewer — which in turn reflect broader power-relationships based on gender, age, 'race' and social class. While these relationships are partly predetermined, they can also be renegotiated in the course of discussion.

Similarly, in the context of the classroom, what children and teachers say will inevitably depend upon the power-relationships which obtain between them — although it will also serve to define and redefine those relationships. For example, students may respond to the propagandist approach of some radical teachers in one of two ways. Either they will choose to play the game, in which case they may learn to reproduce the 'politically correct' responses without necessarily investigating or questioning their own position. Or they will refuse to do so, in which case they will say things they may or may not believe, in order to annoy the teacher and thereby amuse themselves (Buckingham, 1986). A good deal of anti-racist and anti-sexist teaching has foundered on precisely this problem: for the majority of working-class students, it represents another attempt by middle-class teachers to impose their attitudes and beliefs, often backed up by the disciplinary apparatus of the school (Cohen, 1988).

Likewise, using the specialist terminology of academic discourse can serve as a means of demonstrating one's willingness to play the teacher's game, but it does not necessarily reflect 'understanding'. The decision to adopt a critical discourse about 'the media' — rather than talking about the good bits in the video you saw last night, for example — needs to be regarded as a social act, and not merely as evidence of cognitive understanding.

From this perspective, we would need to be much more cautious about the role of language in learning. We would need to question the view of language as a neutral tool for understanding, and the notion of academic discourse as purely 'scientific'. All discourse — including academic discourse — would need to be judged in terms of its *social* functions and effects, rather than merely in terms of its role in cognitive processes. Indeed, there is a significant danger that an academic discourse — however 'radical' — will seek to replace, rather than build upon, the popular discourses through which children already make sense of their experience of the media. The 'subjective' responses of students may be invalidated, in favour of the 'objective' analytical approach of the teacher. By defining the students' discourses as merely 'ideological' — and therefore lacking in legitimate status — the 'scientific' discourse of the teacher may come to serve as the only guarantee of critical authority.

A further problem with Vygotsky's theory here is its privileging of what he terms 'higher mental functions' — in effect, of the intellect — at the expense of the emotions. As I have noted, this is characteristic of cognitive psychology in general, and it is a limitation Vygotsky himself acknowledges (Vygotsky, 1962, p. 8). Even in his essay on play, Vygotsky (1978, Chapter 7) appears to define the 'maximum pleasure' of play as deriving primarily from 'subjection to rules'.

Yet as this research has indicated, questions of preference and pleasure are inextricable from the ways in which children use and make sense of television. While I would reject the deterministic notion that the media 'construct' identity, they are undoubtedly a major resource in the process whereby children define and negotiate their own subjectivity. Binary distinctions between 'ideology' and 'pleasure' or 'reason' and 'emotion' ultimately lead to quite one-dimensional understandings of this process.

Similarly, it is vital to avoid any superficial opposition between 'cognitive' and 'affective' processes in learning. Privileging intellectual, analytical discourses may lead us to neglect much of the significance of what is taking place in learning about the media. If media education is to be effective, it must enable students to explore and to reflect upon their 'subjective' responses, rather than seeking merely to repress them in favour of supposedly 'objective' analysis.

Going Critical: The Social Functions of Critical Discourse

From this perspective, then, we would need to ask some hard questions about the functions and purposes of critical discourses about television. Undoubtedly, children are often extremely critical of what they watch. In this research, children of all ages appeared to be quite adept at 'sending up' television and mocking it for its artificiality. They often complained about bad acting, continuity mistakes and inept storylines, even in programmes they enjoyed a great deal. They constantly questioned the relationship between television and reality, and displayed a considerable degree of scepticism about supposedly 'powerful' influences such as advertising.

Yet as I have shown, children's talk about television crucially depends upon the context in which it occurs, and the ways in which they perceive that context. In talking about television — in selecting what to talk about and how — children are actively defining themselves in relation to others, both in terms of age and in terms of social factors such as class, 'race' and gender.

This is no less the case, I would argue, when it comes to adopting a critical discourse. Children are very aware that adults — and particularly middle-class adults like teachers — often disapprove of them watching television, and believe it has a harmful influence upon them. The fact that these children were being interviewed by an adult in an educational setting was obviously likely to cue more critical responses than might otherwise have been the case.

One characteristic strategy here, which recurred throughout these discussions, was to attempt to displace the 'effects' of television onto 'other people'. Just as adults frequently displace their concerns onto children, so children will often claim that it is those much younger than themselves who are most at risk — while they themselves, by implication, are more 'adult' and thus much less vulnerable. In this context, therefore, the children had a good deal to be gained from presenting themselves as selective, critical viewers, who were able to see through the deceptions and limitations of the medium.

However, there were many instances where the children failed or even actively refused to play the interviewer's game. Proclaiming an exaggerated enthusiasm for gory horror movies, for example, or engaging in wild celebrations of cartoon violence, occasionally seemed to serve as a useful way of subverting the interviewer's power. In choosing to swap anecdotes about favourite programmes or to act out what happened, the children often moved away from the 'educational' agenda, engaging in behaviour which would not be sanctioned in the classroom, and leaving the interviewer way behind. Clearly, the *refusal* of a critical discourse may also serve social functions, and in certain contexts may even (perhaps paradoxically) prove quite subversive.

The extent to which the children adopted this critical discourse therefore depended upon how they were choosing to define the interview context and their relationship to it. Yet it also depended upon their perceptions of their own social position, and their relationships with others in the group. In the case of this research, this was particularly manifested in terms of gender and social class.

Thus, there were certainly instances in which boys chose to deflate what they perceived as 'girls' programmes' such as soap operas, while girls often did the same in the case of 'boys' programmes' such as action-adventure cartoons. Here, the use of a critical discourse — for example, condemning the programmes as 'predictable' or 'unrealistic' — derived primarily from the need to claim or to project a gendered identity.

More broadly, however, it is possible to identify differences between the kinds of critical discourses adopted by boys and girls, especially in single-sex groups. This was particularly apparent in the discussions of television characters (Chapter 8), although it was manifested in a number of other areas of the research. As I have noted, boys in single-sex groups often found it quite difficult to talk about their own pleasure: there was a considerable amount of mutual policing here, and a sense that a great deal was being put at risk. In some cases, the boys appeared to resolve this difficulty by becoming 'critics' — for example, in the case of the middle-class 'film buffs' — or simply by hurling abuse — as in the case of the 'blaring' competition conducted by the working-class boys. While the girls were no less capable of adopting this critical discourse — and indeed in many cases were much more fluent in it — they were also much more willing to acknowledge and to reflect upon their own pleasures. It was among the older middle-class girls that the most complex and sophisticated discussions, for example of modality and representation, took place.

However, these differences were much more apparent in single-sex groups. As I have argued, they need to be seen not as a reflection of a pre-existing gendered identity, but as a construction of that identity for the purposes of a specific social context.

There were also notable differences here in terms of social class. Broadly speaking, the middle-class children here were more likely to adopt this kind of critical discourse about television, particularly in more open-ended discussion. They appeared to be more concerned with questions of modality and representation, and more interested in displaying their knowledge about how television programmes are produced. They were more likely to engage in general discussions and debates about television — rather than, for example, talking about the 'good bits', or about specific programmes. Their judgments appeared to be more self-reflexive and systematic, closer to the discourse of 'scientific concepts'.

Yet again, however, in attempting to explain this difference, it is important to avoid a deterministic account of the role of social class. Here too, we need to account for the different ways in which children perceive the context of discussion. There was certainly evidence that, at least in the early stages of the research, the younger middle-class children were much more likely to perceive and indeed actively to construct the interview situation in 'educational' terms. By contrast, many of the working-class children were more concerned with relationships within the peer group: they seemed to perceive the situation much less formally, and were much less deferent towards the interviewer.

For some of the older middle-class children, the discussions seemed to be perceived primarily as an opportunity for a self-conscious display of their own 'good taste' and critical acumen. There was often a degree of competition here, as children vied to deliver the wittiest put-down of the most awful game shows, or to perform the most damning imitation of bad acting in the soaps. The more criticisms you could offer, the more intelligent and sophisticated you would appear.

Nevertheless, in some of these discussions, the critical discourse often seemed actively to exclude other kinds of talk. While mocking the limitations of television is often a pleasurable activity, it tends to prevent any more sustained discussion of the pleasures of viewing itself. Obviously being able to mock television in sufficient detail depends upon a familiarity with it — yet in many cases, these children would only admit to watching programmes 'to see how stupid they are'. Even programmes that were obviously enjoyed were discussed in extremely distanced, ironical terms. To commit yourself to liking anything — with the exception of documentaries, perhaps, or high-status 'adult' movies — would be to run the risk of aligning yourself with the mass audience, those 'other people' who are stupid enough to watch it and believe it.

While this critical discourse was not explicitly phrased in class terms, it clearly did serve to distinguish the speaker as more sophisticated and knowledgeable than the common viewer. At least to some extent, the discourse served as a vehicle for the middle-class children's attempts to socialize themselves into class membership.

To distance oneself from the pleasures of 'other people' — or indeed from one's own pleasures — is implicitly to assert one's own superiority, and to assert a powerful subject position. Of course, this is not to say that this discourse is incompatible with pleasure, or that it necessarily destroys it for all time. As I have indicated, using this discourse is itself pleasurable — not least because of the impression of power and control that it embodies. Yet we cannot assume that this discourse necessarily reflects the positions which are occupied in viewing itself.

The extent to which we are able to produce critical statements in the context of a research interview — or, crucially, in the context of a classroom — cannot in itself be taken as evidence of what we do outside these contexts. 'Being critical' is a social, discursive practice, not a state of mind.

Nevertheless, in privileging this critical discourse about television, there is a danger of reasserting limited, rationalistic norms of 'critical viewing'. A great deal of media education and of research in this field appears to be based on a notion of the ideal viewer as one who is never persuaded or fooled, who 'sees through' the illusions television provides — in effect, the viewer who is impervious to influence. Yet what is missing from the experience of this 'critical viewer' is the dimension of aesthetic pleasure and of emotional engagement with television. The 'critical viewer' remains unmoved, and can only recognize pleasure as a form of deception, a disguise under which the medium performs its nasty ideological work. From this perspective, pleasure is something we have to 'own up to': it is dangerous and must be intellectualized away (Walkerdine, 1986). The class basis of this approach, and the broader notions of 'taste' that often accompany it, is self-evident (cf. Bourdieu, 1984).

Furthermore, there is a significant danger here that we will continue to compare children with 'adult' norms. Simply to assert that children can be as sophisticated and critical as adults is implicitly to accept a certain definition of what constitutes adult behaviour — a definition which may be inaccurate or even actively undesirable. We need to question the idea that adults are indeed consistently critical viewers — and, more crucially, the assumption that this is either a realistic or necessarily a desirable outcome.

Demonstrating 'Understanding'

This issue of the relationship between discourse and conceptual understanding has emerged as a central theme in recent classroom research in media education. The question of what one takes as *evidence* of conceptual understanding is brought into sharp focus when it comes to evaluation, particularly of students' practical media productions.

The relationship between 'theory' and 'practice' in media education has long been regarded as problematic (see Buckingham, 1987c). Yet while the importance of practical work has increasingly been acknowledged — it forms almost half of most GCSE syllabuses, for example — there remain significant problems in terms of how it is evaluated, not merely by teachers but also by students themselves. Most media syllabuses require a written 'log' or diary to accompany practical projects, yet there is often very little guidance as to the form this should take.

The log appears to serve two main functions. On an instrumental level, it provides a way for examiners to account for the individual contributions of students to what are usually collective projects. More broadly, it should offer students an opportunity to reflect on the experience of practical work — for example, to think about why certain choices were made and the effects these may have had. The written log is intended to encourage students to evaluate their own work, and thereby to draw connections between the 'practical' and 'theoretical' aspects of the course. While conceptual understandings may only be implicit in the practical projects themselves, they should be much more explicit in the written log.

However, as Jenny Grahame (1990) has indicated, there are several problems with this approach. Obviously, the emphasis on a written log discriminates against students who have problems with writing — yet these may be precisely the students who have contributed most effectively to the success of the practical work itself. Yet even for the more 'able' students in Grahame's study, the written evaluation seemed to prove inhibiting and unrewarding. Many of the insights and understandings — especially those relating to the social, interpersonal aspects of the process — which Grahame observed in the course of her students' practical work were lost when it came to writing.

Grahame contrasts this approach to evaluation with a more open-ended follow-up activity, and with informal classroom discussion: here, students were able to set their own agenda, and to draw on their own experience both as producers and as audiences. As she argues, the insistence on written evaluation may derive from a kind of insecurity about what students might be learning from practical work:

> However open-ended the project, we seem to need strategies which bring academic knowledge back to us in a safe and acceptable form. But by insisting that students must locate their individual accounts within a pre-determined 'objective' framework, we may be putting several important learning outcomes at risk. It may be that only by allowing students to write freely and subjectively about their own personal perceptions of the production process can we begin to reconcile our notions of appropriate learning with what they perceive as important to them. (p. 121)

These concerns were also raised in our study of a classroom project about television advertising, undertaken with year 7 students (Buckingham *et al.*, 1990). In this case, we designed a series of lessons in which the critical analysis of advertisements led into a practical simulation, in which students would produce their own. The analytical work was notable for the degree of scepticism which the students displayed towards advertising — although here too, it was the middle-class students who were more adept at employing the discourses of the 'wise consumer'.

Again, one of the major problems here was in attempting to evaluate the students' practical productions. Most of the advertisements they produced appeared to parody dominant conventions, suggesting that they had a very sophisticated understanding of the 'language' of advertising. Nevertheless, it was difficult to know how far to take this material seriously: the use of a simulation seemed to provide a safe space in which potentially difficult issues such as sexuality could be dealt with in a parodic, and thus relatively harmless way.

Yet here too, the students made little *explicit* connection between the 'theoretical' and 'practical' elements of the course: their own evaluations of the practical work focused entirely on the social and interpersonal aspects of the process, and effectively ignored the conceptual aims of the project. Of course, it could well have been unrealistic to expect children of this age to offer an elaborate rationale for their work. On the other hand, we might have been attempting to teach them things they already knew, and were simply so obvious that they didn't need to be stated. Either way, it was clear that our 'conceptual' agenda was much less salient than the social and affective learning which took place.

In my current research (e.g. Buckingham and Sefton-Green, 1992), similar questions have arisen in considering the differences between students' work in English and in Media Studies. In contrast to the often intuitive approach of English (see Buckingham, 1990e), evaluation in Media Studies appears to be much more straightforward: one is assessing students' understanding of the 'key concepts' primarily on the basis of their grasp of the academic discourse of the subject. Yet in practice, the evaluation of students' work — and particularly their practical productions — is much more problematic. The students here were often extremely adept at using dominant media genres and conventions for their own purposes. Yet particularly with 'less able' students, who found it difficult to articulate the rationale for their own work, we were often left guessing about their intentions.

However, over the longer term, at least some students who had difficulty with writing have progressively come to recognize the benefits of written reflection. While there often remains a sense that self-evaluation is a matter of 'stating the obvious', some students have come to acknowledge that writing can enable them to take a more distanced perspective on their own experiences of media production, and to 'discover' things they had not previously recognized. This appears to be much more possible with a more flexible approach to writing, in which theoretical concerns are embedded within more 'personal', expressive language.

Nevertheless, what often seems to count in terms of formal assessment is the students' ability to employ an abstract academic discourse. Yet this discourse may not connect with their existing understandings, or with what they themselves regard as important. In this instance, the work which really succeeded in motivating students was that which offered practical opportunities to articulate and to intervene in their own subcultural concerns — for example, those of black music and street fashion. Yet if those concerns cannot be made explicit and 'theorized' in academic terms, they seem to count for very little in terms of assessment. Here again, there is a distinct danger that privileging critical discourses may lead us to neglect children's social and affective investments in the media.

Not a Conclusion

In this chapter, I have raised a series of questions about the consequences of students gaining access to critical discourses about the media. Ideally, the acquisition of these discourses should make it possible for students to reflect on their own experience of using the media in a systematic and rigorous way. In Vygotsky's terms, an academic discourse provides a body of 'scientific concepts' which progressively transforms children's 'spontaneous concepts', and thereby gives them greater control over their own thought processes.

On the other hand, I have argued that these discourses may also sanction a rationalistic approach to popular culture, which neglects children's subcultural experiences and their emotional engagements with the media. These discourses often embody a form of intellectual cynicism, and a sense of superiority to 'other people'. They may result in a superficial irony or indeed a contempt for popular pleasures which is merely complacent.

The implications of this debate in terms of developing a critical pedagogy in media education remain to be explored. While the classroom research I have considered here represents one starting point, there is an urgent need for further detailed empirical research of this type. We need to know much more about how students acquire academic discourses, and what the consequences and limitations of this might be. Furthermore, any educational conception of 'media literacy' will need to consider children's own media productions as well as their use and interpretation of existing media. It will need to look at children as 'writers' of media, rather than just as 'readers', and at the relationship between these two sets of practices. Here again, this is an area where there has been very little detailed research.

However, this debate will also invoke broader political questions, not merely about what children already know, but also about what we think they ought to know, and why. Despite its limitations, the Vygotskyan perspective may offer a productive alternative to the rather sterile opposition between 'progressive' and 'conservative' approaches to critical pedagogy. While acknowledging the central importance of children's existing knowledge and the need for 'active learning', it also stresses the necessity of students acquiring and participating in dominant academic discourses.

Yet the questions I have raised about the social functions and indeed about the limitations of these discourses also need to be taken on board. Ultimately, while I would agree that giving children access to privileged discourses is vital, it is equally important that they should learn to interrogate them. The claim that academic discourse is inherently 'scientific', and thus superior to the 'ideology' of popular discourse must be open to question. *All* discourses should be questioned in terms of their social functions and consequences; and the concepts and methods of analysis teachers introduce to students must be seen, not as neutral tools for the acquisition of knowledge, but as *themselves* ideological.

As teachers, we need to do more than 'validate' students' readings and pleasures — even assuming that they need us to do so in the first place. We need to encourage them to analyze how those readings and pleasures are produced, and how they might be different. To do otherwise is simply to leave students where they are. Yet at the same time, we need to recover a notion of critical pedagogy which does not reject or underestimate children's affective and social investments in the media, or seek merely to replace these with rationalistic analysis.

This argument implies a view of teaching and learning about the media as essentially *dialectical* and *reflexive* processes — as a constant movement back and forth between action and reflection, between practice and theory, between celebration and critical analysis, and between language use and language study. The relationships between these elements are bound to be complex, and they are far from easy to develop in the classroom. As media education begins to move beyond the stage of pioneering rhetoric, it is precisely these issues that will require honest and detailed investigation.

References

ABELMAN, R. (1983) 'The ABCs of TV literacy', *Television and Children*, **6**, 1, pp. 45–9.

ABELMAN, R. (1986) 'Children's awareness of television's prosocial fare', *Journal of Family Issues*, **7**, 1, pp. 51–66.

ABELMAN, R. and SPARKS, G. (1985) 'How to tell the good guys from the bad guys', *Television and Families*, **8**, 4, pp. 21–4.

ABRAMSON, R. (1976) 'Structure and meaning in the cinema', in NICHOLS, B. (Ed.) *Movies and Methods*, Berkeley, University of California Press.

ADLER, R.P. *et al.* (1980) *The Effects of Television Advertising on Children*, Lexington, Mass., Lexington Books.

ALLEN, R.C. (1989) 'Bursting bubbles: "soap opera", audiences and the limits of genre', in SEITER E. *et al.* (Eds) *Remote Control: Television, Audiences and Cultural Power* London, Routledge.

ALLOR, M. (1988) 'Relocating the site of the audience', *Critical Studies in Mass Communication*, **5**, pp. 217–33.

ALVARADO, M. (1981) 'Television Studies and pedagogy', *Screen Education*, **38**, pp. 56–67.

ALVARADO, M., GUTCH, R. and WOLLEN, T. (1987) *Learning the Media*, London, Macmillan.

ANDERSON, D.R. and LORCH, E.P. (1983) 'Looking at television: action or reaction?', in BRYANT, J. and ANDERSON, D.R. (Eds) *Children's Understanding of Television*, New York, Academic Press.

ANDERSON, J.A. (1980) 'The theoretical lineage of critical viewing curricula', *Journal of Communication*, **30**, 3, pp. 64–70.

ANDERSON, J.A. (1981) 'Research on children and television: a critique', *Journal of Broadcasting*, **25**, pp. 395–400.

ANDERSON, J.A. (1983) 'Television literacy and the critical viewer', in BRYANT, J. and ANDERSON, D.R. (Eds) *Children's Understanding of Television*, New York, Academic Press.

ANDERSON, J.A. (1987) 'Commentary on qualitative research and mediated communication in the family', in LINDLOF, T. (Ed.) *Natural Audiences*, Newbury Park, Calif., Sage.

ANDERSON, J.A. (1990) 'Constitutions of the audience in research and theory: implications for media literacy programs', paper presented at the International Visual Literacy Association Symposium on Verbo-Visual Literacy: Mapping the Field, London.

ANG, I. (1985) *Watching DALLAS: Soap Opera and the Melodramatic Imagination*, London, Methuen.

ANG, I. (1989) 'Wanted: audiences. On the politics of empirical audience studies', in SEITER, E. *et al.* (Eds) *Remote Control: Television, Audiences and Cultural Power*, London, Routledge.

ANG, I. (1991) *Desperately Seeking the Audience*, London, Routledge.

ARIES, P. (1973) *Centuries of Childhood*, Harmondsworth, Penguin.

ASHTON, N.C. (1981) 'The way we see it: a program design for instruction of critical viewing skills', in PLOGHOFT, M.E. and ANDERSON, J.A. (Eds) *Education for the Television Age*, Springfield, Illinois, Charles C. Thomas.

ATKIN, C.K. (1980) 'Effects of television advertising on children', in PALMER, E.L. and DORR, A. (Eds) *Children and the Faces of Television: Teaching, Violence, Selling*, New York, Academic Press.

BAKHTIN, M.M. (1968) *Rabelais and his World*, Cambridge, Mass., M.I.T. Press.

BAKHTIN, M.M. (1981) 'Discourse in the novel', in BAKHTIN, M.M. *The Dialogic Imagination*, Austin, University of Texas Press.

BAKHTIN, M.M. (1986) 'The problem of speech genres', in BAKHTIN, M.M. *Speech Genres and Other Late Essays*, Austin, University of Texas Press.

BANDURA, A. (1965) 'Vicarious processes: A case of no-trial Learning', in BERKOWITZ, L. (Ed.) *Advances in Experimental Social Psychology Vol. 2*, New York, Academic Press.

BARCUS, F.E. (1980) 'The nature of television advertising to children', in PALMER, E.L. and DORR, A. (Eds) *Children and the Faces of Television: Teaching, Violence, Selling*, New York, Academic Press.

BARKER, M. (Ed.) (1984) *The Video Nasties*, London, Pluto.

BARKER, M. (1987) 'Mass media studies and the question of ideology', *Radical Philosophy*, **46**, pp. 27–33.

BARKER, M. (1989) *Comics: Ideology, Power and the Critics*, Manchester, Manchester University Press.

BARKER, M. (1990) Review of Fiske, *Reading the Popular*, and *Understanding Popular Culture, Magazine of Cultural Studies*, **1**, pp. 39–40.

BARRIOS, L. (1988) 'Television, telenovelas and family life in Venezuela' in LULL, J. (Ed.) *World Families Watch Television*, Newbury Park, Calif., Sage.

BARTHES, R. (1977) 'The rhetoric of the image', in BARTHES, R. *Image-Music-Text* (Ed. S. Heath), Glasgow, Fontana.

BAUSINGER, H. (1984) 'Media, technology and daily life', *Media, Culture and Society*, **6**, pp. 343–51.

BAZALGETTE, C. (1988) ' "They changed the picture in the middle of the fight": new kinds of literacy', in MEEK, M. and MILLS, C. (Eds) *Language and Literacy in the Primary School*, London, Falmer Press.

BAZALGETTE, C. (Ed.) (1989) *Primary Media Education: A Curriculum Statement*, London, British Film Institute.

BEE, J. (1989) 'First citizen of the semiotic democracy?' *Cultural Studies*, **3**, 3, pp. 353–59.

BEHL, N. (1988) 'Equalizing status: television and tradition in an Indian village', in LULL, J. (Ed.) *World Families Watch Television*, Newbury Park, Calif., Sage.

BERGER, J. (1972) *Ways of Seeing*, Harmondsworth, Penguin.

BERNDT, T.J. and BERNDT, E.G. (1975) 'Children's use of motives and intentionality in person perception and moral judgment', *Child Development*, **46**, pp. 904–12.

BERNSTEIN, B. (1971) *Class, Codes and Control, Vol. 1*, London, Routledge and Kegan Paul.

BEUF, A. (1974) 'Doctor, lawyer, household drudge', *Journal of Communication*, **24**, 2, pp. 142–5.

BLOOR, D. (1983) *Wittgenstein: A Social Theory of Knowledge*, London, Macmillan.

BLUMER, H. and HAUSER, P.M. (1933) *Movies, Delinquency and Crime*, New York, Macmillan.

References

BLUMLER, J.G. and KATZ, E. (Eds) (1974) *The Uses of Mass Communications*, London, Sage.
BOECKMANN, K. (1991) 'Adolescents' awareness of communicator interests', paper presented to the International Television Studies Conference, London.
BORDWELL, D. (1985) *Narration in the Fiction Film*, London, Methuen.
BORGES, J.L. (1966) *Other Inquisitions 1937–1952*, New York, Washington Square Press.
BOURDIEU, P. (1977) 'The economics of linguistic exchanges', *Social Science Information*, **16**, 6, pp. 645–68.
BOURDIEU, P. (1984) *Distinction: A Social Critique of the Judgment of Taste*, London, Routledge and Kegan Paul.
BOWER, G.H. (1976) 'Experiments on story understanding and recall', *Quarterly Journal of Experimental Psychology*, **28**, pp. 511–34.
BRADLEY, A.C. (1965, first published 1904) *Shakespearean Tragedy*, London, Macmillan.
BRITISH FILM INSTITUTE, WORKING PARTY ON PRIMARY MEDIA EDUCATION (1987) *Working Papers Three* London, British Film Institute, mimeo.
BRITISH FILM INSTITUTE WORKING PARTY ON PRIMARY MEDIA EDUCATION (1988) *Working Papers Four* London, British Film Institute, mimeo.
BRODY, G.H. and STONEMAN, Z. (1983) 'The influence of television viewing on family interactions', *Journal of Family Issues*, **4**, 2, pp. 329–48.
BROWN, R. (Ed.) (1976) *Children and Television*, London, Collier Macmillan.
BRUCKS, M., ARMSTRONG, G.M. and GOLDBERG, M.E. (1988) 'Children's use of cognitive defenses against television advertising: a cognitive response approach', *Journal of Consumer Research*, **14**, pp. 471–82.
BRUNER, J. (1986) *Actual Minds, Possible Worlds*, Cambridge, Mass., Harvard University Press.
BRUNSDON, C. (1989) 'Text and audience', in SEITER, E. *et al.* (Eds) *Remote Control: Television, Audiences and Cultural Power*, London, Routledge.
BRUNSDON, C. (1990) 'Problems with quality', *Screen*, **31**, 1, pp. 67–90.
BRUNSDON, C. and Morley, D. (1978) *Everyday Television: 'Nationwide'*, London, British Film Institute.
BRYANT, J. and ANDERSON, D.R. (Eds) (1983) *Children's Understanding of Television*, New York, Academic Press.
BRYCE, J.W. (1987) 'Family time and television use', in LINDLOF, T. (Ed.) *Natural Audiences*, Newbury Park, Calif., Sage.
BRYCE, J.W. and LEICHTER, M.J. (1983) 'The family and television: forms and mediation', *Journal of Family Issues*, **4**, 2, pp. 309–28.
BUCKINGHAM, D. (1986) 'Against demystification', *Screen*, **27**, 5, pp. 80–95.
BUCKINGHAM, D. (1987a) *Public Secrets: EastEnders and its Audience*, London, British Film Institute.
BUCKINGHAM, D. (1987b) *Children and Television: An Overview of the Research*, British Film Institute, mimeo.
BUCKINGHAM, D. (1987c) *Unit 27: Media Education* (EH207 Communication and Education Course Unit), Milton Keynes, Open University Press.
BUCKINGHAM, D. (Ed.) (1990a) *Watching Media Learning: Making Sense of Media Education*, London, Falmer Press.
BUCKINGHAM, D. (1990b) 'Seeing through TV: children talking about television', in WILLIS, J. and WOLLEN, T. (Eds) *The Neglected Audience*, London, British Film Institute.
BUCKINGHAM, D. (1990c) 'Media education: from pedagogy to practice', in BUCKINGHAM, D. (Ed.) *Watching Media Learning: Making Sense of Media Education*, London, Falmer Press.
BUCKINGHAM, D. (1990d) 'Making it explicit: towards a theory of media learning', in BUCKINGHAM, D. (Ed.) *Watching Media Learning: Making Sense of Media Education*, London, Falmer Press.

BUCKINGHAM, D. (1990e) 'English and Media Studies: making the difference', *The English Magazine*, **23**, pp. 8–12.

BUCKINGHAM, D. (forthcoming) 'Media education and the media industries: bridging the gaps', *British Journal of Education and Work*.

BUCKINGHAM, D. (forthcoming) 'Boys' talk: television and masculinity', in BUCKINGHAM, D. (Ed.) *Reading Audiences: Young People and the Media*, Manchester, Manchester University Press.

BUCKINGHAM, D., FRASER, P. and MAYMAN, N. (1990) 'Stepping into the void: beginning classroom research in media education', in BUCKINGHAM, D. (Ed.) *Watching Media Learning: Making Sense of Media Education*, London, Falmer Press.

BUCKINGHAM, D. and SEFTON-GREEN, J. (1992) 'In other words: evaluation, writing and reflection in media education', *The English and Media Magazine*, **26**, pp. 31–7.

CAMPBELL, B. (1988) *Unofficial Secrets*, London, Virago.

CARBY, H. (1980) 'Multiculture', *Screen Education*, **34**, pp. 62–70.

CARLSSON-PAIGE, N. and LEVIN, D.E. (1990) *Who's Calling the Shots? How to Respond Effectively to Children's Fascination with War Play and War Toys*, Santa Cruz, Calif., New Society.

CASTELL, S., DE, LUKE, A. and MacLENNAN, D. (1986) 'On defining literacy', in CASTELL, S. DE, LUKE, A. and EGAN, K. (Eds) *Literacy, Society and Schooling*, Cambridge, Cambridge University Press.

CERTEAU, M. DE (1984) *The Practice of Everyday Life*, Berkeley, University of California Press.

CHANG, B.G. (1987) 'Deconstructing the audience: who are they and what do we know about them', in McLAUGHLIN, M.L. (Ed.) *Communication Yearbook 10*, Beverly Hills, Sage.

CHRISTOPHER, F.S., FABES, R.A. and WILSON, P.M. (1989) 'Family television viewing: implications for family life education', *Family Relations*, **38**, pp. 210–14.

CLIFFORD, J. and MARCUS, G.E. (Eds) (1986) *Writing Culture: The Poetics and Politics of Ethnography*, Berkeley, University of California Press.

COHEN, A.A. and SALOMON, G. (1979) 'Children's literate television viewing: surprises and possible explanations', *Journal of Communication*, **29**, 3, pp. 156–63.

COHEN, P. (1988) 'The perversions of inheritance', in COHEN, P. and BAINS, H.S. (Eds) *Multi-Racist Britain*, London, Macmillan.

COLE, M. and GRIFFIN, P. (1986) 'A sociohistorical approach to remediation', in CASTELL, S. DE, LUKE, A. and EGAN, K. (Eds) *Literacy, Society and Schooling*, Cambridge, Cambridge University Press.

COLLETT, P. (1986) 'Watching the audience', paper presented to the International Television Studies Conference, London.

COLLINS, W.A. (1970) 'Learning of media content: a developmental study', *Child Development*, **41**, pp. 1133–42.

COLLINS, W.A. (1975) 'The developing child as viewer', *Journal of Communication*, **25**, pp. 35–44.

COLLINS, W.A. (1981) 'Schemata for understanding television', in KELLY, H. and GARDNER, H. (Eds) *Viewing Children Through Television*, San Francisco, Jossey-Bass.

COLLINS, W.A. (1983) 'Social antecedents, cognitive processing and comprehension of social portrayals on television', in HIGGINS, E.T., RUBLE, D.N. and HARTUP, W.W. (Eds) *Social Cognition and Social Development: A Sociocultural Perspective*, Cambridge, Cambridge University Press.

COLLINS, W.A. and WELLMAN, H.M. (1982) 'Social scripts and developmental patterns in comprehension of televised narratives', *Communication Research*, **9**, 3, pp. 380–98.

COLLINS, W.A., BERNDT, T.J. and HESS, V.L. (1974) 'Observational learning of motivations and consequences for television aggression: a developmental study', *Child Development*, **45**, pp. 799–802.

COMSTOCK, G.A. (1980) 'New emphases in research on the effects of television and film violence', in PALMER, E.L. and DORR, A. (Eds) *Children and the Faces of Television: Teaching, Violence, Selling*, New York, Academic Press.

COMSTOCK, G.A. and RUBINSTEIN, E.A. (Eds) (1972) *Television and Social Behavior, Vols 1–5*, Washington, D.C., US Government Printing Office.

CONNELL, I. (1978) 'Ideology/discourse/institution', *Screen*, **19**, 1, pp. 129–34.

CONNELL, I. (1985) 'Fabulous powers: blaming the media', in MASTERMAN, L. (Ed.) *Television Mythologies*, London, Comedia/MK Media Press.

COOK-GUMPERZ, J. (1986) 'Literacy and schooling: an unchanging equation?', in COOK-GUMPERZ, J. (Ed.) *The Social Construction of Literacy*, Cambridge, Cambridge University Press.

CORDER-BOLZ, C.R. (1980) 'Mediation: the role of significant others', *Journal of Communication*, **30**, no. 3, pp. 106–18.

CORDER-BOLZ, C.R. (1982) 'Television literacy and critical television viewing skills', in PEARL, D., BOUTHILET, L. and LAZAR, J. (Eds) *Television and Social Behavior: Ten Years of Scientific Progress and Implications for the Eighties, Vol. 2*, Washington, D.C., US Government Printing Office.

CORNER, J., RICHARDSON, K. and FENTON, N. (1991) *Nuclear Reactions: Form and Response in Public Issue Television*, London, John Libbey.

COSSETTE, A. (1982) 'How pictures speak: a brief introduction to iconics', paper presented to 32nd Conference of the International Communication Association, Boston.

COWAN, R.S. (1976) 'The "industrial revolution" in the home: household technology and social change in the 20th century', *Technology and Culture*, 17, pp. 1–23.

COWARD, R. and ELLIS, J. (1977) *Language and Materialism*, London, Routledge and Kegan Paul.

CULLINGFORD, C. (1984) *Children and Television*, Aldershot, Gower.

DANIEL, J. (1976) 'Metz' grande syntagmatique: summary and critique', *Film Form*, **1**, 1, pp. 78–90.

DAVID, M. (1986) 'Moral and maternal: the family in the Right', in LEVITAS, R. (Ed.) *The Ideology of the New Right*, Cambridge, Polity.

DE FLEUR, M. and BALL-ROKEACH, S. (1982) *Theories of Mass Communication*, London, Longman.

DE MAUSE, L. (Ed.) (1976) *The History of Childhood*, New York, Souvenir Press.

DEMBO, R. and MCCRON, R. (1976) 'Social factors in media use', in BROWN, R. (Ed.) *Children and Television*, London, Collier Macmillan.

DESMOND, R.J. (1985) 'Metacognition: thinking about thoughts in children's comprehension of television', *Critical Studies in Mass Communication*, **2**, 4, pp. 338–51.

DEWDNEY, M. and LISTER, M. (1988) *Youth, Culture and Photography*, London, Macmillan.

DIJK, T.A. VAN (1987) *Communicating Racism: Ethnic Prejudice in Thought and Talk*, London, Sage.

DONALD, J. (1990) Review of R.C. Allen, *Channels of Discourse* and J. Fiske, *Television Culture*, *Screen*, **31**, 1, pp. 113–18.

DONALDSON, M. (1978) *Children's Minds*, Glasgow, Fontana.

DONDIS, D.A. (1973) *A Primer of Visual Literacy*, Cambridge, Mass., M.I.T. Press.

DONOHUE, T.R. (1975) 'Black children's perceptions of favorite TV characters', *Journal of Broadcasting*, **19**, 2, pp. 153–67.

DORR, A. (1980) 'When I was a child, I thought as a child', in WITHEY, S.B. and ABELES, R.P. (Eds) *Television and Social Behavior: Beyond Violence and Children*, Hillsdale, N.J., Lawrence Erlbaum Associates.

DORR, A. (1982) 'Television and affective development and functioning', in PEARL, D.,

BOUTHILET, L. and LAZAR, J. (Eds) *Television and Social Behavior: Ten Years of Scientific Progress and Implications for the Eighties, Vol. 2*, Washington, D.C., US Government Printing Office.

DORR, A. (1983) 'No shortcuts to judging reality', in BRYANT, J. and ANDERSON, D.R. (Eds) *Children's Understanding of Television*, New York, Academic Press.

DORR, A. (1986) *Television and Children: A Special Medium for a Special Audience*, Beverly Hills, Sage.

DORR, A. and KOVARIC, P. (1980) 'Some of the people some of the time — but which people?' in PALMER, E.L. and DORR, A. (Eds) *Children and the Faces of Television: Teaching, Violence, Selling*, New York, Academic Press.

DORR, A., GRAVES, S.B. and PHELPS, E. (1980) 'Television literacy for young children', *Journal of Communication*, **30**, 3, pp. 71–83.

DURKIN, K. (1985) *Television, Sex Roles and Children*, Milton Keynes, Open University Press.

EDWARDS, D. and MERCER, N. (1987) *Common Knowledge: The Growth of Understanding in the Classroom*, London, Methuen.

EDWARDS, D. and MERCER, N. (1989) 'Reconstructing context: the conventionalisation of classroom knowledge', *Discourse Processes*, **12**, pp. 91–104.

EDWARDS, D. and MIDDLETON, D. (1986) 'Joint remembering: constructing an account of a shared experience through conversational discourse', *Discourse Processes*, **9**, 4, pp. 423–59.

EDWARDS, D. and MIDDLETON, D. (1987) 'Conversation and remembering: Bartlett revisited', *Applied Cognitive Psychology*, **1**, pp. 77–92.

EDWARDS, D. and MIDDLETON, D. (1988) 'Conversational remembering and family relationships: how children learn to remember', *Journal of Social and Personal Relationships*, **5**, pp. 3–25.

EDWARDS, V.K. (1979) *The West Indian Language Issue in British Schools*, London, Routledge and Kegan Paul.

EKE, R. (1986) 'Media education issues for classroom investigation in British primary schools', in BRITISH FILM INSTITUTE WORKING PARTY ON PRIMARY MEDIA EDUCATION, *Working Papers Two*, London, British Film Institute, mimeo.

ELLIOT, P. (1974) 'Uses and gratifications research: a critique and a sociological alternative', in BLUMLER, J.G. and KATZ, E. (Eds) *The Uses of Mass Communications*, London, Sage.

ELLIS, J. (1982) *Visible Fictions*, London, Methuen.

ENGELHARDT, T. (1986) 'The shortcake strategy', in GITLIN, T. (Ed.) *Watching Television*, New York, Pantheon.

ENTWISTLE, H. (1979) *Antonio Gramsci: Conservative Schooling for Radical Politics*, London, Routledge and Kegan Paul.

ESSERMAN, J.F. (1981) 'A study of children's defenses against television commercial appeals', in ESSERMAN, J.F. (Ed.) *Television Advertising and Children*, New York, Child Research Service.

FAIRCLOUGH, N. (1989) *Language and Power*, London, Longman.

FELDMAN, S., WOLF, A. and WARMOUTH, D. (1977) 'Parental concern about child-directed commercials', *Journal of Communication*, **27**, 3, pp. 125–37.

FERNIE, D.E. (1981) 'Ordinary and extraordinary people: children's understanding of television and real life models', in KELLY, H. and GARDNER, H. (Eds) *Viewing Children Through Television*, San Francisco, Jossey-Bass.

FEUER, J. (1986) 'Narrative form in American network television', in MACCABE, C. (Ed.) *High Theory/Low Culture*, Manchester, Manchester University Press.

FINE, G.A. and GLASSNER, B. (1979) 'Participant observation with children: promise and problems', *Urban Life*, **8**, 2, pp. 153–74.

FINN, P. (1980) 'Developing critical television viewing skills', *Educational Forum*, **44**, 4, pp. 473–82.

FISH, S. (1980) *Is There a Text in this Class? The Authority of Interpretive Communities*, Cambridge, Mass., Harvard University Press.

FISKE, J. (1987a) *Television Culture*, London, Methuen.

FISKE, J. (1987b) 'British cultural studies', in ALLEN, R.C. (Ed.) *Channels of Discourse: Television and Contemporary Criticism*, Chapel Hill, University of North Carolina Press.

FISKE, J. (1989a) *Understanding Popular Culture*, London, Unwin Hyman.

FISKE, J. (1989b) *Reading the Popular*, London, Unwin Hyman.

FISKE, J. (1989c) 'Moments of television: neither the text nor the audience', in SEITER, E. *et al.* (Eds) *Remote Control: Television, Audiences and Cultural Power*, London, Routledge.

FLITTERMAN-LEWIS, S. (1987) 'Psychoanalysis, film and television', in ALLEN, R.C. (Ed.) *Channels of Discourse: Television and Contemporary Criticism*, Chapel Hill, University of North Carolina Press.

FORSTER, E.M. (1963) (first published 1927) *Aspects of the Novel*, Harmondsworth, Penguin.

FOSTER, H. (1979) *The New Literacy: The Language of Film and Television*, Urbana, Illinois, National Council of Teachers of English.

FOUCAULT, M. (1980) *Power/Knowledge* (in Gordon, C. (Ed.)), Brighton, Harvester.

FOWLER, R., HODGE, B., KRESS, G. and TREW, T. (1979) *Language and Control*, London, Routledge and Kegan Paul.

FRASER, P. (1990) 'How do teachers and students talk about television?' in BUCKINGHAM, D. (Ed.) *Watching Media Learning: Making Sense of Media Education*, London, Falmer Press.

GAINES, L. and ESSERMAN, J.F. (1981) 'A quantitative study of young children's comprehension of television programs and commercials', in ESSERMAN, J.F. (Ed.) *Television Advertising and Children*, New York, Child Research Service.

GALLOP, J. (1982) *Feminism and Psychoanalysis: The Daughter's Seduction*, London, Macmillan.

GARNHAM, A. (1983) 'What's wrong with story grammars', *Cognition*, **15**, pp. 145–54.

GARNHAM, N. (1979) 'Subjectivity, ideology, class and historical materialism', *Screen*, **20**, 1, pp. 121–33.

GERAGHTY, C. (1981) 'The continuing serial: a definition', in DYER, R., GERAGHTY, C., JORDAN, M., LOVELL, T., PATERSON, R. and STEWART, J. *Coronation Street*, London, British Film Institute.

GERAGHTY, C. (1991) *Women and Soap Opera*, Cambridge, Polity.

GERGEN, K.J. and DAVIS, K.E. (1985) (Eds) *The Social Construction of the Person*, New York, Springer.

GIDDENS, A. (1984) *The Constitution of Society*, Cambridge, Polity.

GILLESPIE, M. (1989) 'Technology and tradition: audio-visual culture among South Asian families in West London', *Cultural Studies*, **3**, 2, pp. 226–39.

GILLESPIE, M. (forthcoming) 'The *Mahabharata*: from Sanskrit to sacred soap', in BUCKINGHAM, D. (Ed.) *Reading Audiences: Young People and the Media*, Manchester, Manchester University Press.

GLEDHILL, C. (Ed.) (1988) *Home Is Where the Heart Is*, London, British Film Institute.

GLENN, C.G. (1978) 'The role of episodic structure and of story length in children's recall of simply stories', *Journal of Verbal Learning and Verbal Behavior*, **17**, pp. 229–47.

GOLDBERG, M.E. and GORN, G.J. (1978) 'Some unintended consequences of T.V. advertising to children', *Journal of Consumer Research* Vol. **5**, pp. 22–29.

GOLDBERG, M.E. and GORN, G.J. (1983) 'Researching the effects of television advertising on children: a methodological critique', in HOWE, M.J.A. (Ed.) *Learning from Television: Psychological and Educational Research*, London, Academic Press.

GOLDSEN, R.K. (1977) *The Show and Tell Machine*, New York, Dial Books.

GOODHARDT, G.J., EHRENBERG, A.S. and COLLINS, M.A. (1975) *The Television Audience: Patterns of Viewing*, London, Saxon House.

GOODMAN, N. (1968) *Languages of Art: An Approach to a Theory of Symbols*, New York, Bobbs-Merrill.

GORN, G.J. and GOLDBERG, M.E. (1982) 'Behavioral evidence of the effects of televised food messages on children', *Journal of Consumer Research*, **9**, pp. 200–5.

GRAFF, H.J. (1979) *The Literacy Myth: Literacy and Social Structure in the Nineteenth-Century City*, New York, Academic Press.

GRAFF, H.J. (1986) 'The legacies of literacy: continuities and contradictions in Western society and culture', in CASTELL, S. DE, LUKE, A. and EGAN, K. (Eds) *Literacy, Society and Schooling*, Cambridge, Cambridge University Press.

GRAHAME, J. (1990) *'Playtime*: learning about media institutions through practical work', in BUCKINGHAM, D. (Ed.) *Watching Media Learning: Making Sense of Media Education*, London, Falmer Press.

GRAY, A. (1987) 'Behind closed doors: video recorders in the home', in BAEHR, H. and DYER, G. (Eds) *Boxed In: Women and Television*, London, Pandora.

GREENBERG, B.S. (1972) 'Children's reactions to television blacks', *Journalism Quarterly*, **49**, 1, pp. 5–14.

GREENBERG, B.S. (1974) 'Gratifications for television viewing and their correlates for British children', in BLUMER, J. and KATZ, E. (Eds) *Annual Review of Communication Research, Vol. 3*, Beverly Hills, Sage.

GREENBERG, B.S. and REEVES, B. (1976) 'Children and the perceived reality of television', *Journal of Social Issues*, **32**, 4, pp. 86–97.

GREENFIELD, P.M. (1984) *Mind and Media*, London, Fontana.

GREIMAS, A.J. (1973) 'Les actants, les acteurs et les figures', in CHABROL, C. (Ed.) *Semiotique Narrative et Textuelle*, Paris, Larousse.

GRIESHABER, S. (1989) 'A pilot study of parent and child conflict', paper presented at the International Conference on Early Education and Development, Hong Kong.

GROSSBERG, L. (1987) 'Critical theory and the politics of empirical research', in GUREVITCH, M. and LEVY, M. (Eds) *Mass Communication Review Yearbook 6*, Beverly Hills, Sage.

GROSSBERG, L. (1988) 'Wandering audiences, nomadic critics', *Cultural Studies*, **2**, 3, pp. 377–91.

GUNTER, B. (1985) *Dimensions of Television Violence*, Aldershot, Gower.

GUNTER, B. and SVENNEVIG, M. (1987) *Behind and In Front of the Screen: Television's Involvement with Family Life*, London, John Libbey.

HAKES, D.T. (1980) *The Development of Metalinguistic Abilities in Children*, Berlin, Springer Verlag.

HALL, S., HOBSON, D., LOWE, A. and WILLIS, P. (Eds) (1980) *Culture, Media, Language*, London, Hutchinson.

HALLIDAY, M. (1978) *Language as Social Semiotic*, London, Edward Arnold.

HALLIDAY, M. (1985) *An Introduction to Functional Grammar*, London, Edward Arnold.

HARTLEY, J. (1987) 'Invisible fictions: television audiences, paedocracy, pleasure', *Textual Practice*, **1**, 2, pp. 121–38.

HARTLEY, J. (1988) 'The real world of audiences', *Critical Studies in Mass Communication*, **5**, pp. 234–8.

HARVEY, S. (1978) *May '68 and Film Theory*, London, British Film Institute.

HASTORF, A.H., SCHNEIDER, D.J. and POLEFKA, J. (1970) *Person Perception*, Reading, Mass., Addison-Wesley.

HAWKINS, R.P. (1977) 'The dimensional structure of children's perceptions of television reality', *Communication Research*, **4**, 3, pp. 299–320.

HEATH, S.B. (1983) *Ways with Words*, Cambridge, Cambridge University Press.

HEBDIGE, D. (1982) 'Towards a cartography of taste 1935–1962', in WAITES, B., BENNETT, T. and MARTIN, G. (Eds) *Popular Culture Past and Present*, London, Croom Helm/Open University Press.

HESS, R.D. and GOLDMAN, H. (1962) 'Parents' views of the effect of television on their children', *Child Development*, **33**, pp. 411–26.

HIMMELWEIT, H., OPPENHEIM, A.N. and VINCE, P. (1958) *Television and the Child*, Oxford, Oxford University Press.

HOBSON, D. (1982) *CROSSROADS: The Drama of a Soap Opera*, London, Methuen.

HODGE, B. and KRESS, G. (1988) *Social Semiotics*, London, Macmillan.

HODGE, B. and TRIPP, D. (1986) *Children and Television: A Semiotic Approach*, Cambridge, Polity.

HOFFNER, C. and CANTOR, J. (1985) 'Developmental differences in responses to a television character's appearance and behaviour', *Child Development*, **21**, 6, pp. 1065–74.

HOGG, M.A. and ABRAMS, D. (1988) *Social Identifications: The Social Psychology of Intergroup Relations and Group Processes*, London, Routledge.

HOIKKALA, T., RAHKONEN, O., TIGERSTEDT, C. and TUORMAA, J. (1987) 'Wait a minute, Mr. Postman! Some critical remarks on Neil Postman's childhood theory', *Acta Sociologica*, **30**, 1, pp. 87–99.

HOLMAN, J. and BRAITHWAITE, V.A. (1982) 'Parental lifestyles and children's television viewing', *Australian Journal of Psychology*, **34**, 3, pp. 375–82.

HORTON, D. and WOHL, R.R. (1956) 'Mass communication and para-social interaction', *Psychiatry*, **19**, pp. 215–29.

HOWITT, D. and DEMBO, R. (1974) 'A subcultural account of media effects', *Human Relations*, **27**, 1, pp. 25–41.

HUDAK, G. (1987) 'Student knowledge and the formation of academic discourse: a case study', in SMYTH, J. (Ed.) *Educating Teachers: Changing the Nature of Pedagogical Knowledge*, London, Falmer Press.

HYMES, D. (1972) 'On communicative competence', in PRIDE, J.B. and HOLMES, J. (Eds) *Sociolinguistics*, Harmondsworth, Penguin.

JAGLOM, L.M. and GARDNER, H. (1981) 'The preschool television viewer as anthropologist', in KELLY, H. and GARDNER, H. (Eds) *Viewing Children Through Television*, San Francisco, Jossey-Bass.

JAMES, A. and PROUT, A. (Eds) (1990) *Constructing and Reconstructing Childhood: Contemporary Issues in the Sociological Study of Childhood*, London, Falmer Press.

JONES, M. (1984) *Mass Media Education, Education for Communication and Mass Communication Research*, Leicester, International Association for Mass Communication Research.

JORDIN, M. and BRUNT, R. (1988) 'Constituting the television audience: a problem of method', in DRUMMOND, P. and PATERSON, R. (Eds) *Television and its Audience: International Research Perspectives*, London, British Film Institute.

KATZ, E. and FOULKES, D. (1962) 'Use of mass media as "escape": clarification of a concept', *Public Opinion Quarterly*, **26**, pp. 377–388.

KATZ, E. and LIEBES, T. (1985) 'The export of meaning: cross-cultural readings of American TV', paper presented to the Symposium on Broadcasting, Manchester.

KEY, W.B. (1976) *Media Sexploitation*, New York, Signet.

KITSES, J. (1970) *Horizons West*, London, Secker and Warburg.

KJORUP, S. (1977) 'Film as a meetingplace of multiple codes', in PERKINS, D. and LEONDAR, B. (Eds) *The Arts and Cognition*, Baltimore, Johns Hopkins University Press.

KLAPPER, J. (1960) *The Effects of Mass Communications*, New York, Free Press.

KOLERS, P.A. (1977) 'Reading pictures and reading text', in PERKINS, D. and LEONDAR, B. (Eds) *The Arts and Cognition*, Baltimore, Johns Hopkins University Press.

KRENDL, K.A. and WATKINS, B. (1983) 'Understanding television: an exploratory inquiry into the reconstruction of narrative content', *Educational Communication and Technology Journal*, **31**, 4, pp. 201–12.

KRESS, G. (1985) *Linguistic Processes in Sociocultural Practice*, Oxford, Oxford University Press.

KRESS, G. and HODGE, B. (1979) *Language as Ideology*, London, Routledge and Kegan Paul.

LABOV, W. (1972) *Language in the Inner City*, Philadelphia, University of Pennsylvania Press.

LABOV, W. (1973) (originally published 1969) 'The logic of non-standard English', in KEDDIE, N. (Ed.) *Tinker Tailor: The Myth of Cultural Deprivation*, Harmondsworth, Penguin.

LAKOFF, G. (1987) *Women, Fire and Dangerous Things: What Categories Reveal About the Mind*, Chicago, University of Chicago Press.

LARGE, M. (1980) *Who's Bringing Them Up?*, Gloucester, Alan Sutton.

LEAVIS, F.R. and THOMPSON, D. (1933) *Culture and Environment*, London, Chatto and Windus.

LEICHTER, H.J., AHMED, D., BARRIOS, L., BRYCE, J., LARSEN, E. and MOE, L. (1985) 'Family contexts of television', *Educational Communication and Technology Journal*, **33**, 1, pp. 26–40.

LEISS, W., KLINE, S. and JHALLY, S. (1990) *Social Communication in Advertising*, 2nd ed., London, Routledge.

LEVENE, K. (1986) *The Social Context of Literacy*, London, Routledge and Kegan Paul.

LEVIN, S.R. and ANDERSON, D.R. (1976) 'The development of attention', *Journal of Communication*, **26**, 2, pp. 126–35.

LÉVI-STRAUSS, C. (1963) *Structural Anthropology*, New York, Basic Books.

LIEBES, T. and KATZ, E. (1990) *The Export of Meaning: Cross-Cultural Readings of Dallas*, Oxford, Oxford University Press.

LINDLOF, T. (Ed.) (1987) *Natural Audiences*, Newbury Park, Calif., Sage.

LINDLOF, T.R., SHATZER, M.J. and WILKINSON, D. (1988) 'Accommodation of video and television in the American family', in LULL, J. (Ed.) *World Families Watch Television*, Newbury Park, Calif., Sage.

LINN, M.C., DE BENEDICTIS, T. and DELUCCHI, K. (1982) 'Adolescent reasoning about advertisements: preliminary investigations', *Child Development*, **53**, pp. 1599–1613.

LIST, J.A., COLLINS, W.A. and WESTBY, S. (1983) 'Comprehension and inferences from traditional and nontraditional sex-role portrayals on television', *Child Development*, **54**, pp. 1579–87.

LIVINGSTONE, S. (1990) *Making Sense of Television: The Psychology of Audience Interpretation*, Oxford, Pergamon.

LLOYD-KOLKIN, D., WHEELER, P. and STRAND, T. (1980) 'Developing a curriculum for teenagers', *Journal of Communication*, **30**, 3, pp. 119–25.

LODZIAK, C. (1986) *The Power of Television*, London, Frances Pinter.

LONIAL, S.C. and VAN AUKEN, S. (1986) 'Wishful identification with fictional characters: an assessment of the implications of gender in message dissemination to children', *Journal of Advertising*, **15**, 4, pp. 4–11, 42.

LOVELL, T. (1980) *Pictures of Reality*, London, British Film Institute.

LOWERY, S. and DE FLEUR, M. (1983) *Milestones in Mass Communications Research*, London, Longman.

LUKE, C. (1985) 'Television discourse processing: a schema theoretic approach', *Communication Education*, **34**, pp. 91–105.

LUKE, C. (1990) *Constructing the Child Viewer: A History of the American Discourse on Television and Children, 1950–1980*, New York, Praeger.

LULL, J. (1981) 'Social uses of television in family settings, and a critique of receivership skills', in PLOGHOFT, M.E. and ANDERSON, J.A. (Eds) *Education for the Television Age*, Springfield, Illinois, Charles C. Thomas.

LULL, J. (1982a) 'The social uses of television', in WITHEY, C.D. *et al.* (Eds) *Mass Communication Review Yearbook, Vol. 3*, Beverley Hills, Sage.

LULL, J. (1982b) 'How families choose television programs', *Journal of Broadcasting*, **26**, pp. 801–11.

LULL, J. (Ed.) (1988) *World Families Watch Television*, Newbury Park, Calif., Sage.

LULL, J. (1990) *Inside Family Viewing*, London, Routledge.

LULL, J. and SEN, S.-W. (1988) 'Agent of modernization: television and urban Chinese families', in LULL, J. (Ed.) *World Families Watch Television*, Newbury Park, Calif., Sage.

LUSTED, D. (1985) 'A history of suspicion: educational attitudes to television', in LUSTED, D. and DRUMMOND, P. (Eds) *TV and Schooling*, London, British Film Institute.

LUSTED, D. (1986) 'Why pedagogy?', *Screen*, **27**, 5, pp. 2–14.

MACARTHUR, C. (1972) *Underworld USA*, London, Secker and Warburg.

MACCABE, C. (1974) 'Realism and the cinema: notes on some Brechtian theses', *Screen*, **15**, 2, pp. 7–27.

MACCOBY, E.E. and WILSON, W.C. (1957) 'Identification and Observational Learning from Films', *Journal of Abnormal and Social Psychology*, **55**, pp. 76–87.

MANDLER, J.M. and JOHNSON, N.S. (1977) 'Remembrance of things parsed: story structure and recall', *Cognitive Psychology*, **9**, pp. 111–51.

MARCUSE, H. (1964) *One-Dimensional Man*, Boston, Beacon.

MASTERMAN, L. (1980) *Teaching About Television*, London, Macmillan.

MASTERMAN, L. (1981/2) 'TV pedagogy', *Screen Education*, 40, pp. 88–92.

MASTERMAN, L. (1985) *Teaching the Media*, London, Comedia.

MASTERMAN, L. (1986) 'Reply to David Buckingham', *Screen*, **27**, 5, pp. 96–100.

McGHEE, P.E. and FRUEH, T. (1980) 'Television viewing and the learning of sex-role stereotypes', *Sex Roles*, **6**, pp. 179–88.

McLEOD, J. and BROWN, J.D. (1976) 'The family environment and adolescent television use', in BROWN, R. (Ed.) *Children and Television*, London, Collier Macmillan.

McQUAIL, D. (1983) *Mass Communication Theory: An Introduction*, London, Sage.

MEADOWCROFT, J.M. and REEVES, B. (1989) 'Influence of story schema development on children's attention to television', *Communication Research*, **16**, 3, pp. 352–74.

MERINGOFF, L.K. and LESSER, G. (1980) 'Children's ability to distinguish television commercials from program material', in ADLER, R.P. *et al. The Effects of Television Advertising on Children*, Lexington, Mass., Lexington Books.

MESSARIS, P. and SARRETT, C. (1981) 'On the consequences of TV-related parent-child interaction', *Human Communication Research*, **7**, 3, pp. 226–44.

METZ, C. (1974a) *Film Language: A Semiotics of the Cinema*, New York, Oxford University Press.

METZ, C. (1974b) *Language and Cinema*, The Hague, Mouton.

METZ, C. (1982) *The Imaginary Signifier: Psychoanalysis and the Cinema*, London, Macmillan.

MEYER, T.P. (1973) 'Children's Perceptions of Favorite Television Characters as Behavioral Models', *Educational Broadcasting Review*, **7**, 1, pp. 25–33.

MEYROWITZ, J. (1985) *No Sense of Place: The Impact of Electronic Media on Social Behavior*, New York, Oxford University Press.

MIDDLETON, D. and EDWARDS, D. (Eds) (1990a) *Collective Remembering*, London, Sage.

MIDDLETON, D. and EDWARDS, D. (1990b) 'Introduction', in MIDDLETON, D. and EDWARDS, D. (Eds) *Collective Remembering*, London, Sage.

MIDDLETON, D. and EDWARDS, D. (1990c) 'Conversational remembering: a social psychological approach', in MIDDLETON, D. and EDWARDS, D. (Eds) *Collective Remembering*, London, Sage.

MILLER, M.M. and REEVES, B. (1976) 'Dramatic TV content and children's sex-role stereotypes', *Journal of Broadcasting*, **20**, 1, pp. 35–50.

MORISON, P. and GARDNER, H. (1978) 'Dragons and dinosaurs: the child's capacity to differentiate fantasy from reality', *Child Development*, **49**, pp. 642–8.

MORISON, P., McCARTHY, M. and GARDNER, H. (1979) 'Exploring the realities of television with children', *Journal of Broadcasting*, **23**, 4, pp. 453–63.

MORISON, P., KELLY, H. and GARDNER, H. (1981) 'Reasoning about the realities on television: a developmental study', *Journal of Broadcasting*, **25**, 3, pp. 229–42.

MORLEY, D. (1980a) *The 'Nationwide' Audience*, London, British Film Institute.

MORLEY, D. (1980b) 'Texts, readers, subjects', in HALL, S. *et al.* (Eds) *Culture, Media, Language*, London, Hutchinson.

MORLEY, D. (1981) 'The *Nationwide* Audience: a critical postscript', *Screen Education*, 39, pp. 3–14.

MORLEY, D. (1986) *Family Television: Cultural Power and Domestic Leisure*, London, Comedia.

MORLEY, D. (1991) 'Where the global meets the local: notes from the sitting room', *Screen*, **32**, 1, pp. 1–15.

MORLEY, D. and SILVERSTONE, R. (1990) 'Domestic communication: technologies and meanings', *Media, Culture and Society*, **13**, 1, pp. 31–55.

MORRIS, M. (1990) 'Banality in Cultural Studies', in MELLENCAMP, P. (Ed.) *Logics of Television: Essays in Cultural Criticism*, London, British Film Institute.

MURDOCK, G. (1989) 'Cultural studies at the crossroads', *Australian Journal of Communication*, 16, pp. 37–49.

MURDOCK, G. and McCRON, R. (1979) 'The television and delinquency debate', *Screen Education*, 30, pp. 51–67.

NATIONAL CURRICULUM COUNCIL (1990) *English: Non-Statutory Guidance*, York, National Curriculum Council.

NAVA, M. and NAVA, O. (1990) 'Discriminating or duped? Young people as consumers of advertising/art', *Magazine of Cultural Studies*, 1, pp. 15–21.

NEALE, S. (1980) *Genre*, London, British Film Institute.

NEALE, S. (1990) 'Questions of genre', *Screen*, **31**, 1, pp. 45–66.

NEWCOMB, A.F. and COLLINS, W.A. (1979) 'Children's comprehension of family role portrayals in televised drama: effects of socioeconomic status, ethnicity and age', *Developmental Psychology*, **15**, 4, pp. 417–23.

NEWCOMB, H. (1984) 'On the dialogic aspects of mass communication', *Critical Studies in Mass Communication*, **1**, 1, pp. 34–50.

NICHOLS, B. (1976) 'Style, grammar and the movies', in NICHOLS, B. (Ed.) *Movies and Methods*, Berkeley, University of California Press.

NIGHTINGALE, V. (1989) 'What's "ethnographic" about ethnographic audience research?', *Australian Journal of Communication*, 16, pp. 50–63.

NOBLE, G. (1975) *Children in Front of the Small Screen*, London, Constable.

OLSON, D. (1986a) 'Television and literacy: a comment', in LUKE, C. and MANLEY-CASIMIR, M. (Eds) *Television and Children: A Challenge to Education*, New York, Praeger.

OLSON, D. (1986b) 'Learning to mean what you say: towards a psychology of literacy', in CASTELL, S. DE, LUKE, A. and EGAN, K. (Eds) *Literacy, Society and Schooling*, Cambridge, Cambridge University Press.

ONG, W. (1982) *Orality and Literacy: The Technologizing of the Word*, London, Methuen.

O'SHEA, A. (1989) 'Television as culture: not just texts and readers', *Media, Culture and Society*, **11**, pp. 373–9.

PACKARD, V. (1957) *The Hidden Persuaders*, Harmondsworth, Penguin.

PAGET, K.F., KRITT, D. and BERGEMANN, L. (1984) 'Understanding strategic interactions in television commercials: a developmental study', *Journal of Applied Developmental Psychology*, **5**, pp. 145–61.

PALMER, P. (1986) *The Lively Audience: A Study of Children around the TV Set*, Sydney, Allen and Unwin.

PATTISON, R. (1982) *On Literacy: The Politics of the Word from Homer to the Age of Rock*, Oxford, Oxford University Press.

PEARSON, G. (1984) 'Falling standards: a short, sharp history of moral decline', in BARKER, M. (Ed.) *The Video Nasties*, London, Pluto.

PERKINS, T. (1978) 'Rethinking stereotypes', in BARRETT, M., CORRIGAN, P., KUHN, A. and WOLFF, J. (Eds) *Ideology and Cultural Production*, London, Croom Helm.

PIERCE, C.S. (1940) *Selected Writings*, New York, Harcourt Brace and Co.

PLOGHOFT, M.E. and ANDERSON, J.A. (1982) *Teaching Critical Television Viewing Skills: Towards an Integrated Approach*, Springfield, Illinois, Charles C. Thomas.

POLLOCK, L.A. (1983) *Forgotten Children: Parent-Child Relations from 1500–1900*, Cambridge, Cambridge University Press.

POSTER, M. (1978) *Critical Theory of the Family*, London, Pluto.

POSTMAN, N. (1983) *The Disappearance of Childhood*, London, W.H. Allen.

POTTER, J. and WETHERELL, M. (1987) *Discourse and Social Psychology*, London, Sage.

POULSEN, D., KINTSCH, E., KINTSCH, W. and PREMACK, D. (1979) 'Children's comprehension and memory for stories', *Journal of Experimental Child Psychology*, **28**, pp. 379–403.

PROPP, V. (1968) *Morphology of the Folktale*, Austin, University of Texas Press.

PUDOVKIN, V.I. (1960) *Film Technique and Film Acting*, New York, Grove.

RADWAY, J. (1984) *Reading the Romance*, Chapel Hill, University of North Carolina Press.

RADWAY, J. (1988) 'Reception study: ethnography and the problems of dispersed audiences and nomadic subjects', *Cultural Studies*, **2**, 3, pp. 359–76.

REEVES, B. (1978) 'Perceived TV reality as a predictor of children's social behavior', *Journalism Quarterly*, **55**, pp. 682–9, 695.

REEVES, B. (1979) 'Children's understanding of television people', in WARTELLA, E. (Ed.) *Children Communicating: Media and Development of Thought, Speech, Understanding*, Beverly Hills, Sage.

REEVES, B. and GREENBERG, B.S. (1977) 'Children's Perceptions of Television Characters', *Human Communication Research*, **3**, 2, pp. 113–27.

REEVES, B. and MILLER, M.M. (1978) 'A multidimensional measure of children's identification with television characters', *Journal of Broadcasting*, **22**, 1, pp. 71–86.

REEVES, B. and WARTELLA, E. (1985) 'Historical trends in research on children and the media, 1900–1960', *Journal of Communication*, **35**, 2, pp. 118–33.

REID, L.N. (1979) 'Viewing rules as mediating factors in children's responses to commercials', *Journal of Broadcasting*, **23**, 1, pp. 15–26.

RICHARDS, C. (1990) 'Intervening in popular pleasures: Media Studies and the politics of subjectivity', in BUCKINGHAM, D. (Ed.) *Watching Media Learning: Making Sense of Media Education*, London, Falmer Press.

RICHARDS, M.P.M. (Ed.) (1974) *The Integration of a Child into a Social World*, Cambridge, Cambridge University Press.

RICHARDS, M. and LIGHT, P. (Eds) (1986) *Children of Social Worlds*, Cambridge, Polity.

RICHARDSON, K. and CORNER, J. (1986) 'Reading reception: mediation and transparency in viewers' accounts of a TV programme', *Media, Culture and Society*, **8**, 4, pp. 485–508.

RIMMON-KENAN, S. (1983) *Narrative Fiction: Contemporary Poetics*, London, Methuen.

ROBERTSON, T.S. (1979) 'Parental mediation of television advertising effects', *Journal of Communication*, **25**, 1, pp. 12–25.

ROBERTSON, T.S. and ROSSITER, J.R. (1977) 'Children's responsiveness to commercials', *Journal of Communication*, **27**, pp. 101–6.

ROEDDER, D.L. (1981) 'Age differences in children's responses to television advertising: an information-processing approach', *Journal of Consumer Research*, **8**, pp. 144–53.

ROGGE, J.-U. and JENSEN, K. (1988) 'Everyday life and television in West Germany: an empathetic–interpretive perspective on the family as system', in LULL, J. (Ed.) *World Families Watch Television*, Newbury Park, Calif., Sage.

ROSCH, E. (1978) 'Principles of categorization', in ROSCH, E. and LLOYD, B.B. (Eds) *Cognition and Categorization*, Hillsdale, N.J., Lawrence Erlbaum Associates.

ROSSITER, J.R. (1980) 'Children and television advertising: policy issues, perspectives and the status of research', in PALMER, E.L. and DORR, A. (Eds) *Children and the Faces of Television: Teaching, Violence, Selling*, New York, Academic Press.

ROSSITER, J.R. and ROBERTSON, T.S. (1974) 'Children's TV commercials: testing the defenses', *Journal of Communication*, **24**, 4, pp. 137–44.

ROSSITER, J.R. and ROBERTSON, T.S. (1975) 'Children's television viewing: an examination of parent-child consensus', *Sociometry*, **38**, 2, pp. 308–26.

RUBIN, A.M. (1979) 'Television use by children and adolescents', *Human Communication Research*, **5**, pp. 109–20.

RUMELHART, D. (1975) 'Notes on a schema for stories', in BOBROW, D.G. and COLLINS, A. (Eds) *Representation and Understanding: Studies in Cognitive Science*, New York, Academic Press.

RUMELHART, D. (1977) 'Understanding and summarizing brief stories', in LABERGE, D. and SAMUELS, S.J. (Eds) *Basic Processes in Reading: Perception and Comprehension*, Hillsdale, N.J., Lawrence Erlbaum.

SALOMON, G. (1979a) *Interaction of Media, Cognition and Learning*, San Francisco, Jossey-Bass.

SALOMON, G. (1979b) 'Shape, not only content: how media symbols partake in the development of abilities', in WARTELLA, E. (Ed.) *Children Communicating: Media and the Development of Speech, Thought, Understanding*, Beverly Hills, Sage.

SALOMON, G. (1982) 'Television literacy and television vs. literacy', *Journal of Visual and Verbal Languaging*, **2**, 2, pp. 7–17.

SALOMON, G. (1983a) 'Television watching and mental effort: a social psychological view', in BRYANT, J. and ANDERSON, D.R. (Eds) *Children's Understanding of Television*, New York, Academic Press.

SALOMON, G. (1983b) 'Beyond the formats of television: the effects of students' preconceptions on the experience of televiewing', in MEYER, M. (Ed.) *Children and the Formal Features of Television*, Munich, K.G. Saur.

SCHRAMM, W., LYLE, J. and PARKER, E.B. (1961) *Television in the Lives of Our Children*, Stanford, Stanford University Press.

SCHUETZ, S. and SPRAFKIN, J. (1979) 'Portrayal of prosocial and aggressive behaviors in children's TV commercials', *Journal of Broadcasting*, **23**, 1, pp. 33–40.

SCORAH, K. (1990) *Children and Advertising: A Report by Tilby and Leeves and Kay Scorah*, London, mimeo.

SEDLAK, A.J. (1979) 'Developmental Differences in Understanding Plans and Evaluating Actors', *Child Development*, **50**, pp. 536–60.

SEFTON-GREEN, J. (1990) 'Teaching and learning about representation: culture and *The Cosby Show* in a North London comprehensive', in BUCKINGHAM, D. (Ed.) *Watching Media Learning: Making Sense of Media Education*, London, Falmer Press.

SEITER, E. (1990) 'Making distinctions in TV audience research: case study of a troubling interview', *Cultural Studies*, **4**, 1, pp. 61–84.

SEITER, E., BORCHERS, H., KREUTZNER, G. and WARTH, E.-M. (Eds) (1989) *Remote Control: Television, Audiences and Cultural Power*, London, Routledge.

SHANNON, P. and FERNIE, D.E. (1985) 'Print and television: children's use of the medium is the message', *Elementary School Journal*, **85**, 5, pp. 663–72.

SHEIKH, A.A. and MOLESKI, L.M. (1977a) 'Conflict in the family over commercials', *Journal of Communication*, **27**, 3, pp. 152–7.

SHEIKH, A.A. and MOLESKI, M. (1977b) 'Children's perception of the value of an advertised product', *Journal of Broadcasting*, **21**, 3, pp. 347–54.

SHEPPARD, A. (1990) *Children, Television and Morality*, Research Working Paper 1, London, Broadcasting Standards Council.

SHOTTER, J. and GERGEN, K.J. (Eds) (1988) *Texts of Identity*, London, Sage.

SHOTTER, J. and PARKER, I. (1989) *Deconstructing Social Psychology*, London, Routledge.

SILVERMAN, D. (1985) *Qualitative Methodology and Sociology*, Aldershot, Gower.

SILVERMAN, K. (1983) *The Subject of Semiotics*, Oxford, Oxford University Press.

SILVERSTONE, R. (1989) 'Let us then return to the murmuring of everyday practices: a note on Michel de Certeau, television and everyday life', *Theory, Culture and Society*, **6**, 1, pp. 77–94.

SIMPSON, P. (Ed.) (1987) *Parents Talking Television*, London, Comedia.

SINGER, D.G., ZUCKERMAN, D.M. and SINGER, J.L. (1980) 'Helping elementary school children learn about TV', *Journal of Communication*, **30**, 3, pp. 84–93.

SINGER, J.L., SINGER, D.G., DESMOND, R., HIRSCH, B. and NICOL, A. (1988) 'Family mediation and children's cognition, aggression, and comprehension of television: a longitudinal study', *Journal of Applied Developmental Psychology*, **9**, 3, pp. 329–47.

SMITH, E.E. and MEDIN, D.L. (1981) *Categories and Concepts*, Cambridge, Mass., Harvard University Press.

SMITH, F. (1973) *Understanding Reading*, New York, Holt, Rinehart and Winston.

SOLBERG, A. (1990) 'Negotiating childhood: changing constructions of age for Norwegian children', in JAMES, A. and PROUT, A. (Eds) *Constructing and Reconstructing Childhood: Contemporary Issues in the Sociological Study of Childhood*, London, Falmer Press.

SPEIER, M. (1976) 'The child as conversationalist: some culture contact features of conversational interactions between adults and children', in HAMMERSLEY, M. and WOODS, P. (Eds) *The Process of Schooling*, London, Routledge and Kegan Paul/ Open University Press.

SPENCER, M. (1986) 'Emergent literacies: a site for analysis', *Language Arts*, **63**, 5, pp. 442–53.

SPENDER, D. (1980) *Man Made Language*, London, Routledge and Kegan Paul.

STEEDMAN, C. (1982) *The Tidy House*, London, Virago.

STEIN, N.L. and GLENN, C.G. (1979) 'An analysis of story comprehension in elementary school children', in FREEDLE, R.O. (Ed.) *New Directions in Discourse Processing*, Norwood, N.J., Ablex.

STREET, B.V. (1984) *Literacy in Theory and Practice*, Cambridge, Cambridge University Press.

STUBBS, M. (1983) *Discourse Analysis*, Oxford, Basil Blackwell.

SULLIVAN, E.V. (1987) 'Critical pedagogy and television', in LIVINGSTONE, D.W. and contributors, *Critical Pedagogy and Cultural Power*, London, Macmillan.

TAN, A.S. (1979) 'TV beauty ads and role expectations of adolescent female viewers', *Journalism Quarterly*, **56**, pp. 283–8.

TANNEN, D. (1980) 'A comparative analysis of oral narrative strategies: Athenian Greek and American English', in CHAFE, W.L. (Ed.) *The Pear Stories: Cognitive, Cultural and Linguistic Aspects of Narrative Production*, Norwood, N.J., Ablex.

THORNDYKE, P.W. (1977) 'Cognitive structures in comprehension and memory of narrative discourse', *Cognitive Science*, **9**, pp. 77–110.

TODOROV, T. (1977) *The Poetics of Prose*, Ithaca, N.Y., Cornell University Press.

TRACEY, M. and MORRISON, D. (1979) *Whitehouse*, London, Macmillan.

TRAUDT, P.J. and LONT, C.M. (1987) 'Media-logic-in-use: the family as locus of study', in LINDLOF, T. (Ed.) *Natural Audiences*, Newbury Park, Calif., Sage.

TRELEASE, J. (1984) *The Read Aloud Handbook*, Harmondsworth, Penguin.

TUDOR, A. (1973) *Theories of Film*, London, Secker and Warburg.

TURNER, G. (1990) *British Cultural Studies: An Introduction*, London, Unwin Hyman.

URWIN, C. (1985) 'Constructing motherhood: the persuasion of normal development', in STEEDMAN, C., URWIN, C. and WALKERDINE, V. (Eds) *Language, Gender and Child-hood*, London, Routledge and Kegan Paul.

VOLOSINOV, V.N. (1973) *Marxism and the Philosophy of Language*, Cambridge, Mass., Harvard University Press.

VYGOTSKY, L. (1962) *Thought and Language*, Cambridge, Mass., M.I.T. Press.

VYGOTSKY, L. (1978) *Mind and Society*, Cambridge, Mass., Harvard University Press.

WALKERDINE, V. (1984) 'Developmental psychology and the child-centred pedagogy: the insertion of Piaget into early education', in HENRIQUES, J., HOLLWAY, W., URWIN, C., VENN, C. and WALKERDINE,V., *Changing the Subject: Psychology, Social Regulation and Subjectivity*, London, Methuen.

WALKERDINE, V. (1986) 'Video replay: families, films and fantasy', in BURGIN, V., DONALD, J. and KAPLAN, C. (Eds) *Formations of Fantasy*, London, Routledge and Kegan Paul.

WALKERDINE, V. and LUCEY, H. (1989) *Democracy in the Kitchen*, London, Virago.

WAND, B. (1968) 'Television viewing and family choice differences', *Public Opinion Quarterly*, **32**, pp. 84–94.

WARTELLA, E. (Ed.) (1979) *Children Communicating: Media and Development of Thought, Speech, Understanding*, Beverly Hills, Sage.

WARTELLA, E. (1980) 'Individual differences in children's responses to television adver-tising', in PALMER, E.L. and DORR, A. (Eds) *Children and the Faces of Television: Teaching, Violence, Selling*, New York, Academic Press.

WARTELLA, E. (1984) 'Cognitive and affective factors of TV advertising's influence on children', *Western Journal of Speech Communication*, **48**, pp. 171–83.

WARTELLA, E. and ALEXANDER, A. (1978) 'Children's organization of impressions of television characters', paper presented to the International Communication Asso-ciation, Chicago.

WARTELLA, E. and ETTEMA, J.S. (1974) 'A cognitive developmental study of children's attention to television commercials', *Communication Research*, **1**, 1, pp. 69–88.

WERTSCH, J. (1985) *Vygotsky and the Social Formation of Mind*, Cambridge, Mass., Harvard University Press.

WILLEMEN, P. (1978) 'Notes on subjectivity: on reading Edward Branigan's "Subjec-tivity Under Siege"', *Screen*, **19**, 1, pp. 41–69.

WILLIAMS, F. (1969) 'Social class differences in how children talk about television', *Journal of Broadcasting*, **13**, 4, pp. 345–57.

WILLIAMS, R. (1980) (originally published 1960) 'Advertising: the magic system', in WILLIAMS, R., *Problems in Materialism and Culture*, London, Verso.

WILLIAMSON, J. (1978) *Decoding Advertisements*, London, Marion Boyars.

WILLIAMSON, J. (1981/2) 'How does girl number twenty understand ideology?', *Screen Education*, 40, pp. 80–7.

WILLIAMSON, J. (1985) 'Is there anyone here from a classroom?', *Screen*, **26**, 1, pp. 90–5.

WINN, M. (1985) *The Plug-In Drug* (revised edition), Harmondsworth, Penguin.

WOBER, J.M., FAZAL, S. and REARDON, G. (1986) *Parental Control of Children's Viewing: Patterns of Discipline and of Viewing Experience*, London, Independent Broadcasting Authority.

WREN-LEWIS, J. (1983) 'The encoding/decoding model: criticisms and redevelopments for research on decoding', *Media, Culture and Society*, **5**, 2, pp. 179–97.

WREN-LEWIS, J. (1985) 'Decoding television news', in DRUMMOND, P. and PATERSON, R. (Eds) *Television in Transition*, London, British Film Institute.

YADAVA, J.S. and REDDI, U.V. (1988) 'In the midst of diversity: television in urban Indian homes', in LULL, J. (Ed.) *World Families Watch Television*, Newbury Park, Calif., Sage.

YOUNG, B.M. (1986) 'New approaches to old problems: the growth of advertising literacy', in WARD, S., ROBERTSON, T. and BROWN, R. (Eds) *Commercial Television and European Children*, Aldershot, Gower.

References

YOUNG, B.M. (1990) *Television Advertising and Children*, Oxford, Clarendon.

ZADEH, L. (1965) 'Fuzzy sets', *Information and Control*, 8, pp. 338–53.

ZUCKERMAN, P. and GIANNINO, L. (1981) 'Measuring children's responses to television advertising', in ESSERMAN, J.F. (Ed.) *Television Advertising and Children*, New York, Child Research Service.

ZUCKERMAN, P., ZIEGLER, M. and STEVENSON, H.W. (1978) 'Children's viewing of television and recognition memory of commercials', *Child Development*, **49**, pp. 96–104.

Index